THE WAY
OF ALL
WOMEN

THE WAY OF ALL WOMEN

a psychological interpretation by M. Esther Harding

with an introduction by C.G. Jung

published by G. P. Putnam's Sons
for the
C. G. Jung Foundation for
Analytical Psychology

Acknowledgment and thanks are due the following publishers for the use of passages quoted:

To Little, Brown and Company for the poem from *Final Harvest* by Emily Dickinson;

Princeton University Press for passages from *The Collected Works of C. G. Jung,* Bollingen Series XX, ed. by G. Adler, M. Fordham and H. Read, transl. by R. F. C. Hull: Vol. 7, *Two Essays on Analytical Psychology* (Copyright 1953 by Bollingen Foundation; 2nd. ed., 1966); Vol. 10, *Civilization in Transition* (Copyright © 1964 by Bollingen Foundation); Vol. 17, *The Development of Personality* (Copyright 1954 by Bollingen Foundation); and from *The I Ching, or Book of Changes,* translated by R. Wilhelm and C. F. Baynes, Bollingen Series XIX, (3rd edn., 1967. Copyright © 1950, 1967 by Bollingen Foundation, New York).

Routledge and Kegan Paul Ltd. for material from Jung's *Psychological Types;*

Stanford University Press for the passage from *Tibet's Great Yogi Milarepa* by Evans-Wentz;

University Books Inc. for the quotation from Mead's *Fragments of a Faith Forgotten;*

Vincent Stuart and John M. Watkins Ltd. for the quotation from *Anna Kingsford* by Edward Maitland.

Published on the same day in the Dominion of Canada
by Longmans Green Canada Limited, Toronto.

Printed in the United States of America

Production by Bob Vari

Library of Congress Catalog Number 78-97582.

Second Printing, 1970

"The modern woman
stands before a great cultural task,
which means perhaps,
the beginning of a new Era."
—C. G. Jung, Women in Europe

Contents

Preface
to the
Revised Edition

It is thirty-seven years since this book was written and many things have happened during that time. A spirit of revolution is in the air, affecting almost every field of human endeavor — science, politics, morals, even religion, have changed almost out of recognition. And yet on re-reading this book I was amazed to find how few changes were needed to bring it up to date. Some of the books and plays cited in illustration are no longer read as they were in the 1920s, and the referehces to the feminist movement are no longer relevant, but beyond these the thesis is still valid. For while the form of life changes, human nature does not change, or only very slowly. As the Chinese *Book of Changes* says:

> The Town may be changed,
> But the well cannot be changed. [1]

And the commentator adds: "The style of architecture changed in the course of centuries, but the shape of the well has remained the same from ancient times to this day . . . Political structures change, as do nations, but the life of man with its needs remains eternally the same . . . The foundations of human nature are

---

1 *I Ching,* p. 197.

the same in everyone. And every human being can draw . . . from the inexhaustible wellspring of the divine in man's nature."[2]

In addition to the acknowledgments in the original Preface I should like to add my appreciation to Mr. Edward Mills, editor of Longmans Green and later of David Mackay, for the sustained interest he has taken in this little book during the years.

M. E. H.
1970

---

2 *Ibid.*, p. 198.

Preface
to the
First Edition

The ideas underlying the present volume are based on the teachings of C. G. Jung who has opened to us a new realm of thought and experience which promises a solution of many of the fundamental cultural problems of our day. These ideas, however, are not always easily translated into the terms of daily life. In this book an attempt has been made to perform the entirely feminine task of showing how the knowledge of human nature made available through the study of the unconscious may be applied to everyday experience in a helpful way.

Those who consult a psychologist usually do so with the hope of finding a means of dealing with their practical difficulties. If these people are merely instructed in theory they may well say, "This is very interesting, but how does it help me?" Many books today point out the problems of both social and personal life; many analyze the causes of prevalent modern problems; few undertake to demonstrate a method of living by which the individual may find a workable solution of his own difficulties.

In the following pages I have not attempted to offer a panacea for life's ills. I do not claim any superior knowledge of how the moral or social difficulties of our day may be met, but I do present certain suggestions for action through which each individual who is interested in truth may come to find it more fully in his own life and, through the practical application of the modern knowledge of the psyche, may perhaps build for himself a firmer structure.

In these days when the outer props onto which man has pinned his faith seem to be crumbling, it is all the more necessary that an inner security be built up which will be able to withstand the shock of outer misfortune. All the world over the dark forces of the "downgoing" are making their power felt. No longer can we reassure ourselves with the thought of a bank balance. All too often we build a fortune as a child builds sand castles before a rising tide. Outer security seems to be undermined. Is there any other kind of security to which we can turn? Those who are religious have in all ages turned to the spiritual realm, in times of misfortune, discounting the values of this world. Such an otherworldliness no longer suffices the modern man who desires a more complete and satisfying life here and now. He wishes to realize his spirituality in this life rather than in a problematical hereafter. Yet exclusive concern with the outer world has proved as unsatisfying as the denial of its existence. Today we see arising a new evaluation of a different kind of reality, based on the psychological understanding of human nature, which perhaps contains the germ of a middle way between the extremes of materialism and of otherworldliness.

Understanding is invaluable, but for many people, and especially for women, understanding must be supplemented by a workable practice if life is not to be lived in vain. For man creates the idea and woman transforms it into a living reality.

To those who seek such a practical way of life I dedicate this book.

I want to take this opportunity to express my thanks to Dr. Jung, through whose sympathy and encouragement the book was conceived, and to my colleagues, Dr. Eleanor Bertine and Dr. Kristine Mann, who have discussed the material in every stage of its growth and to whom I am indebted for illustrations and suggestions and without whose constant help the book would hardly have been possible. Dr. Bertine particularly has been untiring in her assistance and generous cooperation. Dr. Jung's Introduction was written in German and I am grateful to Mrs. Cary Baynes for her excellent translation. I also want to express my thanks to those who have permitted me to quote from their dreams and other private material; and also to Messrs. Dodd, Mead & Company, Inc., for permission to quote from *Two Essays on Analytical Psychology* by C. G. Jung; and to Messrs. Harcourt, Brace and Company, Inc., for permission to quote from *Psychological Types* and *Contributions to Analytical Psychology* by C. G. Jung; and to The Oxford University Press for permission to quote from *Tibet's Great Yogi Milarepa* by Evans-Wentz.

M. E. H.

1933

Introduction

It is a pleasure to comply with the author's wish that I should write an introduction to her book. I have read her work in manuscript with the greatest interest and am gratified to find that it does not belong in the category of certain priggish books which expatiate on the psychology of women with as much prejudiced one-sidedness as loquacity and finally overflow in a sentimental hymn to "holy motherhood." Such books have another unpleasant characteristic: They never speak of things as they are but rather as they should be, and instead of taking the problem of the feminine soul seriously they benevolently gloss over dark, and therefore unpleasant, truths with advice which is as good as it is ineffectual. Such books are by no means always written by men— if they were they might be excusable—but many are written by women who seem to know as little about feminine feelings as men do.

It is a foregone conclusion among the initiated that men understand nothing of women's psychology as it actually is, but it is astonishing to find that women do not know themselves. However we are only surprised as long as we naively and optimistically imagine that mankind understands anything fundamental about the soul. Such knowledge and understanding belong to the most difficult tasks an investigating mind can set itself. The newest developments in psychology show with an ever greater clarity that not only are there no simple formulas from which the world of the soul might be derived, but also that we have never yet succeeded in defining the psychic field of experience with adequate certainty. Indeed, scientific psychology, despite its immense extension on the surface, has not even begun to free itself from a mountain-high mass of prejudices which persistently bars its entrance to the real soul. Psychology as the youngest of the sciences has only just developed and, therefore, is suffering from all those children's diseases which afflicted the adolescence of the other sciences in the late Middle Ages. There still exist psychologies which limit the psychic field of experience to consciousness and its contents or which understand the psychic to be only a phenomenon of reaction without any trace of autonomy. The existence of an unconscious psyche has not yet attained undisputed validity, despite the presence of an overwhelming amount of empirical material which could prove beyond the peradventure of a doubt that there can be no psychology of consciousness without the recognition of the unconscious. Without this foundation, no datum of psychology, if it be in any way complex in nature, can be dealt with. Moreover, the actual soul with which we have to deal in life and in reality is complexity itself. For example, a psychology of woman cannot be written without an adequate knowledge of the unconscious backgrounds of the mind.

On the basis of a rich psychotherapeutic experience, Dr. Harding has drawn up a picture of the feminine psyche which, in extent and thoroughness, far surpasses previous works in this field. Her presentation is refreshingly free of prejudice and remarkable in the love of truth it displays. Her expositions never lose themselves in dead theories nor in fanatical fads which unfortunately are so frequently to be met with in just this field. In this way she has succeeded in penetrating with the light of knowledge into backgrounds and depths where before darkness prevailed. Only one half of feminine psychology can be covered by biological and social concepts. But in this book it becomes clear that woman possesses also a peculiar spirituality very strange to man. Without knowledge of the unconscious this new point of view, so essential to the psychology of woman, could never have been brought out in such completeness. But also in many other places in the book the fructifying influence of the psychology of unconscious processes is evident.

At a time when the frequency of divorce reaches a record

number, when the question of the relation of the sexes has become a perplexing problem, a book like this seems to me to be of the greatest help. To be sure, it does not provide the one thing that all expect, that is, a generally accepted recipe by which this dreadful complex of questions might be solved in a simple and practical way so that we need rack our brains about it no longer. On the other hand, the book contains an ample store of what we actually need very badly, namely understanding — understanding of psychic facts and conditions with the help of which we can orientate ourselves in the complicated situations of life.

After all, why do we have a psychology? Why is it that just now especially we interest ourselves in psychology? The answer is, everyone is in dire need of it. Humanity seems to have reached today a point where previous concepts are no longer adequate and where we begin to realize that we are confronted with something strange, the language of which we no longer understand. We live in a time when there dawns upon us a realization that the people living on the other side of the mountain are not made up exclusively of red-headed devils responsible for all the evil on this side of the mountain. A sign of this dim intuition has also penetrated the relation between the sexes; we do not all of us say to ourselves, "Everything good dwells within me, everything evil within thee."

Today there already exist super-moderns who ask themselves in all seriousness if something or other is not out of joint, if we are not perhaps somewhat too unconscious, somewhat antiquated, and whether this may not be the reason why when confronted with difficulties in relationship between the sexes we still continue to apply with disastrous results methods of the Middle Ages if not those of the cave man. There are people indeed who read with horror the Pope's encyclical on Christian marriage, though they can admit that to cave men the so-called "Christian" marriage means a cultural advance. But although we are far from having overcome our prehistoric mentality, and although it is just in the field of sexuality that man becomes most vividly aware of his mammalian nature and also experiences its most signal triumphs, nonetheless certain ethical refinements have entered in which permit the man who has behind him ten to fifteen centuries of Christian education to progress toward a somewhat higher level.

On this level, spirit—from the biological point of view an incomprehensible psychic phenomenon—plays no small psychological role. Spirit had an important word to say in the idea of Christian marriage itself, and in the modern questioning and depreciation of marriage the question of spirit enters vigorously into the discussion. It appears in a negative way as counsel for the instincts, and in a positive way as defender of human dignity. Small wonder then that a wild and confusing conflict arises between man as an instinctual creature of nature and as a spiritually conditioned, cultural being. The worst thing about it is that the one is forever trying to do violence to the other, in order to bring about a so-called harmonious and unified solution of the conflict. Unfortunately, too many persons still believe in this method which continues to be all-powerful in the world of politics; there are only a few here and there who condemn it as barbaric and who would rather set up in its place a just compromise whereby each side of man's nature would receive a hearing.

But unhappily, in the problem between the sexes, no one can bring about a compromise by himself alone; it can only be brought about in relation to the other sex. Therefore the necessity of psychology! On this level psychology becomes a kind of special pleading or, rather, a method of relationship. Psychology guarantees real knowledge of the other sex and thus supplants arbitrary opinions which are the source of the incurable misunderstandings now undermining in increasing numbers the marriages of our time.

Dr. Harding's book is an important contribution to this striving of our time for a deeper knowledge of the human being and for a clarification of the confusion existing in the relationship between the sexes.

C. G. Jung
Zurich, February 1932

THE WAY
OF ALL
WOMEN

1. All things to all Men

In childhood we are taught certain stories and myths telling of the origin of the world and of mankind and giving a general view of life and of conduct. It is as though they said: "This is the way things came into being, and this shows their essential nature and relationship." These legends and tales which appeal so immediately to the child are for the most part as old as historical man and hark back to the infancy of the race. The views they express, insofar as they are still binding today, must represent something deeply embedded in the mind of man. Man has corrected and refined these beliefs in certain realms; in other spheres they remain powers in the background, determining his conduct. In no way are these unseen and unrecognized forces more strikingly manifested than in man's general attitude toward woman.

"In the beginning"—according to the record in Genesis—"God created the heaven and the earth" with all that they contained. The summit of his creation was mankind—"male and female created He them." In this statement is expressed a belief in divine creation, but the statement is also intended to account for the simple fact that mankind is *both* male and female. The first chapter of Genesis contains, however, another and a better known version of the making of man: it is the story of Adam's sleep and of the creation of Eve by the removal of one of his ribs. This story shows woman conceived of as a part of man, taken out of his side while he is unconscious. It is a myth which represents woman as an unconscious part of man, wholly secondary to him, without any living spirit or soul of her own. This myth illustrates an attitude fundamental in man's view of woman. If the story had been told by women we should have had a different account of the creation. For instance, in a school examination paper the question was set: "Give an account of the creation of man." A little girl wrote: "First God created Adam. Then He looked at him and said, 'I think if I tried again I could do better.' Then He created Eve." Here we have a perfectly naive feminine version of the story.

There is a great discrepancy, I admit, between a myth hallowed by age and religious tradition and this school child's version of it. But from the psychological point of view they are nonetheless valid examples of the rift between two attitudes. This rift is illustrated, on the one hand, by man's still prevalent way of regarding woman and, on the other, by the worst exaggeration of the feminist movement.

Where does the truth lie? Is it to be found somewhere between the two points of view or is it necessary to approach the whole subject from an entirely different angle?

The first condition for an impartial investigation into the relationships between men and women is to rule out old assumptions of the superiority or the inferiority of one to the other. We must not hold the view that woman is man's inferior, nor must we take our stand on the little girl's version of the creation and assume that man is a creature who has not yet evolved to the female standard. This latter view is secretly held by many women, but they never express it directly, for to do so would be heresy. Indeed, the majority of women who hold it most firmly would deny it if challenged. But if we talk with them we can see this assumption underlying such simple comments as: "Men are so stupid," "Men, poor things, they can't help it," "They are all children," and so on. The implication is that women are wiser and more adult than men, but this is kept secret. It is not only not talked about, it is not even formulated, and the women who say such things about men do not really *think* them in their heads.

It is not the woman who resembles the aggressive woman of the feminist movement who makes such comments. She is too concerned with trying to be man's equal and so discounts all differences, physiological as well as psychological. She never depreciates man, for her aim is to be like a man, equal to a man, no whit his inferior. She no longer has any standpoint for criticism of him, because she has sold her birthright, her feminine inheritance, her uniqueness, by cancelling the difference arising from the fact that she is female. It is only the very feminine women who in secret speak so condescendingly of men. Such women are strong in their feminine position; they make no attempt to rival men; they do not want an individual position in the world, for they are wanted by men who, indeed, are even willing to support them.

Just what, then, is the difference between the woman who is the man's woman and the woman who is not the man's woman? Men have often commented upon it. Their attention has been caught by the latter type of woman only because of her competition, which threatens them in business or in the professions, or because of her insistence on her political rights. But their deeper interest has been in the man's woman, primarily on account of what she has meant to them personally. She has been repeatedly portrayed in plays and novels and we can sense her peculiar influence in lyric poetry which so often celebrates her. She figures in myths and legends, but she is always shown from the man's point of view. And even when, as in these modern days, attempts are made to give a more objective picture of human beings, we find that such women are still described, for the most part, from the masculine point of view. There is, for instance, no outstanding autobiography written by a woman of this type which presents to our closer scrutiny her own inner experience of life. For these women most often present themselves to us solely in terms of their external experience; they recount outer events and the part they played in them but fail to convey a picture of their inner experience. Possibly they are not sufficiently aware of themselves to be able to give a picture of what their subjective life is like. For this type of woman is generally very unselfconscious; she does not analyze herself or her motives; she just *is*; and for the most she is inarticulate. Furthermore she has, as a rule, no urge to make herself understood by a large audience. Her interest and her life lie in her relation to one man or perhaps to two or three men; hers is a *personal* interest, not one which concerns itself with a larger group. Hence it is that women of this type, numerous as they are — for, indeed, they may be considered to make up the primary type of womanhood — have never been interpreted truly. Their silence has become their "mystery." A mass of literature has grown up about them which purports to explain them, but the explanation is always based on the man's idea of the woman; it is never the woman's interpretation of herself.

C. G. Jung faced this problem more effectively than any other psychologist. Not only did he analyze the problem of the significance of woman from the point of view of the man, but he, alone among psychologists, clearly differentiated between this subjective significance and the objective reality of the woman herself and defined clearly the type which can most readily carry for the man the significance of his own subjective and unconscious values. But here Jung's further discussion of the subject necessarily meets a blank wall. He, as a man, can tell us relatively little of the woman herself and of her part in the proceeding. Only from the point of view of an observer can he tell us what value, if any, *she* gains from carrying the image of the man's unconscious values and from associating with the man who thus glorifies her.

Such a woman, who is peculiarly adapted through her own natural gifts to be man's partner, in the fashion implied in the Genesis idyl, is the primary type of woman *in nature*. She is the female human animal, whose whole attention is focussed instinctively on her mate. She adapts herself to his wishes, makes herself beautiful in his eyes, charms him, pleases him. These things are naturally a manifestation of the fundamental biological relation between the sexes. But where these instinctive reactions appear in modern women the aim of Mother Nature is masked, in accordance with the conventional code, while the woman herself may be quite unaware of the hidden meaning of her actions.

Primitive woman was doubtless quite content with the role the Genesis myth assigned to her, for in primitive situations, where the biological aim is the sole guide in life, that the woman shall be attractive to the man and shall call forth and hold his interest is all that is important for life and for her. Even until today some women have remained almost as unconscious as their most remote ancestress and are still content to be only man's helpmeet and counterpart. But humanity at large has moved since those days toward a greater consciousness, chiefly through the emergence of a conscious and personal ego whose aims have conflicted with the simple urges which Mother Nature first implanted in our breasts. Thus, as woman has evolved and become more aware of herself as a separate entity—an ego—a conflict has arisen within her psyche between the individual values which she has attained and the ancient, collective, feminine trends—and conflict is the beginning of consciousness.

There are three typical stages of development through which the human being passes in the gradual evolution of consciousness. These may be called the *naive,* the *sophisticated* and the *conscious.* The first, or naive, is related to nature only. It is a way of functioning which is entirely unselfconscious. It is, so to speak, the state of man before the Fall, when he was entirely innocent and at one with himself. In this stage there is hardly any differentiation between conscious and unconscious, for selfconsciousness has not arisen. The individual lives in a primitive union with nature, a state broken only by the emergence of the ego. This is a change of great importance in the development of the personality and is a definite step toward consciousness.

From this point the individual enters the period of sophistication. The natural powers within him and the resources of the world without are gradually explored and exploited, and the capacities and powers thus gained are organized under the leadership of the ego. Personal aggrandizement and the satisfaction of the ego arise and form a new life-motive. The lust for power comes to occupy an increasing place. But at this point a new factor may come into the picture. The selfishness of the power attitude may obtrude itself on consciousness. Love perhaps arises which will dispute the dominant position of the ego, or some other value which transcends personal considerations may replace those formerly held. This change in emphasis inaugurates a gradual redemption of the personality from the dominance of the ego, and the third stage—the stage of consciousness—begins.

In the innocent play of domestic animals we may see certain ways of acting which we recognize as fundamentally masculine or feminine. The arts and wiles which the female uses to attract the male are so nearly akin to the ways of a pretty woman that we cannot help smiling. These things are manifestations of primitive femininity. They can be seen too in tiny children. A little girl, while still quite young, begins to act in a different way from a little boy. Where he is independent and aggressive, she is coy and winsome. She begins very eary in life to gain her ends through coaxing or merely through being adorable. Her whole way of functioning is in relation to someone else from whom she may attract attention or care or love. In many grown women we see the same process at work. The woman herself is doubtless unaware of what she is doing. She may have no deeper motive than eagerness to *please,* to do what is expected of her, to fulfill another person's ideal of her. This other person is usually a man. She rarely stops to ask what she herself wants or how she feels. She is content if he is content, provided his contentment is only to be attained through her. In this way she makes of herself a sort of mirror which reflects the man's mood, his half-unrealized feelings. If he is sad, she is melancholy. If he is joyous, she bubbles with mirth. And, indeed, so subtle is her unconscious, or half-unconscious, intuition of his mood that often she will react to it while he himself is still unaware of what his mood is. So it is that he seems to discover what should be his own feeling *in her*. For men tend to be exceedingly unconscious of their own feeling moods. Even though a man may have suffered an intense personal loss he is very likely to react to it as an almost *impersonal* emergency, requiring a practical adaptation only, and to remain entirely unaware that he has also a feeling reaction to it as a *personal* experience. All he knows is that he feels out of harmony with himself. In this state he goes to see a woman such as we have been describing. She senses his mood almost before he speaks to her. Regardless of what she had been thinking or feeling before his arrival she now reflects the feeling of which he is unaware. If he has had a blow which he does not recognize as an emotional one, it is melancholy she reflects — a great vague, contentless yearning. As he does not know what there is to be sorry about, her melancholy cannot have much point or content, but this very vagueness allows his own sorrow or regret to find a place in her. He can project his unconscious feeling on to her, and no matter what it may be it can flow into her and so find its own form, undisturbed by any preconceptions on her part. He feels his personal sorrow raised to the level of a universal grief and is relieved of his own pain in contemplating the pain of mankind. By his contact with her he has gained a contact with his own feeling, and through the generalization of her mood he has found a way of adapting to his own grief which, left unrealized, might have overwhelmed him.

So it is that a man can find in such a woman an image or picture of the other part of himself, otherwise unknown to him, which indeed he does not recognize as belonging to himself. This image seems to be in her; he perceives it, but as though it were her feeling, not his own. When a subjective content is experienced in this way it is commonly spoken of as *projected*. The fact that its subjective source is not recognized means that it is in a sense *unconscious*. When projected by a man upon a woman it is like a mirage, an illusion, concealing the woman who is there; his own unconscious feeling-contents meet him in personified form.

The sum of these contents make up the unrecognized part of man's psyche and when brought together into a whole constitue the man's feminine soul,[1] which exercises over him an irresistible fascination and appears variously as *La Desirée* or *La Belle Dame sans Merci*. This feminine soul of the man Jung has called *anima*.

Men with the same inherited background have anima figures which are strangely similar, so that the anima herself can be recognized by her characteristics, which are universal and collective. In imaginative writings, especially in novels and plays the anima is often drawn unmistakably. Anima figures form the central characters in such imaginative stories as *She* by Rider Haggard, *Green Mansions* by W. H. Hudson, and many others. She-who-must-be-obeyed and the Bird Girl represent the anima of their authors. They have certain characteristics in common: they are only part human (each is both more and less than a real woman), they carry feeling values, and each has a quality which makes her lightest word a command, absolutely binding on the hero.

These are portrayals of the anima herself, the collective soul of man, which we feel to be non-human, but many women, both in fiction and in real life, show certain anima characteristics which are more or less modified by human traits. For although it is true that a man's anima as a rule becomes apparent to him only when it is projected onto a woman, yet the anima herself is not a real woman. She represents rather a collective, or universalized, picture of woman as she has appeared through the centuries of

---

1 *Soul* is here used in a psychological, not a theological, sense. When Jung speaks of the *soul* he is concerned "with the psychological recognition of the existence of a semiconscious psychic complex, having partial autonomy of function. . . .The autonomy of the soul-complex naturally lends support to the notion of an invisible, personal entity that apparently lives in a world very different from ours." (*Two Essays on Analytical Psychology*, pp. 188-189.) The reader is referred to Jung's discussion of this whole subject in the *Two Essays* and to the definitions of soul and soul-image in the chapter "Definitions" in *Psychological Types*. Wherever in this book technical terms have been used, the author has endeavored to use them in the sense in which Jung has defined them, either in the chapter on definitons referred to or scattered throughout his other writings.

human experience *in relation to man*. This last factor is important. All that a man sees is colored for him by his own subjective contents. And inasmuch as woman, throughout the ages, has been to man the symbol of his unknown feminine soul, his eyes have been peculiarly blinded when he has looked at her. A man without a soul is but half a man, consequently when his soul is projected onto another human being it is as though half of himself were in her. The woman becomes enormously important as well as enormously attractive to him. He longs to get into relation with her, for by so doing he will come into relation once more with his own soul, which is otherwise lost to him.

Certain women have a peculiar aptitude for reflecting the man's anima. However, not all women have this gift. Those who are so endowed form a definite group, although naturally the women comprising it differ markedly from one another in many particulars, for this group makes up a large proportion of womanhood throughout the world and contains women of many qualities. Yet there are certain characteristics held by all these women in common—a fact which justifies our speaking of them as forming a distinct anima type.

The general characteristics of the anima woman change as she passes through the different stages of psychological development. In the first, or naive, stage she is a natural, instinctive creature. She manifests in her every action the innocent functioning of feminine instinct. Her whole attention is directed, albeit without her conscious knowledge, to the effects she produces on men. She is completely naive. She has no conscious critique of her own actions and motives; she has no objective standard or criterion at all. It never occurs to her to judge herself by an external standard, or, indeed, to view herself as object. She is just female creature, as unconscious of herself and as innocent as the domestic animals. If a man projects his anima onto her, she is unaware of it. She simply lives what she feels and what she is. She is related to herself and to her own instinctive satisfactions, just as the animals are. She is a nature product. And for this reason she never knows beforehand what she wants. She is ambiguous. "She will and she won't." The opposites in her sleep side by side, so that she has a certain bivalent quality, like nature. The man senses his soul in her and seeks to be united with her. His anima is also, like nature, bivalent. So her ambiguity fits in with his need.

In time the ego awakes in her and the second stage of development begins. She finds that by living instinctively she attracts the attention of a man or of men. The man, finding in her a symbol or picture of his soul, wants a close relationship with her so that he may be reunited to his own soul. Because of this urgent need he is willing to give her almost anything she asks. She wants a relationship with him too, or perhaps we should say "Nature in her" wants it for biological ends. But because she is, as a rule, unaware of this natural urge within her she acts as though she were indifferent, with the result that the man pays further court to her. Then if her ego comes to consciousness she makes a discovery, namely that this seeming indifference makes her more desirable from the man's point of view; and she begins to use it as a definite trick, of which she is at least partly aware, to attract the man's attention and gifts. Or perhaps the woman is truly indifferent and cold. She may really not want the man's attentions but she realizes that the power she has over him is a great asset. If she then, either deliberately or half-unconsciously, begins to exploit the man's projection using his need to her own advantage, the flirt gradually emerges, who in her worst aspect becomes the "gold digger."

Ego development in the anima woman, however, may show itself in a much more adapted and social form. For instance, a woman may use her charm and the attraction she has for men in a socially desirable and acceptable way, which is yet a conscious use of her gifts to attain an end. If she is married she develops skill in managing her husband and the whole situation between them. She is always at hand, she always anticipates his wishes, she makes home so pleasant that he of necessity has to fall in with her plans and do what is expected of him. A woman of this type makes what is popularly called a "wise wife." Her ego orientation is not directed to such purely personal and selfish ends as in the case of the flirt and the gold digger, but to ends which are seemingly legitimate, namely making her husband happy and her marriage a success. The danger of this orientation becomes apparent, however, when we sense a subtle emphasis on the possessive pronoun. It is *her* husband, *her* marriage! In order to keep her husband happy such a woman almost inevitably has to reserve a part of her reactions. She gives him only as much of her feelings as is calculated to be good for him, and by skillful management she keeps him unaware not only of a certain lack of reality in her reactions but also of the fact that life is humdrum and dull. If, however, she should be ill or obliged to be away from home it may be that the husband will wake up and begin to find life apart from his all-loving wife far more interesting than when he was perpetually lapped about by her solicitous care. Then he becomes aware that her kindness and unselfishness are not all they seemed, and the egocentric attitude behind her mask of the "good wife" peeps out.

If such a woman is to develop beyond the stage of egocentricity something more is needed than the refinement of her desires for personal success and happiness. Her natural capacity to attract the man's anima projection gives her an importance and power which are in a certain sense fictitious, for she has done nothing to merit them. They depend solely on the man's illusion. It is like a fortune put into her hands for which she has not had to work. To sacrifice this power requires real devotion to a purpose or value which is superior to her own ego. Redemption from primitive instinct, on the one hand, and the domination of the egotistic attitude, on the other, demand first that the woman become aware of her own instinct and of the part she plays in relation to the man. If she truly loves him or if a deeper relation to life develops within her, then the whole current of her desire may be diverted toward a non-personal goal — to one which supersedes the goal of personal satisfaction and superiority. Thus a fresh step is made in the conscious development of the individual —a step toward individuation. [2]

It is the primitive, feminine element in woman which catches the projection of the man's anima in actual life. There is in all women a streak or thread of this primitive femininity, although in some women it may be almost entirely repressed and in others kept out of sight by a conscious effort. Our Western education of girls seeks to eradicate its manifestations as far as possible; hence with the majority of our women it remains a trend, a factor of their psychology, but not the dominating one. This trend, however, is the ruling factor in the personality of certain women and girls who make up the groups of anima women. It is interesting to note how such a woman functions in life and how she affects those around her.

When a woman of marked anima type comes into a community, all the young men, unmarried and married alike, are immediately fascinated by her. Their heads are turned and they cannot say too much in her praise, while they vie with each other in showing her attentions. The women, however, have a different opinion of her. At first they are merely cold and aloof but soon become

2 It is necessary here to distinguish between the use of the terms *collective, individual* and *personal*. As far as possible Jung's usage has been followed. For example, in *Psychological Types* Jung says that "men who in public life are extremely energetic, bold, obstinate, willful, and inconsiderate" may at home "appear good-natured, mild, accommodating, even weak" (p. 589). He asks "which, then, is the true character, the real personality?" and answers, "According to my view. . .such a man has no real character at all, i.e., he is not *individual* but *collective*, i.e., he corresponds with general circumstances and expectations. . .He is an individual, of course, like every being: but an unconscious one. Through his more or less complete identification with the attitude of the moment, he at least deceives others, and also often himself, as to his real character. He puts on a *mask*. . . .A man who is identified with this mask I would call 'personal' (as opposed to 'individual')" (p. 590). "The psychological individual is characterized by its peculiar, unique psychology. . . .The psychological individual, or individuality, has an a priori unconscious existence. . . .A conscious process of differentiation is required to bring the individuality to consciousness" (pp. 560-61).

critical and blame her for the defections of their husbands and lovers. They usually make the mistake of criticizing her to their men and are horrified to find that the men defend her. Or if masculine courage is lacking for that—and it takes a courage of no mean order for a man to defend a woman when feminine public opinion condemns her—the men compensate for what they consider injustice and prejudice on the part of their women by redoubling their attentions to her. This merely adds to the feminine fury against the "depraved woman," the "hussy." But what of the woman herself? She will say: "I only want to be left alone, to go my own way and live my own life. I do not set out to attract men, and I certainly do not want to estrange them from their wives and sweethearts. Why do all the women shun me and mistrust me? I am lonely and want a woman friend. I want to be good. But wherever I go men follow me, they offer to see me home and even make improper advances to me. Is it my fault? I do not want it. But the poor things are so unhappy I simply must comfort them as far as I can; only a woman with a heart of stone could do less. But I always send them home to their wives or sweethearts. Can I help it if they come back?" Such, at all events, is her way of putting the case.

Now here are three different estimates of the same situation. The man's estimate is based on the value he finds through being able to project his anima and in that way to make a relation to his own unconscious. The wives, on the other hand, hate one who acts the part of anima, as they think, shamelessly. Their resistance to her is doubtless strengthened because they would all like to have her power over men, but their moral code prevents them from exercising even such powers as they have. It is a case of "they could if they would but they dare not." And their involuntary renunciation makes them bitter as it did the fox who called the grapes sour.

Meanwhile the woman herself remains quite unconscious of what she is doing. She feels herself to be entirely innocent. Her actions and their results have no connection. She cannot see herself as a whole. When talking with such a woman one gets a sense of the most amazing ambiguity and of the extraordinary ambivalence of her every word and action. She does not know in the least that she invites the attentions of the men who flock around her or that she plays them off one against another. She just *is*. And no one is more amazed at the result of her actions than she herself. I remember once seeing a girl of this type who was saying goodby to a group of admirers clustered around her. She shook hands with all but one. As it gradually dawned on him that she was passing him by, he looked more and more crestfallen and slipped away from the group to open the door for her. As she came out he said in the greatest dejection, "Aren't you going to say goodby to me?" "Oh, I thought you were going to see me home," she replied. Needless to say the young man went with her, although up to that moment he had had no intention of leaving the party so early. But—and here we come to the interesting part of the incident—the girl had had no intention of asking him to leave with her. Her oversight of him had been purely accidental, it was not till she saw his dejected attitude that it occurred to her to ask him to accompany her. Further, she had no idea that he would interpret her action as singling him out from her admirers. She was later both hurt and puzzled to discover that he had construed her action as encouragement and that, on this basis, he expected her to accept a greater intimacy with him. She was more puzzled to find that the other admirers were jealous of the preference she had unwittingly shown him.

A girl of this type will say the most provocative things and will allow herself to become involved in a compromising situation with one whom, perhaps, she really dislikes, only to be amazed and hurt when he takes her words and actions at their face value. Or perhaps she wishes to dismiss an admirer. She really wants to be rid of him, but instead of taking a definite stand, telling him plainly that she does not like his attentions, she compromises, put him off. She runs away, as it were, but always gives him a final glance over her shoulder, with a "come hither" look in her eye. If one challenges this attitude she defends it by saying, "It would be so cruel to dismiss him finally; I am only trying to get him to accept the idea of separation gradually." It never occurs to her that she is like the good lady who, on being told that the puppy's tail had been docked, said, "Oh, how cruel to cut it all off at once. Why didn't they do it a bit at a time so that the puppy could get used to it." The anima woman is kind, but her kindness is cruelty, and her innocent goodness makes her act as the most sophisticated man-killer would. For this type of woman is a nature product, and nature is always bivalent—good and bad, kind and cruel.

All these ways of acting are purely feminine; they are collective, not individual, and occur whenever masculine interests and desires —masculine libido in short—is brought into contact with feminine libido. Women in whom this way of functioning is strong find the same attitude in *all* the men they meet. To them all men are alike. Therefore *all* men may find in such a woman a collective feminine attitude which can accept every man and his masculine libido no matter what form it takes. Such a woman is truly "all things to all men."

But certain women of the anima type are curiously aware of their own lack of inner oneness. Such a woman has an intuitive perception of the bivalence and ambiguity of her own nature. She may indeed ascribe it to a subjective sense of being not one woman but many women. For instance, Anna Kingsford, an exceedingly intuitive and subjective woman, said in one of her talks with her biographer: "I am such a puzzle to myself and I want to be explained . . . I want to know . . . especially how it is that I am so many and such different kinds of people and which of them all I am or ought to be. For the many mes in me are not even in agreement among themselves; but some of them actually hate each other, and some are as bad as others are good." [3] Later, in trying to account for her sense of plurality, she became convinced that she was a reincarnation of many women who had

3 Maitland, *The Life of Anna Kingsford*, Vol. I, Chap. IV.

lived ages before her and that she had carried over memories of these previous incarnations. I have often encountered this phenomenon in an anima woman. The splitting up of the one woman into many women is the obverse of being "all things to all men," for one of the women within her is called out by her contact with one man and another by the next. She is like a many-sided crystal which turns automatically without any volition on her part under the influence of changes in her environment. By this unconscious adaptation, first one facet and then another is presented to view and always that facet which best reflects his anima is presented to the gazer.

Women who function primarily as the anima of men are not by any means all alike in character or personality, but beneath their external differences a fundamental similarity in psychological attitude and reaction can be found which accounts for the effect they produce in life and especially on men. Three kinds of women will be described who apparently are poles asunder, as different from each other as women could be, and yet on deeper investigation it will become clear that they all have a basic attitude to life which is characteristic of the anima woman and differentiates her from others.

First, we have the innocent flower-like maiden who is generally fair and pretty, who always suggests innocence and who, regardless of what her age may be, invariably plays the part of a child. She is the heroine of many books. She is always pure and good; she may be sinned against, but she never sins. She is man's good angel. Dora in *David Copperfield* is just such a person. She is ignorant of the world and its ways, yet she is often engaged in trying to reform some reprobate who, whatever his faults may be, has at least ventured into the struggle of life instead of remaining on the outskirts as she has done. Such a girl is glorified out of all semblance to reality by the projection of the man's anima, for when he sees his anima — his soul — in her, she becomes to him an "angel child." To one who is not under this illusion, she appears a dull enough little thing. Her education is often defective and generally consists of a knowledge of how to dress and how to hold her tongue, though in the latter accomplishment she may be deficient! She rarely has anything to offer in the way of achievement, yet her charm and good looks and her "influence for good" undoubtedly have their place in the world. Under this flower-like innocence, however, one may often glimpse a "something" which suggests that the girl is not so innocent and disinterested as she appears. Her gestures seem to hint that she perhaps fancies herself in the role of guardian angel, or she shows a tendency, scarcely recognized by herself, to seek the center of the stage. The dreams and fantasies of such girls may unmistakably show the ego trend in the unconscious. One girl dreamed that she was dressed like little Lord Fauntleroy coming down a wide staircase into a large hall where a group of people, all gazing at her in silent admiration, awaited her. The analysis of such a girl often reveals deeply hidden away a cherished fantasy of herself as a princess. In real life women of this type nearly always select from their group of admirers the important men as recipients of their favors and, as a rule, make what is called a good marriage. All these things indicate that the ego which is so conspicuously absent from the conscious personality is not entirely missing but is in the unconscious, so that an ego trend poisons, as it were, the purity of the girl's motives in every situation.

The flower-like anima girl is doomed to be a child to the end of her days. Childishness may be charming enough while she is still young; it may be tolerable even through her thirties; but after that it becomes pathetic or boresome, for she goes through life as the mummy of a child in a painted casket. She is condemned to be a perpetual Ophelia, counting her flowers while others around her are concerned with the possibly tragic destiny of men and states. Novelists have recognized that this type of woman must always be young and have, indeed, resorted to the device of keeping her eternally youthful by making her die early — a fate, which strange to say, frequently happens to her in real life.

The next instance is apparently the exact opposite of the child anima. She is dark, full-blooded, passionate; she lives all of her feelings and instincts entirely uncensored. The innocent flower-like girl has no consciousness of her own instinct, she may well be entirely cold or unawakened, but this woman is passion personified. Her tempestuous moods lure and hold the man. He never knows where he will find her from one day to the next—whether he will be received with passionate embraces or with a stiletto! Such a woman lives exactly as she feels, without any calculation as to the effects of her action, and she always feels strongly. She personifies "Nature, red in tooth and claw." Kipling's line, "The female of the species is more deadly than the male," characterizes her. Apart from the violence of her reactions to men, she may be domestically minded; she may wish to "be good" and to live a quiet and ordered life; but ever and again men come around her and something within her is stirred and acts automatically, quite regardless of her own conscious wishes in the matter. Carmen is a good example of the passionate anima woman, but with her the ego trend in the unconscious is dominant for she delights to gain power over men in order to flaunt them.

A woman of this kind whether egotistic or not is enormously attractive to certain types of men. It is as though her abandonment to her emotions releases in them their over-restrained feelings and permits them to experience that irrationality of nature which they have held under too rational a rule. They may not even need to abandon themselves to their more irrational passions; for many a man it may be sufficient to have the woman abandon herself. For, in her abandonment, it is as though for a little while his untamed irrational anima finds release.

Finally, there is the woman who stands in marked contrast to both the flower-like anima girl and the passionate anima woman. She is cold and distant and unreachable. By her very passivity she releases the man, in certain instances, from a too great intensity. She is usually without emotional expression and is utterly impersonal. She gives no indication of her own wishes, answers a question either by silence or by a cold phrase which may have various interpretations.

Galsworthy, in portraying Irene in the *Forsyte Saga,* has drawn a woman of this type with great skill. It has been said that Irene was frigid to the wrong man and glowing to the right man, but this does not alter the fact that she played the cold anima to Soames. Irene could not by will power, it is true, give a sexual response to Soames, whom she did not love, but she failed none-theless to live up to what was required of her by the law of relatedness. She lived for several years in marriage with him and made herself into a statue. In spite of the fact that the respon-sibility for the related side of life belongs principally to the woman, Irene withheld her feeling reactions in all the episodes of everyday life and so gave Soames no opportunity to develop a better kind of relationship with her. She continued in the marriage and did nothing about it. Even in the final scene (which doubtless rouses the indignation of every male reader of the book) when Soames forced her to an unwelcome intimacy she still maintained the passive role of the injured wife. Why didn't she fight him? But this would have meant taking a stand, something of which she was hardly capable. She preferred to maintain the role of injured innocence. As a result of her passivity, Soames was virtually tied to a corpse through all the years of his marriage. I hold no brief for Soames. He is not painted in attractive colors. But one must ask why Irene did not play the game *or* end the situation. The answer is that she was afraid. As Soames' wife she had a home and a position of wealth. If she left him she would have had to support herself and face the condemnation of society. This she was not strong enough to face alone. She needed the support of Bossiny and the strength born of her love for him, in order to free herself from her bondage. By remaining with Soames she could get what she wanted without giving anything in return. Her action depended on an unconscious ego-power motive.

When we come close to such a woman to find out what she

is really like we shall probably discover that, like her sisters described above, she is entirely innocent of any conscious wish to tyrannize over the man. She is probably a very nebulous person who is not clearly conscious of her own wishes, quite unable to say what she feels at any moment and liable, as Irene was, to be thrust into a marriage which she only subsequently discovers is distasteful to her. She probably spends most of her time in a half-twilight state—not fully aware of what is going on around her—never really rousing herself to make a definite decision which she is prepared to stand by. She has perhaps assumed her cold, distant manner as a convenient shield between herself and reality, having found it to be the most effective armor against those importunate persons and circumstances, irritating because always recalling to her the obligation to wake up and make a decision. She too is bivalent—she will and she won't; and rather than rouse herself to definite action she will endure anything. Here again we have this ambiguous quality of the anima woman.

These typical anima women are, in each instance, naive and unconscious. They act in this way because this is the way "it" acts in them. Such a woman is a nature product and in this stage of consciousness, at all events, is innocent of any deliberate attempt to gain power over the man whom her charms have attracted. She does not realize that her power over him is due to his anima projection which her own nebulous quality has mirrored. For him the relation with her is weighted through his anima; while for her the situation holds the possibility of the fulfillment of her biological needs, an aspect, however, which is frequently neglected. Beyond that it holds the possibilities of personal satisfaction because of the fictitious position of importance she occupies on account of his absorption in her.

The woman, however, may grow tired of carrying the man's anima. She may become increasingly aware that her husband does not really love *her* but is always seeing something over her shoulder, as it were. She may say that she does not want this any longer and that she wishes to be loved for herself but that she cannot prevent his seeing her as other than she is. This "cannot," however, is not altogether true. If she would show herself in her true colors by giving her reaction at the time, he would soon begin to discriminate between her and his anima. If asked why she does not do this, she will almost invariably admit that she is afraid of losing him. In other words she is not really prepared to give up the advantages she gains by carrying his anima projection, although she may also want greater liberty in order to develop her own personality. For to play the anima role means to act, think and feel *only* as feminine being. It is a role which is entirely collective, representing a biological and instinctive reaction to the male.

But woman is, after all, not only a nature product, not only an instinctive feminine creature; she is also a human being. In the Western world, at all cultural levels above the peasant, there is present, at least potentially, an ego, a center of consciousness which says "I" and which prevents the woman from being *only* nature. Yet if she lives only as anima, the ego remains relatively unconscious. If this is the case, her actions are all tinged by ego-power motives which can be unmasked by looking below the surface. Thus every woman who neglects her real reaction in too great compliance to the wishes of the man plays to catch the projection of the man's anima. She has a motive, although, it is true, the motive may be an unconscious one. No reaction is over-ridden except by a stronger one; action follows the strongest motive. If a woman allows her wish or impulse to be over-ridden, there must be a stronger motive at work than her conscious wish. If, in complying with the man's wishes, she represses her own desire, she does it in order to catch the man's anima—in the last analysis to catch the man—and her motive is the wish for power or prestige or support, even though she herself may not be aware of this fact.

When this ego motive, latent in the unconscious, becomes dominant and rises to consciousness in any one of these women, she embarks on the second stage in the evolution of consciousness.

The naive woman becomes the sophisticated woman of the world. She is frankly intent on power and superiority and exploits men for money or for prestige or for the satisfaction of her instincts. The flirt, the gold digger, the scalphunter, the courtesan are all types of the anima woman who has gone wrong, as it were, whose natural gifts have been organized under the ego. These women are, or become, almost always cold and aloof. Even the passionate type learns to use her instinct for the gaining of power. She does not give herself even to her own passion, for the deepest interest lies elsewhere.

Some readers may be disturbed because so often the so-called lower types of women have been chosen as illustrations. Naturally extreme cases are chosen in order to point out a particular psychological trend. They have also been chosen because they show unmistakably the traits of character which always exist to some degree in the woman who reacts only as anima, even though the characteristics may be so completely masked that the woman herself remains unaware of their existence.

But these two stages of consciousness, the naive state and the sophisticated or ego state, do not represent the psychological condition in all women. In the naive state consciousness is diffuse, not clearly centered, and the natural impulses and instincts function unchecked by any development of individual conscious aims in the woman herself. In the sophisticated stage the individual aims of the woman, which in many cases may even go contrary to the natural impulses or biological aims, come to the fore and gradually dominate consciousness. In the third stage both the natural impulses and the dominance of ego-power are superseded by a newly recognized value or object which the woman accepts as of greater worth and significance than either the biological urge or the impulse to acquire personal power and satisfaction. This may be called a suprapersonal value or object because it is accepted by the individual as being above personal needs and wishes, thus claiming complete and unconditional allegiance.

Such a suprapersonal value has been found by some in a dom-

inating idea such as the ideal of Liberty or of Fraternity, or of
the Love of God, ideas which have claimed at times from men
and women a devotion superseding the claims of their own biological and personal needs, superseding even the claims of family
duty and love.

In all ages seers have recognized abstract ideas or principles
as the supreme values in life, but before they can become powerful forces or motives for man in general they have to be demonstrated in a concrete situation. For example, liberty as an ideal
can inspire a man like Lincoln, whose character was gradually
redeemed from ambition and the desire for personal power and
aggrandizement through the value which he saw in this idea.
But before the average citizen of the United States could be moved
by it, it had to be concretized in the actual endangering of the
liberties of the Union. In a somewhat different but still comparable
way mystics have devoted their lives to an inner concept of God.
Only, however, when the inner truths men serve have been expressed in a religion which is a more or less concrete embodiment
of their ideals have the majority of men been stirred to enthusiasm.

But today these ideas have lost their old power of redemption
for the majority of people. We recognize this and from all sides
comes the question: Is there some other object or aim which
carries with it a similar value? Or is it our doom to live and
die under the dominance of the ego? An intellectually chosen
ideal, however worthy, cannot release us from the powerful forces
of nature and the ego. An object or value which is to redeem
us must have the power to release within us energies superior to
those wielded by either sexuality or the ego. The solution is not
to be found in a rational idealism, nor for most seekers is the
solution to be found in the modern churches. Some people have
found a solution for this modern problem through analytical psychology. Jung has shown that when a human being explores the
hidden depths of his own psyche he finds primordial images,
pictures of racial experience, archetypes, ancient powerful forces
which have influenced his character and actions all unseen and

unknown. His personal ego no longer dominates the scene, his personal satisfactions fade into relative insignificance and he becomes aware for the first time of the drama of inherited forces within himself. He realizes that the ego is no longer the center of his psyche, the king of life. His consciousness enlarges and as the work of exploration proceeds and he strives for and attains a relationship to these inner figures, a new center of consciousness gradually emerges. This is not a new ego—a kind of Super-I— for it includes racial and suprapersonal trends which are not identical with the personal wishes and needs of the individual, though these also are represented. On the contrary, it has a non-personal quality which would prevent the individual from using the term "I" to express this new center or Self. In this new Self may be found a suprapersonal value which has for us moderns the power and validity which men in other times found through an ideal related to the external world or through the experience of a concretized religion.

On account of its subjective character the problem of a suprapersonal value is a peculiarly difficult one to discuss intelligibly. It is not a question of any esoteric doctrine but only of the facts of psychological experience which I have observed sufficiently often to convince me of their validity. But when an inner psychological experience of a suprapersonal value is to be discussed, there is difficulty in finding suitable terms; the language has necessarily to be metaphorical.

The majority of people get along perfectly well without making the effort to acquire a degree of consciousness beyond the ego stage. Psychologically those individuals who are well adapted to this world and to their own environment live in a state of peace. Therefore this discussion of a suprapersonal value may be, to them, incomprehensible. But for others who are, for whatever reason, maladapted, it is as though their fatherland were threatened; they are compelled to develop a new state of consciousness, to seek for a suprapersonal value, just as the inhabitants of an invaded country have patriotism forced upon them.

A not inconsiderable number of the well adapted whose experience of life is yet not satisfactory to them want something more than comfort, refinement and amusement. To such people, as well as to the maladapted, comes the challenge to seek for themselves that spring of vitality which has been choked by our material civilization. They, too, like the inhabitants of an invaded country, must seek a value above their own personal aims if all is not to be lost. But as this is not a fact of personal experience for all my readers I shall leave the more theoretical aspect of the subject and content myself with describing briefly the observable effects that result from the substitution of a suprapersonal value for those of the ego.

The anima woman must find her suprapersonal value, not through an intellectually accepted ideal but through a deeper experience of her own nature which leads her into relation to the woman's spirituality, the feminine principle itself. Jung has used the old Greek philosophic concept of Eros or relatedness to express this feminine principle, in contrast to the Logos which is the masculine principle dealing with factual knowledge and wisdom.

In ordinary life examples of this substitution of a higher value for personal ones can be recognized, and the new psychological orientation which this implies is shown by a certain change which takes place in the woman's attitude.

Take for example the *femme inspiratrice*. She has been worshipped and adored by men. The good things of life come to her easily. She has been put on a pedestal and been considered almost divinely wise. Like the anima woman in general she is quite fluid, having few solid attitudes or points of consciousness of her own, which would only distort the reflection of the man's unconscious contents. She is like a deep pool of water which only reflects what passes before it. The man sees in her, however, images and pictures of great definiteness and detail, much as one may see pictures in the clouds or in the fire. We recognize that the picture image does not exist as such in the plastic material, but that the many changing shapes and forms allow those things which are still in symbol form in the unconscious of the observer to become manifest to him. In a similar way a *femme inspiratrice,* through her plasticity and unconscious behavior, allows the man to see in her a reflection of his own unconscious thought forms. These are accessible to him only through the stirring of instinct aroused by his attraction to the woman. Usually men do not recognize that this is the case but are deceived as to the part the woman plays in their inspiration. They ascribe to her a much more active role than she as a rule is capable of taking.

Certain women, however, who have advanced beyond the sophisticated stage are yet particularly well fitted for this role of *femme inspiratrice* on account of their own contact with the deeper things within them. Such a woman can lead a man whom she loves into touch with the hidden truths of life because of the reality of her own inner experience. She herself could not write the book or paint the picture which the man creates through his relation to her, but on account of her contact with her own inner truth, which is a truth of life and of relationship, she can open the gates for him. Such a woman is in a different category from one who is nothing but anima, for she gives of herself and is not playing a role in which her unconscious motive is to hold the man. She is a "redeemed" anima woman — redeemed, that is, from the hold of her own biological instincts, on the one hand, and from self-seeking and egotistic motives, on the other.

But the *femme inspiratrice* who is just anima also plays an indispensable part in the man's inspiration. A man can rarely view his unconscious contents directly; they are only perceptible to him through fantasy or when they are projected into the objective world. Therefore, if a man finds them only in the woman, he needs the woman if he is to find them! But truth demands that we recognize *what* part she plays, namely whether she is an active agent or whether she is entirely passive, a mere reflector of his unconscious thoughts and, when left to herself, a creature destitute of all that he found through his association with her.

To play this role, even successfully, may not indicate an inner development in the woman herself. It may be just one way of playing anima.

For many a woman there is a great lure in the thought of inspiring her man, of being his guardian angel, indispensable to him. I remember the case of a girl of about fifteen who was brought for analysis on account of her exceedingly unsatisfactory adaptation. She would not go to school or submit to any kind of discipline but was running quite wild. An older man of some prominence in the artistic world was in love with her and the girl thought of herself as his inspiration and his guardian angel. He was of somewhat dissipated habits and she considered it her mission to reform him, so that, on the one hand, she was sprouting wings while, on the other, she was being a naughty little girl! And yet the artist actually did find inspiration from his assocation with her. This might be all very well for the artist, but it was bound to spell ruin for a girl in such a position. For, instead of going on with her own education and development, she was reduced to being nothing but a psychological function of the man. She was limited to being his "soul," just as Eve was for Adam, instead of taking up her own task of becoming an individual woman in her own right. An added element of danger is the probability that such a man will always require a *young* girl to play this part for him, so that in a very few years this particular girl will find herself replaced by another victim of his psychological need.

When a man has a relation with a woman who is to him *femme inspiratrice* he gains from the relationship the inspiration to create. To him his creation is the child of his love for the woman. Often he expects her also to regard his work in this light. But if she does so her attention is directed to the *thing*, and she comes to maintain her relationship to him *in order* to get a certain result. This is a power attitude. It means that she seeks her satisfaction at the wrong source. For to her the *relationship* is the child of her love — her creation — and in it she must seek her satisfaction and fulfillment, not in any "good" that may come out of it. For this value of relationship is her suprapersonal value.

The substitution of a suprapersonal value for ego values may be seen in certain women's attitude toward dress. To the anima woman dress is very important. She has to dress for the part that she is to play in every situation. It is not simply that she wants to dress becomingly. It is something more than this, even granted she has her share of natural vanity. Rather, it is as if she considers *herself* a work of art which she will take infinite pains to make as perfect and as fully expressive of the inner meaning it is intended to convey as her material resources will allow. In other words, it is as though the anima woman does not regard herself and her life experiences as belonging only to herself, but as though in some way they have a general or collective significance which demands for their every expression her greatest care and attention. This is just what the artist feels about his product. It represents his own personal experience of life, but by his art he raises it from the merely personal into a form which expresses general or even universal truth.

This capacity to generalize her emotions may be exploited by the ego, for such a generalization allows many women to express, or to portray falsely, an emotion which they do not really feel but which is calculated to catch the projection of the man's anima by its very generalization. We see such a dramatization in the case of woman who may play to perfection the role of the bereaved widow, even when those who know her intimately realize that far from being desolate she is really relieved at the death of a husband whom she did not love. We see her dressed in deep, but not ostentatious, mourning, her cheeks pale with powder if not with anxiety, her eyes large with unshed tears, her manner gentle, yet dignified — so brave, so sweet, so to be pitied! Perhaps the whole thing is unconscious. Possibly she is just playing the role of widow, as she imagines it should be played. Or it may be that she is more sophisticated. She may have her attention fixed entirely on an impression which she wishes to produce in a particular quarter and which with consummate skill she brings to pass.

But it is not only in her clothes that the anima woman dresses for a part. She very frequently makes up her face and has her hair dressed according to an accepted mode. It is almost as though she wears a mask. She takes great pains to eradicate or to disguise all individual marks, both in features and in expression, and to present to the world only a collective mask which does not vary with the coming and going of her actual feelings but only according to her conception of what the situation requires. This also, in its simplest form, is done in order to express that part of her personality which is universal or collective, and in its less naive form is done in order to catch the projection of the man's anima which is always generalized or collective.

The anima woman carries her acting even beyond this point. Not only is her dress a work of art, not only is her version, so to say, of her own face an artistic creation, but (the conviction is forced upon one) her presentation of her emotions is also, as Jung once said of her tears, purposive. Her laughter, her tears, her facial expression, the tones of her voice all seem to be directed toward an end. The woman herself may be completely unconscious of this orientation, or she may be dimly aware that "now is the time to cry." The more difficult and tragic the circumstances of a coming interview may be, the more careful is her selection of exactly the right dress and make-up. She always has one eye on effect. She always has to act her emotion — to make of it a work of art. She never completely *has* her own experience unless by presenting the picture of it to others she receives it again through their response.

Women who are developed on the individual side despise such arts and wiles. Possibly the indifference to dress which many of these women display comes from a reaction against the dramatization so characteristic of the anima type. The dramatization comes from an unconscious mechanism and is a reaction of female to male. While this may not be apparent to men, women, of whatever type, are quite aware of the unreality of the action, and the more frank and outspoken among them are naturally repelled and refuse to have anything to do with what seems to them deception. In discarding these arts, however, they perhaps throw out the wheat with the chaff, for the tendency to play a part is quite instinctive and is related also to the carrying of the projection of the man's anima. Since this performs a very important function, both biologically and psychologically, we must ask what is the deeper significance and value of the woman's dramatization?

May it not be that the woman is compelled to dress for the part, and to act it, in order to find the inner meaning of her own experience? Perhaps she can only consciously *get* the thing that lives in her through observing her own gestures and instinctive acts. Kipling reports that when Riki-Tiki-Tavi, the mongoose, first saw a cobra he felt that his eyes were red and *so* knew that he was angry. Similarly, it is only when a woman finds herself instinctively doing certain things that she realizes what it is that is within her. Often women have said to me, "I found the tears running down my cheeks, and so I knew that what he said hurt me badly." To so great an extent woman *is* instinct! Her actions, her gestures, her words may all voice or embody instinct, femininity. If she will only let herself act uncensored, then she can observe in herself, in her own actions, the working of pure nature. It is as though she herself is her own work of art, which she creates by working with the plastic materials of her own life, often toward ends which she does not as yet comprehend. And by a kind of afterthought she is enabled to discern, through viewing her actions objectively, what it was that life wanted of her. Psychological development takes place when she looks at herself in this objective way and so comes to understand the deeper aspects of her own nature and incorporates them consciously into the totality of her character and attitude. This is by no means an easy thing to do, for it makes the woman herself her own "animal of experiment." However, if she allows these quite instinctual things to take their course she may find something functioning within her which is intrinsic to her and yet is not her personal ego. The second century Gnostics had a text in their books which bears on this way of experiencing oneself: "Learn whence is sorrow and joy, and love and hate, and waking though one would not, and sleeping though one would not, and getting angry though one would not, and falling in love though one would not. And if thou shouldst closely investigate these things, thou wilt find *Him* in thyself, one and many, just as the atom; thus finding from thyself a way out of thyself." [4]

If a woman seeks for consciousness by this route she will find two major difficulties to be overcome. First, the instinctive things which spontaneously occur to her to do may not correspond to her own idea of herself or to the attitude toward life which she has consciously taken. A conflict will then inevitably arise within her and, if she is not to repress the instinctual side once more, she will find it essential to change her attitude; she may even be compelled to admit that she has been mistaken in her estimate of herself — an admission no one likes to make.

The second difficulty lies in the very real danger that the woman may drop back into being "just nature" once more. This danger is immanent and ever-present, since she has so recently climbed out from her instinctual state. This step was accomplished, moreover, only through a revulsion of feeling against the old ways, and a fear of a relapse to that old state is betrayed by a tendency toward rigidity in her new attitude. It is impossible to go back as though the change had never been. She has gained a degree of consciousness; a going back would be a regression; she cannot achieve again the innocence of the child. When Adam and Eve were driven out of the garden because of their new consciousness of good and evil, born from eating of the tree of knowledge, an angel with a fiery sword was placed before the gate to prevent their going back. That sword is still there, and a woman who

4 Mead, *Fragments of a Faith Forgotten*, p. 223.

has achieved a certain degree of consciousness cannot go back to the stage of the naive anima woman; the regression would inevitably lead her to licentiousness. Nevertheless, she has to beware of an excessive rigidity. If she is to gain a position of balance through a wider consciousness of both sides of her nature, she must let her instinct — for instance, the instinct to play a part — show itself, while at the same time she reminds herself continously, "This is not all." A remarkable expression of this double need occurred once in a woman's dream. The dream said to her, "Let us live strongly and devotedly whatever comes, and afterwards let us analyze it." By this means she can become aware of the deeper workings of instinct within herself and yet not lose touch with her conscious attitude.

What then is the significance, psychologically speaking, of the anima role which women play? For the man, to find and love a woman who bears for him the symbol of his soul, whose qualities reflect his unconscious feminine side, is, potentially, an experience of deep spiritual significance, holding for him the possibility of development through the integration of parts of his psyche which were previously unrealized. For the woman who carries this symbol, however, the subjective experience is necessarily very different. Its value for her lies in evoking and tending the man's interest — his love. The richer and more creative parts of her own feminine nature lie deeply buried within her, hidden even from herself. It is almost as though another woman (perhaps Mother Nature herself?) lies sleeping within her, inaccessible except as she may be quickened into life by the man, as Brunnhilde was awakened by Siegfried's kiss. The man is more aware of the flow of his energy, that is, of his libido, than the woman is; she is always a little indefinite, a little vague and unfocused. But he does not experience instinct (nature) in himself, as the woman must. Yet this experiencing of nature is revivifying, like a plunge into the ocean from which all life arises. If a man is to reach these hidden depths, it must be by awakening nature in the woman through his love. His instinctual libido flows out. He is aware of it primarily as an outflowing, a searching for a home outside himself. No wonder that he desires and loves a woman who can satisfy this longing. But the woman is nearly always a little aloof from the situation. She lives *in herself,* away from him. She finds life, it is true, because of his interest in her; it is this which wakes life in her, yet she lives it *in herself.*

Anima women who are still in either the naive or the sophisticated stage of development often show this aloofness and preoccupation with themselves and their own reactions. With them it is an autoerotic manifestation. This is so because the woman uses the man's anima projection and his consequent interest in her for her own pleasure and satisfaction. Certain women even deliberately act the role of anima in order to catch the man's projection and exploit it for their own benefit. But the aloofness of the woman is not necessarily autoerotic. In Eugene O'Neill's play, *The Great God Brown,* the characters all have masks which they put on whenever they dare not show their real selves. Sibyl, the harlot, has such a mask which is painted like the conventional anima woman. But she, in her real self, is something greater than she appears to be. She wears her mask less and less frequently as the play proceeds, for she lives in such a relation to her own instinct that she is able to draw out and cherish the best that each man has in him. She accepts his libido and cares for it, but she never tries to possess or exploit it. She is related to something deeper than the ego and its satisfactions. Her devotion is given to some greater value that she senses in life; as a result no one needs to wear a mask when he is with her but can show himself for what he really is. Such an attitude brings for the woman redemption from the overwhelming power of nature, on the one hand, and from the dominance of the ego, on the other. To attain such an attitude requires from her a recognition that she does not possess the man's libido, but that it is, as it were, lent to her in trust and when the time comes she must return it to him. Her own gain comes not through possessing the man's libido but through giving herself to the deeper significance of life and truth made available through the emotional experience. Thus a value which she estimates as above any personal gain or satisfaction comes to hold the central place for her, and redemption of her personality is brought about through the recognition of a suprapersonal value.

There is another way in which a woman may be redeemed from the bondage of instinct and of the ego, namely through a worked-out relationship with a man. If the woman falls in love with the man who has projected his anima onto her, she is no longer aloof and indifferent. The projection of her animus is caught by him. She, as well as he, is under an inner obligation to get in touch with her soul. She can no longer play unscathed in a situation which may well be a matter of life and death to him, for she also is involved. However little the situation may be to her liking, she is compelled to come back to him over and over again and to try to work out the difficulties between them. By this means reality can gradually be made to replace the illusion of the animus and anima projections, a process which involves psychological development and an extension of consciousness through the assimilation of that unconscious side of the psyche which previously lived in the projected animus or anima. In this case the value that is superordinated to the personal wishes and satisfactions is that of the conscious relationship.

The coming of a suprapersonal value changes the very nature of the experience of life for the individual. While personal motives ruled, the life was lived under the pleasure-pain principle. Happiness and personal satisfaction were the aims of life. To some, happiness was interpreted in a purely selfish way, perhaps even on an animal plane. To others, more developed and more cultured, these aims involved a more refined, more esthetic, even more altruistic way of life; but still, in the final analysis, that was good which gave pleasure, and that was bad which caused pain. When, however, a value arises which is above the personal level this standard of appraisal is overstepped. Pleasure and pain, realities though they undoubtedly are, become relative. What is pleasurable when regarded from the personal point of view may be neither good nor desirable when viewed from a different standpoint. And pain may cease to be an unmitigated evil when it is realized as a necessary step in attaining a value which is greater than the personal loss involved. For the sake of an inner relation to the spring of life or for the sake of gaining consciousness and reality in a relationship, a woman may indeed be content to accept pain. She may even be willing to go voluntarily to meet pain and perhaps to inflict it on a loved one if, by taking the painful course, truth may be served. In this way what is evil on the personal level may minister to what is good on the suprapersonal plane.

Thus we see that instinctual libido which arises from the hidden depths of human nature is, at first, just one of the manifestations of nature forces; it has nothing of individuality about it. Presently, when the ego arises, this nature force may be brought up to consciousness and held there under the dominance of the ego. But later a further step in consciousness may be taken. This happens either when the woman becomes aware of a value which transcends her ego and to which she voluntarily submits herself, or when she gets caught into life by falling in love and being obliged through a binding relationship to work on the difficulties and problems that arise between herself and her lover. In either case a step may be taken which results in a deeper and broader consciousness and the emergence of an individuality out of the welter of collective and personal impulses which have been until now her sole motivation.

2. The Ghostly Lover

To be "in love" with a man is more than to "love" him. The state of being in love carries with it a certain element of compulsion, and one who is in love, however enraptured he may be, is certainly not free. Love is proverbially blind. Indeed, a girl may be in love with a man whom, in the absence of the glamor resulting from her state of mind, she might find not even likable or attractive. The glamor and attraction are effects produced by forces in her unconscious which have been stirred to activity through her contact with the man. She projects onto him some important element from her unconscious and then is attracted or repelled by that which she sees in him, quite unaware that it has originated deep within her own psyche. It is her masculine soul, her *animus,* which she has projected. This mechanism is the exact equivalent of the projection of the man's feminine soul, or anima, which formed the subject of the last chapter. When a woman is in love we can either say that she *loves,* that is, she is active, or we can put it the other way round and say that she is attracted, that is, she is passive. In other words her animus, projected to the outside world, draws her irresistibly. Regardless of whether the man loves her or not, the fascination makes it appear as though he were the active party—as though *he* loved her. From her subjective point of view it seems to her that she is attracted from without, while in reality the thing which attracts her is from *within*—in her unconscious.

The possibility of this occurrence is occasionally shown in a play or novel where the girl is portrayed as having a lover who is not of this world but belongs, instead, to the spirit or ghost world. This was the case in the old Jewish legend of the dybbuk, which was made the subject of a drama by Solomon Rappaport and performed both in Yiddish and English.

In this legend the lover who lures his beloved away from reality into union with himself is shown quite objectively as the ghost of a dead youth with whom the heroine was in love. In certain scenes in the play the girl is represented as possessed by the ghost; he enters into her and takes possession of her and she is shown to be temporarily insane, which is to say she is suffering from a psychological illness. In these scenes the ghost has no objective reality but lives nonetheless as a subjective reality in the girl's psyche. She is entirely absorbed in him and by him. She is lost to the real world about her, for she is living only in her own subjective world with her ghostly lover.

In Eugene O'Neill's *Strange Interlude* the same subject is dwelt upon. But here the ghost does not appear at all; his presence must be inferred from the effects he has upon his lover-victim; that is, he appears *only* as a subjective factor in the girl's psychology. The heroine had been in love with a young soldier, an airman, and when he is killed in the war she, as it were, loses her soul and, as a result, can give nothing of her real self to her life. She marries and is loved by many men, but her devotion always goes to her lost lover.

In both instances the lover is portrayed as the ghost or as the still-living influence of an actual man with whom the heroine had had a real relationship, however slender and frustrated it may have been. This influence which effects the woman as though it came from the action or desire of a man, when the truth is he is inactive or perhaps dead or may never have existed as an objective reality, must be a subjective effect within the woman's psyche— hence the term, *Ghostly Lover*. Manifestations of a ghostly lover may occur not only as the ghost of a real man but also in cases

where an actual flesh-and-blood lover has never been in the picture.
We may see instances of this in real life as well as in plays and
novels. Barrie has shown the situation very clearly in his play
Mary Rose, in which strange music lures Mary Rose away from
her husband and child to the Island-that-wants-to-be-visited. This
is a not unusual retreat which one frequently comes upon in the
subjective life of real people. I have known many individuals
who have built up an elaborate fantasy island or castle to which
they retire when life is dull or difficult. Here they often spend
endless time and energy constructing in fantasy a world more to
their liking than the humdrum one to which they find it so hard
to adapt. They "rebuild the world nearer to the Heart's desire."
A fantasy world where everything is as one wishes is enormously
alluring and exerts a fascination calling one away from reality;
it becomes increasingly hard to resist, the more it is indulged in.
This also is the work of the Ghostly Lover.

In talking about the Ghostly Lover we are not dealing with
something which is remote or unusual or which occurs only in
abnormal or pathological conditions. On the contrary the Ghostly
Lover, in his psychological or subjective aspect, is a living reality
to every woman. He holds his power and exerts his lure because
he is a psychological entity, part of that conglomerate of
autonomous, or relatively autonomous, factors which make up
her psyche. As he is a part of her so she is bound to him; she
must find him and consciously assimilate him if she is not to
suffer the pain and distress of disintegration. For he is her soul
mate, her "other half," the invisible companion who accompanies
her throughout life. Jung has named this soul-figure of the woman
animus. The animus is the equivalent of the man's anima, but the
two figures differ markedly in their characteristics and in their
manifestations. [1]

The term Ghostly Lover has been devised to denote the destructive aspect of the animus, but it must be borne in mind that

1 For a further discussion of this subject the reader is referred to C.G.
Jung's essay, "Anima and Animus" in *Two Essays on Analytical
Psychology.*

this is only one aspect, for he does not always function destruc-
tively. As *Ghostly Lover* he *always* acts as one who lures his
victim away from reality by promises of bliss in another world.
In the woman's psychology he is the counterpart of the siren
in the man's. In the man's psychology, as in mythology, the
siren by her music and charm lures the man to a watery grave.
The Ghostly Lover, by the promise of untold bliss, entices the
woman to seek his arms in the air.

The Ghostly Lover, however, is not merely an abstraction of
the psychologist; he is manifested in actual, everyday life. In the
first two of the plays mentioned above, the Ghostly Lover is
personified and acts his part, a dominating one, as do the other
persons in the play. He appears as a reality with power to act
independently and autonomously. His psychological connection with
the woman whose animus he represents is clearly shown by the
curious and almost magical bond between them. In this way is
expressed the autonomy of the animus, composed as he is of
psychological contents of which the woman is unaware or over
which her conscious ego exerts no control, for they belong to
her unconscious. If she should become aware of these psychological
contents, she would be in a position to dissolve the personification
of the animus and thus to divest it of its power while she would
be released from the "magical" influence which the Ghostly Lover
previously wielded.

The form of presentation in the plays is the result of the intuitive perception of the artist, who actually perceives the various
psychological tendencies of his characters in personified form, as
though they were separate people. In his artistic product he shares
with us, the audience, the fruits of his insight, but—and here is
a strange fact—he may not know himself that the characters
he depicts are psychological tendencies and complexes. He himself may take the play as being a simple narration of objective
fact. In much the same way, in real life the Ghostly Lover is
occasionally personified in the memory of a dead or absent lover.
More often it happens that in consciousness he is not personified;
the woman victim herself does not know it is a ghostly lover

who calls her away from reality to an unreal world, although in these cases her unconscious material, her dreams and daytime fantasies show clearly the real situation. In either case, however, when the Ghostly Lover calls and the woman follows she disappears, as it were, from reality, much as Mary Rose did. To those about her she becomes vague, falls into a brown study, is perhaps cross or irritable; or she may wear a baffling or propitiatory smile. To herself it seems that she has become absorbed in an inner experience of great beauty and value which she cannot by any means share with another. At a moment when she is actually trying to share her inner experience with a friend such a mood may overtake her; and not realizing how vague and meaningless her remarks have become it may seem to her that her friend is unsympathetic or willfully misunderstands.

Sometimes such a mood is associated with thoughts of an actual, absent or dead friend. I recall a woman who wore black for twenty years for a man to whom she had refused to become engaged while he was living. She used this man as an absolute shield between herself and all reality. On the yearly anniversary of his death her friends sent her flowers. Because of the grief she was still supposedly suffering for his loss, she managed to get herself excused from making even the ordinary efforts toward friendship that society demands. Her attitude to life asserted that she was sad, bereaved and must be carried by her circle of acquaintances for the rest of her life.

In another instance a woman suddenly widowed refused to weep for her husband. She felt that he had merely disappeared for a moment and was not really dead. She felt too that this attitude was in some way very noble and brave, and her friends sustained her in it by their comments on her wonderful courage. She did what was necessary toward readjusting to the outer world, but she held secretly to her fantasy that her husband was still alive and made no inner readjustment. Her attitude influenced her children who lost their old ability to make friends. Gradually their lives began to sink into emptiness, a kind of vacuum in which their mother existed. Meantime, she lived in the thought of her husband; her eyes held a curiously vacant, yet expectant, look, for to her he was still alive and might appear at any moment. One day, when she was half asleep, she thought he was standing by her. Throughout the rest of the day she went through the motions of living, but she wore a strange smile and was apparently far away. Again he came to her, and again and again. Sometimes she caught a glimpse of him, but more often she was merely overwhelmingly aware of his nearness. Gradually he seemed to grow bolder, until she came to have the feeling, when she looked up suddenly at almost any time, that he had only that instant stepped out of sight. At this point she became frightened, began to wonder if she were going insane or were really seeing a ghost. On psychological investigation the "ghost" proved to be "Ghostly Lover," that is, the appearance arose from the projection of the woman's animus, which in the absence of her dearly loved husband had become personified, as it were, in space. The condition cleared up completely under psychological treatment.

The idea of the Ghostly or Spiritual Lover is not a new one. Religious mystics of all ages and creeds—the Sufis, the Shaktas, the Christian mystics—have all sought for union with a Divine Lover. Rabia, the Islamic woman mystic, knew God as the Divine Lover, the Beloved of her Soul, as did St. Bernard of Clairvaux, while many women saints of medieval Christianity tell us that their religious experience was of God as a Lover. Even today when a nun takes the veil, she is dedicated to this Divine Lover. She wears the bridal veil and is given a ring, as the Bride of Christ.

Religious experiences of this sort have been highly valued not only among Christians but also with peoples of other religions, such as Mohammedans, Buddhists and Hindus. Individuals having them have been regarded as saints, possessing a wisdom different in character from the wisdom to be gained by knowledge of the world and having achieved a development of character which makes them in very truth superior human beings.

We can hardly dismiss as hysterical nonsense all the evidence concerned with these religous experiences, nor can we say that it is entirely in the nature of unreal fantasy, as in the case of Mary Rose. How much of it is of that nature, it is hard to say. Undoubtedly there are many who "have professed religion" as a means of escaping from the burdens and difficulties of life in the world. The inner experience of such people would, in all probability, be of a lover who lured them away from the world of reality into a dream world. In other words, if anyone chooses a life of seculsion and introversion as an escape from the difficulties of life, he must expect to get lost in that inner world where as many difficulties and dangers await the adventurer as beset the explorer of the outer world. Indeed, the outer world is safe and protected compared with the inner world of the unconscious. But the pseudoadventurers do not represent all who have explored the inner world.

Since the fifteenth century adventurous souls have exercised their courage and audacity in exploring the unknown parts of the earth. Today the exploration of the globe has been practically completed by the conquest of Everest and all the more remote areas, notably the Antarctic. In two remaining spheres, however, man is setting himself a further task of exploration. In the realm of the air fearless and undaunted young men are setting out on ever more daring enterprises, even into interplanetary space. In the sphere of the inner life, with less advertisement and general talk, other men and women, no less courageous, are setting out on the adventure of exploring the hidden world that lies behind consciousness. But in this inner world, as in the outer, the adventurer who travels without knowledge or expreience or true seriousness of purpose goes forward only to his own undoing. For nature knows no pity. If one goes to the polar regions without due preparation, merely to escape from some difficulty in life, he will inevitably meet with a most unpleasant awakening. In just the same way, if one seeks the inner world in order to escape from life's tasks he will without doubt be overwhelmed and will perish. A similar fate will overtake anyone who chooses a religious life of contemplation as a means of escape from life's tasks. It is the purpose that counts. For instance, to take up the religious life of contemplation as a means of escape from life's burdens is not to experience God, but rather to fall into the unconscious and gradually be swallowed up. The visions or fantasies that come to such a man will be of a very different character from those of the true mystic and will not stand the test of analysis. The Church has always been careful to differentiate between the two and to warn against false religious experiences.

Milarepa, a great yogi and teacher, who lived in Tibet during the end of the eleventh and the beginning of the twelfth centuries, also warned his disciples to differentiate between the true and the false experience. In his last discourse to his pupils he said:

> The true dawning of the Voidness in one's mind,
> And illusory obsessions of the consciousness,
> Appear to be alike, but beware, and confuse them not.
>
> The knowing of the Pure, the Unalloyed State, by meditation,
> And the fondness for the Tranquil State born of the
>   trance ecstatic of Quiescence,
> Appear to be alike, but beware, and confuse them not.
>
> The Flood-tide of the Deep of Intuition,
> And other deep convictions that "This seemeth right,"
>   "That seemeth true,"
> Appear to be alike, but beware, and confuse them not.
>
> The clear perception of the Mind Unmodified,
> And the noble impulse to serve others,
> Appear to be alike, but beware, and confuse them not.
>
> The spiritual boon which shineth on one as resultant of
>   Connected Causes,
> And merit temporal, which bringeth much of worldly goods,
> Appear alike, but beware, and confuse them not. [2]

2 Evans-Wentz, *Tibet's Great Yogi, Milarepa*, p. 298.

So we see that inner fantasies and visions, daydreams and religious experiences fall into two groups which, as Milarepa says, "appear to be alike" and yet are so different in their results that while one leads to the greatest unreality and, indeed, is to be seen at the point of its fullest development in mental hospitals, the other is a true and valid experience of an inner reality which is as "real" and as powerful as any external reality.

This statement will meet with skepticism, I am sure, or even frank ridicule from some of my readers. To many the phenomena of the outer world with their direct appeal to the senses constitute the only reality. Unless a thing can be seen and felt and handled, it is for them ephemeral and unreal. Yet even such concrete-minded and practical people are compelled to recognize the existence of many unseen and impalpable forces which manifest themselves in the material world. Electricity cannot be seen; radio and television waves are invisible. Yet their reality has been demonstrated beyond any question by their effects in the world. These are physical forces, but there are also psychological forces which by their manifestations in the concrete world convince us in exactly the same way of their reality. For example, fear, for no external reason, may take hold of a crowd, and a panic develop. Or an idea originating with one or two individuals may spread through whole nations with farreaching results. Christianity is an outstanding example of an idea which swept through the world. The religious experience felt at first by a few affected the lives of many; as a result European civilization and culture were entirely changed.

But the concrete-minded man always tends to discount such things; he characterizes the inner experience of one to whom such things are the *great* reality as idle fantasies or repressed instincts. A psychologist once asserted that all mystical experiences arose from repressed sexuality and challenged any mystic to lay bare his inner experiences, asserting that he could prove, even to a mystic, the sexual origin of every mystical "reality." I know of no mystic who took up the challenge, which is hardly to be wondered at. To the concrete-minded man all inner experience is of the nature of fantasies, vapors, wish fulfillments, or is a sort of illness of which a man can be *cured* by bringing his interest into the "reality" of the external world.

On the other hand, the man whose chief orientation is to the inner world of thought and of the spirit tends to depreciate the external world and to overappreciate the inner experiences. He also needs Milarepa's warning. Just as the concrete-minded man confuses the true with the false and says that all inner experiences are "silly and wasteful," so the man with inner vision tends to confuse the true with the false and to say that *all* his fantasies are "beautiful and significant." Each attitude is biased and leads to a one-sided and unstable position. How can we follow Milarepa's advice to "beware and confuse them not"?

The first step in making such a discrimination is to examine the data more closely and determine what the actual experience of the Ghostly, or Divine, Lover is. The experience of the Ghostly Lover is an inner or subjective one. Whether we conceive of the lover as being the woman's animus, her masculine soul, or whether we conceive of the Divine Lover as God, in either case he may be perceived by her as a being outside her conscious personality, and yet he is one with whom she can converse only subjectively, that is to say, within herself. Even where, as in the case quoted above, there is a hallucination of an external presence or, as in the cases which we shall shortly consider, where an actual man carries the values of the Ghostly Lover, it is still possible in every case to demonstrate the subjective or psychological character of the energy which the Ghostly Lover wields.

The inner experience may be perceived in various ways. It may be experienced as a *mood,* either with or without conscious content and fantasy pictures; or as a *projection* in the outer world, when some actual person or circumstance is endowed with the meaning and value of the inner experience; or as a *dream* or *vision,* which may form the basis for an artistic or some other creative product. The mood, the projection, or the vision represents the part of the experience which is perceived in consciousness, while beyond this there may—almost certainly will—also be phenomena, dreams or fantasies, appearing from the unconscious, which will show the situation viewed, as it were, from the other side. For instance, I have known more than one case where a woman, retreating from life into her subjective moods, has dreamed of *an airman flying overhead.* In the typical dream *he comes close to the ground and the dreamer catches hold of a part of the airplane and is carried up and away like the tail of a kite.* I say this is a typical dream for I have met with it repeatedly in patients who are being caught away from life into the unconscious.

Fantasies with an emotional tone which bring their own satisfaction are a normal part of psychological life. Only when the preoccupation with this fantasy material withdraws attention from the world of reality does it become a menace. In particular, fantasies and visions of an imaginary lover play a necessary part in the psychological changes of puberty.

But this absorption with the dream of love should be a passing phase, giving place to the interests and activities of real friendships. Frequently, however, girls show a tendency to cling to such fantasies. Where outer contacts are not easily made or where an incipient attachment is checked by external difficulties, we often find the young girl retreating into the world of dreams where the suitor is more to her liking and plays his role more as she would have it played. Here we have the birth of the Ghostly Lover. Such a fantasy inevitably stands between the girl and all the boys and men whom she meets. It is as though her acquaintances have an unseen rival whom they must surpass before they can hope to win her attention. As time goes on the developing woman may forget her fantasy; she occupies herself with her life tasks and thinks no more about her girlhood dreams. But that does not mean that her problem is solved. The Ghostly Lover has fallen into the unconscious. He is not conquered or dispossessed. He is still the Beau Ideal, the Prince Charming, before whose attractions all other men seem insignificant. He is invisible, but his presence can be inferred from the reactions of the woman who possesses him or, rather, who is possessed by him. She will have what appears to the onlooker to be a perfectly arbitrary standard by which she judges every man she meets. She will say, "Oh yes, he's a nice enough fellow, but I like tall men" or fair men or dark men or thin men or what not. Or, making her judgment from the head, she will say, "He is too intellectual," or "He hasn't any ideas."

This "opinionating" is not be be confused with a real judgment based on external facts. It is true that in certain cases a man may be so occupied with his intellectual life that he has nothing to put into a relationship with a woman. But the falsity in the case I am considering rests in the *a priori* nature of the judgment that allows nothing to the situation. It is not that the woman has tried to find values in the relationship and failed, but that by her *a priori* judgment she blots out the man in one stroke. If a woman makes a critical atmosphere in the beginning, the man will certainly hesitate to leave his own masculine sphere where he feels himself secure. In the realm of feeling, which is properly the woman's world, a man tends to feel hesitant, rather at a disadvantage, and if the woman's attitude is critical he is forced over to the intellectual side and is prevented from functioning on any but the most impersonal basis.

This unseen hero may show himself only through the woman's depreciation of real men. But this depreciation is proof of his presence in her unconscious as a criterion. He holds for the woman such overwhelming values that all other men pale in comparison. The trouble is that the values of the Ghostly Lover in such a form are unrealizable, for he remains only an "impossible possibility." The woman cannot bring these values into life through a living relation to the man, for he only exists in her unconscious, nor, while he thus keeps her from life, can she obtain his values in any other way. An actual case may serve to illustrate this point.

A certain woman had become interested in a man whom she knew only slightly. He represented for her the unknown hero, although he actually did not come up to her expectation nor act in the way she wanted. She met him one day at a reception and sat and talked with him for some time. When she got home she found herself much depressed and filled with a vague dissatisfaction. She could not understand her own mood because outwardly the situation had gone very well, even though up to that time the man had shown no disposition to play the part she wished. That night she dreamed that *she was ironing a sleeve. Inside the sleeve, instead of the ironing board, there was a little wooden egg such as is used for darning stockings.* Her associations to the dream were illuminating. She said that the sleeve is used metaphorically in the term to "have something up your sleeve," while an egg is a possibility. We say, for instance, "Don't count your chickens before they are hatched." But this egg is a *wooden* egg, it can never hatch. It may be used perhaps as a nest egg to induce the hen to lay a real egg, but it itself is hard and uncompromising. It is a rigidly held "possibility" that is in fact no possibility at all! The woman had in her talk with the man unconsciously tried to coerce the situation into being what she wanted it to be, with the result that the life had been sucked out of the real living possibilities which were inherent in the situation, while she had substituted a wooden egg which she had kept up her sleeve.

In this situation the possibility which was held as a rigid demand on life was the work of the Ghostly Lover. But the example serves also as an introduction to the next form in which the hero in the unconscious may show himself. Unconscious contents have a great tendency to be projected to the outer world, where they fasten onto any convenient carrier which presents a suitable hook. When this occurs the mantle of Prince Charming falls upon some man in the outer world and the woman falls violently under the spell of this current incarnation of the prince. The nature of the spell varies. She may project intellectual values and find a Great Teacher; she may project erotic values and find her Beau Ideal.

In the first chapter the projection of the values of the man's anima and the nature of his involvement with the woman who carries these values for him were discussed at length. When the woman's soul, or animus, is projected, in a similar way, it is as though the values of the animus were transferred to the man. The emotional involvement which results is spoken of as a *transference*. A transference of this variety may occur in widely different circumstances. The amount of reality underlying it may vary from a mere nothing up to an intimacy that ends in marriage. But if the attraction, the charm, the spell in each case is the result of a projection of the values of the Ghostly Lover, the result will be a situation which is not based on reality, with a consequent liability to crumbling and disillusion.

This is the nature of the transferences which women and girls so often make to heroes in books and plays, to popular preachers, to movie stars, or to men of adventure and to political leaders. Take, for example, the hero-worship of Rudolph Valentino. Probably not one of the thousands of women who flocked to his lying-in-state had ever even so much as exchanged one word with him. A particular example of this kind of hero worship occurred in 1928 when Col. Charles Lindbergh made the first solo transatlantic flight in his plane "The Spirit of St. Louis." To his admirers their hero was a symbol; it was the man's action, his role, which appealed to his admirers, not primarily the man himself. The same may be said of those who were attracted to the strong personal charisma of John F. Kennedy. We might, indeed, infer this from the fact that so many women are attracted by the *same* man. Love based on a reality-relatedness is more discriminating. If either a man or a woman is *generally* attractive to the other sex (attractive, I mean, in a general or universal way) we may well suspect that this factor of the projection of the Ghostly Lover (of the animus or anima) enters into the situation. Certain men and women lend themselves to this kind of transference. Sometimes the effect is produced by the role that the man actually plays, as, for instance, in the case of Valentino. He acted the part of the hero in many a film drama and it was in the guise of hero that he appeared to his devoted admirers. It was as though Prince Charming had indeed taken on flesh and blood, and every girl who saw his films could identify herself with the heroine of the play and so feel him in very truth her lover. In the cases of "Lindy" and JFK, the mechanism was a little different. They both lived in a reality world, not a movie world. Lindbergh's deeds of daring and Kennedy's revitalizing of the image of the American presidency were accomplished amid the stern realities of life, not in the safety of a studio. But here again the profession renders the individual particularly susceptible to the transference of the woman's animus.

Jung, in his commentary on *The Secret of the Golden Flower,* [3] speaks of the anima as the earth spirit, while the animus is the air spirit. [4] In accordance with this we find that men are attracted by the siren, the woman who is half fish living in the depths of the water, or by the earth spirit, who lives deep within the earth. For instance, Ulysses is lured by the sirens, and Tannhauser by Venus, who is represented in the legend as living in the Venusberg, a mountain in the depths of the earth. On the other hand, women are caught up into the air by the Ghostly Lover. The Flying Dutchman is such a Ghostly Lover to Senta. In Eugene O'Neill's *Strange Interlude,* it is an airman who becomes Nina's Ghostly Lover. In *Lohengrin* a rather different aspect of the animus is shown. For Lohengrin is the spiritual, or sky, animus who comes on the swan to aid Elsa in her extremity. He does not carry her away with him, but he disappears when she doubts him, showing that it is the woman's attitude which has power to convert the Ghostly Lover into spiritual animus. Then, if her attitude becomes tinged with power motives, he degenerates again into the Ghostly Lover from which he evolved. To the woman her animus *is* up in the air; if she goes with him, it is to meet him in realms above

---

3 Harcourt edition, pp. 81-149; *Alchemical Studies,* pp. 1-55.

4 *Secret,* pp. 115-116; *Alchemical,* par. 57.

the earth, and we feel of her that she is "all up in the air." Hence it is that a man who conquers the air, a flying man, is a particularly appropriate holder of this kind of animus transference.

In this hero worship of Valentino, Lindbergh and Kennedy we have examples of transferences made by many women to men of renown where the reality contact is practically nil and the attraction arises only from the role played by the hero. When, however, a man or woman in ordinary life regularly attracts admiration or love from a large number of people, it is not so easy to see what the situation really is. There are doubtless men and women who are lovable in themselves and who, by their very good qualities, attract the transference of their whole circle. If they express themselves clearly and show their preferences plainly, however, matters generally right themselves and the disappointed among their admirers can go their way without permanently broken hearts. The trouble comes when such generally attractive people are unwilling or unable to show what they really are like, and assume the role that the admiring circle would impose upon them. Such an assumption of a role may be completely unconscious or it may be a partly conscious pose. In Gilbert and Sullivan's *Patience* we have an excellent caricature of the sort of situation that arises when a pose is assumed in this way. Here the young man who poses as the Fleshly Poet, on the one hand, and the one who assumes the role of the Idyllic Poet, on the other, catch in turn the transference of all the young ladies of the chorus. The method by which this illusion can be resolved in real life is shown in the play. The young man who hides his own reality continues to be caught in the role; the fact that he deliberately acts a part for his own ends does not prevent his imprisonment. The other who clearly expresses himself and his own position, declaring that he loves Patience and no one else, is released from his embarassing situation and the other young ladies are promptly cured of their love sickness. "A hammer came up and drove them home," as the song about the magnetic qualities of the hero puts it.

The general, or collective, character of the animus transference in these cases is shown by the large number of women who are attracted to the same man. For the individual woman partakes of the ancestral experience through the animus who is racial rather than personal in his character, which accounts for the extraordinary similarity in the description given of him by different people.

Thus it happens that when the one man fulfills the ideal of many women his appeal obviously rests not on his individual qualities but on those which are generally attractive to many women; that is to say, he carries those values of the animus which are not personal to any one of his admirers but are common to them all. This does not mean that his admirers do not feel themselves to be personally involved; they do. Jealousy and rivalry frequently arise among them, and the least hint of preference or of attention from the object of their admiration is treasured and used as a basis for quite unwarranted assumptions of his involvement. To the onlooker, the collective, non-individual character of the phenomenon is clear, even when the individuals concerned are completely or partially blind to it.

There is another aspect of transferences of this character where the collective nature of the involvement is not quite so easy to recognize. In the instances we have just discussed, one man carried the transference for many women, but we also find cases where a series of love objects carry the selfsame values for *one* lover. This, too, results from the transference of unconscious values to a human being, the anima in the case of a man, the animus in that of a woman. While the transference lasts, the loved one is all-perfect; there is a curious sense of fitness, even of predestination, in the choice. "I feel this woman to be my woman," a man once said of a woman whom he had met only two or three times, "I feel myself to be her man." There is a magic rightness about it. But if for any reason the love object should fail to satisfy the requirements of the transference carrier, the illusion is broken and the garment of love, torn from the first object, slips easily over the shoulders of the next, and the illusion of rightness and predestination begins over again.

It is just this kind of relationship, seemingly so unique, so personal, which is most subject to sudden disillusionment. For it is in fact no more than an illusion—an illusion produced by the projection of the anima or animus onto another being. There is a hint of this in an expression frequently used of relationships of this character, "She is my soul mate," which in psychological terms should not be interpreted, "She is the mate of my soul," but, "She is my soul, my mate."

The factor of illusion or "magic" in love of this nature is recognized in legend and myth. For instance, love takes possession of the lovers as the result of drinking a magic potion. If both the man and the woman drink, a mutual animus-anima transference takes place, such as is depicted in *Tristan and Isolde.* Here the two love each other with the same kind of love, but in spite of this fact their love cannot be lived in the reality world, they must flee from reality, must forego their honor and ignore their obligations to King Mark. In cases where only one person drinks the draught, the philtre may be deliberately prepared for gaining power over the victim, as in *Götterdämmerung,* where Siegfried is lured to dishonor and death, or, as in *A Midsummer Night's Dream,* when Titania falls in love with Bottom who is wearing the head of an ass.

Animus transference of this type is a very common occurrence. A woman falls in love; she is enthusiastic over the man; her emotions are strongly aroused; there is no doubt that mighty forces are brought into play. But the odd thing is that nothing happens; the situation always falls flat. The man may be intrigued for a little while; he is certainly flattered, and he may even take advantage of the woman's involvement with him. But sooner or later disillusion creeps in; the spell is broken, the glamor gone; the beloved becomes only ordinary man. A few weeks, or perhaps only a few days, elapse, and the process begins all over again. Another man looms on the woman's horizon and becomes the hero of the hour. Again the woman is aglow with the re-emergence of her animus values. It may be that this episode will be more satisfactory, that more of reality will be brought into it and that the affair will last a little longer, but it is foredoomed to failure. Sooner or later it will be replaced by another similar projection.

Such a woman seems to be bound to the wheel which drags her through an endless series of projections, bound on it by one of the greatest laws of her being—the necessity to seek her own soul, her animus. But it is her fate to see him only as a projection upon one man after another. She loves him in one man, but she soon discovers she has been deceived, for the man and her animus are not the same thing. She loves him in another, lives through a brief period of illusion and awakens again. This time she metaphorically rubs her eyes and looks around, only to see her animus masquerading in the person of another man. Disillusion gives place to illusion and the whole experience is repeated. She realizes that this sort of thing leads nowhere, that she is following a chimera—the Ghostly Lover who lures his victim away from life and reality. And the question arises: How can this hopeless quest be checked? She may understand perfectly what is happening to her, yet be powerless to help herself. Her emotions are too deep and too powerful to be amenable to the commands of her conscious will.

A third way in which the Ghostly Lover may show himself is in the form of visions or values which are seen or sensed deep in the unconscious, the inner world. Many people are lured by such fantasies. For instance the would-be artist who sees marvellous pictures which she never paints, or the author whose poem or novel remains unwritten, or the theosophist who lives in a world which can never be realized in practical life—all are lured away from reality by the Ghostly Lover. If the artist tries to paint her picture, the meagerness of the reality-product discourages her. She feels it is better that one person, namely herself, should keep the beauty of the vision unspoiled by an inadequate expression of it. She "catches Leviathan with an hook," it is true, but instead of pulling out Leviathan she herself is pulled in and lost to the reality world. Surely it is better to catch a little fish and land it than to hook a great fish and be pulled under the water. At times the only wisdom may be for her to let go of these things and turn her attention to establishing a hold on reality. At others, by a supreme effort, the hidden value can be caught and brought to birth in the world; then the Ghostly Lover will change his character and become the spiritual animus. He is vanquished as Ghostly Lover; he no longer acts as dybbuk, but becomes the woman's strength and guide; that is to say, he performs his right function of relating her to the unconscious.

The same mechanism which takes the would-be artist away from real life may function in other women who make no pretensions to artistic ability. Whenever it seems easier to enjoy an idea or an interpretation alone, rather than to present it to the world, one should suspect that it is the work of the Ghostly Lover. Reality is the great test of value; if a thing works it is real and not a dream. This is the test that the world applies to one who claims to be an inventor. If he can make a model which will work, he is no idle dreamer. So, too, visions and thoughts can prove themselves of value through their application in the world, even though they may relate to conduct and relationship rather than to the material world. A vision which can bridge the gap between two human beings is no more an idle dream than was the vision through which the George Washington Bridge was conceived.

The constellation of the animus, whether as Prince Charming through a projection onto a living man or in the vision of inner values, is always important. For at such times potential values, which are ordinarily hidden away beyond reach in the depths of the unconscious, are stirred from their slumber and become available for consciousness. Our reach usually exceeds our grasp. Nevertheless, at the very moment when the animus values are glimpsed, energy is always released. This energy generally shows itself as emotion, but all too often the moving of the waters passes before one can stretch out a hand and make the value his own. Even when a woman is sufficiently aware to seize upon the treasure, it may be only to find it more firmly anchored in the primordial depths than she herself is in reality. In consequence she will be in danger of being engulfed, if she does not take counsel of wisdom and relinquish for the moment her hold on that most desirable treasure. But the power and attraction of the animus are such that she is compelled, even against her will, to return to it again and again, just as a woman who, having fallen in love with a man who has represented animus to her and having resolved never to repeat the experience, is nonetheless irresistibly drawn into another affair which is a duplication of the first. Her burnt fingers do not save her any more than singed wings save the moth from the flame.

Therefore the question of whether there is any way in which these values of the animus can be brought into reality and made to enhance the value of the conscious personality becomes urgent. Is there any technique by which the Ghostly Lover can be made to change his form and become a psychological function creating for the woman a relation between the conscious and the unconscious worlds? In a chapter on the anima and the animus, [5] Jung has outlined in general how this may be done and has discussed at length the advantages gained by the individual who succeeds in wresting the values from the anima and animus. The ways in which this method may be applied in the various situations already discussed must be more fully described.

When the animus appears only as a mood, based on the memory of a dead or lost lover or on a conscious or unconscious fantasy of "Prince Charming," obviously nothing external can be done directly in relation to the man concerned, for he lives only in the woman's inner world. But something *can* be done to counteract the effects in the outer world, which result from the woman's possession by the Ghostly Lover. For instance, she may set her-

5 *Two Essays on Analytical Psychology*, pars. 296-340.

self the task of becoming aware of the functioning of the critical attitude by which she depreciates all men whom she meets. She can attempt to undercut the animus by criticizing her own critical attitude. When she makes a snap judgment about a man or a situation or is swayed by an unfounded opinion she must ask herself *why* she thinks this. To the onlooker this task appears easy. But if a woman who is possessed by the animus tries to reach consciousness in this way she will discover how difficult it is. For these opinions are in their nature perceived as *a priori* truths; they are not reached by a process of logic or argument. If they were, it would be relatively easy to detect the false step leading to the untenable position.

How then can such a woman become conscious of what she is doing? To only a very small extent can she become aware by exercising a conscious critique; only in rare instances can she be made aware by the protest of her friends. If she goes to an analyst she may become aware to a certain extent, from a simple discussion of the incidents of her daily life. But for a real understanding of the situation, an analysis of the unconscious aspect of the incidents is necessary. There the work of the animus will be clearly shown, and he will be unmasked in his true aspect. Such evidence, coming as it does from the patient's own material, is convincing in a way that no exposition and no criticism from another can ever be, for the conviction of truth born of one's own unconscious material, to be appreciated, must be experienced.

When the source of her critical attitude is recognized in this way and the woman has released herself from the spell put upon her by the Ghostly Lover, she will be able to meet whatever human contacts life brings her in a more humble and accepting spirit than before. Such a change in attitude has an effect that is almost magical. Over and over again, women have told me that no sooner have they changed in their attitude than everyone changes toward them. People who formerly were resistant become receptive; those who were hostile or indifferent become sympathetic. It is as though some "magic" is working, and working, too, beyond the sphere of immediate contact. One woman, for instance, whose critical and possessive attitude had so alienated her best friend that he had come to avoid her, gradually perceived during the course of analysis where she had been at fault in expecting him to fulfill her ideal and realized that this was really an effect of her possession by the animus. Hardly had she come to this realization when her telephone rang; it was her friend calling up to ask her to go out with him—the first spontaneous move he had made in her direction for weeks.

Many instances could be cited showing that when a woman releases herself from the hold of the Ghostly Lover she finds emotional value and new life in contacts which were previously sterile. This is one way in which the problem of the Ghostly Lover may be resolved.

Something of the same result may be achieved in cases where the animus is projected onto a living man. Here again the chief difficulty lies in unawareness of the real situation. When a woman makes a projection of her animus she does not know what she is doing. On the contrary, to the woman the *fact* is that she meets a man who to her *is* this marvellous person. She *perceives* him to be such, and only by a careful analysis of the situation in both its conscious and its unconscious aspects can the true nature of the case be recognized *while the projection lasts.* This is a very important point, for often the true nature of a situation can be readily recognized *after* it is past, since then the outcome gives evidence of its true nature—it is seen historically. Its hidden tendencies manifested through the life process are still nascent in the earlier stages; they are but germs hidden in the womb which shall bring forth the future, a future already inherent in the situation. This womb which holds the seed of the future is the unconscious. If the unconscious is analyzed, the germs latent in any situation will be brought to light. Thus by analyzing the unconscious content we can view the present, as it were, historically; we can get a fourth dimensional point of view. It enables us to see things "as they are" and at the same time to see things "as they will be." We outwit time, for we see the future in embryo.

This "foresight" surely is the significance of the third of the Three Fates, the Norn who spins the future from the past and the present. To see life in this way, not only "as it is" but "as it will be," carries with it a new responsibility for our actions which to many may seem too costly to acquire and too heavy to bear. Wotan, we remember, paid for this privilege with the sight of one eye. We humans also pay heavily, for we can no longer be wafted along under the spell of an animus projection. It is delight and intoxication to be in love with a man who carries the animus values. He is our Beau Ideal, our "soul mate"! To analyze and to understand this as a psychological illusion rather than as a piece of heaven on earth requires courage and the willingness to pay a great price. The price we must pay is to assume consciously the responsibility for our actions. No longer can we blame fate or the man, nor can we consider ourselves injured innocents and sink back into illusion again, where

> Each owns a paradise of glass . . .
> Like fauns embossed in our domain
> We look abroad and our calm eyes
> Mark how the goatish Gods of pain
> Revel; and if by grim surprise
> They break into our paradise
> Patient we build its beauty up again. [6]

Nor can we ever again experience a sublimated state like that in which Emily Dickinson wrote of herself, after the break-up of her own love affair:

> Title divine — is mine!
> The Wife — without the Sign!
> Acute Degree — conferred on me —
> Empress of Calvary! [7]

---

6 *English Review*, June, 1923, p. 546.
7 *Final Harvest*, p. 240.

In this poem there is certainly no sign of any attempt to understand the psychological problem that her love had brought. We see here the very inception of the Ghostly Lover as memory of the lost man; and we see him in his true character, masquerading as Christ, while the poetess is his Queen. How could a woman look twice at an ordinary mortal man while that fantasy held her!

When a woman finds herself in love with a man onto whom she has projected the Ghostly Lover, she can release herself from the dominance of her animus if she can work through the transference element in her love and make a real relationship with the man. This outcome is naturally more feasible if the involvement is mutual. There is obviously no possibility of relationship where the hero is adored by thousands of women, as in the case of Rudolph Valentino, but in an ordinary social situation when a man and woman are attracted to each other, on account of a mutual anima-animus projection, it is possible to redeem the values which have been projected, by building up a relationship based on reality, in place of the illusion of the transferred values. The problem of the Ghostly Lover is most frequently resolved in this way. When a man and woman marry there is almost invariably some element of an animus-anima projection in their love. After the first glamor has worn off, each begins to realize that his partner does not see him as he is, but that in some strange way he is distorted in the other's eyes, for in certain ways each is glorified and in others depreciated. But the whole mechanism is subtle and may not come clearly into conscious focus. There is, moreover, a great tendency to let things slide and not to make an issue of slight misunderstandings. After a few protests and a more or less prolonged conflict, the young couple generally settles down to the business of life and allows these misconceptions to go on practically unchallenged. In such a case the projections of anima and animus persists and no real relatedness can develop.

One might think this was an ideal solution of the situation, were it not that the garment of the projected animus or anima, so docilely accepted in the early days of marriage, becomes increasingly hard to throw off, and the man and woman find themselves progressively forced to wear the mask which was not repudiated at first. Such a situation formed the theme of Eugene O'Neill's play *The Great God Brown*. The mask so slightly assumed by Dion in order that he might fulfill his fiancee's ideal gradually hardens on him, crushing out his spontaneity and initiative. The second danger point now arises. The partner who has been submerged by the weight of the animus or the anima projection rebels and refuses to carry it any longer but forcibly reveals himself for what he is. If the whole situation does not disintegrate from the effects of the explosion, another opportunity is offered for building up something of reality-relatedness. But, once again, this outcome is, in the sense used above, historical; only the sequence of events brings the opportunity, and that generally not for many years. The obligation, in such a case, to work on the problem of relationship is the work of fate; it is not the free choice of the individuals concerned. If, however, instead of merely living along, carried by the energy and desire created by the projected animus or anima values, this man and woman had sought out the intimations from the unconscious, it would have been possible to discover where the animus or anima projections obscured the situation. By this means they could have established at each point a small measure of relatedness to each other in their own true persons. As a result there would have been built up gradually through the years a reality in place of the illusion based on projection. Dealing with the problems of life in this way has a double value, for not only is reality substituted for illusion, but the anima or animus values, dissolved from their projection in the outer world, are also realized in the character and personality of the man or woman. The maturity which may sometimes be seen in a couple who have lived together for a lifetime, learning to know and accept each other, comes in no small measure from this assimilation of the anima and animus.

In other instances the values of the Ghostly Lover may be realized through the creation of a work of art, although here I speak with more reservation. For the production of a work of art, even when it embodies the values made available through the anima or the animus, does not always mean that these values are really incorporated into the personality of the artist. If this were so, every great artist and every great poet would be a great individuality, a really developed human being. We should like to believe this, but unfortunately we cannot. For, lamentable as it is, a great poet or artist is frequently an all-too-human personality. It seems as though some poets have paid, with their characters, the price of their genius. The work of art is often but another way in which the values of the animus are projected to the external world. Instead, however, of their being found in a loved object, they are projected in the form of an image of the inner drama. By this means something is gained; the world is richer in art; and the artist, through making actual the vision of his inner fantasy, has submitted himself to the discipline of hard work and to the appraisal of his fellowmen. He is no idle dreamer; he has made good on the reality side. Nevertheless, if he does not assimilate the psychological significance of his own work, he cannot obtain for his own personal development the values of the soul image which have inspired his creation. He has seen his vision as a vision only. He does not realize that it is the drama of his own inner life, and so he gains no development from his "artist's" insight.

And here we come to what is perhaps the most important part of the whole subject, namely the assimilation of the values of the Ghostly Lover. At first when these values are unconscious they are completely unavailable for development. Then they are projected, and the individual becomes aware of them, but they are outside the personality. The problem is: How can they be brought back within the psyche in such a form that their energy may be available for conscious life-development?

If a woman whose animus values are constellated in a projection onto a man is analyzed, a moment comes when the projection is broken. The psychological energy, or libido, formerly occupied with the projection is released and sinks down into the unconscious where it begins to activate the primordial images that lie hidden there. At this moment it sometimes happens that she begins to produce spontaneous fantasies and visions, which represent the transformations which the libido is undergoing in the unconscious. If the woman takes these fantasies seriously as representing a certain kind of reality, she can begin to take a part in the fantasy, that is, she can "get into" the fantasy and participate in its development, instead of merely being obsessed by the mood of unhappiness into which such a disappointment is only too apt to throw her. Jung has described this method in his *Two Essays.* He says:

> Now this is the direct opposite of succumbing to a mood, which is so typical of neurosis. It is no weakness, no spineless surrender, but a hard achievement, the essence of which consists in keeping your objectivity despite the temptations of the mood, and in making the mood your object, instead of allowing it to become in you the dominating subject. So the patient must try to get his mood to speak to him; his mood must tell him all about itself and show him through what kind of fantastic analogies it is expressing itself. [8]

Through allowing the mood to unfold itself in this fashion a picture of the situation in the unconscious is revealed in which the subject can come to participate. If this participation can be achieved, a gradual development of the fantasy material takes place in such a way that the values, previously caught in the projection, are assimilated and serve to create a new center for

---

8 *Two Essays*, par. 348.

the personality which, as Jung says, "ensures for the personality a new and more solid foundation." [9] In the *Two Essays* he gives a most striking instance of this use of the fantasy as a means of so getting in touch with the images of the unconscious as to wrest their energy from them for utilization in the building up of the personality. In the following piece of fantasy material, something of the same sort is taking place. A woman who had projected her animus onto a man with whom she had fallen in love did not recognize that her involvement was due to an animus transference, but the man was apparently aware of danger. She met with a rebuff which threw her back upon herself. She was undergoing analysis at the time, hence, instead of falling into a depression, she tried to get her mood to talk to her and to show her in fantasy the movement of the images of the unconscious, hoping by this to understand the significance of the frustration of her love. This was the fantasy or waking vision that came to her. I quote it in her own words:

Out of the woods into a sunny field I came. Fresh cool breezes from the surrounding mountains blew across the stretch of green sunlit meadow. I seemed to be in a shallow bowl held high to heaven. I was alone. There was only the sound of the long grass swaying in the breeze.

Suddenly from the woods behind me galloped four horses, two black and two white. On them rode four knights in armor, each bearing a lance from which streamed a silken pennant. A knight in black armor with a dragon in rubies on his breast rode one white horse and carried a golden lance with a flaming red pennant that curled and twisted in the breeze like a tongue of flame. On the other white horse rode a knight in steel armor, with a blazing sun of sapphires on his breast, carrying a lance of steel, from which streamed a tongue of blue flame. A knight in gold armor with a topaz heart on his breast and a golden lance in his hand from which curled a tongue of yellow flame,

9 *Ibid.*, par. 365.

rode one black horse. On the other rode a knight in silver armor with a crescent of emeralds on his breast and in his hand a silver lance with a long narrow pointed green flame streaming far behind.

The four horsemen galloped to the center of the field. They dismounted and, leaving their horses, paced off one hundred paces in oppisite directions: the knight of the dragon one hundred paces to the north; the golden knight one hundred paces to the east; the knight of the emerald crescent one hundred paces to the south; and the knight of the sapphire sun one hundred paces to the west. They drove their lances into the earth, called their horses to them, mounted and drew their swords of flaming steel from their scabbards. At a shout, brandishing their swords in the sunlight, they spurred their horses and dashed headlong to meet their opponents. I fell to the earth and covered my eyes. I heard the heavy impact of the horses' bodies, heard the ring of steel on steel and got on my knees to pray. I must have fainted as I knelt. When I regained consciousness I opened my eyes and there before me in the center of the field was an alter. On it was a shallow bowl of silver studded with rubies and emeralds and sapphires and topaz, in which burned a clear flame which shot to heaven. I staggered to my feet and drew near to the altar, and fell on my knees and bowed my head in prayer. Suddenly I heard a voice. I looked up and there in the flame, poised as if for flight, was a magnificent eagle.

To give anything like a full interpretation of such a fantasy is far beyond the scope of this book; the psychological problems that are touched upon would lead too far afield. But a general interpretation will show something of the course which the libido takes in its transormation.

The woman is in a bowl of the mountains, in a sort of earth-womb where she has drawn back in deep introversion. This drawing back into the womb of nature is a typical movement whenever the libido, which was streaming out forcefully toward an outer object, is suddenly checked. Here in the inner world she sees the heroes, the glorious personifications of the animus, come galloping. They are four in number and are related to the four fundamental colors and to the four points of the horizon. They represent the four divisions of the microcosm no less than of the macrocosm. We might speak of them as the four functions [10] of the psyche. They appear here as figures of chivalry. Their jewels and regal appearance indicate how important are the values that have been stirred to activity by a situation which, judged from external standards, is relatively trivial. This woman has made many animus transferences before, but this is the first time she has realized what she was doing *while she was doing it*. The annihilation of the unconscious figures in the conflict is the result of that realization.

Within the circle of the hills the knights trace out a square, one hundred paces each way. This is related to the age-old problem of the attempt to square the circle, to measure the incommensurable. The knights delimit a portion of the field which is measurable and, therefore, knowable. Psychologically this means that the animus projections measure off a segment of the illimitable cosmos which should rightly belong to the human psyche of the woman. When the animus is not dealt with and is not brought to consciousness he functions as the Ghostly Lover who lures the woman away from known and knowable reality to limitless regions. Therefore this delimiting activity of the four knights is very important. It means that while the human psyche is still incommensurable by virtue of its contact with the unconscious, yet, in this instance, the animus figures delimit it and make it, as it were, available for experience through the function of relating the human being to the world of the collective unconscious.

Thus the patterns of this fantasy form a kind of diagram of the psyche. The similarity of such diagrams to the mandalas or magic circles of China, Tibet and India has been discussed by Jung in *The Secret of the Golden Flower* and in *The Archetypes of the Collective Unconscious*. The pattern drawn here is a mandala. In the Orient such mandalas are used in meditation and other

---

10 See Jung, *Psychological Types*, pp. 412-517.

religious practices, in order to find the central point of the personality, which is not the ego, but is non-personal. And here through a psychological process the woman is doing a similar thing.

After the knights clash the woman finds that they have disappeared. What remains is a central altar with a bowl upon it, ornamented with the jewels previously worn by the knights; that is to say, the animus values are transferred to the bowl on the altar. Within the bowl is a flame (energy), the energy which was manifested before in the conflict of the knights, and, on the objective plane, in the intensity of the woman's involvement with the man onto whom she had made the animus projection. From the bowl arises, phoenix-like, an eagle, the bird of long flight, who soars up to the sun.

During the transformation the woman loses consciousness, an evidence that such a change cannot be understood or grasped by the conscious intellect. It is and will always remain a mystery — one of the miracles of life. This unconsciousness is also a kind of death. It signifies that the conscious ego is being displaced as the center of the personality. It is a kind of death of the ego.

The bowl on the altar is like the bowl of the hills. Here within the four-square area which the knights measured off and delimited from the unknown circle in the hills, another circle appears, suggesting that this new center of the microcosm has a certain similarity to the macrocosm. It too is a bowl or circle, not to be measured by our rule of measure. (Note that the area of a circle πr^2 is unknowable, except as an imaginary figure owing to the nature of π, which cannot be worked out exactly.) This means that this new center of the psyche is beyond complete comprehension by the conscious. It partakes of the nature of the cosmos. It is as though a fragment of the cosmos became crystallized in the very center of the human psyche. And just as a drop of water is the ocean in miniature, so this central crystallization is the cosmos in miniature. In terms of religion it is God within the human being. Such a concept has been the central mystery of many great religions, and we meet the same idea coming directly from the unconscious in the fantasy of a modern American woman. The form of the fantasy shows plainly that the bowl and its contents carry for this woman the values of a religious object, for at sight of them she falls on her knees to pray.

The eagle which rises from the flame is, like the phoenix, the promise of the renewal of life. It is analogous to the dove, the Holy Spirit, which descended upon the disciples in tongues of flame. In the Christian story the Holy Spirit, which was to bring God to dwell within the hearts of the believers, descended only after Christ, the incarnation of God as Hero, had departed from the world. Psychologically it is also true that the spiritual animus comes to dwell within the psyche only after the projection of the animus, the incarnation of the Ghostly Lover, has been overcome. Thus it is that the Ghostly Lover disappears and in his stead is born a new spiritual power transforming the life of the individual. Through this redeemed animus the woman gains a relation to the masculine principle within herself. This masculine principle is the Logos, or wisdom. When she is identified with the animus she is possessed by opinions and rationalizations and so-called principles which do not represent true wisdom at all. These are the work of the Ghostly Lover. True wisdom can be known only through the spiritual, or redeemed, animus who is a mediator between conscious and unconscious. He brings the values of the creative sources of the unconscious within reach of that human being who has had the courage and the strength to overcome the Ghostly Lover.

3. Work

In the first chapter we spoke of woman as she finds her life and satisfaction in relation to man. She follows the pattern laid down by Eve. She is maid, wife, mother or widow, which are aspects of life that suffice for her. She hardly knows of any other possibilities. Life in relation to her man and to society is fulfilled for her in the living of her feminine functions. She lives as *woman*. But, if she is to become an independent personality, instead of being only the feminine counterpart of a man, she must bring up to consciousness her own masculine qualities. Practically, this means as a rule that she must go out into the world and submit to the discipline such a step implies. She is able to take a place in the world of affairs only through the exercise of these masculine qualities which are ordinarily latent or unconscious, consequently many a woman who enters business or a profession is characterized by a more or less masculine appearance and habits which bear witness to the change which has taken place in her psychological attitude.

In the beginning of their struggle for independence women were obliged to identify themselves without reservation with their masculine adaptation, and for the most part they sacrificed their love life to it completely. They were obsessed by the desire to prove the equality of the sexes. They could see no reason why men should not accept them on the basis of their real accomplishment in life; they did not realize that a man cannot accept a woman who rejects her own feminine nature. Professionally trained women tend to judge each other by their achievements, in the same way that men judge men. But men cannot so judge a woman. It is really impossible for them to estimate a woman's value except on the basis of her feeling quality. Women, most of them, cannot understand why feminine values should be brought into a professional question at all. But if women are to progress further in the man's world of work, they must recognize it is a case of "This ought ye to have done and not to have left the other undone."

The need to fight for the right to independence had passed its initial stages before 1914. With the coming of the First World War woman's "right" to work was established and consequently her attitude largely changed. The bitterness and belligerence which were characteristic of the early feminist women disappeared and instead the professional woman of the nineteen twenties emerged. This woman, freed from the conflict, assured in her right to a place in the business world, could put all her energy into her professional achievement. She had the poise and emotional calm which the earlier women so often lost in the heat of the struggle for independence. But in devoting themselves heart and soul to their work these women rarely had time or energy for the emotional side of life. For them it was necessarily a choice between marriage and a career. But lately this antithesis has become much less marked and the third stage of the conscious development of women is under way. For today many young women achieve marriage *and* a career. The voluntary control of her family which modern science has made possible is one very important factor in this change, but a modification in the woman's own attitude which has taken place during the last 30 or 40 years must not be overlooked.

The woman's problem is not yet solved, however. She has won the right to live her life in the man's world, but the necessity to devote time and energy to her education and later to her profession still forces her to pull away from the life of wife and mother which would fulfill her feminine and biological needs, unless, as is frequently the case, she marries as soon as she is out of college, or even before. She may then take a job so that her husband can continue his studies and professional training. Then when he becomes able to support the family she leaves her job and undertakes motherhood. So far so good. But a second crisis not uncommonly occurs after the children have gone to school, when she finds time on her hands and wants to go back to professional work and the society of her peers instead of being almost entirely restricted to the society of children. For to the woman these two ways of life stand in opposition.

Yet if any human being is to reach full maturity both the masculine and the feminine sides of the personality must be brought up into consciousness. Each part must then undergo a discipline which will produce a gradual development on that particular side. The stages through which the individual passes in the progress toward psychological maturity, as they affect the development of woman in her feminine role, have already been spoken of in the first chapter. The same stages, namely the naive, the sophisticated and the conscious, must be experienced also in the evolution of the masculine values of a professional woman.

When a woman first brings her masculine qualities up into consciousness, she lives through a stage of identification with this side of her personality. The personal ego becomes a determining factor in her life, for education has as its aim the increasing of power through knowledge. Instead of being gentle and pliant and led by her feelings, instead of acting, in other words, as a feminine being, she begins to recognize a goal, as a man does, and in many instances becomes aggressive, dominating and opinionated. The undeveloped and undisciplined masculine qualities in the background of her psyche take control of her personality. She is no longer guided by her feminine impulse and feelings without a conscious knowledge of where they are leading her, but is guided instead by a masculine authority which directs her from the unconscious. She has views and opinions about everything.

These opinions are not logically thought out judgments, but seem to her obvious truths, as though "everyone must think so." Often they will be based on an assumption of what some authoritative person such as the father or a teacher or even a columnist would think. In other cases, they may be quite indefinite in their origin. For instance, more than once when I have questioned the accuracy of a statement of fact from such a woman she has replied, "But I have seen it in print." Much of the success of modern advertising is based on this psychological prejudice.

To those who come in contact with a woman in this phase of development, she seems extremely dogmatic. It is useless to argue with her, although she often delights in argument, for always with her the conclusion is already reached before the argument begins. As a matter of fact, she never argues in order to reach the truth, but only in order to convince her opponent of her view of the matter. For her the ego, the sense of a personal I, has become identified with the promptings which come from the animus. The woman is not able to hold in consciousness at the same time the feminine and the masculine voices within her psyche; she allows the masculine to override the feminine and exclude it. Such a woman is said to be identified with the animus. Animus identification is not limited to the professional groups of women. On the contrary, many examples of this condition may be found in the ranks of the married.

Jung speaks of masculinity as meaning "knowing what one wants and doing what is necessary to achieve it." [1] So the animus-identified woman, living as she does on the masculine side of her nature, aims directly at what she wants. If she wants marriage, she goes after it and may succeed in "catching a man." Her direct approach, however, as a rule only attracts the rather vague, inefficient and somewhat feminine man, or indeed, apart from attraction, she may succeed with such a man simply because he is too vacillating and indeterminate to escape, while a more mas-

---

1 *Civilization in Transition*, par. 260.

culine man would be repelled. When she is married, the era of petticoat rule begins and the man finds himself more and more dominated, his masculine sphere being progressively usurped by his aggressive and efficient wife. Some men under this regime have been known to take to drink, others have become domestic pets, while yet others have found refuge in invalidism. The trouble with this masculinity of the woman is that it is quite undisciplined. In the old days if a man found himself married to an animus-identified woman, he resorted to physical violence, and it was doubtless on account of this problem that wife-beating was allowed by law! If an animus woman today should marry a really stalwart husband, it might be that her animus could be disciplined by his masculine strength even apart from physical violence, but, as was said above, generally speaking, the animus type of woman marries a rather diffident, weak man, who is quite unable to attempt singlehanded the discipline of a woman's animus. The result is that if such a woman marries, her "devil" usually rules the household. She is upheld in her tyranny by her husband's submissive attitude while in any conflict with the outside world she does not hesitate to use him as a shield. In external situations, where the impact of the world might bring some discipline, and indeed would do so if she were single, she resorts to the married woman's defence and compels her husband to protect her.

Naturally all animus-identified women are not so obviously outrageous as this picture would suggest. Many women may conceal their dominance under an exterior of kindliness and good nature. But you have only to cross them, or even to go your own way, and you will find out that in spite of its appearance of softness and conciliation their rule is a very real one.

Women whose masculine qualities come to the fore and who find for themselves a career in the world where they can exercise their individual aptitudes have a far greater chance of redeeming this side of their characters from the hold of the unconscious than the woman who marries. For in order to learn a profession or trade and to practice it successfully, a woman has to meet certain reality demands. If she is too aggressive or opinionated she will lose her position. If her opinions do not tally with the facts she must either change her opinions or find herself disregarded. The world with its inexorability becomes her schoolmaster. Instead of being, like her married sister, face to face only with a husband who is presumably in love with her and who can be coerced by many wiles, the unmarried woman must adapt herself to a reality which is not at all under the necessity of obliging or humoring her. For she has undertaken to make herself economically independent in a world previously occupied only by men, where the conditions of life and acitivty have been created by men for men, with no attention given to the women's attitude or point of view. Under this discipline she may really develop many of the virtues which were considered formerly as the exclusive acquirements of men—courage, honesty, dependability, the power to co-operate, to be impersonal in her attitude, and to make decisions with impartiality and fairness. But as these things are acquired through a discipline of her animus and not through a spontaneous functioning of her feminine characteristics, they always tend to be a little excessive, a little inflexible; her justice tends to scrupulosity, her courage will not stop short of martyrizing herself.

Of the general run of women whom one meets in business and the professions, all of the more efficient and successful have won for themselves something of this development of the animus which makes it possible for them to function adequately in life on their masculine qualities. Such women acquire a new self-respect from doing a piece of work, worth-while in itself. To do a good "job," even if it is mechanical, and far more if it takes a larger share of her creative energy, brings to a woman, as to a man, the consciousness of being an independent member of society. She gains a real release of energy by learning to do her work whether she feels like it or not. The voluntary submission to discipline, the ability to hold herself to her daily task, even though she may be in trouble, brings very real rewards, and indeed the necessity to apply herself has proved a stablizing point to many a woman when her world was in flux. Through these things a woman's character develops and her will power, which Jung has defined as the "ability to do gladly that which I must do," grows. This phase of the woman corresponds to the second stage of development, that of ego-consciousness, or sophistication.

The world of work, however, is essentially a world of competition which forces the ego into consciousness. In the case of the anima woman the ego often hides almost entirely in the unconscious. This woman gets what she wants indirectly through the man. The professional woman, however, is compelled to work directly for what she wants; consequently her ego develops and is forced too much to the fore. Sometimes this unfortunate overemphasis is quite apparent and blatant, but often the ego trend is not so obvious and she herself may be quite unaware of her true motive, not realizing that the desire for personal power and prestige runs through everything she does. She may, for instance, be devoted to a cause; she may give her time and her energy for an ideal, most unselfishly as it seems, but the apparent devotion to an impersonal cause or ideal may be but a trick of the animus. It is of the very nature of the animus to present what appears to be truth under the guise of generalized principles, high sounding words or great ideals, which have a peculiar attraction for women functioning through the animus. For instance, I once met a woman who told me in all seriousness that she was going to devote her life to "the progress of the universe"! It had never occurred to her to ask herself in what direction progress for the universe lay, nor yet what effect her efforts were likely to have on the universe at large! When a woman becomes identified with a cause, she can devote all her energies to its furtherance without realizing the part her ego plays in the matter.

A woman who is related to a cause in this unconscious way is, however, very vulnerable. Any criticism of the cause seems to be directed against her personally, and it is naturally impossible for her to take an impersonal attitude. If her official connection with it is broken, her interest, which previously appeared to be with the principle involved, may suddenly cease. Her real motive — a natural interest in her own power and prestige — is then exposed unmistakably. A woman who passes her whole life on this level of development may be successful while she is still young and the power and influence which she attains may satisfy her during middle life, but when she is faced with the problem of old age she will inevitably find herself at a loss.

If a further stage of development is reached, however, the animus woman may find her redemption, just as men do, from personal aims in seeking for a general ideal to which she is willing to sacrifice herself. "Certainly the courage and capacity for self-sacrifice of such women is admirable," writes Jung, "and only the blind could fail to see the good that has come out of all these efforts. But no one can get round the fact that by taking up a masculine profession, studying and working like a man, woman is doing something not wholly in accord with, if not directly injurious to, her feminine nature." [2] For always her psychological center of gravity is too high. Nothing really strikes to the depths of her being. Her emotional nature remains untouched.

At first her work and her interests satisfy her, but later she is likely to become aware of her loneliness. Her sexuality awakens. She is stirred by a passing man and reaches out after the proffered companionship and satisfaction. To her amazement the man withdraws. She does not know why, for she is prepared to love him, to give him everything in her power. She does not realize that he is repelled by her very intensity. He might enjoy a flirtation with her, provided it is clearly understood that there are to be no obligations and no broken hearts, but he is afraid he will have her round his neck for the rest of his life. This difference between the man's expectation and the woman's as to the implications of a love affair constitutes a very real problem. For he usually takes it as a passing incident to be enjoyed while it lasts, but always kept as a light affair which he intends to break

---

2 *Civilization in Transition*, par. 243.

off just as soon as it shows signs of becoming inconvenient. While she, consciously or unconsciously, takes it as a relation which potentially, at least, may become permanent, and indeed she often disconcerts him by falling in love and taking it *au grand serieux.* Even when the woman has lain in wait for him, not at all because she loves this particular man, but simply because she wants an affair, this result may still overtake them. Her initial attitude to the affair seems like his, impersonal, but a difficulty arises because they each attempt to make the situation fulfill an *a priori* conception of *what it should be,* instead of allowing the relationship to evolve according to its inherent character. The man is afraid to leave things to run their own course for fear of getting involved in a relationship which may demand too much of him. He finds it awkward to become really involved; he hates to be obliged to take seriously what might be just a pleasant pastime, for nothing curtails freedom so badly. The woman, on the other hand, also fears to get her feelings involved. It seems to her that if she should do so almost anything might happen to her. Her professional adaptation, for instance, might go to pieces, leaving her stranded without the ability to continue to earn her living. Only with great difficulty have women extricated themselves from the feminine role which history has prescribed for them and learned a new self-respect and independence. But this lesson could only by acquired by keeping their feelings strictly under control. All their energies have been engaged in developing the masculine side of their natures, and nothing meantime has been done toward disciplining and developing the feminine instinct which yet remains a most powerful force within them. The professional woman who embarks upon an affair fears that if she should concede anything to the instinctual side, she might fall straightway into a pit of the instincts. And so she holds fast to the superiority won through her intellectual achievements.

Before going further it is worthwhile to ask: What is the position that women have won for themselves in the world of work? It is now generally recognized that women, certainly some women, do as well as men in school and college work. A very fair proportion of women can be found at the upper end of examination lists, whether in the purely academic or in the more technical fields such as medicine, law, economics and so forth. These women go out into the world to compete on equal terms with men. We should, therefore, expect to find women scattered in similar proportion throughout the upper ranks of workers. But this is not the case. For the most part, women are not found filling the biggest and most responsible positions, either in industry or in the professions. Over and over again one hears the complaint that an efficient and well-trained woman has been passed over in favor of a younger and less well-trained man, that women must content themselves with routine and less remunerative positions. This state of affairs has been accounted for along two lines of reasoning. Women say that they are deliberately passed over because of men's jealousy and prejudice. On the other hand, it is argued that the higher paid posts ought to be held by men because they have a family to support. But are these the only explanations? If men are asked why women are compelled to occupy the inferior positions in industry, they often allege inefficiency and an inability in general to take the initiative. They admit exceptions but on the whole they consider it unwise to give positions of great responsibility to women, not only for this reason but also because they harbor a fear that a woman may marry at any moment and throw over her obligations.

The amount of really creative and original work women have produced is indeed relatively slight. The number of outstanding women writers, artists, musicians, scientists or financiers is amazingly small. Why is this? Are women really not so creative as men? This is a question that only the future can answer. But certain factors in the psychology of women have a bearing on the problem.

In the first place, from the very beginning of our civilization there has been a widespread conviction that women cannot create, a conviction that it is in some obscure way almost indecent for them to do so. The conventional attitude suggests that creativeness is the prerogative of the man while for a woman to put forth something she herself has conceived and created is to disregard her instinctive reticence and modesty. In the last century writers such as George Eliot and George Sand felt themselves obliged to assume masculine names to conceal their identity. In these days of free education no woman consciously *thinks* that she must not create. But still the sense that women *shall* not create remains; it is almost like a taboo, which always works from a much deeper level than does a conscious prejudice. A woman *thinks* that women can create, that she herself has something to say well worth the saying, yet she may be quite unable to say it. Her state is like that of the woman who thinks she has freed herself from the sexual taboos of the last generation. She may consciously believe in free love and yet find herself in terrible conflict if she becomes involved in a situation in actual life where her theories are put to the test. It almost looks as though women believed the world of work and achievement to belong to men only, that these things represent the man's world. Intellectually and consciously women strive against this prejudice, sometimes with rancor and bitterness. But the prejudice persists and deep down in the unconscious many women have given it credence.

I am speaking here of a woman's creative abilities only in relation to the external world of objective reality, which has been considered the man's world. In the woman's world naturally woman is the chief creator, and no Victorian prejudice hampers her in the exercise of her creative abilities, whether in the biological realm—the creation of new life—or in the realm of Eros, where she creates relationship and that feeling atmosphere best illustrated by the word home. In these places a woman creates from the feminine side of her nature, and her creation and its method of presentation need only accord with the laws and customs which women make to guide their own feminine activity.

When a woman tries to make a creative contribution in the world outside the home, she is tempted to make it in the man's way, the only way she has been taught. But the woman's way is different. Before she can tap the source of her own creativity and be able to contribute something really original to the world, she must have experienced deeply her own feminine nature; otherwise, she is bound to speak from the animus. It is in the head only! We have an exceedingly clear example of this in the life of Elizabeth Barrett Browning. She had written many beautiful and charming poems before she met Robert Browning, but these early poems were all intellectual in type. During her engagement to Browning she wrote the sonnets which were afterwards published under the title, *Sonnets from the Portuguese.* In these she expressed her own love experience and for the first time showed herself as really creative, a really great poet. "They [the sonnets] were intimate outpourings of a full heart meant for his eye alone," writes one of her biographers.

> Elizabeth had never been one to share her emotions with the world; she was an intellectual, not a lyric poet. As her husband read . . . he was the more impressed with the universality of these poems in which she had, without restraint, expressed her innermost self. . . At first when he suggested publication Elizabeth was adamant . . . . She could and did share with the world her intellectual ideas; she could write for the world a fictitious love story; her emotions and her own love story were not public property . . . . Had they been written originally for publication, she could not thus have shown her heart . . . . Her emotions were personal, not of the stuff of which public poems are made. To publish his heart's deepest outpourings the poet must, unless he be insincere, divorce the idea of himself from the emotion; he must universalize his emotional experience. Elizabeth wrote these sonnets as the outcome of her emotional crisis. It is because the experience, though rare in such perfect form, is the universal idea that her poems remain the perpetual voice of true lovers. [3]

---

3 Boas, *Elizabeth Barrett Browning,* p. 131.

A woman's creation is not an abstraction; it is a very personal thing, based primarily on her own subjective experience and not on objective experiences of the external world. If a woman is to create in the man's world, she needs not only to bring up into consciousness her masculine qualities, but also to experience deeply her feminine nature. If the man is not to live exclusively in the world of affairs, he too needs to develop both sides of his personality so that he may take his share in creating in the woman's realm. In much of woman's creative activity he cannot participate —she alone can be mother. But in the making of a conscious, that is, a psychological, relationship between them he must take part. To do this he must domesticate and discipline his own feminine qualities which are personified in his anima. At the same time the demand upon him to develop his masculine powers to their greatest capacity will not be abated. Concerning this Jung says that "man will be forced to develop his feminine side, to open his eyes to the psyche and to Eros. It is a task he cannot avoid, unless he prefers to go trailing after woman in a hopelessly boyish fashion, worshipping from afar but always in danger of being stowed away in her pocket."[4] But the man who tries to become a "great lover" or to establish himself in the world of men through his feelings will be hopelessly lost. He becomes just a phenomenon, not a man at all. In D. H. Lawrence's *Lady Chatterley's Lover* the hero is of this type; because of the blows life has dealt him, he has withdrawn from the world and hidden himself in a lowly position. He tries to make a new life based entirely on feeling values, but he is quite unable to establish any relation to the woman other than a sexual one, for he cannot uphold the masculine end of the relationship. One does not wonder that Lawrence has to end the book without describing the marriage which he yet suggests is to be so perfect.

For the woman to achieve anything of value and permanence in the masculine world, she must be developed on both sides of

4 *Civilization in Transition*, par. 259.

her nature, but even when this has been done and she feels herself ready to put forth in a creative work the wisdom she has gained she will probably meet another barrier within herself. For, in order to speak openly about woman's secret knowledge, she must overcome her fundamental instincts of modesty, passivity and reserve. To most women this seems well-nigh impossible. For it is the woman's nature to hold herself in the background, to maintain a passive attitude, and, psychologically speaking, to veil herself and her reactions and to seek her goal only by a devious and largely unconscious route. For a woman to show herself clearly as an individual, to come into the open and say what she has to say, demands that she go contrary to this natural tendency. To do such a thing with real integrity involves a complete sacrifice to her ego and she can bring herself to make this sacrifice only for some very potent reason. We respect the Lady Godiva who, to save the lives of her people, could disregard her inherent modesty and ride naked through the streets, but we have a different attitude toward women who display their charms for a livelihood, for the motives are different. Lady Godivas are, however, relatively rare; few women sacrifice their innate sense of reserve for reasons comparable to hers. Ordinarily, the woman releases herself from the restraints of her modesty through an animus opinion, telling herself: "It is absurd to feel this way. Men do not feel so. Why then should I be hampered by so silly a prejudice?" Through this argument she divides herself into two distinct parts. She becomes overfrank and outspoken, acting on her rationalized opinion, but this apparent frankness is achieved by repressing her real feeling, which means that she reserves the real essence of the matter. As a consequence, what she does or says often fails to convince. Realizing this, she tries to supply the lack in her presentation with a certain urgency; having taken out feeling, she puts in passion, which naturally raises resistances in her audience.

This is the mechanism which lies behind the modern cult of frankness and simplicity in sexual and other matters. The woman says, "The prudery of the Victorian age is stuffy and ridiculous. Let us be frank and get rid of all this hypermodesty." But her very instinct is to be modest. The feminine essence must be concealed; it may show itself only when the situation is exactly right on the feeling side. Hence, overfrankness is just as hampering as overmodesty. The important point is this: A woman's revealing of herself is a matter of feeling rapport, it is not at all a matter of reason or logic. So when through her animus a woman assumes a pose of frankness in these matters, it necessarily follows that she must repress her deeper feeling as well as her sexuality and act as though sexuality did not exist. This effect can be seen, for example, in the repression of sexuality which must accompany the current fashion in nude and near-nude sunbathing, and which can extend in a similar way to other less promiscuous situations where sexuality *is* appropriate. The result may be that even in a friendship with one man where feeling might well ripen into love a woman who has practiced the modern overfrankness may find herself quite unable to respond on the deeper level. Or the repressed sexuality may show itself in various disturbances of the unconscious, as for instance in nightmares, fears or other neurotic symptoms.

Consequently, when a woman's manner toward men is characterized by great frankness, it is to be expected that she will make comradely relations to men, but without any really deep contacts on the feeling side, for her own feeling has been of necessity repressed and, therefore, cannot touch the man's feeling. For such a woman it is a significant turning point in her relation to a man when she finds that she can no longer look him frankly in the eyes, for it means that her real feeling which may not be shown openly has begun to stir.

And so the circle is complete and once more the woman finds herself confronting a man in the earlier primitive situation—woman to man. Has nothing, then, been accomplished by this half century and more of search for freedom and independence, of rebellion from the old ways? Is woman to fall back once again into her old role of man's counterpart? Or is it a different woman who comes back to the primal relationship? She turns back to her problem more profundly herself. In seeking for a solution of her personal problem she has accomplished more than she set out to do. For society today begins to sense possibilities inherent in the relation between men and women which would hardly have happened without this new consciousness on the part of women. Indeed, the change in woman herself is perhaps the key to the significance of the feminist movement.

In looking for the significance of a cultural movement, it is necessary to free oneself from the prejudice that the aims consciously held by the participants are identical with the aims or goal of the movement itself. It will be readily granted, for instance, that Henry VIII's reasons for favoring the separation of the Anglican from the Roman Church had little to do with Protestantism *per se*. His desire for a divorce and a new wife was entirely personal and its satisfaction was personal. Historically speaking, however, it matters not at all that his connubial wishes were gratified; what matters is that the separation between the two branches of the Church occurred. So in the movement which we are considering, it is a small point that the individual lives of certain women have been enlarged and fulfilled. The great point is that as a result of their efforts the Western nations as a whole have gained a new insight regarding the very nature of the relationship which men and women can establish between themselves.

Jung, speaking of the relations between men and women, has this significant thing to say:

> The discussion of the sexual problem is, however, only a somewhat crude prelude to a far deeper question, and that is the question of the psychological relationship between the sexes. In comparison with this the other pales into insignificance, and with it we enter the real domain of woman.
>
> Woman's psychology is founded on the principle of Eros,

the great binder and loosener, whereas from ancient times the ruling principle ascribed to man is Logos. The concept of Eros could be expressed in modern terms as psychic relatedness, and that of Logos as objective interest. [5]

If we look back over the last hundred years, we can clearly discern that the aim of womanhood, as shown in the feminist movement, has been to reach the goal of a more conscious relationship between the sexes. The individual women concerned may not have realized this, but the historic sequence betrays the unrecognized aim. The way of woman is always to go by devious routes to her goal. You will rarely discover what a woman's objective is by asking her a direct quetion, nor yet by observing what she attempts first and deducing her intentions from that, for she is herself often unconscious of her real aim. She will begin to look for a spool of thread and end by cleaning the whole house. She may have been quite unaware that it was her intention to houseclean. But on further investigation it is obvious that preparations have been quietly going forward for some time for a spring cleaning, although she was unaware of it herself.

Because of her relative weakness, woman has learned to bring things to pass by strategy rather than by direct attack. This use of strategy is not a consciously thought-out diplomacy as it is with a man, but is an instinctive reaction to a situation which calls for greater strength than she possesses. One can see the same thing in animals. The door of my room is open. The dog wants to run out and bark at a stranger in the hall. I tell her not to do so. She knows that if she goes directly to the door I shall use my superior strength and prevent her from going. So she waits till I am occupied with my book. Then she gets up and saunters behind a chair, which is in the opposite direction from the door. Then very quietly, keeping a piece of furniture always between herself and me, she goes completely round the room and so reaches the open door. In the same way women, when faced by a situation which they are unable to overcome by strength, resort to subterfuge and strategy. And lastly, the indefiniteness and unconsciousness of the woman, which Jung has spoken of as being the complement of the man's more conscious purpose, play their part in her tendency to seek a goal by devious ways.

The bluestocking attitude and the feminist movement generally were parts of this deviousness. Women do not really want complete independence of men in any sense which implies isolation. What woman really wants is relationship, and for that a certain separateness is necessary. There cannot be any real relationship between a dominant and a dependent member of a group, any more than there can be real relationship between masters and their slaves. Further, the independent or individual side of woman's psyche was so completely neglected that it was incredibly undeveloped and childish. The most complete concentration and devotion were required for a period in order to compensate for the former neglect. In the early days of the feminist movement no woman who was not devoted heart and soul to the achievement of independence and education could possibly have made any headway against the enormous weight of public opinion from without and the inertia of custom from within which combined to hold her down in the accustomed grooves of what was *right and proper* for a woman. When such a view is universally held in a community it comes to have the significance of a divinely instituted order. Women in breaking with custom had also to break with what they had been taught was God's will for them. Only those who are singlehearted in their devotion can free themselves from such bonds. We get the sense of this complete concentration of purpose in Strachey's *Life of Florence Nightingale.* Instead of living only for herself and her personal satisfactions this remarkable woman surrendered family, ease, social position, wealth, even love and marriage to her urgent need to work in the world and make herself a useful and valuable member of society.

But woman, as always, was then and still is unconscious of her true aim. She thought she wanted independence and a career. This was a subsidiary though a very necessary phase in the movement toward her real goal, namely the creation of the possibility of psychic, or psychological, relation to man.

If woman herself has not understood her own goal, is it any wonder that her aim has been misunderstood? A few discriminating men have encouraged her, because they have understood, perhaps better than she did herself, what her goal really was. Outstanding among such farsighted men was Jung. He has repeatedly reminded us that man and woman together make up humanity, that if woman remains in a state of primitive unconsciousness suitable to the days of medieval Europe, man alone cannot progress very far in the quest for greater consciousness. The woman's problem is her problem, yes! But it is also a problem which concerns humanity. If she does not solve *her* problem, mankind is held back to her level of unconsciousness.

It is imperative then that woman bring up the masculine side of her nature, that she learn to love a thing, or an idea, even, though this is primarily a man's prerogative, and even though her attitude toward the thing or idea will never be his. For however completely she has succeeded in this task, she will care more about the *application* of the idea than for the idea itself, though she will still call it the idea. So it is, her love finds its way through the thing to the human being back of the thing.

There is a certain kind of impersonality which kills a woman's interest. If her work is purely mechanical, such as filing index cards, or moving a lever to and fro on a machine, her interest is, as a rule, not satisfied, as a man's perhaps might be, in working out a new system, or in discovering *how* it is done, or even in coming to love the machine. She will either become a sort of robot or she will turn away from the task and occupy herself with the person for whom she is doing it.

But a personal motive will carry a woman through an almost unlimited amount of monotonous work without the risk of losing her soul. For instance, she can make an infinite number of stitches if the embroidery is for a special place in her house or she can knit sweaters and socks indefinitely for her husband and boys. But if she is to find a satisfactory adaptation in the world where the personal motive is no longer operative, she needs a new kind of impersonality, one characteristic of the best masculine work. For the woman, however, there is always the danger that she may become identified with her attitude of impersonality and as a result push her feminine values into the unconscious. She can avoid this danger only through greater consciousness.

Many young women start out in life with a real desire to serve their generation, and their high idealism appears at first sight very like the man's devotion to an idea. They are eager for instance to serve the cause of justice or mercy or freedom. But their love of these things is subtly different from the man's. Year by year they fill the ranks of teachers, nurses and social workers. Such a young woman starts on her career with a fund of sympathy for others. She tries to relate herself to the sorrows of the world through her feeling. Just as in the ordinary domestic circle the woman knows a thousand things to do in case of trouble, while the man merely feels embarrassed or in the way (unless the trouble is one that a check can cure), so in the larger circle of a hospital or social workers' bureau, she tries to alleviate suffering by giving of herself and her feeling. But such suffering is endless and she is soon in danger of being overwhelmed by the crushing weight of misery that she meets day after day. The more sensitive girls are crushed by the problem and either seek a different sphere of activity or fall into neurosis. The more sturdy may react by developing a protective hardness, which no misery and no appeal can penetrate. In this case fear of the intensity of her own feeling reactions may throw the woman over into an animus attitude: she will attempt to meet the suffering of the patients and indeed her own "softness," as she would call it, by animus opinions. She may say, "It is the lot of man to suffer. What are you making such a fuss about?" Only a minority of women find that real adaptation to life and to humanity at large which comes by no other way than through the recognition of a value which is superior to those personal ones which guide a woman in her individual life.

A suprapersonal value has power to rescue a woman from the impasse, on the one hand of being overwhelmed or on the other of becoming hard, when this value is accepted as supreme, for then it transcends not only her own personal life and desires but also the personal needs of those whose suffering has so painfully affected her. In bygone days women found such a suprapersonal value in their religion. They found relief from their too great suffering by casting their burden on the Lord or by communing with Our Lady of Sorrows. Today in the realm of psychology we recognize that it is only by something which we must call a "religious attitude" that a woman can differentiate between her own personal feeling and "the Whole Great World's Sorrow." Her share of this great world burden she must be prepared to assume, but she cannot carry it all. The "dewdrop slips into the shining sea" and loses itself yet finds itself for it is filled by that same water whose bulk makes up the sea. Just as the dewdrop surrenders itself in the ocean so can a woman, when an emotional experience of something greater than the individual threatens to overwhelm her, perhaps find herself through a voluntary surrender of herself and her own personal wishes for the fulfillment of life itself. This surrender is not a self-martyrdom. To surrender herself to life is profoundly right for the woman. It is her way and brings her joy. For life is only fulfilled through the little life of each individual, through the historic sequence of individuals. This impersonal life lives in herself no less than in all humanity. By putting the fulfillment of life before her personal needs and satisfactions, she takes a step toward the solution of the problem of sorrow and evil.

I recall a dream which illustrates this point. The dreamer was a woman whose work had led her into close contact with the sufferers in a widespread calamity. At first she had been crushed by the suffering which she could not relieve. Then she had tried to repress her feeling, thinking it the only way in which she could carry on. Later it became necessary for her to try to assimilate the whole experience. As a first step in this process the repressed feeling came up and threatened again to crush her; it was as though each incident she had witnessed was her own personal grief. One day she dreamed that *she saw horses circling through the sky.* This reminded her of a picture of the zodiac which she had seen the preceding day. Then she dreamed of *a race track on earth like that in the sky, with animals going round in the different segments of the track. There were various kinds of animals — a sheep, a bull and the like. She noticed particularly a horse. This scene faded, and in her dream she found herself at home. She picked up her watch from the floor and saw that it was broken completely in two.* Her associations to the dream were that the race track was like a sundial, and also like the circle of the zodiac. It thus represented a year clock, a measure of time by years; she spoke of the precession of the equinoxes which refers to time in terms of centuries. This clock is, as it were, the clock of history. In her dream this clock of history is functioning, but she discovers that her own personal timepiece, which would ordinarily mark out the days of her life, has been completely broken. The dream marked the beginning of a change of attitude toward the suffering she had witnessed.

If women are to see their personal problems in true perspective, it is absolutely essential that they learn to take things impersonally while not losing touch with their own feeling. Otherwise they are hopelessly caught in the network of the personal and have to suffer, as though they were a personal fate or even a personal fault, things which really belong to the fate of a generation and are rightfully the burden of society.

To our dreamer the unconscious said, "You must not look at life any longer from the point of view only of your personal life span. Life from the point of view of history has other meanings."

4. Friendship

In her close relations with men a woman is always tempted to play the part of anima. Pressure comes to her both from without and from within to play this role, for the man wants a woman to fulfill his ideal of womanhood. He has a pattern of what a woman should be and how she should react to him, which is either held as a conscious ideal or functions as an unconscious compulsion of which he himself is unaware. This pattern is perpetually held up to the woman. If she does not fill it, he will have none of her or will try to force her into conformity. She is compelled by his set purpose and at the same time by an inner urge, to give him what he wants, to fit herself to his requirements. She wants to play anima to him exactly as much as he wants it, for this is the pattern through which the biological needs of both man and woman have been cared for throughout the ages.

But a relation based on the projection of the anima must, of necessity, remain largely unconscious, a tendency which is increased by the functioning of the woman's animus. If her relation to her animus has not undergone a process of redemption, it always lures her to look for values over the horizon. The Ghostly Lover calls her to follow him up into the clouds on a false scent. The man of promise, the man "with the words," enchants her so that she does not stop to make actual the values which she senses, but, like the dog in Aesop's fable, throws away the reality, hoping to grasp the reflection which looks so much larger. Her instinct to play anima to the man and her own inner tendency to follow the Ghostly Lover combine to keep the relation between man and woman *unreal.*

So strong are the powers of unconsciousness wielded by anima and animus that any human relationship would seem to have been doomed to remain unreal were it not that another factor bringing potentialities of development as yet untried came into the situation. Had the relation between man and woman remained the only vitally significant one, the progress of humanity might have been blocked and the path to the evolution of consciousness which relationship opens up might have remained closed. But times changed. Women were forced out into the world. Marriage no longer offered the only career for them. Many women, and those by no means only the failures and the "leftovers," remained unmarried for a part of their adult lives, in many cases for the whole. These women, far from being the weaklings, the stupid or unattractive members of their generation, may be the most vital and enterprising, the ones with greatest intelligence and initiative.

Among women of this class friendship has come to hold a place of unprecedented importance. The relationships that are to be found between such women are often of a very high type, and may be exceedingly free both psychologically and materially — free, that is, from ulterior motives. For unlike a relation of equal importance between a man and a woman, these relationships do not involve financial dependence of one on the other, nor do they involve any obligation for the mutual satisfaction of instinct. There is no legal tie, no contract, no social demand. The association is based on human liking and on the attraction of one personality for another, on mutual interests and on an inner psychological or spiritual accord which is more important in friendship than either sexual involvement or mutual interests.

This psychological or human factor is, however, very vulnerable. If it is to be safeguarded from the destructive effects of projections and illusions, definite work has to be done on the *structure* of the relationship itself. The relationship has to be given body — to be made actual or concrete. This is peculiarly the woman's task. It means the bringing to birth of feminine values as a reality in the world of reality.

In speaking of feminine values and of woman's cultural task one is open to the criticism of using empty phrases. It is so easy to *say* that woman must bring into life specifically feminine values which shall release her from dependence on man or competition with him, but it is exceedingly difficult to define with any clarity exactly what these are or where they may be found. The difficulty is increased because of the very nature of these values which are so different from the masculine ones that they can neither be appreciated when judged from the masculine point of view nor, indeed, can they in many cases be recognized as values at all. Women's values do not enter into competition with those which men have differentiated through the ages. Women's values are dependent on those which men have delineated only to the extent that a woman cannot act as a pioneer in differentiating conscious feminine or Eros values from the realm dominated by unconscious instinct unless she has in some measure acquired the capacity for thought, judgment and efficiency, which belong to the Logos sphere. To this extent the new values *are* dependent on the old.

It was essential that these new Eros values should be differentiated from the instinctual feminine of the anima role before they could enjoy a separate existence. For this reason it is not surprising to find that they make their first independent appearance in a realm where instinct plays a lesser part than in the relation between men and women, namely in the sphere of women's friendships.

Certain women find it diffuclt to get onto an understanding basis with men, but with women they are at ease and readily establish a friendship. Attraction between members of the same sex, based on a feeling rapport, is a usual condition among both boys and girls during their adolescent years, when these friendships form their closest emotional ties; they are living through a homosexual phase which is entirely normal. Later in life friendship and love for some member of the other sex usually displaces this earlier love but the phase of emotional development which gives rise to these friendships is not confined to early youth. The instinctual love of which it is a manifestation may yield its *primary* place to another instinctual bond, but love for friends usually persists throughout life and is often of great importance in the emotional experience of the individual.

In these modern times when the period of immaturity is greatly prolonged, the emotional development of young people is often correspondingly retarded. If in adult life the love of friends continues to take first place, the condition is often due to a prolongation of an emotional phase normal to adolescence, which passes when it has· been lived through. Retarded development of this kind will account for a certain number of homosexual friendships among women, but hardly for all.

At certain periods in the past the tendency of men to seek the friendship of men increased to a remarkable degree. For instance, at the time of the foundation of the *polis,* the independent city state, Greek civilization witnessed a movement of this kind. The love of men for boys was exalted in the cultural idea above even the love of man for maid. Plato's *Symposium* on this subject has remained through the ages as the outstanding example of the spiritual heights to which human love might attain. Some centuries later, in Europe, a similar condition prevailed. Men in the Age of Chivalry congregated in guilds of knights—Knights of the Round Table or Knights Templars—and it was the ambition of every promising boy to become page and later squire to some knight of renown.

The result of these periods of devotion between men was a great increase in the strength and significance of the manly virtues and a corresponding decrease in the purely physical involvement of men in instinctual satisfaction with women. It was an integral part of the movement of chivalry that the European woman's position underwent a marked change. Up to that time, she had been considered by men principally in the light of a household necessity; she was housewife, sexual object, bearer of children. When men's interest started on a new phase of development, centering around their activities with their men friends, they began simultaneously to idealize woman; she became for them a carrier of spiritual values, a symbol of the life of the soul. The emotional friendships between men characteristic of the time were a part of a cultural movement resulting, on the one hand, in a development of sex-solidarity and, on the other, in a change in man's attitude toward woman.

In the last few decades friendships between women have come in a similar way to hold a place of unprecendented importance in the community. This change in the emotional life of women is significant not only for the individual but also for our whole civilization, for we are passing today through a distinct phase of culture like those which affected men so profoundly in the past.

One cause of this phase is the weakness and lack of development of the specifically feminine values, inevitable while women were exclusively occupied with men; the outcome promises an increased solidarity among women, resulting in an entirely new development of those values which have to do with feeling and relationship. This change in women, according to the historical precedent, should also modify and revivify the relations of men and women to each other.

Friendships between women sufficiently important to warrant the formation of a family or household unit are exceedingly numerous today. It is an extraordinary change in the structure of society which leads many hundreds of women, instead of marrying and raising a family, to make a major relationship with another woman. Many causes—economic, educational and social— have contributed to produce this phenomenon. But if we are to understand its meaning, we must look below these external conditions to find the psychological changes which perhaps predetermine them.

The terms cause and effect must be abandoned while we occupy ourselves with the attempt to differentiate the various strands, whose interweaving has brought about a modern revolution—a revolution which affects not only the lives of individuals but also the life of society. If this were dealt with merely as a personal problem its cultural significance would be lost sight of and so the individual would be compelled to bear the burden of responsibility for a collective movement, a gradual change in the race of which the individual is but a manifestation. Viewed from this standpoint, those people whose experiences are limited to relationships with their own sex must be regarded as victims of a changing instinct, which may be sickness, or may be, for all we know, only the awkwardness of an adolescent civilization changing from childhood to adult life. If this latter is the case, the instinctual frustration with its inevitable suffering, which these individuals have to bear, must be considered the growing pains of society.

The social change must, however, be studied in individuals. During this cultural epoch at the time of the movement for higher education and economic emancipation, a certain modification of character toward a masculine type began to be noticeable in many women. This movement was caused partly by a turning away from the frivolities of social life or from a home in which, because of modern inventions, there remained so little creative domestic work to interest them. In addition, there was also a very real turning away from the temptation to live on the purely domestic and instinctual side of life, which was the result of a psychological reorientation; it signified development in a direction new to that generation of women. Their greater seriousness of purpose was expressed in a greater simplicity of dress and in a surrender of the mannerisms and weaknesses which women had formerly cultivated to attract the attention of men. The early professional women affected, instead, a somewhat masculinized dress and manner, as well as certain masculine characteristics, which were not assumed but which really expressed a psychological fact, namely that in these women there was developing an attitude of mind which had formerly been considered to belong typically and exclusively to men.

These changes in dress, manner and interest have gone side by side with the increase in women's friendships which we are considering. They are all manifestations of the need of a certain independence from men during the period in which woman was finding a new aspect of herself. But let us try to understand the significance of this need, instead of merely noting the incidental economic and social changes which accompany it, for from the historical point of view this phase of social behavior must have an evolutionary significance which is both biological and psychological in its nature. Its biological significance I must leave to the eugenicists. Its psychological significance bears strongly, however, on the theme of this book — the contribution which women have to bring to the new era of consciousness whose evolution characterizes our time.

Let us first consider the facts as they can be observed in everyday life. On every hand are to be seen instances where two women who have formerly lived alone in a club or residential hotel join forces and begin housekeeping together, at first, perhaps, largely as a matter of convenience. Women have a great need to take a hand in their own domestic affairs, but the cost of living by oneself may be prohibitive. By uniting their resources two women may be able to make a home where they can entertain their friends and also satisfy their need for domesticity.

Now this is a very curious and amusing swing around the circle, for women went out of the home in revolt against the drudgery and monotony of domestic work. But the fact remains that from the very dawn of human life it has been woman's task to make the home and to care for it. Indeed, it is probably owing to woman's peculiar genius that such a thing as a home could be created at all. For countless generations and in all countries women have found their chief satisfaction in cooking, sewing and supplying the bodily needs of themselves and their households. These tasks fulfill that side of woman's nature which is related to the Earth Mother as universal provider, and when she is cut off entirely from this kind of activity, one side of her nature starves. So, sooner or later, many a woman who has been living in a collective institution decides that she can no longer be just an insignificant member of the hive. She wishes to have a home of her own.

A menage started with another woman in this way, as a matter of convenience, may be the beginning of a friendship between the two which gradually strengthens through the months until a real family unit is formed. Many women, however, set up house-keeping together on a different basis. The link between them is primarily one of friendship. Perhaps when they first met, they were deeply attracted to each other and on account of their feeling elected to make a home together. The bond between such friends is one not of convenience but of mutual love and their life together is consequently likely to be very rich, attaining a permanence and a stability equalled only in marriage.

The values of such a relationship, the daily companionship, the shared life interest, the home, are in many ways comparable to those found in marriage. The necessity, also, of recognizing the shadow side of one's own personality which close contact with another human being imposes is a factor in women's relation-ships, as in marriage. But the sexual love and mutual dependence of marriage make a far closer bond than is at all usual between friends. For instance, if the husband and wife should not be in harmony on various matters, even important ones, or if their interests are far apart the gap between them can still be bridged if their love is passionate. The situation between two women friends is very different. By their very nature women need above all things to keep the feeling atmosphere clear. If a misunder-standing arises they cannot be content to lay the problem aside or to gloss over the difficulty. They need, instead, to come to a mutual comprehension of each other: each must clarify her own attitude and reach an understanding of the other's motives and standpoint. This can only be done through a thorough discussion of the incident, whatever it may be. Such a discussion is hard work; it is by no means easy. But it leads to a recognition of the *truth* of the matter—the truth not so much of *fact* as of *feeling*. This kind of work on relationship lies peculiarly in the woman's sphere. It both bores and frightens most men, but through it a development of character in regard to Eros, or relatedness, is brought about which can only rarely be achieved in any other way. Women, through their mutual relationships, are beginning to evolve a new consciousness along these lines, comparable perhaps to the evolution of thinking which men have brought to pass through their concentrated attention to facts and truth.

Women who form their major relationship together not because of love but as a matter primarily of social or economic convenience find themselves also caught up into this cultural movement which is expressed in the mode of the day, but they have no understanding of its psychological significance. They "fall into" the mode, they do not consciously *choose* to mold their lives on this pattern in any directed way or for any conscious reason. Their action furnishes an example of the way in which "circumstances" and "the time" fulfill themselves. The cultural significance of women's friendships is more than personal, but these women fall into line with the times for personal reasons. Those who see a value beyond the merely personal participate in the development of the culture of their time more consciously. They seek in their friendships for a new kind of relationship—for a *truth* in human situations which has a significance beyond personal likes or expediency, and through seeking this value they consciously take part in the movement directed toward building up those feminine values which our culture has neglected.

This new attitude to relationships and feeling-truth is naturally applicable to the relations of men and women as well as to those between women. But these new values are emerging in our day chiefly on account of the close associations of women, so largely brought about by social and economic forces. Women themselves are, for the most part, exceedingly undeveloped in their relationships and need the concentration of feminine interests. For in our culture the feminine values of Eros have remained in a primitive and unconscious state. It is hardly conceivable that any step forward could have been taken unless women had been forced to seek each other's company. Women, as well as men, would have perforce remained content with that degree of relatedness which could be produced by the sexual bond in an unconscious or instinctive way, without any aid from conscious and directed work.

As these new qualities begin to emerge, women are learning to value their women friends in an entirely new way. Men have not, up to the present, been forced by circumstance to make this exceedingly modern step in consciousness and are still, for the most part, quite unable to give women the kind of emotional satisfaction and security which they can find with their women friends. This is not unnatural. Men have had to be leaders and teachers in the realms of thinking and in all those things which belong to the man's sphere. Women must take the lead and be prepared to teach in feeling matters, for these belong to her sphere and form an essential part of her genius.

Women who have found these values of relationship for themselves want to bring them into their relations with men, but men rarely want them of their own accord. When a man, however, has been intrigued into learning the lesson, he recognizes the enhanced values which the deeper understanding brings to the relationship and would not voluntarily go back to the old unconsciousness. This is a hard road, however, for men, and one so foreign to their own instinct that they can hardly be expected to be enthusiastic about it. For the sake of a dearly loved woman a man may be willing to essay it, but it will be a long time before men set out on their own initiative to create conscious relationships of this kind. Women do not, even after a century of higher education, evolve new sciences or new philosophic systems. It is hardly likely that men will immediately embrace the new realm which women are here and there beginning to evolve.

Nevertheless as women enter more and more into business and the professions and so are thrown into daily contact with men on a basis of work and cooperation the necessity for comradely relationships inevitably develops. Such friendships between men and women may be very valuable indeed, producing a psychological intimacy that is yet without overt sexual or erotic overtones. The exchange of ideas, the sharing not only of interests centering on their mutual work but also perhaps concerning music, literature, the arts or outdoor activities, can be very rewarding. If neither of them is married and has no erotic involvement other than marriage, it is quite possible that a different and more exclusive intimacy will develop. If that should happen, it will be found that the months of comradeship have served to consolidate a stable foundation for an unusually satisfactory marriage partnership, even if there has not been the deep constellation of the affections characteristic of projection of anima and animus. The values of a psychological relationship which have been developed through the years of comradeship will serve the couple well in the greater intimacy of marriage with all its problems of mutual adjustment.

These values of relationship, genuine and real though they are when developed in an actual living friendship, are, nevertheless, quite difficult to describe in abstract or general terms. A writer who uses such terms is always open to the reproach of using high-sounding words which have no actual or concrete meaning. This is a disadvantage that always dogs the expounder of new ways, for words have a meaning only to those who have themselves experienced the values for which the words stand. For those who have experienced this new kind of relationship, even in small measure, my words will have meaning. Those who have not made their relationships conscious may not understand at all what I am talking about. But if such a one is interested and will make the attempt to get reality into his nearest relationship he will, I venture to predict, find the key to what I have to say, through his own experience. In order to avoid using such apparently meaningless generalities, I will give concrete instances of situations which are sufficiently common to be within the personal experience of most of my readers.

In an association between two women, which begins as a matter of convenience, only the more superficial layers of the psyche are involved at first. The problems incidental to daily life and close quarters can be met by the exercise of ordinary politeness and good feeling. As the friendship grows, however, deeper layers of the psyche may come to be involved. The daily contacts may have reverberations beyond the surface reactions so that if the pitfall of repression is to be avoided a greater frankness will be necessary, together with a willingness to accept and work on the emotions brought to light in the relationship, whatever they may be. If, for instance, a compulsive desire to dominate threatens the harmony of the situation, this must be clearly recognized and tackled, not only in its manifestations, the specific instances which brought it to light, but in its cause, namely the determination to have one's own way at all costs. Only by such an attitude of frankness can the friends be sure that the situation between them is not being falsified by repression.

If the friendship between two women becomes permeated by love of a more emotional and instinctual character, there is a strong tendency to ignore the new element and, indeed, actually to remain unaware of its presence. When we come to speak of love between two people of the same sex, we immediately touch on a subject which is hedged about with prejudices and taboos. The word *homosexual* is used today, however, in many senses, so that in any discussion of friendships between two people of the same sex it is necessary to make clear exactly what is meant.

The emotional involvement in a friendship may be intense in its character and yet be without physical expression. For love between women does not necessarily involve physical sexuality.

Viewed from one angle such a friendship would not be called homosexual. Yet for women who have no sexual expression in their lives the repressed instinct is bound to color their major relationship and give it that quality of emotionality which is the earmark of erotic involvement even though no overt sexual acts or even conscious sexual impulses are present. Thus from a broader point of view it must be recognized that the emotion involved in such friendships is instinctual or sexual in its character. In other cases the love between friends may find its expression in a more specifically sexual fashion which, however, cannot be considered perverted if their actions are motivated by love.

There is unfortunately no word in general use which makes clear the distinction between these two situations. If it were not for the sinister connotation which clings to the term *homosexuality,* it might not be necessary to make a clear-cut distinction, but it does not seem right to refer to friendships of either character by a term which is linked in the mind of the public with debased practices and criminality, for they are often of a high moral and ethical quality. Yet in the absence of any other term, *homosexual* must serve.

In judging of any sexual relationship, whether homosexual or heterosexual, it must always be borne in mind that the quality of the emotion involved is the criterion of value rather than the nature of the accompanying physical expression. It is necessary to be cautious how we apply the term *perversion.* In a friendship between women there is a natural tendency to repress the element of erotic love, a tendency which is strengthened by the conventional aversion which is felt toward the very idea of sexual love between women.

It is not that the friends consciously repress something which they really know. The problem goes deeper than this, for the sexuality may be repressed at a level below consciousness. Many people, women especially, never even dream of the possibility of this kind of involvement. Though in a literal sense I make a mistake in saying they do not dream of it; they are very likely to dream of it, but the possibility itself is simply unthinkable. It cannot be entertained in consciousness and any evidence of its presence is ignored. The instinctual involvement, being repressed in this way, shows itself in a certain compulsive element which enters into the situation. The two women seem to be driven by an unseen force and compelled to create an emotional problem which is constantly present between them. The intensity which is not recognized in its true colors and is repressed disappears from consciousness but reappears in all sorts of other manifestations. For instance, it may show itself as an undue solicitude in regard to health or comfort; one friend may pamper and tend the other. "Dear, do put on your sweater," or "Eat a little more." The point gained may be quite unimportant, its significance lies in the emotional satisfaction gained through the personal involvement. The emotional concern may find its vent in disagreements and quarrels and in attempts at domination, both direct and indirect. Often the cause of the quarrel is trivial in the extreme. Each party would be content with a solution in either direction. The intensity of interest is not in winning the argument, but in the mutual involvement which a quarrel permits.

Disputes of this nature may go on to a violent explosion or even to the point of an actual rupture of the friendship. The friends do not know why they quarrel, for the sexual element is entirely repressed, but they are urged on by a power beyond their control to strain at their bonds and to hurt one another, each, as it were, trying "to get something" out of the other. When a friendship breaks up in this way, the details may be most surprisingly sordid. Women whom one had thought of as gentle and cultured will suddenly show some of the characteristics of the wildcat. The compulsion to "get something" out of a friend, which has it roots in repressed sexuality, may find its expression in all sorts of demands. Quarrels may arise, for instance, about business affairs or about the division of their common possessions which could be easily arranged with a little common sense and good will were it not for the unrecognized instinctual involvement.

When friendship goes deeper than mere comradeship and the sexual element is frankly accepted, a more fundamental rapport becomes possible, and a relationship of greater depth and stability can be achieved. But in order to work out a conscious—a psychological—relationship, the greatest honesty is necessary in regard to the true nature of the feeling held for each other. If the friends do not refuse to face the problem it presents, the instinctual bond which arises between them may even strengthen their love. If they are willing to struggle along trying to understand the true motives and purposes of their impulses, they will probably find that the physical attraction, as such, recedes in power and proves to have been nature's way of forcing them to a realization of the importance of the bit of life they are to experience through each other. Psychologically speaking, the purpose of this kind of union is to strengthen the power of the feminine element in both women. When this is accomplished the natural polarity of the sexes begins to reassert itself, and they each turn toward men for this side of their fulfillment.

The friendship, however, usually survives this reorientation and continues to hold for the friends certain values which are rarely, if ever, experienced in a heterosexual relationship. The inner essence of friendship defies treatment in a psychological essay; it might be better depicted in a psychological novel, but for any real appreciation of its value it must be experienced. It is only possible, therefore, in this discussion to hint at its living value and for the rest to speak of those everyday events and problems from whose right handling relationship can be built up between two human beings who love each other.

Certain difficulties are more evident in a relation between two women than in one between a man and a woman. For instance, a tendency to rivalry may exist; or each may want the exclusive government on the feminine side and may try to force her partner to play the man's role; also the tendency to identification, which dogs all couples who live together, is likely to be particularly strong. If two people love each other, they quite naturally want to be constantly together; they want to do the same things, they come to think in the same way, they entertain together, and indeed discuss everything together, even their friends' actions, and so come to hold the same views and in the end present a single face to society. A classical example of this kind of identification is to be seen in Ruth's love for Naomi. When she threw in her lot with the older woman she said, "Entreat me not to leave thee, or to return from following after thee, for whither thou goest, I will go; and where thou lodgest, I will lodge: thy people shall be my people, and thy God my God: Where thou diest, will I die, and there will I be buried." It is in this spirit that many friends start out in life together. Their acquaintances come to think of them as inseparable, they are dealt with as a unit; one is never invited out without the other. Neither ever comes home with fresh interests, for each has been to the same place, has met the same people. All of this increases their identification and leads to a sterilizing of the relationship. It is as though they have only one life between them, instead of two related lives. Only things which are separate, however, can be related — a point emphasized by Jung in his essay on marriage, where he says, "In order to be conscious of myself, I must be able to distinguish myself from others. Relationship can only take place where the distinction exists. . . . As no distinction can be made with regard to unconscious contents, on this terrain no relationship can be established; here there still reigns the original unconscious condition of the ego's primitive identity with others, in other words a complete absence of relationship."[1] If two things are identical, they cannot be related. They flow into a sameness which is without energy or interest.

The question arises then: What can be done to forestall this stagnation in identification? Is there any way of preventing it, or is this the inevitable grave of relationship between any two individuals who are very closely associated? Human nature so

---

[1] *The Development of Personality*, par. 326.

intensely desires intimacy and union and longs so ardently to be understood that it is difficult to build up any real independence and uniqueness; loneliness and isolation are too hard to bear. Indeed, isolation and withdrawal from human companionship have their dangers too, which are as serious as those of too close association. To be remote and isolated brings no development. The problem then comes down to this: How can two people keep a sufficient distance and separateness so as not to lose themselves in identification with each other, and yet live sufficiently intimately so as not to fall into the egotism and unrelatedness of isolation. within themselves?

This is a problem which naturally cannot be solved merely by sitting down and thinking it out. It involves time and growth. It is not a problem of a static adjustment; it is a problem in *life.* An adjustment between two individuals which is satisfactory today may be outgrown in a few years or even in a few weeks. Such a problem can only be solved "in the living"—*solvitur in ambulando.* Psychological development results through working on such a problem. All who wish their relationship to grow will encounter certain points of difficulty, however, which will need adjustment. Perhaps some of the pitfalls might be avoided if these were taken into consideration in the beginning.

One of the most frequent mistakes that women make in the arrangement of their lives together is in failing to provide for a sufficient separateness. For example, they arrange to share all the rooms in common, a mistake hardly avoidable if they have to live in the confined space of a modern apartment. But even where entirely separate rooms are available, each may want to be always accessible to her friend and so falls into the habit of leaving her door open. The time will come, however, when she wishes to be quite alone; then she hesitates to close the door for fear her friend will think the action a gesture intended to keep her out in a personal way, with a certain negative feeling. So the door is left open, and an unspoken rule grows up that "doors are left open," the only exception being when one friend is annoyed at the other or withdraws herself with a hostile implication. As a result each sooner or later begins to feel, if she is a sensitive person, that she can have no privacy from the other, that her very thoughts are not her own, that she may have no secrets from her friend.

But the fact is, the deepest experiences of our inner life cannot be communicated. If one cannot have a secret, there are certain secret things from which one is shut out. Certain things in one's own psyche will not tolerate exposure. For instance, unformed thought-germs are like embryos, they must live for a long while in the hidden depths of a human psyche if they are to grow and mature. Therefore, if a woman persists in living constantly in the publicity of a relationship without secrets, the result is that she will know only those things in herself which are suitable for publication. Inevitably her consciousness becomes shallow. If the woman is an introvert, whose inner life is of great importance to her, there will in the course of time grow up within her either a conscious or an unconscious reaction to this devastating publicity. She will find herself becoming the victim of thoughts which, indeed, must be kept secret. She will begin to have great resistances against her friend, will begin to hate the sight of her, to wish her out of the house, perhaps even to wish her dead. Now she cannot withdraw herself, for the negative feeling just below the surface would surely become evident to her friend whom she does not really hate, whom indeed she really loves and cherishes and around whose love and companionship her very life is built. She will probably force herself to openness and accessibility once more, and go even a step further into identification in order to compensate for her feelings of violent withdrawal. In such a case as this the bonds of love become in very truth bonds which are hard to break and ill to bear.

Obviously this kind of situation contains dynamite and it is only a matter of time before something destructive will happen. An arrangement for separateness made at the beginning of the association would have avoided much of the difficulty. If the two had realized that a relationship can only be formed between separate individuals they would have made an agreement to leave each other some privacy. But the very need for privacy, for separateness, is an outcome of psychological growth. Undeveloped people and children are collective in their needs. They may be able to live and work and sleep in groups without violating anything within them. There is in America today almost a cult of the "group." The houses are frequently built with all the rooms opening one out of another, often only curtains divide them. All of the family share all of the rooms. It is part of the national quest of the "best for all," instead of something less than the best for each, which some would much prefer. Many who live in this collective fashion are content not only to live in houses whose rooms are all public, but even when they are alone to allow their privacy to be intruded upon by an unseen visitor who keeps up a perpetual conversation via the radio. In such an atmosphere psychological development of the individual is impossible. For privacy is a fundamental human need without which there is no individuality; anyone who lives always with others can only function collectively. By collective functioning I mean functioning according to a role whose characteristics and limits are already defined, having been laid down by custom. For instance a woman functions collectively as "a wife" or "a mother," "a friend," "a citizen," "a lady" or "a good sport." In order to live her life according to one of these roles a woman must know, either consciously or unconsciously, the rules, so to speak, of the collective pattern, but no demand is made on her for consciousness of what the situation really is or of how she really feels. She needs only to know how things "ought to be," how she "ought to act," what feelings are "appropriate."

The collective side of her psyche can function in a general situation up to this point, by making use of the rules of the average or the normal. No living creature, however, is quite average—every human being only approximates the normal. If two women live together at close quarters, the failure of each to live up to her standard will sooner or later become apparent. Consciousness of her own deviations from the conventional picture of "a good friend" or "a cultured woman," or whatever the collective pattern may be, forces on the woman a choice of attitude. If she is unconscious of its true significance, she can discount her deviation from her standard as a part of the weakness of human nature, to be explained to her friend as a mistake, a failure to live up to an ideal; or if she senses that much is at stake, she may regard the deviation as more important. For in this very deviation she demonstrates that she does *not* function as a collective being—*a* woman—but as an individual—*this* particular woman. The adjustment with her friend must be based on the recognition that she is a separate entity with the right to an individual name, and is shown to be so by her very failure to live according to a collective standard. Thus out of close contact with another human being and the disillusion which results, the possibility arises of recognizing both herself and her partner as individuals.

If a woman lives only as a member of a group she may retain her ideal of herself but she lives only collectively. The only things she may recognize and approve in herself are those which are similar to or identical with the general characteristics. She is reduced to the least common denominator of the group. She may be a good member or a bad member, yet in the final analysis she is just *a* woman. As soon, however, as she begins to live in a close relationship, apart, with one other human being, she is compelled to differentiate within herself *the* individual woman. Stated in reverse and with equal logic: As soon as a woman begins to differentiate herself from the other members of the group, *not by personal peculiarities but by individual reactions,* the possibility and, indeed, necessity arises of developing relationships in place of her former identifications. The original state of primitive unconscious oneness in the group is identification. When the individual members of the group begin to develop a consciousness of themselves as separate, this oneness is split up into a duality, a pair of opposites, which are bound together just as all the other opposites—for instance, "above and below" or "right and wrong" —are bound together. The opposites into which identification is split are *individuality* and *relationship*. Most people have a longing for close friendship and intimacy, indeed, for a relationship, a longing which has deeper roots than we are accustomed to think. The reason for this urge or longing is perhaps to be understood in the light of a craving of the psyche for individual differentiation. The longing for sexual love, marriage and children is based, we are all aware, on more fundamental necessities than the fulfillment of the needs and desires of the individual. Here we recognize the workings of a racial or evolutionary law which gives the biological aims of life precedence over the personal aims of the individual. Over and over again, it may be seen how an individual man or woman can be caught by this biological urge and carried forward over all obstacles until the biological aim of the instinct for reproduction is satisfied, even if it leads him into a marriage which personally speaking may be disastrous. But man is not only an animal with biological life aims. He is also a psychological being. Yet he did not invent or create his own psychological nature. The mind, the spirit, the psyche of man is a result of an evolutionary life process, similar, we must suppose, to that which resulted in his bodily form. This psyche appeared without the volition or intervention of man and indeed without his conscious knowledge of what was taking place. This side of man's nature arose and developed, so far as we know, autonomously and by a self-regulating process, similar to the biological life processes. Thus in this realm we are justified in saying that man is subject to the workings of psychological life aims. We speak of a *biological* life aim without postulating a conscious, a personified or an anthropomorphic mind or will in physical evolution. Similarly, when I speak of a *psychological* life aim, it must be understood that I am not postulating a conscious mind or will, either in man or in a deity which, as it were, conceives or holds the "aim," but, using the analogy of the biological life aim, I am suggesting that there is also a psychological life aim which can be observed empirically in individuals. If we are permitted to observe the inner life of any individual, we shall find that even as the young man or young woman is hurried into marriage by the pressure of the biological urge of which he may, nonetheless, be unaware, so in the psychological realm also events follow in a sequence which urges him forward unerringly toward a psychological goal.

The longing which most people have for companionship is a psychological urge comparable to the biological ones; it functions after the pattern of a life aim, pushing the individual forward into a relationship. The woman acting on such an urge may explain her action to herself in terms of expediency. "It is more convenient than to live alone." "It is less expensive." "It is generally advisable." And the like. These are her conscious motives. But life has other axes to grind. No sooner has she entered into a close association than she finds herself caught with an important decision to make. If she cannot face the demand the situation puts upon her for consciousness of herself as apart from, other than, a representative of the collective standard, she may choose to retire from the situation, but she must then withdraw into isolation again. That she cannot do without serious regression. She *has* to go on. She *must* work on the relationship or choose regression, which is psychological death. If she decides to go on and face the difficulties of the relationship she will immediately find herself obliged to initiate a separation—a conscious discrimination—between herself and her friend. She is compelled to find herself as an individual. Each step which she takes in differentiating herself from the collective pattern forces her, whether she will or not, to "go at it again" with her friend, and so to differentiate the relationship a little further. Life has caught her. She has become the tool of one of life's purposes. It is apparently a law of life that living things may not stagnate—they must evolve. Thus we see that her isolation and loneliness force a woman to companionship and that companionship, in its turn, compels her to find what and who she really is. This dual movement toward differentiation and development in the psychological realm is apparently a life aim which functions regularly. In the lives of some the psychological life aim moves in the same direction as the biological life aim. For them, fulfillment in both realms of life can be attained simultaneously. But in some instances the two urges are opposed. When this is the case, the opposition produces a conflict in the individual, which may be devastatingly severe. As an example, I shall cite a typical situation, several instances of which have come to my notice.

A woman has a friend of her own sex—perhaps she is living with her—when a man appears on the scene who asks her to marry him. Loyalty to her friend and the greater consciousness which in certain instances is promised in the relationship call her to devote her life to her friendship. On the other hand, the biological urge and conventional opinion combine to persuade her to marriage, even though, because of the particular relation with the man, consciousness and psychological development may have to take a very secondary place. I do not mean to imply that in every case the friendship holds more psychological values than the marriage, for the reverse may be true. But I instance a situation where the weight of the psychological values is in favor of the friendship. For when these two things—friendship and marriage—come into conflict there is always a great tendency to choose marriage, not only on account of the biological urge to fulfill the fate of wife and mother, but also on account of the weight of the conventional evaluation which works from within the individual's psyche no less than through the opinion of society. In such a conflict the individual must make a choice, and from the severity of the conflict which often results in such a dilemma we can glimpse the strength of this psychological life aim which is here in direct opposition to one of the strongest and most imperious of the biological life aims. The fact that it is impossible in any given instance to foretell which aim will get the upper hand and be followed, or to foretell whether subsequent events will or will not justify the choice, demonstrates that these psychological life aims have a validity for life, which in their own sphere is paramount.

In those cases where the friendship is chosen the relation between the woman and her friend carries a weight and importance which cannot be lightly dismissed. These two women choose to make their major relation in life together. Their friendship will tend to follow some general or archetypal pattern until such time as they have developed a conscious differentiation of their own individualities in the way described above. Two distinct types of relation can commonly be observed. In the first, based on the pattern of a marriage, the masculine role is played persistently by one, while the feminine part is played by the other. Unless through this experience the masculine woman can capture her own feminine values, her emotional development has a great tendency to remain static. Usually she lives in the joy and rapture of the transference to her friend of the moment and refuses to work on the difficulties which arise between them, becoming involved instead with one woman after another. She is unwilling to sacrifice the pleasure which the condition of being "in love" brings to her and so cannot assimilate the feminine values projected onto her friend. When during the process of living in a close relationship her projection is challenged in the way described above, she withdraws, hurt, and will even break the relationship rather than make any inner change. In a short time she will be caught in a similar situation with another woman. This type of woman is never termed "manly," whatever her age may be; she is spoken of as "boyish," implying that on this side of her character she is held in an adolescent stage. Her failure to assimilate the feminine principle is like an eternal youth. The recurrent transference to a woman followed by the inevitable breakup is of the nature of a regression. Such women are persistently adolescent; they will not or cannot grow up.

The other woman, who has played the feminine role, does not, as a rule, function after the psychological pattern of wife but is either child or mother to her boyish friend. Her condition resembles that to be found in the other type of close friendship between two women, based on the relation between mother and daughter. In this situation neither woman is markedly masculine in appearance or in interests, and neither plays exclusively the active part in the relationship. The pattern of mother-daughter constitutes a perpetual danger, however, to the psychological growth of the friends, for it tends to hold at least one of them, and generally each of them alternately, in the position of child to mother.

If a woman has not had a satisfactory relation to her own mother, she is unable to learn what her mother might perhaps have taught her of the heritage of feminine wisdom, which can only be taught through close association and understanding, not through percept. Or, if the mother herself is not a very feminine person, she may be quite unable to give her daughter what she needs. In either case there results for the daughter a weakness on the feminine side, so that if she is to grow to full maturity she needs a relation to a woman.

But the maternal factor in the relation between two friends has dangers as well as undoubted values. For every human being has within his breast a great regressive longing, a reaching back to the mother. We are all not unlike the little girl who at the age of two went to stay with her grandmother. When her mother came to take her home, as was to be expected, she regressed to the baby phase she had just begun to outgrow and refused to feed herself. She snuggled up against her mother who promptly began to feed her. Her grandmother said to her, "Why, Lucy, you are a big girl now. Why don't you eat up your cereal?" The child made no reply, but a little later she was heard to say to her doll: "Dolly, some folks thinks you ought to be a big girl now, but I doesn't think you need quite yet." Just as this little girl was afraid to break her childish relation to her mother so a woman may dread the thought of breaking her childish relation to her mother-friend, for fear of losing the love and warmth which the relation to a womanly woman has brought to her, perhaps for the first time in her life. But only by working out of her dependent state and so redeeming her childish love can she acquire her own feminine and feeling values.

If, however, the friends are willing to make conscious their reactions in every situation which arises between them, these "patterns" will soon prove to be inadequate and the necessity will arise to transcend the unconscious form and create a conscious psychological relationship with each other. This is a new creation and inaugurates a new phase of emotional development and experience of which only the higher types of women are capable. Friendships of this kind are commonest among self-supporting women who have devoted much of their energy to making an adaptation in the world of work. It is in such cases that the exclusive orientation to women is most likely to be temporary, although the friendship between the two may be stable and permanent. For it is women of this type who gain most readily the values to be won from a love relationship with another woman. The very qualities which enabled them as young women to launch out on an independent career guarantee that they will work for reality and consciousness in their intimate relationships, and by so doing they will gain for themselves the feminine and feeling values which they formerly sacrificed when they chose a career instead of marriage.

Among married women friendships with women are not usually regarded as very important, but they may occasionally loom large and through them a consciousness of values in relationship may be developed which can be applied to the marriage relation in a way which enhances its significance. It is rather unusual, however, for a married woman to take feelings of this nature very seriously. For when once she has established herself in a marriage with the love of husband and children and all the associated social prestige, she has little urge to take up the undeveloped side of her psyche. It is, indeed, an exceptional woman who attempts it. Life's good things come to her without effort; there is no urgent call to strive for that development which would enable her to create them for herself. The married woman rarely realizes the lack of individual development which makes her but a dull friend to the woman who is developed on this side. Yet occasionally, perhaps in later life when her children have left her or when she is thrown back on her own resources by the death of her husband, a married woman may take up her own psychological development and so may be led to explore those parts of her psyche which are conventionally less acceptable.

If we question the vigorous unmarried women characteristic of today, we shall find that a large proportion of them could have married. They refused because they wanted something different from the usual conventional marriage or they wanted first to try their own wings in college or work. They looked at the lives of their married sisters and friends and found them unutterably dull. They put marriage off till some day in the future, but did not realize at the time the difficulty they were letting themselves in for. They wanted the relationship when they should marry to be deeper and more real, and so through the years of their work they sought for maturity and development. But the men of their group continued to make the old type of marriage with all its collective values and its lack of demand on the side of relationship. So, when these women found themselves, at the age of thirty or thirty-five, at last ready for marriage, the men of their own age were already married.

Three choices for the fulfillment of the emotional side of life were still open to them. They could enter into an extra-marital relation with a man. They could marry a man much younger than themselves (this solution of the problem is a very frequent one in America today). Or they could turn to their women friends and seek through friendship to satisfy their emotional needs. This is the road which many of them have taken.

Thus friendships among women are a part of the same trend which became manifest in the social revolution of the last eighty or one hundred years. They have their roots in social and generally human movements of far-reaching significance, such as the changed economic conditions resulting from the mechanization of industry, in the education and financial emancipation of women, and also in the related psychological changes which took place in the women themselves. The increase of homosexual friendships among women must be considered as a transitional phase of civilization. Perhaps it is *womanhood* that is passing through adolescence in regard to individual development. This trend in society is, perhaps, a symptom of human evolution, while in each particular friendship, the friends may become mature—rounded out psychologically— through this very experience.

These movements must be regarded without prejudice. We must seek their psychological goal and significance—their creative quota —and not regard them from the *a priori* standards with which they conflict. When we find large numbers of responsible, vigorous and adequate women rejecting marriage, which has been considered the most developed state, and "regressing" to intense relationships with other women, we recognize that they must be searching for something whether they are aware of it or not. Marriage represents an adaptation to the sexual and reproductive instincts of humanity and is, without question, a mature adaptation on the biological plane. But the step back is, as we have seen, related to a move- ment directed toward a psychological development in women by which a more conscious and differentiated relationship becomes possible. The movement is biologically a regression, but psy- chologically has a progressive significance. In the old type of marriage a woman lived only for the collective values of wife and mother, and apart from marriage had practically no place in society; the individual side of her nature was entirely un- developed and was represented in her unconscious masculine soul, her animus, which was projected onto her husband. When, how- ever, she began to develop her own individual and masculine values, she lived the masculine side of herself in reality, submitting it to discipline. She no longer projected it in the old exclusive way upon a man. As a result, she found herself no longer able to live just as his anima, his counterpart, but was obliged to set out in the world for herself. In this phase of her evolution, for psychological as well as social reasons, friendship with another woman was the only form of emotional experience open to her. Consequently, relationships became very common among those women who were seeking a fuller development and maturity.

From the biological standpoint this movement toward friendship must be considered a regressive phase of civilization, for on account of it many potential wives and mothers have remained unmarried. Yet regarded from a psychological and cultural angle, it reveals itself as a *reculer pour mieux sauter* — a drawing back to get a fresh start. For through this step many a woman in the past has succeeded in escaping from the condition which demanded that she live only as man's counterpart, personifying his anima, into a life of fuller opportunity for personal development. This movement of society may foreshadow the development of the woman of the future — indeed of womanhood itself — out of the condition of psychological onesidedness which her unconscious relation to man has imposed, into a freer life in which she will find herself as a conscious and complete individual.

A new thing never arises from the highest place but always from a lower. The change in relation between men and women, brewing for many years, has been preceded by a step back from the stage of conventional marriage in order that a new and more individual capacity might be developed in woman in her own realm. Only when this has been attained can she achieve conscious relationship with a man.

5. Marriage

Almost every woman wants to marry, for marriage seems to offer the best opportunity for fulfillment in life. Not only does it promise the daily companionship of the man she loves, with a satisfaction deeper and richer than mere companionship, and give her the right to bear and rear their children and so satisfy her own maternal instinct, but it promises also, when the glamor of youth and the struggle of middle life are past, the hope of evening years of closest intimacy with the one who is dearer to her even than herself. Through a shared life-experience, the opportunity arises to explore the hidden depths of another individual — to learn to know and love another in his weakness and in his strength. The beautiful words of the marriage service: "For richer, for poorer, in sickness and in health until death," refer not only to the material world but to the psychological as well, not only to the outer life but also to the inner.

A picture of marriage drawn on such ample lines, the lights and shadows giving scope for the exploration of love in all its varieties — love that is joyous, love that is tender, love that gives and love that receives — forms a cherished part of the dream of most girls. Sometimes the marriage which the young woman actually finds fulfills her ideal, but such marriages go their way without noise or notoriety. It has been said that the country which is without history is the happiest, and the same is perhaps true of that lesser "state," the family. These marriages do not come directly under the scrutiny of the practicing psychotherapist.

Other marriages, however, fall short not only of the ideal but also of a more modest requirement. The girl sees so clearly what she would like her marriage to be, but only rarely has she any idea how to make her dream come true. She does not know how to bring to pass—to make concrete—the vision of love and mutual helpfulness, of intimacy and companionship, which forms the very core of marriage as she pictures it.

The question of marriage as a whole is too comprehensive to be discussed here, and this is not the place to consider the advantages of marriage over any other association between men and women, such as "companionate marriage" or "free love." Certain problems, however, which a woman encounters in adjusting herself to the position of wife in an ordinary, average marriage do need consideration here. Some of her problems will depend upon the nature of the individual relationship, others on general considerations which are taken for granted by everyone as a valid foundation for life. But beyond these, subsequent events frequently show, either in domestic difficulties or in the revelations of a divorce proceeding, that illusion and misunderstanding can come between two people—even the best meaning and most good-hearted—in matters which each had considered covered by the categories of personal relationship and love on the one hand, and generally accepted standards of conduct on the other.

When we see two young people pledging their troth at their wedding we assume that the experience of one will be the reciprocal of the other, that they are "entering life together." This attitude implies that marriage is a thing in itself, an institution, and that the experience of it will be the same, or approximately the same, for the man as for the woman. A very little reflection, however, will convince us that this idea does not tally with the facts.

To the man, marriage belongs to his personal life. It has relatively little to do with his position in the community or with his relation to his work. But to a woman the situation is entirely different; marriage is much more far-reaching in its effects. Her whole life is altered by it, her social status completely changed. There is a world of difference between whether she is Mrs. or Miss. As Mrs. So-and-so she is accepted by the world and accorded a deference and attention which she would never receive if she were still Miss. Marriage to a woman is an achievement; some women take it as the one thing required of them; having thus far succeeded, they may for the rest of their lives sit back and "take it easy." Whether her husband is satisfactory or not, a married woman nevertheless shows to the world the contented face of a human being who has arrived. A cynic is said to have remarked that many a woman has no other claim to personal distinction beyond this: that she once induced some man to marry her. One might add "God help him."

A woman who marries to gain a position in life proceeds, as a rule, to identify herself completely with her husband, taking his achievements as though they were her own. If *he* has done anything worthy of distinction, *she* puts on airs. If he is elected to a postion of honor she expects to receive a full share of the deference and respect he has won. I have heard such women say, "*We* are writing a book." "*We* built the new State House." They are upheld in this attitude by society. No matter how stupid or uninteresting the wife of a prominent man may be, or how disagreeable, she is invited by all those who welcome her husband to their homes. Her position in the world does not depend upon her own efforts, either of work or of character, but only upon the achievements of her husband. The converse of this is also true. If the husband is a ne'er-do-well, the wife may be industrious, efficient and charming, but their friends will only say, "Poor Mrs. So-and-so! It is too bad she has such an unsatisfactory husband; she deserved something better than that." But they will not ask her to dinner when they are expecting guests whose husbands have been more successful.

On this account a woman's choice of a husband is influenced, consciously or unconsciously, by many factors—wealth, position, social prestige and the like—which influence the man far less. It is true that a man's choice of a bride may also be affected by these considerations, but as a rule the man looks for his fulfillment on the instinctual and love side of his nature in his marriage, and for his individual and ego fulfillment in his work and in the world. In considering marriage, a woman must take into account not only her personal inclinations but also whether or not the man will be able to support her and her children; whether, too, he is likely to make good in the community. For in most instances, the woman looks to her marriage for the source of her entire satisfaction.

Until two or three generations ago these questions were considered quite openly by the parents of the girl. More recently they have been pushed into the background. Arranged marriages have been discarded in favor of those dependent on personal inclination; the love match, especially in Anglo-Saxon countries, carries the popular sentiment. Marriage settlements and the young man's prospects, which occupied such a large place in marriage arrangements a hundred years ago, are now left largely to chance.

The importance of these things was formerly held clearly in consciousness, but they were arranged by the parents, not by the girl herself, for the bride must not appear worldly-minded. Today the girl makes her own arrangements far more often than formerly, but still she must not *appear* worldly-minded. Her marriage must be a love match; personal inclination must ostensibly be all that guides her. Yet these questions of money and social position are as important as ever. If they are not consciously taken care of, they will drop into the unconscious and control the situation from a hidden vantage point. This means a definite loss from the point of view of the individual's social adaptation: If a girl disregards the worldly aspects of marriage, her preferences for certain men may well be guided by motives of which she is herself unaware. She may really be unconscious of the reasons for her likes and dislikes. She actually may not know that she prefers A because of his position in the world although his temper is vile, and she will be equally unaware that B, whom she might love, fails to get a response from her becaue "he is an artistic sort of chap, who is not likely to settle down permanently." If the matter stopped there, this might be all very well. But there is a grave risk that, having married A and secured a good home and social position, she may become aware of her starved feelings and then, if B is anywhere about, complications may ensue.

The woman *must* take these things into account. Only in this way can she be freed from their unconscious compulsion and be enabled to examine the state of her feelings honestly. If a woman who is about to make a worldly marriage acknowledges frankly to herself that she does not love her husband but that she wants the position he can give her, disaster is far less likely to follow than if she lets herself be duped into thinking she loves him by keeping her worldly wisdom in the background. But naturally many women who might be betrayed through their own unconsciousness into making a worldly marriage would be horrified at this cold-blooded exploitation of the man's affections if they realized what their own motives were. Perhaps Nature, who is more concerned for the race than for the individual, plays a part in keeping the woman unaware of her true feelings, for if she will not take the worldly advantages into conscious consideration the welfare of herself and her children can best be assured through her ignorance of her true feeling for the man.

The woman who is really conscious of these social considerations and yet loves a man whose characteristics do not hold out very good social prospects may be able to forego the worldly advantages and choose to marry the poor man, provided she knows what she is doing and counts the cost.

From the point of view of society, marriage is a social institution like the family and the church and, as such, comes under the ruling of certain general laws. The laws and customs which govern the general case apply also to the individual instance, but they cannot be expected to give complete guidance in regard to its management. Thus everyone has in the background of his mind an idea of marriage and its obligations, but most men and women would find it exceedingly difficult to formulate their ideas. As a legal contract, marriage and its requirements have been formulated in the statutes. But these rules and laws are necessarily generalized and refer only to external action, they cannot touch the more subtle realms of implicit action — thoughts, feelings or even words. Faithfulness, for instance, is considered in terms of physical sexuality; support is considered in terms of shelter, food and clothing. But these things represent the very minimum in our code of honor as it affects marriage. In the picture which each one has of marriage, these formulated obligations have their place, but there are many others which are taken for granted — assumed as *of course* — although they remain unstated. If these assumptions were conscious they could be discussed before marriage, but their very *of course* character makes it seem unnecessary, even impertinent, to bring them into the open.

The idea of marriage is a generalized concept, but the generalization is not uniform. Each social group, each racial group and each geographic group has its own assumptions regarding the structure of the "institution of marriage," and the idea of marriage varies in different small groups within the community to an amazing extent. The picture that each individual holds is modified by family tradition, by superimposed pictures of marriage gleaned from novels and plays, by his own observations of the marriages of relatives and friends and, especially, of the marriage of his parents. From such diverse sources an idea of marriage and its obligations is built up for each individual, an idea which he takes to be not the highly personal and almost accidental composite it really is, but a universally valid standard. Because the underlying assumptions and prejudices are hardly recognized, they cannot be discussed by the pair before marriage, but they will surely lead to actions which to an onlooker may appear arbitrary or unreasonable. The total assumptions of any two people never tally exactly, and indeed masculine and feminine assumptions differ so that a clash of opinion between husband and wife is almost inevitable sooner or later—and this on some point which they have each assumed is accepted by all right-thinking people.

For instance, a young woman marries the man she loves because of his charm, his ability to say the right thing and, perhaps not a little, because of the way he has in lovemaking. She may have agreed to accept "love in a cottage." After the first glamor of their love has passed, however, old assumptions begin to reassert themselves. Something whispers that as wife she ought to be supported in the same style as her sisters or friends, that she has a right to expect the comforts she was used to at home, that if she has a baby—well, certainly her health must not be allowed to suffer! In accordance with her feminine nature, she will probably bring these opinions to bear indirectly. While still saying that she accepts poverty, she yet makes her husband feel that he is a failure if he cannot give her the comforts and necessities that her friends have without question.

Possibly the difficulty takes another form, arising from unconsciousness or temperamental differences. If, for instance, her husband is of a thoughtful turn of mind and likes to round out his day of work with an evening's reading while she is more sociable, her assumption that *of course* her husband should go out with her to parties or that *of course* he must dress for dinner and play the good host to her friends may be the source of endless controversy. This adjustment may never have been discussed before marriage. It was not a problem to her because she took his sociability for granted; it was not a problem to him because sociability of that order had never crossed his horizon.

His assumptions of what is naturally to be expected of a wife may prove just as disconcerting to her. His masculine tendency to systematize and to organize may drive her "nearly crazy." More than one woman has said to me: "It is golf on Saturday afternoon, and lovemaking on Sunday morning! If he makes love to me again on a Sunday I shall scream!" But the man doubtless takes it as *of course* that when he is tired and concerned over business affairs he cannot be expected to make love to his wife.

This does not mean he does not love her. But a woman feels that love which is regulated by the calendar is only habit, and not *love* at all.

The man perhaps assumes that *of course* he can bring his friends home without warning and that his wife should be prepared to entertain them and make them welcome. It is true that it is his home as well as hers, but he forgets that the burden of the extra work falls on her or that she may have other plans. For instance, if the unexpected guests arrive on the maid's evening out his wife may feel hurt and resentful. These "little" things need very careful talking out, for each of the partners can so easily become a tyrant to the other, all unwittingly. A man, in speaking of just such a problem between himself and his wife said, "Mary a tyrant? No, Mary is not a tyrant!" Then with raised voice, "Mary is tyranny!"

The problem, however, goes deeper than this. It is not just a question of an adjustment which shall be fair to them both. A more subtle assumption underlies the masculine disregard for feminine values. A man may bring home not only his friends but also his business associates with whom he has no particular friendship. When he brings his friends he presumably wants his wife to make their acquaintance and her feminine values of relatedness are given a place, but when he brings home business associates he does not want her to make friends with them, he simply wants her to look pretty and give a touch of feminine charm to the situation which is really a business and not a social one. He acts as if she were only a delightful part of his equipment and he expects her to be satisfied if the entertainment furthers his business enterprises. A woman can only fill this role by assuming an artificial manner. If she consents to play this part she must wear a mask, while the deeper side of her nature which requires her to create something of personal relatedness is repudiated. If her social life is built up largely on this pattern she becomes identified with the social mask, which Jung has called *persona*. *Persona* is the name of the mask which the Greek actors wore to depict the character they represented in the play. The choice of the term is particularly happy because the characters in the Greek theater were all representations of social or collective roles—as the *happy lover,* the *jealous wife,* the *well-loved father.* Oedipus, Electra and Jocasta are not individuals but types and each would have had a typical mask or persona. In daily life everyone has some mask or persona which he assumes whenever he feels obliged to hide his real features. If he wears it too often or too continuously, however, he loses his ability to discard it. The mask, his chosen role, becomes a permanent and invariable attribute. The man himself grows to be identical with his persona. This is the danger that threatens a wife who too often plays hostess to strangers with whom she can have nothing in common, while for reasons of expediency she acts as though they were her friends.

The masculine assumption that she should be willing to make use of her charms in this way seems to exclude her fundamental need; to her it is an exploitation of her feminine nature—yes, of her very soul—for the furtherance of her husband's business. Only rarely does a woman realize why she is so annoyed at his assumption that she will *of course* be charming to his business acquaintances; she only feels exploited. He cannot for his part understand her unwillingness to comply with his wishes and thinks her selfish and uncooperative, which makes her angry and tends to alienate her. If she were aware of the causes of her own re-action, she could explain her point of view to her husband and a better understanding would result. Or if he had confided in her at first he would probably have enlisted her cooperation, for his success in business concerns her also—their interests are iden-tical—and her need for relationship would have been satisfied through the sense of partnership with him.

These assumptions, conscious and unconscious alike, may seriously jeopardize the harmony between married couples through the misunderstandings which they cause, but they frequently have another unfortunate effect on the relationship, on account of a curiously compulsive influence which they exert on the situation and which is stronger when the assumption is unconscious than when it is conscious: The psychical energy tied up in the assumption acts as a vortex, so that everything in its neighborhood is distorted. This center of irresistible attraction produces an almost uncanny sense of unspoken demand—an unexpressed will to power.

For instance, an ambitious or dominant woman may unwittingly make a tremendous claim on her hsuband because she has to find her entire satisfaction through her marriage. He may feel her like a millstone around his neck, as though she were making a power demand on him which he could neither tolerate nor escape. This effect is sometimes increased by a deliberately undertaken policy. For example, the energies of many men have been forced into the single channel of moneymaking to satisfy the ambition of their wives, while on the other hand many a promising and efficient girl has been reduced to a mere shadow by the man's assumption that he, and he alone, is "head of the house."

The condition known as "falling in love" furnishes fertile soil for all these assumptions to grow up and flourish, for it carries with it a certain sense of identity with the loved object which makes the lovers feel that they are in some mysterious way akin, that they were meant for each other, that they understand each other even without the medium of speech. I once knew a couple who scarcely ever communicated with each other except by grunts and changes of facial expression. They said, "Words are so clumsy and spoil everything." These two believed that they knew each other through and through and that no understanding between two human beings could be deeper.

A unity which is not based on experience of each other but depends on a mysterious sense of kinship comes from the projection of an unconscious part of the psyche upon the partner. The man sees in the woman his feminine counterpart, the reflection of his anima, his soul; while she sees in him her animus. The feeling of identity which arises between two people who love each other is very highly prized, for it rescues them from that sense of isolation and loneliness which is the portion of all who live as isolated individuals in the midst of the huge and indifferent crowd which makes up society. But since this sense of identity comes from a psychological projection and does not necessarily accord with facts, it lures the two into a false security. Neither is aware of any need to explore the territory between them and so each continues in complete ignorance of the partner's real character.

The illusion of at-oneness is increased by the woman's tendency to fulfill the man's expectation of her. Every woman in love unconsciously adapts herself to the anima role. Even a woman who would be classed as an animus type, with a clear idea of what she wants and a direct and frank way of going after it, will often drop her clear-cut manner when she falls in love and will become soft and pliant, sensitive to the man's every mood and responsive to all his wishes, expressed or implied. But a dramatic change of this kind is only a passing phase. Once she is safely married, the other side of her personality will reassert itself, and she may be as dismayed as her husband is to find that she has very definite ideas about many things which, formerly, she was quite willing to leave to his decision.

This tendency of the woman to accommodate herself to the man's idea of her is often augmented by a conscious attempt to "fit herself to be his wife," not only by perfecting herself in the domestic arts but also in the subjects that belong to his sphere! I remember one girl, a charming, pretty little thing, who became engaged to a professor of physics and believed it her duty to become a complete helpmeet for him. Her attempts to master the intricacies of mathematics did not enhance the value of the relationship, however, for he was not interested in discussing such things with her, but wanted something very different as a counterpoise to his overacademic life.

When a girl passes through a temporary change in personality due to her involvement with her lover, she unconsciously deceives him as to her true character and disposition. The involuntary deception is increased by the illusion of love's proverbial blindness and constitutes a very real, though hidden, danger to the safety and permanence of her marriage. Unconsciousness of this sort is most extensive with young people whose experience of life and of themselves is limited, but it is less dangerous for them than for more mature people, for as life challenges their assumptions the couple will replace them by more valid judgments which they have formed together.

Indeed the relative age and maturity of husband and wife determine the psychological situation of marriage to an extent insufficiently realized. The bride of fifty will have to meet problems unknown to a child wife of fifteen and the reverse is no less true. Several strange marriages have come to my notice where a discrepancy in age has been an outstanding feature. In one case a widower and his son married a widow and her daughter. At first sight there seems to be nothing very strange about the situation, except for the identification between parent and child, shown by their marrying into the same family. But it is quite startling to hear that the father married the daughter and the mother the son! The problems of these two households, close as they were, would be utterly different, just as they would in another case where a father and son married two sisters. In these situations we have examples of three different kinds of marriage: the marriage of two young people, the marriage of a young woman and an older man, and the marriage of a young man and an older woman. I shall consider the outstanding problems in marriages of these types, but to complete the classification according to age, I must add the marriage of two older people.

Each of these four marriages has a typical problem and a particular psychological task. I speak of a marriage task beyond the generally recognized one of creating a means for the social and emotional adaptation of two people and of bringing children into the world and so caring for them that they shall be adapted socially and emotionally, for marriage also imposes tasks which have to do with the inner life and culture of individuals.

The marriage of a young couple who start life together in their later teens or early twenties will be considered first. The young man and woman in such a case have had little or no previous experience of life. This is probably their first close friendship. They will explore the world of love and of ideas hand in hand and will make their friends together. The only life they know apart from the home in which they grew up is the one they themselves build. Their love for each other starts as a mutual projection of anima and animus, which in their case often makes a successful basis for marriage. The assumption that they think alike on all questions matters relatively little here, for the ideas and attitudes of both are as yet hardly formed, but are still fluid and will take definite shape only as a result of the experiences they will later encounter together.

But a marriage of this kind, stable and happy as it may prove to be, does not as a rule foster the psychological development of the two individuals, for it is based on identification, not on a conscious or psychological relationship. External problems tend to keep the man and woman who marry young very much occupied. As a rule the task of making a home, of providing an income sufficient for their increasing needs, and of building up a social life take all of their time and energy. The chances, too, are that babies will shortly arrive, necessitating a further expenditure of time and attention not only by the young mother who must bear them and tend them, but by the father who must provide the wherewithal for their support. Little leisure remains in which to become aware of the more subtle aspects of life. The problem, for instance, of their own psychological relationship does not obtrude itself very insistently until middle life when the children are off their hands and their financial position is established. During the middle forties many apparently stable and satisfactory marriages come to a place of great strain. [1] Not in-

1 For a further discussion of this subject the reader is referred to an essay on marriage in C.G. Jung's *The Development of Personality.*

frequently a husband and wife after having lived together for fifteen years or more and having brought up a family discover quite suddenly that "they are no longer in love with each other." The realization of their fundamental lack of harmony and relationship may lead them even to the point of discussing the possibility of divorce. Many divorces, indeed, are actually obtained at this time.—for no reason that seems to the onlooker either very apparent or very urgent. To those principally concerned it may seem sufficient to say, "But I am no longer in love with him" or "with her." They do not seem to realize that "love" which has died in this fashion overnight has never been love at all. Certainly it is not a conscious relationship; it results from a projection, and when the projection is removed, or its illusion of reality dissipated, each finds himself confronting a complete stranger. The outcome shows that they have not successfully accomplished their life task which lies in resolving the projections of anima and animus and thereby integrating the personality by gradually absorbing the projected elements into the psyche. By a resolution of the projection the man gains his anima, his soul, as a complementary part of himself, of his own psyche, instead of its being merely reflected to him from his wife; and the woman, in the same way, takes into herself her animus which formerly she found only in the person of her husband. This is the typical problem of the adolescent marriage.

The second type may be called the adult marriage. The man and woman are again approximately of the same age. In the adolescent group the boy is usually a little older than the girl; in the adult group there may be a similar age difference, but it is not so regularly in favor of the men. Marriages of men and women over thirty are a phenomenon of recent times. Until the middle of the last century, if a girl was not married before twenty-five, she was considered a hopeless old maid; today the number of women who marry after thirty-five is by no means inconsiderable. But marriage at this age is very different from the marriage of adolescents. The man and woman who have reached adult life unmarried have more life experience: their ideas on most subjects are more or less clearly formed; their characters and habits are already crystallized; each has a circle of friends and activities which may be very different from or even incompatible with the other's. The woman who marries late in life belongs, as a rule, to the group of business or professional women. She has made a career for herself, she is self-supporting and has been living an independent life away from her family. She is by no means willing to take her ideas secondhand from her husband. She has her own well-organized opinions on politics, religion, business, society and all other matters of general interest including divorce and free love. The marriage of these two does not mean, as it would if they were younger, that they will experience life and form their views together. They come to their marriage already experienced and if they are to get along together harmoniously they must form either a relationship which shall leave them free to hold their individual opinions or one which shall be built up through an understanding and respect for each other's views— a relationship based on their differences and not on their identity.

As a first step, it is most essential that the partners should talk out, as far as possible, all the ramifications of their association— finance, privacy, the right to see their friends alone, the obligations to unify their personal habits. These and many other matters must be discussed and, at the very least, a tentative agreement must be reached if the marriage is to escape shipwreck. Men and women about to marry often say: "We believe in a free marriage." When asked what they mean by a free marriage, they will put forward some advanced theories such as, "We do not consider ourselves bound to each other by any pledge of fidelity." But you may find that on all other points they are completely conventional in their assumptions, while remaining unaware that they assume anything.

As a rule, the man has one set of assumptions, the woman another, which further complicates matters. Take for instance the matter of finance. They may have agreed that the woman shall continue in her career and their incomes be shared. "But," they may be asked, "what will you do if there are children?" The woman will reply, "Of course, my husband will support me while I am incapacitated, and naturally he will support the child afterwards." But the husband may say, "We have agreed that I am to supply half" — or two-thirds, or whatever the proportion may be — "of the household expenses, and that is all I am prepared to give." When the first child comes, the man will realize that he must support his wife, at least for a time; but now, far from acting on any "liberal" or "modern" theory of sharing alike, he quite likely falls back on an old model and does as his grandfather did before him — supplying his wife with money for housekeeping only. Consequently, she must ask him for every penny she spends for her own necessities. His assumptions of the obligations of marriage are entirely different from hers.

Another couple, when questioned about privacy, assert that *of course* married people share a room, although they may have been accustomed for many years to a room of their own and to being entirely alone for a large part of every twenty-four hours. If they allow themselves to be guided by their assumption of what married people *should* do a sense of suffocation is likely to arise owing to the too great intimacy. When this happens they cannot bring the problem up, or insist on greater separation, for fear of making real the breach which is already undermining their inner sense of union. The ways in which unconscious assumptions undermine the understanding of man and wife could be multiplied indefinitely, the cure in each case can only be found through greater frankness.

Adults generally begin their problem at the point which those who marry young reach only later. They, like the young people, will also have to take up the problem of the projection of anima and animus in some measure, but this comes to them usually as a minor rather than the major problem, which is the relation between them. The fact that the marriage is more likely to be childless than is a youthful marriage emphasizes the necessity of working on their intrinsic relationship. Children are a bond between the parents, but also serve as a "buffer state," keeping them apart. All too often parents avail themselves, perhaps unconsciously, of the presence of children to evade a direct psychological contact with each other which would necessitate their taking a step toward greater consciousness. This is not possible in a childless marriage where the typical problem is to work out a psychological relationship through which each may find himself and his partner as unique and conscious individuals. Thus the task is here to attain consciousness through relationship.

In the marriage between a young woman and a much older man, one of the chief motives influencing the girl is likely to be the desire to gain security. She wants to marry "a man whom she can trust," one already established in the community and of proved ability to provide for her. Generally speaking, in such a marriage affection takes the place of passion. The girl feels assured that not much will be demanded of her sexually. Her husband is almost like a father, the transition is easy, her whole girlhood's adaptation can be transferred intact to the new home. She gives affection and deference to her husband just as she did to her father. The pattern of the relation between father and daughter is carried on. The daughter-wife expects to be petted and humored. The father-husband gives security and expects in return to keep all decisions in his own hands, while having a devoted but irresponsible child about the house. Psychologically this means that the girl has never released herself from the tie to her father, and that the man's anima is as childlike and undeveloped as in his child wife. This type of marriage, though still common, was perhaps the most usual up to the middle of the nineteenth century. It reflected the extreme childishness of women on the individual side and of men on the side of relationship, which the whole organization of society fostered. Dickens — and indeed most of the novelists of his period — described it as the ideal marriage, but it has become less universal as women have developed their own masculine and individual capacities. Now many women can win security for themselves through their own efforts and capabilities and do not need, in the same way, to seek for it in a husband. When a woman has learned to make her own decisions and to bring to pass by her own efforts what is necessary for her comfort and well-being she does not relish the idea of having these things decided for her, nor does she like to be dependent for their gratification on the bounty and good nature of a father-husband. Most significant of all, she is profoundly dissatisfied with the meagerness of a relationship which leaves her in the position of a child.

The typical problem in the father-daughter marriage lies in the necessity to resolve this psychological situation. The wife is caught in a position where her adaptation depends on remaining a child, while her own evolution demands that she become adult. As long as she looks for security outside herself, in her husband, she cannot win her own individual values. Her task is to gain a relation to the masculine principle, or Logos, within herself and so to achieve her own maturity. In this way she will become a separate psychological entity, and the marriage will pass on to a different phase where the problems of psychological relationship can be taken up as between two individuals who are both mature even though there is a considerable difference between their ages.

The polar opposite of this type of marriage, in which an older woman marries a younger man, is by no means uncommon in America today. Women, who, instead of marrying, have chosen a profession and built up a place in society for themselves by their own work, may find that the problem of marriage recurs when they reach thirty-five or forty, but on another plane. The motives for marriage have changed. These women do not need support, for they can secure for themselves a satisfactory income, but they do need companionship and affection. In addition, they frequently become increasingly aware of sexual starvation. Several different ways present themselves for the solution of this problem. When the pressure of sexuality is not too great many a woman solves her emotional problem by a friendship with another woman. Or she jumps, as it were, over the sexual aspect of her difficulty and arrives directly at the maternal. She adopts a child whom she supports and to whom she is both father and mother. If her sexual problem is more urgent and her emotional needs cannot be satisfied by the love of friend or children, she makes a relationship with a man. As a rule, there are no unmarried men of her own age available, for this problem of late marriage is peculiarly the problem of women. She is therefore left with two alternatives: she can have an extramarital relation with a married man (a problem which will be considered later) or she can marry a man who is her junior and generally also less mature psychologically.

One of the factors accounting for an older woman's interest in a man much younger than herself lies in her own emotional immaturity. Such a woman has put all her energies and attention into developing her professional qualities and but little into developing her feminine values. As a rule, she is very unconscious of her own feeling reactions. Except for an all-embracing maternal kindliness she is exceedingly undifferentiated on the emotional side of her nature. This is one reason why she is satisfied with an undeveloped man, and also why she is attracted to him, for the type of relation possible with him reflects her own lack of development in relationship.

As a rule, the man of her choice is not only her junior but also her inferior in adaptation to the world. I have known many instances where a competent and successful business or professional woman has married a man much younger than herself and has then partially or entirely supported him—the traditional role of the man and woman being reversed.

This social phenomenon, common as it is coming to be, is a

very strange one. It almost seems that America is moving toward a matriarchal state of society, in which a strong efficient woman marries a rather undeveloped and feminine man who takes a filial relation to her. The woman is everything—mother, provider, organizer—and the man merely an adjunct, however necessary, to the household.

From the psychological point of view the relationship between such a man and such a woman is not at all satisfactory. The marriage is similar to the old conventional Victorian one, but with the roles reversed, which increases the disadvantages of the arrangement. In the patriarchal marriage of Victorian days, the woman, childish though she was in many ways, yet remained mistress in her own sphere. She cared for the feminine side of the household and fulfilled her particular function of childbearer. But in these modern matriarchal marriages, the man is practically a nonentity. He is supported and yet takes no responsibility for the domestic side of the home. In the past, the woman's biological functions filled her life with interest and work and affection in a way that his cannot. So he becomes entirely dependent on her, but dependence is not relationship. No real psychological relationship is possible between a dominant and a dependent individual.

Unless the man can solve the problem of his masculine adaptation to the world, in his marriage he can be nothing but a son to the dominant mother-wife. Even in the place which has been left to him, he will soon fail to satisfy her emotionally. For when a man is sexually involved with a woman who is psychologically his mother-provider, he is psychologically imprisoned, being held on that infantile level where pleasure and satisfaction represent happiness, and happiness *for him* remains a goal in itself. The sexuality of men is so closely linked with physical needs and satisfactions that a long discipline is always required to gain release on that plane from the dominance of the pleasure principle. In the case we are considering, where the woman to whom the young man goes for his satisfaction stands in the place of a mother, it is hardly to be expected that he will be able to release himself from the compulsion of his need which creates a sort of "cup-board-love." [2]

The woman in such a case is compelled to fill the role of mother, for an older woman naturally fears that she may not be able to hold the allegiance of a younger man, feeling that if she refuses to give him what he wants, he may go off after younger and more desirable women. So she feels under compulsion to give him, or to appear to give him, all he asks. Rarely is a woman brave enough to lay aside all ulterior motives and react as woman to man, directly from her own feeling. Yet only such a genuine reaction can compel him to sacrifice his give-it-to-me-because-I-need-it attitude, and few women caught in such a situation are brave enough or sufficiently disinterested to take such a risk. Even if the mother-wife were sufficiently courageous, she is rarely aware enough of her own feelings to be able to express them. A woman who marries a son-husband is as a rule un-developed in her feminine nature, and is unconscious of her reac-tions, which may well be undeveloped, childish and egotistic. She does not know how she feels but projects her dissatisfactions onto the man and complains of "how much he demands" and "how impossible he is" and "how little he gives in return for all she does for him"—all in the tone of the mother who has failed to bring up her child properly and when his behavior is un-satisfactory lays all the blame on him or on "the Lord" for giving her such unsatisfactory progeny.

So long as her own emotional nature is immature, she will continue to seek her fulfillment by making someone else dependent on her, her own inner childishness being projected onto or re-flected in the man to whom she is attracted. If a marriage of this kind is not to be a complete failure, however, she is compelled to work on the difficulties that arise through his immaturity. In releasing him from his dependence on her, she effects at the same

---

2 An English phrase referring to a love which is focused on the cookies in the cupboard rather than on the person who dispenses them.

time a change in her own childish and dependent emotional nature. She grows inwardly, and that side of her psyche neglected during youth may now reach maturity through her marriage. Thus the typical problem of this form of marriage is met, for her task is to gain a relation to the feminine principle, the principle of Eros, within herself.

Naturally the emotional factors which have been made the basis of this classification of marriage do not appear in isolated form in real life. On the contrary, the problems peculiar to them usually appear in various combinations. For instance, there is hardly a marriage, certainly not a successful one, where the woman does not feel maternal toward her husband at some time or in some fields, nor is there likely to be a marriage of any duration in the course of which the woman does not have occasion to turn to her husband for help or support in some crisis. The marriage of adolescents will, in the long run, encounter the problems of differentiating the individual needs of the man and the woman, while the marriage of adults will not escape those issues arising from psychological identification. Nonetheless, in these typical marriage patterns outstanding and typical problems may be discerned which of course do not necessarily form an absolute contraindication to marriage or, indeed, to successful marriage; but each presents a particular type of problem which if not met may prove fatal to the partnership.

The more developed the man or woman is, however, the less do these external conditions matter. Conventional standards, representing as they do the generalized wisdom of society, are the rules by which a woman must guide her life until she has something better — something more adapted, more individual — with which to replace them. To one who is only collective in his psychological development, the collective error stands as an inevitable pitfall. If a woman has not become a separate individual but is still collective in her attitudes and standards, that is, in her psychological development, she is well advised to keep within conventional bounds in her marriage, for to do that which is a mistake from the collective standpoint is a mistake for her. But another, who has developed within herself those characteristics which enable her to extricate herself from the collective pattern, may overstep the conventionally held restrictions for individual reasons which seem to her sufficient, and may successfully attempt in her marriage what would, for the average conventional person, bring failure.

After the turmoil and excitement of the wedding are over and the bride and groom start off on their honeymoon, the first thing that confronts them is the fact that they are alone. Marriage may be an institution; their particular marriage may be a social event of some importance in their circle; but as far as they themselves are concerned, marriage — *in the living* — reduces itself to a relationship between two human beings. This is an aspect that young people are very apt to overlook in the glamorous days of courtship. They look forward to playtime together such as they have enjoyed during their engagement, and anticipate, perhaps, to an extent dependent on their previous experience, the fulfillment of passion. But the extent of the intimacy involved in marriage is rarely anticipated. During the courtship, the man, for instance, brings into the relation those interests which he feels will please his beloved and which fit in with her wishes and character, leaving other interests in the dark. He does not necessarily feel that he is deceiving her. These other interests do not arise to be lived with her and he perhaps remains unaware that he is withholding them from her knowledge.

The whole situation is changed, however, after the wedding. From now on the entire time of the husband and wife may have to be accounted for to the other, and their thoughts and opinions on each and every subject may be questioned. If one withholds opinions, a practice which may be disconcerting in the extreme to the other, this becomes no longer a matter of expediency unconsciously indulged in but a conscious deception. Thus arises the necessity to choose a course of action which will — little as the young people realize it — largely determine the character of the marriage. The man may decide to keep inconvenient facts to himself and tell his wife only "what it is good for her to know," or he may have the courage and honesty to put all his cards on the table and fight the matter out with her. The wife will also have the same problem to decide. She, also, must either deliberately keep certain things to herself or take what may be a considerable risk and tell him about them. The first of these alternatives leads, needless to say, to a situation foredoomed to become more and more false as the years go on; it is purchasing present peace at the cost of inevitable and increasing estrangement. The second alternative offers at least a prospect of improved understanding and a growing relatedness. It is true that if the love between the young people has little basis of real relatedness, being based on the illusion of an animus-anima projection, the impact of reality may prove too destructive for the love to hold at all. But usually when two people love each other, they are compelled by their love to come back again and again and make repeated efforts to understand the nature of the difficulty between them. Each time this occurs the bond is strengthened and as the years go on they can strike out for truth with more confidence because of the increasing area of really worked-out understanding which nothing can destroy.

In attempting to work out such a mutual understanding certain problems in connection with the instinctual side of their life together will almost inevitably arise. If the sexual relation between husband and wife is to be right and alive, it is necessary that each make an adjustment to the other on both the physical and the psychological planes. The physical adjustment requires much patience and good will on the part of both. As a rule, the woman is far less conscious of this side of her nature than is the man. She, more often than he, comes to her marriage inexperienced. She submits to the man, in many cases, with the sense that this is something which is expected of her and is for his satisfaction rather than hers. I have known of instances where the girl has actually been told by her mother or by some other adviser that women do not enjoy sexuality but that she must submit to her husband's desire in the matter, and if she wishes to hold his love she must pretend to enjoy his embraces and must appear to respond to them. Such advice leads to a falsification of her sexual feelings which is devastating both to the husband and to herself. He may not realize what the trouble is, why he has such a deep sense of dissatisfaction or why his unsatisfied desire returns so quickly. Unless something deeper of her own instinctual nature awakens within her, the wife is likely to go on "submitting" with ever-increasing reluctance and a growing inner resistance to her husband, while he, with a certain dogged attitude based on his idea of "marriage rights," may perhaps persist in his demands, entirely forgetting, if he ever knew, that this legal term was originally spelled "rites" and has in its primary significance nothing to do with "rights." But he also forgets that it is not in the nature of things for him to continue for long to enjoy what gives his wife no pleasure.

Or, perhaps, in a case where at the beginning of marriage the woman appears frigid, the couple may take her indifference too seriously and consider it as a permanent defect, while in reality it comes from her inexperience which a few months of patience will cure. If from their first unsatisfactory experience they both jump to the conclusion that she is temperamentally frigid, their expectation of failure may prevent the success of future attempts. For love after all is an art which can only be acquired through long experience; those who practice it sincerely will increase in the range and the depth of their expression, much as an artist's capacity for expression grows. But the art of love cannot be practiced successfully if it is viewed only as a technique—the expression of love must be a genuine expression of an emotion which is actually felt. The man is usually more aware of his physical emotion and quicker in his responses than the woman, so that he may get his physical satisfaction before she is fully aroused, but if he learns through love of her to control his own reactions, he can give her also fuller satisfaction. If the physical side of their love is to grow unhindered, they must talk to each other about it. For only by so doing can they learn about love and about themselves through comparing their experiences and reactions. But this is a very difficult thing to do because love gestures and reactions are so personal and so instinctive that both men and women are exceedingly sensitive on the subject. By attempting to talk about these intimate matters, they are brought face to face with the conventional prejudice within themselves. They may be willing *to do* unconventional things provided they are not compelled to recognize or to acknowledge them. This very common characteristic is especially true in matters of love. Many are hampered in their love-making by a prejudice that they hardly know exists. Those who are more conscious may look with critical eyes at what they are doing; then the fear of overstepping the bounds of "normal" sexuality may cast a shadow over the freedom of their love-making. Or they may have an *opinion* that love should be made in such and such a way and that all other gestures or actions are wrong. A woman once said to me, "A kiss on the face from husband to wife is all right, but a kiss below the neck is unthinkable." If love is not to be restricted by all sorts of unspoken prohibitions there must be a willingness on the part of both husband and wife to experiment, and a realization that anything which is a real expression of love may be acceptable between two people. There is, however, another and more subtle conventionality which may suck the life out of a love relationship. This is the attitude which makes a convention or a precedent even out of one's own experience, as though each experience of love had to follow the pattern laid down on a previous occasion. Love-making is the expression of a living feeling; it cannot be bound but must be left free so that the living spirit can find for itself the expression which will alone reveal to the man and the woman the nature of their love.

The experience of sexuality is not the same for the man as it is for the woman, either physically or psychologically. The physical differences between them are obvious; the psychological differences are just as great and require a no less delicate adjustment. But these differences are far more subtle. Many people seem completely unaware of them, merely experiencing the irritation and estrangement consequent on their neglect.

Sexual union to the man is the concrete symbol of relationship; it represents the spiritual union of love. To him sexuality presents itself as the obvious means of attaining a real union with his beloved, and also as the one way in which he may hope to subdue that vagrant and illusive spirit which he glimpses in the woman because she carries the values of his anima. The man is convinced that if a misunderstanding, a difference of opinion, or an intrusion of undisciplined ego demands or selfish attitudes have broken the rapport between himself and his loved one, it will be restored if only he can come to her sexually. He argues that the feeling between them after intercourse has so often been deepened and strengthened in a way that to him seems little short of miraculous. "When the feeling between us is broken or strained," he says, "intercourse will put it right."

But the woman, whether she knows it with her head or not, knows deep down within her woman's nature that to have intercourse when the feeling between them is not right violates her, and in consenting to it she consents to an assault upon herself. For her it is absolutely essential that the feeling difficulty be cleared up first, that the domination and selfishness be laid aside. She may be willing to leave the practical points of the dispute unsettled till later, if good feeling and a sense of understanding and acceptance of each other is reestablished, for then she can without violation of her own nature receive her husband's physical love and respond to it.

These matters cannot, of course, be adjusted in a few weeks or months, they require years of close intimacy and painstaking work. Through working on such problems the man and woman may gradually become more conscious of their own natures and in this way build up a solid structure of relatedness each to the other. But a very disturbing factor which will interrupt this growth and development, although it brings also its own peculiar values to the relationship, is likely before long to make its appearance. The woman becomes pregnant. To her this is a deeply significant experience for it affects her in every phase of her being. A new instinct, the instinct of maternity, possesses her.

The reproductive instinct in woman is only partly sexual; another part, for some women perhaps the major part, is maternal, while only a relatively small part of a man's reproductive instinct is paternal. Thus when a husband learns that his wife is pregnant, he realizes that it is a fact of great importance to him, but it is a fact outside himself, the significance of which he senses chiefly through its effect on her. At this stage, while the woman is going through an experience which affects her vitally in her own person, he participates only in imagination and through sympathy. During this period and the subsequent ones of the child's infancy, when her instinct is directed almost entirely into the maternal stream, his instinct continues to be primarily sexual in its needs and manifestations. Her absorption in the maternal process leaves him with unsatisfied or "loose" libido, for she is not available to him emotionally in the same way as she was before. The difficulty in adjustment which results is accentuated by the fact that the paternal instinct in most men is hardly aroused at all before the birth of the child, while the maternal instinct takes possession of most women from the very beginning of pregnancy.

This difference in the instinct of husband and wife frequently gives rise to serious problems between them, especially in those cases where the sexual interest of the woman is far overbalanced by the maternal. In such cases not only is she occupied during pregnancy with those mysterious changes which are going on within her, but after the birth of the child she is likely to put its interests always before her husband's and to allow her maternal solicitude for her baby to deprive him of her time and attention.

Sometimes a woman whose sexuality has remained childish and undeveloped, who therefore finds little pleasure or satisfaction in her sexual relation to her husband, takes refuge in maternity, almost, it seems, with unconscious deliberation, with the perhaps unrecognized intention of preventing her husband from making any further sexual demands upon her. Is it any wonder if the husband, whose instinct is not occupied with children, begins to look for consolation elsewhere? The wife, however, does not realize what part her neglect of him has played in the situation. She ignores her own fault and blames him for his defection. Instead of taking the first sign that he is becoming interested in other women as a danger signal, indicating that she is letting the value of her marriage slip through her fingers, she tries to hold him by all sorts of tricks or by appeals to his loyalty. This reaction is perfectly instinctive — a self-protective mechanism — but it is more than that, for society has decreed that it is a woman's business to "hold her husband." Thus another conventional *of course* enters into the picture. It is at this point, indeed, that many women become both demanding and possessive. A woman will seek, for instance, to prevent her husband from going anywhere alone. If she must stay at home in the evening to care for the babies, he must stay at home too; if he but speaks to another woman, she becomes jealous and fault-finding. She will do all in her power to hold him — except the one thing which might be efficacious: to revive the reality of their relationship which is fast suffocating under the dust of habit.

The following incident illustrates what may happen when the woman is courageous enough to put reality in the place of artifice. Boredom between a certain man and his wife had become so unendurable that they felt divorce was the only possible cure for the impasse they faced. It was suggested that, as a last expedient, they try the effect of expressing their real reactions. This involved breaking the habit of years, for they had consistently repressed their feelings, "taking it out," as the saying is, in an inner bitterness against each other. The plan worked like a charm. On the very first occasion when the woman brought out her negative reaction to some unconsciously selfish act on the part of her husband, he sat up and looked at her with a new attention, saying, "Why, you're interesting when you talk like that!" His words threw fresh light for her on the whole situation. She realized in a flash how mistaken the old way had been, how mistaken the fear that she would lose his affection if she would express her real feelings.

It is by no means uncommon to find that the woman has built up a conscious system or technique for holding the man's interest and love, and we cannot altogether blame her for this, however insincere her method. For in the event of the failure of her marriage, she bears most of the blame. In England, this is true to a far greater extent than in America, where divorce is so common. But even in America society is still swayed by something of the old *feeling,* although many people no longer hold strictly to the old *opinions.* Consequently, married women tend to be too much oriented to their husband's interest and reactions. One woman, for instance, is concerned almost exclusively with the effect her actions and words will have on her husband, with the result that she consciously tries to "manage" him. Another, in revolt against this exclusive concern, puts all her ardor into rebellion. But whichever form her concern takes, it results in a too complete absorption in the man and his reactions. As a consequence, too much of the woman's attention is withdrawn from her own task of finding herself, or discovering the inner center of her own being and her own path in life.

This diversion of the wife's attention is almost inevitable, for from the point of view of society, she *must* make a success of her marriage. Conventionally, she must always appear to be on good terms with her husband regardless of any private difficulties and must always be available to their social circle. In addition to the personal and instinctual concerns, her relationship to her husband has to carry all the social and comradely interests. For marriage is not only an institution, not only an intimate personal relationship; it is also quite literally a social function. The family is the unit of society; its days are filled with duties and amusements *on the everyday plane*—these are the staples of life. To make a success of marriage in this sense demands from each a certain easygoing tolerance, and a certain amount of affection and understanding. But this type of "successful marriage" never touches the deeper levels of the psyche, where dwell the dark, the unknown, the passionate instincts and emotions. Indeed, the very necessity of maintaining an easy workaday comradeship demands that the dark and unknown and violent forces in the depths be kept well in check. It is therefore unusual for the polarization between husband and wife to become very great. For many people—and they are doubtless of the most normal and perhaps the happiest type—such an experience of life and love suffices; in the affection and companionship of the home situation they find all that they need. But there are others who are impelled by something intense in their own natures to seek for greater heights and depths of emotional experience. I have spoken above of how the woman's absorption in her children may leave her husband unsatisfied. In such a case certain men may be driven by their own intensity and by an inner need to experience themselves more deeply to seek with some other woman what they have failed to find in their marriages.

A situation of this kind raises a very difficult emotional problem for the wife. She feels, not unnaturally, that her whole position is jeopardized. She believes that if her husband is interested in another woman he can no longer love her. If the other woman is of an obviously inferior type, one with whom the wife realizes he can have only a very limited affair, she is likely to be less alarmed than she would be if a woman of a superior type had attracted him. In the former case the wife feels the affair to be disgusting enough and humiliating for her, quite apart from the very real and deep suffering she endures, but if it does not obtrude itself on her attention, that is, if she does not have to recognize it, she can let it take its course in the hope that, ignored, it will soon pass over. But in the latter case, if the husband is attracted to a woman of character—his equal in culture and in moral development—then the wife is likely to be much more alarmed. She fears, and rightly, that a relationship with such a woman may be more enduring than an affair with one of light morals and no culture; yet the marriage is in certain ways more endangered by the man's involvement in light affairs than by an extramarital relationship which is more seriously undertaken. For the man's development along Eros lines—that is, on the side of his nature through which he is related to women—depends on the *character* of his relationships; the things he learns outside of marriage will inevitably react on his attitude to his wife. If he has an inferior type of relationship with an inferior type of woman, he will assuredly expect to manage his affairs with his wife after the pattern learned from his mistress. If his mistress is a woman who can be picked up and put down at will, one with whom he never has to work out any difficulty, one whose hurts are cured by gifts, one with whom he never has to measure up to any standard of responsibility, and one toward whom he can act always according to his own pleasure and convenience, then the lessons learned with this "light-of-love" will be practiced in his associations with his wife. For as the *I Ching* says in speaking of the "bold maiden" who comes to meet the man: "The inferior thing seems so harmless and inviting that a man delights in it; it looks so small and weak that he imagines he may dally with it and come to no harm." [3] But no man has much experience with such women without learning to his cost that they exact a heavy price for their favors, and in a quarter perhaps where it is most unexpected; he finds that they are, invariably, at least as self-seeking as he and that their resources for getting what they want are inexhaustible. These lessons, too, he will take home with him. He will expect his wife to act when crossed as his mistress acts and he will arm himself in advance against the demands he fully expects her to make. She will naturally enough be incensed at the low opinion he holds of her. But she

---

3 *I Ching*, p. 171

would hardly be human if she did not sooner or later justify him in it and come to say, "Well if he thinks that sort of thing of me, I will just show him what it is like."

Occasionally it happens, however, that a man has an extramarital affair with a woman of different type, one who is his equal in culture, morals and social standing. In this case perhaps the new relationship relieves the home situation of a good deal of tension. In certain instances the man's extramarital relation seems to be the counterpart of the wife's absorption in her children. She, through her maternal experience, may learn much that is of value in her relation to her husband, and he, through his love for another woman, may likewise learn much that is of value in his relation to his wife. For in his relation to a woman to whom he is not married, he is obliged to submit to the laws of feeling relationship; he has no contract with her, he has to make good all along the line—not in his own judgment but from the woman's point of view—or he finds himself dismissed. If her feelings are not of the kind to be soothed by a gift, he is compelled to meet her on her own ground and to accept a measure of responsibility for psychological relationship—a responsibility which his wife may have been quite unable to elicit from him.

The absence of the social obligations of marriage and the absence of the bond which children make between husband and wife serve to concentrate the attention of lover and mistress on the varying shades of their feeling for each other in every situation as it arises. The lover and mistress are entirely separate entities; they are not identified. A certain collective obligation, however, always exists between husband and wife which prevents a similar concentration of attention and indeed fosters unconsciousness of the actual feeling situation between them. They form a unit and must always present a united front to society. They move in the same social circle. No matter how serious the problem just arisen between them, they must appear among their friends as a harmonious pair. Their home must have a certain unification of aim. Their children necessitate a further simplification and unification of their relation to each other. The routine of their lives leaves little opportunity for attending with sufficient concentration to the emotional side of their relationship. The intensity of love or the urgency of disagreement each requires time if it is to be assimilated. Many married people find it easier to repress both under the mask which they habitually wear before the family. Thus a certain unreality creeps in and their association tends toward an easygoing unconsciousness. This kind of relationship has, however, many rules; it makes up everyday life, so to speak, while a relationship outside of marriage is rather in the nature of a school where much can be learned which may subsequently be applied to marriage.

In these days of easy marriage and easy divorce, there is a great tendency to take the whole subject of matrimony very lightly. The modern attitude is: since divorce is so easy, why should marriage be taken seriously? A woman in her early thirties who had made a terrible mistake in her marriage once actually said to me: "Well, why *should* one take marriage so seriously?" This is an attitude almost inconceivable to one who realizes the significance of marriage. Its very essence implies permanence. The man and woman who marry declare their intention to take this one relationship out of all other possible relationships, in order to work on it and make it permanent—lifelong. It is the most far-reaching of relationships. If a woman marries without taking its obligations seriously, it follows that she does not take any relationship seriously. Only through relationship, however, can her psychological boundaries be defined: only thus can she find herself. If she does not take her marriage seriously, she does not take herself seriously at all. Such an attitude is the beginning of the disintegration of society.

It may, however, be urged that no one can undertake to promise that his affections will persist unimpaired for a lifetime, that it is impossible to pledge the permanence of one's feelings through even one year. This is true and it is also true that to modern consciousness it is more moral to break a contract, one of whose most essential features, love, can no longer be fulfilled, rather than to go on indefinitely substituting duty for love. But the fact remains that if a woman marries without the heartfelt intention of permanence, if she allows a certain mental reservation to creep in—"If it is not satisfactory there is always divorce!"—she is not likely to make a success of her marriage. No determined adventurer about to embark upon a hazardous enterprise holds any commerce with a voice which whispers, "If all does not go well, I can always turn back." Mental reservations like this do not lead to success.

So, if a woman undertakes the adventure of marriage with a backdoor of escape—easy divorce—left open, the adventure is all but doomed at the outset. The difficulties and dangers of any close relationship demand the mobilization of all our forces. It is a well-known psychological fact that if the attitude be secretly taken that "we can always turn back," it is impossible to mobilize all of our forces. Only after a woman has made every effort to solve her difficulties, has left not a stone unturned, and still her marriage has failed, only then should she turn, perhaps, to divorce. Judging from my own knowledge of many marriages, I believe that many divorces have really been unnecessary, that they have *solved* no psychological problem of the marriage.

If, however, a woman must seek this way of escape from an intolerable marriage, she ought to bring to it the same seriousness of purpose and the same close consideration of all the factors concerned which should have been given originally to the question of marriage. There are many things a wife would do well to take into account before she turns to divorce as the remedy for her troubles, for the clock cannot be put back. Even if she has no children—and unquestionably if she has—she must carry with her throughout life the imprint of this relationship. If her marriage is cut short, leaving unsolved problems in which her libido is still bound up, she will continue to bear the burden of an unfinished relationship which will crop up to be dealt with at every point in her life whenever she comes close to a man. It will become a kind of ghost which she can exorcise only through working out that problem which her release from her first husband left unsolved.

Marriage *must* be taken seriously. It is as though to become wife to any man means, in a certain psychological sense, to become his other half. It means to take upon one's self something of responsibility for his anima. The attraction leading to marriage is an indication that the man has projected his anima to this particular woman, while some quality or complex of qualities in her really reflects this aspect of his psyche. The woman, therefore, in working on her relation to her husband, is also working on that part of herself which reflected his anima. If she cannot make a satisfactory adjustment with him, she must seriously ask herself whether it may not be that at least part of the fault lies in her where there lurks, perhaps, something which really resembles those qualities she so much resents in him. Certainly it is not until she has dealt with her own possessiveness, her own selfishness, her own unconsciousness, that she is able to help him with his problem. For his faults toward her lie in that realm of his psyche furthest from his conscious concerns, namely on the side of Eros or psychological relationship, which should be mediated by feeling; if the woman does not help him here, it is well-nigh impossible for him to become conscious.

If, then, a woman runs away from one marriage because of the man's lack of Eros development, she is likely in a second marriage to find herself involved with a man who is no more satisfactory. In other words, not until the woman has done everything possible toward making herself conscious in the relationship to her husband and has left no stone unturned to work out something of reality between them, unblurred by assumptions, illusions and projections, is she justified in violently breaking her association with him. For the relation between husband and wife is a unique relation. It carries with it the possibility of development on more planes than any other which life offers. Once undertaken, if its values are to be garnered, it must be carried through to the furthest possible limit, even though compromises may be necessary and cherished illusions and assumptions must be discarded. For the woman who can do this there is a great reward, both in terms of her own personal development and growth and in terms of an established relationship which none of the hazards of life can overthrow.

6. Maternity

The relation of mother and child is so simple that every peasant woman takes it for granted; so full of emotional content that artists, poets and storytellers have been lured by it in every age; so complicated that psychologists are kept busy tracing out its subtle currents and enduring effects. The exploration of the fundamental relation of a child to his mother has led to a widespread consciousness of the factors which go into the building up of an adult's character and which influence his motives and actions, sometimes consciously, but far more often in a way and to a degree of which he is profoundly unconscious. The conclusions first drawn by psychologists, who based their theories on observations of the unconscious, have now become facts of such common knowledge that modern plays and novels not only take them into account but often base the entire plot on problems arising out of the relation existing between a mother and her child. I say "modern plays." I might have saved myself the use of the adjective, for not a few classical plays deal likewise with the same fundamental subject. To give typical examples of plots concerned chiefly with this relation, I have but to mention, among classical stories, *Oedipus Rex, Elektra, Hamlet* and *Ruth,* and among modern plays and novels, *The Silver Cord, Sons and Lovers* and *Mourning Becomes Electra.* But—and here is a strange phenomenon—these examples reflect for the most part the situation from the point of view of the child. It is not easy to find a novel or

157

play which treats the relation from the point of view of the mother. And—a stranger phenomenon still—our textbooks of psychology are concerned chiefly with the complexes and conflicts in the child and deal with these to the almost complete exclusion of the mother's side of the problem. Women are not unaware today that this discussion is so largely a one-sided affair and they are puzzled by it. "It is hard to be a mother these days," a woman once said to me. "If you are a 'bad' mother your child naturally reproaches you and lays all the blame for his difficulties on your inexpert treatment of him. But if you are a 'good' mother you will still not escape blame and reproach. For now it is said that by your very kindness and skillful handling you have bound him to you in an inescapable fixation."

This is indeed the Scylla and Charybdis of the mother's problem, for if she is "all mother," devoting herself to her children's needs when they are young and identifying herself with their interests as they grow older, she will find that they remain bound to her and to their own childishness. She has been a "good mother" and the result has proved to be "bad." Or if she is a "bad mother" giving the children not special consideration but continuing her own life with as little interruption as possible, she may still find that they cling to her apron strings, or perhaps "fling off" in an infantile search for freedom of a kind which does not exist. It almost seems that there is no way of avoiding these conflicting difficulties. The role of mother appears to be doomed in advance. Those who apotheosize the "mother" as well as those who revile her predict for her task nothing but failure.

The question arises then: How can a woman deal with this dilemma? Is the peculiar relation between a mother and her child to be considered only a liability? Is there not some way by which the dangers and difficulties of this fundamental relation of child to mother can be adequately met? Since we are dealing here with the problems of women, the subject will naturally be approached from the mother's point of view. After all, this is the primary aspect, for the relation of the mother to her child begins long before consciousness dawns for the infant, and the main lines of the relationship are already firmly established before the child himself has much power to influence them. The woman's relation to her offspring and to herself *as mother* are the predetermining factors whose influence on subsequent events cannot be over-estimated.

In considering the mother's problem, however, we must not for one instant lose sight of the child's own personal standpoint, for any real solution *must* take into full account both child and mother. The relationship between them is so deep and so funda-mental that we should surely begin on an *a priori* belief that their interests cannot be inherently opposed, and this in spite of the fact that if we listen to certain psychologists and novelists we might well conclude that the interests of mother and child *are* fundamentally opposed—many people seem to think that it is necessarily a case of the mother exploiting the child or of the child flouting and overcoming the mother. But surely these are not the only alternatives. Each generation, it is true, must be superseded by the next; but in this historic fulfillment are we to conceive of life as casting aside and trampling on each generation as it passes—much as certain primitives erect a "suicide pole" for the aged or bury them alive when they are no longer of use to the tribe? We are too much individualists today to give our allegiance to such a non-individualistic creed. The solution of all the problems with which this book deals points away from the kind of psychological interdependence which makes the freedom of one a necessary sacrifice to the happiness of another, and is directed instead toward a value which is above personal satisfac-tions and egotistic ambitions. In the recognition that the true fulfillment of each individual is not to be found through the satisfaction of his personal desires alone, but also through an allegiance to the aims of another part of his psyche which is in harmony with the movement of life through the generations, lies a possible solution of the problem. If the divergent aims of mother and child are to be met in such a way as to satisfy the essential individuality of both, each must recognize this suprapersonal law which transcends personal impulses and wishes and which yet does not override or disregard the right of each to psychological development and fulfillment in this life.

The experience of motherhood begins with pregnancy. When a woman first realizes that she is carrying new life within her womb, her joy and sense of fulfillment may be mingled with wonder, but the pregnancy itself seems quite natural to her. When the man learns of the situation, however, it seems to him an almost unbelievable miracle—a fabulous thing which he cannot grasp. But to the *woman* pregnancy and giving birth to children is an integral part of her nature. If she is at all in touch with the "earth woman" within herself, she takes it, after the first amazement that this thing should have come to *her,* very much as a matter of course. It is as though something within her said, "This is the way it is to be a woman."

Women vary greatly, however, in their way of reacting to pregnancy. For the primitive or naive woman the whole process may be completed almost entirely on an instinctive level. Such women want babies and feel at their best, both physically and psychologically, when carrying a child. They are *physically* maternal, and their love goes out quite simply and naturally to their children.

Until recently it has been assumed with a kind of blind sentimentality that this is the one normal type of woman; that *of course* any true woman must rejoice at the prospect of becoming a mother. Certain feelings are expected of her and she herself may feel guilty at their absence. Yet the actual experience of maternity is not always so easy and free from conflict as this expectation would suggest. For civilization brings with it a development of the individual ego with its sense of *personal* importance. A woman who is aware of her own ego will not react to pregnancy in a purely instinctive fashion. The recognition of the fact may come as a shock, or as an unexpected experience which has to be met by a conscious attitude. It may be that her emotional response is one of joy and acceptance; or, again, she may regard it, as a terrible nuisance, interfering with her life's pattern and plans in a way she had not counted on.

Her objections may rest on purely selfish grounds. She wants to be able to enjoy herself, she resents losing her figure and youthful energy, she may anticipate with terror the suffering entailed, and she may look forward to the time of caring for the baby, with its disturbed nights and fully occupied days, with resistance and distaste. Emotionally such a young woman is still a child; her whole orientation to life is in pleasure-seeking. Such a woman will find within herself neither strength nor courage to meet the ordeal of maternity, for it has to be met *alone!*

Another woman may wish to avoid pregnancy for more serious reasons. She may have a less selfish outlook and yet dislike intensely the interruption in her life which motherhood involves. The whole scheme of life of not a few modern young people is seriously interfered with by the woman's pregnancy. For instance where the couple married counting on the woman's earning to make their joint income sufficient for their needs, the realization that the wife is pregnant brings urgent and severe problems. For the husband the matter of income may be serious enough. But for him it is, after all, a problem belonging to the outer world — one chiefly in ways and means. For the woman, however, it is a living crisis within her which causes a violent conflict or split in her own nature. It may seem as though her body had turned traitor to her. She does not want pregnancy for reasons which seem to her most important; but deep within her something rejoices that once again a human being is about to fulfill the ancient commandment, "Be fruitful and multiply."

Occasionally the woman's resistance to pregnancy turns into resentment against her husband. She may feel as if he had betrayed her, had forced this experience upon her against her will. I remember one woman who harbored for years, from the date of her first pregnancy, the most intense resistance against her husband, feeling that her sufferings were his fault. Consequently she resented his approaching her and became almost entirely frigid toward him. Fortunately, however, the majority of women are able to accept the problem of maternity as a part of their own nature and so avoid this impasse.

When a woman resents her pregnancy she is very apt to suffer from various disorders—as vomiting or a threatened miscarriage—which are, at least in part, the result of her psychological attitude. If she can be made aware of the nature of her resistances and can recognize that her pregnancy is the fulfillment of her own fate, belonging to *her* and not forced upon her, the symptoms usually clear up and do not return.

The woman who has a developed ego sense does not necessarily resent pregnancy. In the majority of cases she treats it as *of course,* "all in the day's work." At first she is concerned chiefly in concealing the fact from observation; later she becomes involved in the preparations it entails and in anticipations of the baby and in loving plans for its future. A women who is in this way preoccupied with the external aspect of her experience may yet remain completely unconscious of the *significance* of the event which is taking place within her. I have known women, mothers of several children, who have never become aware in any profound sense of what was taking place, who never realized in the least degree that an act of creation was being performed through them. Something more is needed beyond fulfilling the biological instinct and adapting to the needs of the child, if a woman is to experience *in herself* the significance of maternity, if she is to be conscious of herself as woman and as mother.

In the past, as was said above, it was assumed that *of course* every woman wanted a child, but today young married couples often frankly admit that they do not want or cannot afford babies. If conception takes place in spite of their intention to avoid pregnancy, they may take matters into their own hands and interfere with its continuance. This course of action is undertaken quite lightly in many instances, as though it were of little consequence. The voice of Nature and any understanding of the significance of the act are alike blotted out by the rational and materialistic attitude which they take toward life.

Abortion and infanticide, so abhorrent to the Christian standpoint, have not always been condemned. They are freely practiced among primitive tribes and were by no means uncommon in ancient civilizations, as, for instance, in China. Abortion was extremely common also in Europe up to the Middle Ages and the present world trend is toward legalization under prescribed circumstances. But there remains a deep-seated sense that such an action is wrong. This sense of the wrongness of abortion is generally explained in terms of the taking of life—as a sort of murder. When an embryo sufficiently developed to be viable is destroyed, the act approximates infanticide and the majority of people so regard it, although opinions vary greatly about the destruction of a less developed embryo. Yet any fertilized ovum is a potential new life and a strictly logical attitude would draw no distinction between the youngest embryo and a fully formed child. Some people even carry the desire for protecting life to the extreme point of condemning the use of contraceptives on the ground that, if it is evil to destroy an ovum after fertilization, it must also be wrong to prevent its meeting with the sperm cell.

The common sense attitude of today rejects these arguments against contraception as absurd on the ground that there is an acknowledged necessity to bring into the world only those children who can be adequately cared for and equipped for modern life and its hazards. Thus the attempt to solve the problem from the angle of conventional morality inevitably leads to a *reductio ad absurdum*. Is there to be found in a study of the psychological reaction of individuals to contraceptives, on the one hand, and to abortion, on the other, a deeper, more fundamental, more individual morality which can be taken as a guide to action in this most difficult realm of life?

Modern people usually hold that pregnancy should be voluntary, a task undertaken consciously at the most favorable time, an attitude which certainly seems to have common sense as its basis.

But this plan does not always work out, for unintentional conception occasionally occurs. If this possibility has not been taken into account, the young couple may find themselves in a serious dilemma. Under such circumstances they sometimes argue that it is far better not to allow the pregnancy to go on as they cannot afford the present expense, much less provide adequately for a child. To terminate it seems to be the easy way out of their difficulty, a superficial view which is nevertheless often taken. That this course of action involves a certain amount of pain and risk and a good deal of expense they recognize. They are less likely to consider seriously that it is an offense punishable by law; its psychological effects are the last they take into account. For they seem to think that when the pregnancy is terminated all will be as before. They do not realize that the clock cannot be put back, that a situation which has come into being can never be recalled.

An instance, one of many which have come to my attention, will serve to illustrate this point. A woman in the middle thirties came to consult me because she felt herself to be at the breaking point. She did not know why. In reviewing her history she told me that at the age of sixteen she had "got into trouble" with a man whom she met casually while traveling. She had concealed her condition from her parents for some time and when they discovered it, they were overwhelmed. The man was quite unknown to them and the girl knew nothing of his whereabouts at the time. Realizing that the family's good name would be disgraced by the appearance of an illegitimate child, fearing that their daughter's life would be ruined, and feeling, too, the terrible responsibility of bringing an unwanted child into the world, the parents took nothing more into account, but went with their daughter to a distant city and had the pregnancy terminated. This happened some ten or fifteen years before this woman consulted me and she was not aware that her present difficulties were in any way connected with this, as she would say, "little trouble" of so many years back, which had nonetheless done violence to her inmost nature and had alienated her from her own deepest womanhood.

She had been caught in an almost insoluble dilemma. She followed the advice of her parents who judged it better to do as they did rather than to permit an innocent child, whose very existence would embarrass and compromise the mother, to be brought into the world. She took the easiest and quickest way out of the difficulty and tried only too successfully, to blind herself to the real significance of her action. She did not realize that she was interfering with a process which goes far deeper than the conscious wish. As a modern woman she could not bear young, unthinking, like an animal. She was not able to support a child and felt it would not be fair to involve one in her own difficulties. But here her consciousness of the situation ended. She was not aware that something deep within her had stirred — that the maternal instinct had begun to take possession of her. This, however, was exactly the case. When she began to search for the cause of her subsequent breakdown she found just below consciousness an accumulation of repressed and unrealized emotion bound up with her dead baby. At the time she had passed over the whole experience with a sigh of relief that she had freed herself from the fate which threatened to overwhelm her. But ten years later she was compelled to weep for the infant who, in her necessity, she had repudiated without a tear.

There is no royal road out! In a case such as this, where a young girl becomes involved in a situation whose significance she does not realize and where, no matter what she does, wrong is involved, to let nature take its course and bear the child does not solve the problem. On the one hand, such a child should never have been conceived and it cannot be right to compel an innocent child to bear the burden of its mother's fault. On the other hand, to terminate the pregnancy is an act directly in opposition not only to the law of the land but also to a law of nature. To act in haste does not put matters right, nor make the situation as though the pregnancy had never been. A girl who has been through such an ordeal is inevitably cut off psychologically from friends of her own age, and to pretend that she is the same as she was before it happened is the merest hypocrisy. If an experience of this character is repressed, unrealized, it acts as a center of irritation in the unconscious which may later threaten the girl's whole adaptation to life.

How such a situation should be met is naturally a very difficult question. This girl found herself trapped. The course she took seemed to be forced upon her by fate. Her premature plunge into the realities of life had precipitated a problem too big for her to handle. By taking the road her parents suggested, she evaded the moral conflict involved in her predicament and so remained unconscious. If instead of searching wildly for a way out she had made an attempt to grapple deliberately with the evil in the situation, she might, through facing the conflict, have come to a greater degree of consciousness. Through this, instead of being pushed by fate into something whose significance she did not realize, she would have been able to make a voluntary decision as to her course of action.

When the choice is made with full consciousness of what it involves the outcome will not be *all* evil. For it is through just such moral conflicts courageously borne that psychological growth is brought about. This problem forms the theme of Hawthorne's *Scarlet Letter* and Lynne Reid Banks' *The L Shaped Room.* In each case the heroine bore an illigitimate child and, through accepting the burden and responsibility entailed, developed and matured in a way which would hardly have been possible if her life had followed a more usual course. The same result may be achieved by a woman who decides to take the other road, if she chooses it not to escape from the consequences of her own folly but rather with a conscious determination to bear the whole burden herself and not involve a child in her dilemma. If this is her motive she will not incur irrevocable moral or psychological injury but, instead, may gain development of character through the suffering she consciously assumes.

This incident of a successfully terminated pregnancy furnishes a most striking example of the importance of the inner aspect of the experience. Inasmuch as there were no external results, it might be supposed that nothing of importance could be happening within. Yet even where the external situation has been passed over merely as a disagreeable necessity, much like an illness, its inner effects do not so pass. Any other minor operation is an experience which can be accepted at its face value, and after the pain, anxiety and convalescence are over it falls into the background, leaving no long train of inner consequences. But an interference with pregnancy does not act in this way, for pregnancy involves more than physical changes. The bearing of children is a biological task. The roots of the maternal instinct reach back into the deepest layers of a woman's nature, touching forces of which she may be profoundly unconscious. When a woman becomes pregnant these ancient powers stir within her, whether she knows it or not, and she disregards them only at her peril.

The stirring of the maternal instinct is clearly shown in the following story. It is the more remarkable because the woman herself had no idea that she was pregnant and indeed since her marriage had taken every precaution to prevent pregnancy as she wished to continue in her profession. One night, however, she dreamed a most significant dream, which was repeated three times, indicating its great importance. The dream is quoted here in her own words.

"There was a delightful big mother elephant. She seemed so big and warm by contrast, because she was leading a tiny youthful figure, a girl, who was trying her best to follow and keep up with her. Occasionally because of fatigue or things of interest along the road she would stop. Then the big friendly elephant would stop, just long enough to turn her head around and smile (the way elephants can only do in dreams) and motion not to be discouraged, to come on, and not give up. Then again the figure would hop up and follow gaily after. It was a pleasant trip the two journeyed together. The elephant so wise, the figure so young

and happy. When the figure started again on the road after hesitating, I awoke, finding myself cold and shivering and to my great surprise I was out of bed walking across the room as though I were myself that little figure who was being called to follow the elephant across the continent. This happened twice. The third time I dreamed it they reached their journey's end. *The two arrived at the Golden Gate of California and then the elephant sat on a tiny island directly in front of the setting sun. The little figure just watched, waiting, directly in front of her. The sun sank rapidly.* This was the end of my dream. Through my work with the analyst we dug out all the associations that elephants have for me, in particular their religious significance in India. Then the question arose: What did they mean to me? What was this quest or journey on which the mother elephant would take me? What was my attitude going to be?''

The little figure in the dream was undoubtedly a part of the dreamer. This "part" had to follow the elephant and take up the burden of the journey. She could do so only after much hesitation and, indeed, she needed a good deal of encouragement. So urgent was this call from the unconscious depths of her being that she actually got out of bed in her sleep to follow (the dreamer is not usually a sleepwalker). Not until she had been asked, "What is this quest to which the elephant is calling you?" did the dreamer begin to suspect that she might be pregnant, which indeed proved to be the case. Then the meaning of the dream at once began to be clear. The great mother elephant had come to lead her to the experience of maternity. She must lay down the professional work she had proposed for herself, follow the mother elephant to the edge of the continent and, through the experience of pain and danger which awaited her, descend with the sun and with the sun arise again in the East to a new phase of life.

This exceedingly significant dream had a profound effect on the dreamer. Up to the time she dreamed it she had been a child playing at life (her attitude is shown in the little figure who stops to see everything of interest on the road) but pregnancy is already upon her, all unknown to herself. Life is calling to her to undertake a responsible task, perhaps the most responsible anyone can undertake — to bring another living being into the world. The Mother from deep within her calls to her to cease being a child and to take up her task.

As soon as a woman reaches a stage of consciousness which permits her to realize the experience of maternity as a task, something which transcends personal likes and dislikes enters the picture and the woman is thereby freed to realize herself consciously through her function of mother.

It may be well to pause for a moment to ask what the significance of maternity is when viewed as a *task*. On the biological plane the reproduction of the species is a function common to all living things. Together with the task of obtaining food and shelter, it uses practically the entire energy of all species below the human level, and for a large part of the human race these two occupations absorb most of the individual's available energy. With the increase in control of the physical world, however, the task of reproduction has become less and less formidable. In order to keep the population adequately supplied with recruits, not so many women need to have children and no woman needs to have many children.

The social significance of childbearing has thus been considerably restricted. Nevertheless, to the woman herself the bearing of a child has, apart from the fulfillment of her biological instincts, other no less important significances. The child is, in a sense, a completion both of herself and of her husband. Immortality of a certain kind is attained in the child. He perpetuates, as it were, the life of his parents, of which he is a living embodiment. For this reason to found a family is for many people an undertaking of great importance. On another plane — a more subjective one — the mother herself is reproduced through the *experience* of maternity, and so gains a symbolic immortality in that the physical child to whom she gives birth may be to her the symbol of a new self, re-created through the act by which she has fulfilled her own nature. So, in the dream quoted above, the going down of the sun for its *night journey* under the sea may result in the birth of an inner child, a new Sun Hero, who arises in the East. On this plane of interpretation, the dream is then this woman's individual version of the myth of the birth of the Hero, that is, it foreshadows the rebirth of the woman herself, re-created through the experience of pregnancy and parturition.

Many women sense dimly that in the experience of childbirth more happens than they are entirely conscious of. They know intuitively that the significance of childbearing is deeper than the production of the actual physical child. The infant means to them far more than they can explain. There enters into their love of the child an emotion which belongs to deeper and more subjective significances, for the child represents the promise of the renewal of life—of immortality and of re-creation. The physical child is to his mother another self, a non-personal, an "object" self. The spiritual child born of the experience of maternity is in the same way not the mother's personal ego reborn, but is non-personal, a new center of the psyche, which Jung has called the Self.

When a woman becomes pregnant her attention, both biological and emotional, is claimed for the new and vital creative process taking place within her. She withdraws into herself. Life demands that she surrender her own body, almost her own entity, to the child. She can no longer give herself completely to the life with her husband. He feels this withdrawal of her interest and may resent it. After his first efforts to draw her back into their mutual concerns have met with scant success, he in turn may withdraw. Or, if he is a more understanding person, he may realize the claims of the child and also put his energy and interest into the creative enterprise which is the fruit of their marriage, although the child cannot mean as much to him as to the mother in this intrauterine stage of its existence.

It is difficult moreover for him to distinguish between the personal or egotistic demands of his wife and the legitimate demands of her pregnancy. Indeed, there is a grave risk that the woman herself may fail to make this differentiation. She may magnify her disabilities, perhaps unconsciously, to gain attention from her husband, claiming care and solicitude for *herself,* instead of for *herself as mother*—the priestess of life; or she may underestimate them in a determination not to be selfish.

The false attitude which arises from self-pity or from fear of losing her husband's love during the time when she cannot be all wife to him is peculiarly baffling to the man, for it is very difficult for him to estimate justly the pains and restrictions a pregnant woman suffers. Some men, being unable to imagine an ordeal which by the nature of the case can never touch themselves, discount these disabilities completely. Others, perhaps the majority, overestimate the sufferings of motherhood, not realizing that this is woman's share of the discipline of life which is as necessary for her spiritual well-being as work is for a man's.

If the woman is not chiefly concerned during this process with the discomforts and limitations pregnancy imposes but is willing to allow life to be lived through her, she may experience an entirely new phase of consciousness, for she becomes complete in herself, independent of man. She is all mother and offspring. She attains, biologically and psychologically, to the completeness of the Virgin Mother Goddess. She regains something of the separateness of virginity. The pregnant woman has been worshipped from antiquity as representing something "in herself," something individual. Paradoxically, this aspect of individuality is attained through completely fulfilling a collective role; a pregnant woman is no longer what she has been—the embodiment of the personal —she is one of "the Mothers."

When maternity is accepted in this spirit, the woman experiences something of her own *individual* separateness. Her pregnancy becomes for her a profound psychological adventure. Through it she feels her oneness with the creative Mother and at the same time her own identity. For this is a road which she has to travel *alone*—she and the new life within her—the new life, inarticulate, helpless, unborn, yet commanding with an imperiousness which cannot be denied.

Then when her hour comes she must give herself up to be merely the medium for this new life, her body merely the prison whose doors must yield to the violent assault of the being who would live free. In that hour the woman must experience a gradual descent into the depths; the distinguishing marks of her personality, of her social grade, of her race, are stripped off, until she like her remote ancestress of old is revealed only as woman—as female creature engaged in her most fundamental task.

For the superficial and egotistic woman, this is a terrible and humiliating ordeal. To those whose natures are more profound, it brings a knowledge of the significance of life which is seldom found in any other way. Hence, in spite of the pain, childbearing is most deeply desired by many women because of the contact with the deepest meaning of life which has come to them by this road and by it alone.

But with the birth of the child the task of motherhood has only begun. For its adequate fulfillment years of devoted service are necessary. The task is so long and exacting that many women become completely absorbed in it. Thinking of it as a lifelong task, they lose all sense of perspective and allow their whole personalities to be merged in the role of mother. This is a mistake, for in the life of a woman the period given over to the bearing and rearing of children, important though it undoubtedly is, represents but one phase. Even during this period she is not only mother but also wife. If she identifies herself with her function of mother, she not only disregards the rights and claims of her husband and seriously hampers her children in their development, but her own life loses its right proportions as well.

Maternity is a task of twenty to thirty years' duration only—a long time, but not interminable—and the wise woman will look toward its termination even while she is in the midst of its

duties and will plan for the transition period when her own interests must be freed from the children to be invested in other
fields.

While love for their children may form a real bond between
husband and wife, there is nonetheless a danger that the mother's
preoccupation in the physical care of the babies, especially while
they are very young, may act as a barrier separating them. For
the most intimate contacts with the child, the actual physical
delight which the personal care of the infant brings, especially
the stimulation of maternal love through the physical act of
suckling the infant as well as bearing it, are experiences of the
mother alone.

It is through his complete dependence and weakness that the
infant is most closely endeared to the mother. This very dependence
is paradoxically the great power of the weak. The child becomes
"King Baby"! He can tyrannize over his mother by his appeal
to her pity and if he is not taught progressively to satisfy his
own needs his weakness will be a millstone around the mother's
neck. Yet in bearing with the necessary weakness of her child,
a mother learns to be merciful. The weak know no mercy. Their
weakness makes demands on the strength of the strong until the
last gasp, and the strong cannot turn and throw them off. Their
very strength hands them over, bound to those dependent on
them.

But a mother who allows her children to enchain her too long
will find the positions reversed — she becomes the weak one. When
they grow up and cease to need her, she cannot let them go.
If she has sacrificed herself to them till there is no self left except
the part which lives in them, she will instinctively cling to them,
and they will be compelled in self-defense to throw off her con-
vulsively grasping fingers. Awareness of this danger would help
a mother to encourage her children to be self-dependent. When
the temptation comes to do something for a child who is slow
or clumsy, if by any possibility he can manage for himself, she
should refrain. Even if he gets into difficulties, it is time enough

to offer help when he is at the end of his own resources. This rule applies not only to physical matters but to intellectual and emotional concerns as well. If there is a relation of mutual trust and respect between them, he will come and ask for help when he needs it. Until that time it is the part of wisdom to let reality do its educative work. In this way the individuality of both mother and child is given free scope, neither encroaching on the domain of the other.

The early years of maternity are, of course, the most absorbing. When the children are young there is no respite from the constant care their physical needs and training demand. The mother who loves her children undertakes this task with a gallant spirit. Her deepest wish is to give them the very best. This is her ideal and she is resolved to live up to it. "This is how a mother ought to feel!" But in the daily accomplishment of her unending task there comes to many a mother a secret knowledge that she does not live up to her own ideal. There are times when the children and their demands become almost intolerable. As a rule, she passes over these lapses in maternal feeling, considering them as the weakness of human nature resulting from overfatigue or some other indisposition, or else she reproaches herself for selfishness and weakness, not recognizing that these fluctuations in her mood are absolutely inevitable. She takes no account of the rest of her personality but forces herself into being the all-loving and all-giving mother of her ideal. By this attitude she compels her children always to be the recipients, they become not only all-receiving, but also all-taking. For an overindulgent mother invariably produces a selfish and exacting child, whose helplessness makes further demands upon the mother's attention. The child remains dependent for all initiative upon the mother whose interest is focused entirely upon him. A "do-it-for-mother" attitude toward matters which should be his own concern develops and produces in the child a quite false orientation to the mother's wishes and desires, instead of to his own satisfactions. This may often be seen in the nursery problems of eating and the natural functions. A healthy child eats, or should eat, because he is hungry and for the satisfaction which eating gives him. This is an independent goal, apart from "being good" or doing what he is told. But if his meal is made an occasion by which he gains the attention of his mother, his interest is diverted from his body satisfaction to an emotional satisfaction gained by compelling her attention. This false emotional relation is often carried over into the schoolroom and playground, and we hear the child calling every moment of the day: "Mother, see what I've done!" "Mother, look what I've made!" When children turn constantly in this way to their mother, she naturally finds great pleasure in their devotion and dependence, but she is gradually swallowed up by them and is laying up trouble for herself against the time when they will leave her. She has become dependent upon their dependence and she will hardly know how to live without them, for her friends have dropped off from neglect and her own activities have rusted from disuse. Her whole attention has been occupied by her children; when they leave her she will be without occupation at an age when, depleted by their continual demands through the years, she has no energy or initiative to seek new interests. When she ceases to be "mother," she may find she has lost all significance in the social order.

This outcome is inevitable unless the mother's attitude toward her child can be purified from unconscious motives which make demands upon him to fill the gaps in her own life. Overindulgence of the child is merely a mask for the suppression of his interests in favor of her own. For if she is looking to the child to give significance to a life otherwise empty and without purpose, she puts upon him a great burden and makes demands which he can hardly be expected to fulfill. By such an attitude the mother really devours the child, a situation which is by no means uncommon. It is to be seen perhaps in its most flagrant form in cases of adopted children, where the demand for the child's gratitude is more openly expressed and indeed seems more justified than in the case of an "own" child, for whose advent the parents are alone responsible. But even here it is quite common for parents under the guise of love to demand a lifelong devotion and service from their children which amounts to psychological slavery. The maternal attitude is dual. The mother loves her children and makes great sacrifices for them, but if she expects them to fill her life, her love for them is largely a mask for self-love. Her seeming kindness is really cruelty.

If the mother takes the opposite path and does not expect her children to fill all of her life, that part of her interest which cannot be poured out in maternal love must seek its satisfaction elsewhere. She loves her children, it is true, and cares greatly for their welfare; but she also has a life apart from them, comprising her love for her husband, her need for friends and for interests of her own. These calls on her time and attention are all legitimate and necessary. If she identifies herself with her mother role, assuming that she ought to give herself up entirely to her children's requirements, she will find herself sooner or later resenting their demands and being torn by conflicting impulses in regard to them. If she does not repress these resentments but recognizes their cause, she will find some way to meet the problem. For if a woman is not to lose *herself,* she must keep a sense of proportion even during the children's infancy, or their demands will grow more and more exacting. Surely it is better to let the standard of perfection by which they are tended slide occasionally than for her to become nothing but an automaton. Even when viewed from the angle of the children's own welfare this is the better way. It is of little use to them to have the most perfect physical care unless their mother is a vital woman deeply fulfilled in her own life.

In emphasizing the need for a mother to make time and opportunity for her own life I do not wish to give the impression that the child's interests can always be relegated to second place. Maternity is a serious and arduous undertaking and those who are not prepared to make personal sacrifices for it are in no position to attempt it. But in the family the individuality of each member must have due consideration, that of the mother no less than that of the child.

To this end it is possible to train the child from the very first to be alone. Children readily learn to amuse themselves happily and safely without constant supervision. Even quite tiny tots can be left alone for a part of each day with advantage. The tendency to overstimulation inherent in modern life and modern educational methods can be balanced by solitude and the child be given an opportunity to develop initiative and self-reliance. For the mother such a regime may be lifesaving. It leaves her free for a little while to think her own thoughts uninterrupted, to get on with her work and to attend to adult interests in a way practically impossible if the children are with her all the time.

During the infancy and early childhood of her family the mother runs a great risk of losing all contact with interests which occupy the time and attention of those who are not exclusively concerned as she is with the needs of babies. Her preoccupation with children and their interests fills many years of a mother's life. Under other circumstances these are the years when she would be most active intellectually. Her sisters who launch out into the world grapple at this age with all the current problems of the day—religion, social and intellectual questions, politics, and so forth. The mother of young children has no time for such interests and so justifies the view that she is like a child in her inability to form valid judgments on the affairs of the world. The caustic remark of a young college graduate—"When a girl marries she is lost as an interesting companion"—carries an unpleasant grain of truth. Then, too, the stultifying effect of exclusive contact with children does not stop short at the arrest of intellectual development which so often overtakes the young mother. It has a consequence even more far-reaching and destructive. The woman who goes out into a world of adults has to meet problems of relationship—adult emotional involvements. The woman concerned with children is likely to become and to remain childish in her emotional reactions and in her capacity for relationship. This effect is particularly unfortunate, since the major responsibility for carrying out and developing this side of life rests on the woman. It is true that the mother is not just a child with children. Her maternal attitude to the child is in itself an adult adaptation, but so long as it remains a merely instinctive attitude it does not lead to any real psychological development. Only as the mother's instinctive attitude to the child is replaced by a consciously worked-out relationship which does not overbalance the other aspects of her psyche can it produce profound development in her personality.

It must be admitted that the urgency of never ending duties is sometimes so inescapable as to force the devoted mother, at least for some years, to make with open eyes the sacrifice of all other cultural interests. Yet even so, development need not cease if she is able to realize an inner value which is served in serving the children. If she does what she does of her own free will, in loyalty to her own love or in the spirit of a deep acceptance of *her* way, she will not, when her children go, be left inert and empty nor will she be compelled to demand emotional recompense from them. If she redeems the instinctive maternal in herself, building it up into the whole structure of her psyche, her recompense will come through the growth and development which this brings. It is the experience of her own maternity, not the bringing forth and rearing of children, which has redeeming power for herself.

To understand what this *experience of maternity* is it is necessary to inquire into the nature of maternal feeling and find if possible that essential element which differentiates it from other instinctual emotions. The desire for the conservation of life, and that at all costs, is the outstanding characteristic of mother love. The mother's task is to tend and rear her child no matter what he is like. She has to work with the material given her and make the best of that. In all other spheres of activity man is free to change the material with which he works. If the material proves unsatisfactory, although the work is half completed, it can be discarded. But a child may be quite different from what the mother would have chosen, he may even be physically or mentally defective, but she cannot discard this material for a better kind. She *must* conserve it — work with it over long years and make out of it the best that she can. This entails a far-reaching discipline which has its reward in the development it brings about in the mother's character.

In many women, however, love of the offspring remains of an almost animal-like quality, which cannot be called love of the *child,* of the person, at all. The child represents to such a mother a little piece of herself which has become partly separated and which she passionately loves on account of the still unbroken bond with herself. I remember going some years ago to see a peasant woman whose infant had just died. I found her sitting in front of the fire, rocking herself to and fro and holding her swollen and aching breasts. Tears were rolling down her cheeks and she was moaning to herself in grief and discomfort, her emotional and physical pain all mixed and confused in her consciousness. As I leaned over, I caught the words repeated over and over again: "Oh, if only my baby were here, he could suck a bit and ease me." Here is the primitive mother who is "wailing for her children and will not be comforted" — until the next baby comes and fills her empty arms.

During the period of infancy mother and child form a natural unit, unbreakable except at the cost of great violence to both. As time goes on, however, this oneness, at least on the physical side, is gradually broken up. Simultaneously the child should win for himself an emotional, or psychological, separateness, but the achievement of independence is a difficult task in which the mother must share if it is to be successfully accomplished. Unfortunately the union between them, instead of being lessened by the physical growth and development of the child, may merely recede from view as the conscious evidence of its presence is outgrown. In this way it takes on a more subtle, and for that reason a more dangerous, form, which may develop into a permanent identification.

The difference between identification and real love can be clearly seen in certain rather marked cases, while in others the elements may be almost inextricably mixed. No one then is more deceived than the woman herself as to the nature of her — so-called — love for her children. For instance, the mother of a four-year-old boy said to me one day, "My son is going to be a great statesman." One pities the poor little fellow with such a task before him. Perhaps he will grow up having no outstanding gifts, and those he has may turn to mechanics or music rather than to politics. But the mother's ambition and unfulfilled potentialities — she was a woman with considerable ability, both social and intellectual — had fastened themselves onto the child; therefore, he must be trained to live the life she would have chosen, had she been a man. It had never occurred to her that she was doing anything unfair, that she was not leaving the boy free to live his own life, but that she was bringing subtle pressure to bear in order to induce him to live her life for her.

This kind of identification is extremely common. It may be masked while the children are quite young, but shows more and more clearly as they reach adolescence and becomes increasingly pernicious the longer the child is unable to break through it and assert his own personality. The trouble with the child is that he has not yet found himself. Unless he is an exceptionally well-centered individual, his real trends and capacitites are buried in the nebulousness of youth. The pressure from his mother's desires either distracts him from discovering his own wishes or pushes him into abandoning them. He may, for instance, prepare himself for a role in life for which he is not naturally fitted, with a consequent stultification of his real capacities and the possibility of a breakdown in his adaptation should he realize later the true state of the case. In other instances the achievements a mother covets for her daughter may be a substitute for the fulfillment of her own ambitions. For example, she may want her to become a "social success" or to "make a good marriage," regardless of the girl's own wishes. She may be temperamentally unfitted for a life in society, may indeed long for an intellectual life, or she may fall in love with a poor man, instead of a rich one — but her identification with the mother hangs over her ominously. She is threatened with strangulation whichever way she turns. If she gives up her own wishes she will sink into lethargy and resentment; if she stands up for herself the unconscious bond to the mother may reduce her to neurosis through the sense of guilt which she suffers.

A mother whose ambitions are tied up in this way with her daughter may be exceedingly fond of her and may lavish affection upon her so that the girl feels herself a criminal if she denies her mother anything. In other cases the mother may find to her great bewilderment that the girl holds herself aloof from all attentions and becomes sullen or resistant. She tries to overcome her daughter's coldness with increased demonstrations of love and redoubles her efforts to create a congenial atmosphere between them, but all to no end. She has no understanding of the girl's difficulty, and even less that her own "love" may hide an unconscious power attitude — a demand that her daughter abandon any attempt to find herself as an individual, remaining instead an appendage, a possession of the mother. The girl's aloofness is a reaction to the possessiveness of which the mother is unconscious, not to her obvious affection. But as the mother is unaware of her own motives, she naturally lacks the key to the understanding of her daughter's coldness. Such cases often become clear when explained from the daughter's point of view.

More than one young woman whose emotions and feelings were pitiably repressed has told me that her mother's lavish expressions of affection were simply terrifying to her and that the more she withdrew, the more demonstrative the mother became. Further questioning made it clear that the mother was, perhaps unknown to herself, loving an ideal — "my daughter" — upon which she put her own connotation, never realizing that her unconscious self-seeking was making an unfair demand upon the girl to sacrifice her own individuality and become what the mother wished. The daughter, feeling herself to be totally unlike her mother's image of her and unconsciously sensing the tremendous possessiveness behind the love, had retreated into her shell like a turtle. It was her only way of combating the mother's manifestation of emotion; she feared that, were she to accept the love, she would be compelled to make return in the form so subtly demanded—a payment which would cost her her very soul.

Feeling which is truly maternal, which takes what is given to it and makes the best of it, is in marked contrast to this mother-child identification, however much it wears the mask of maternal love. A mature woman actuated by disciplined maternal feeling takes stock of her child's capacities, develops them, gives them full opportunity to grow. The more unlike his parents he is, the more care must be taken to give him freedom to develop his own aptitudes and to grow within his own limits.

If his capacity is below the expectation of his parents they are faced with a serious problem: Just what shall be their attitude toward him? Two cases, illustrating different ways of dealing with this situation, present themselves to my memory. In each the family was cultured and intellectual, and the son anything but mentally gifted. In the first instance, the boy was definitely defective and as he grew older his difficulties became more marked; even untrained observers could see there was something seriously wrong. But the father, ambitious and successful, was completely blinded by his own desires. He would not, or could not, see his son as he was—a young man but with the mentality of a child of six. As the boy grew, the father continued to engage expensive tutors and insisted that he should be entered at one of the more prominent universities. How far the father's attitude contributed to the son's difficulties it is impossible to say, but it undoubtedly fostered them through the emotional atmosphere it created, and in a more obvious way. For on account of the father's blindness the boy was kept in an entirely false environment, being unable to take advantage of the education provided for him and not being provided with any training which would have been really educative. Yet this father was convinced that he loved his son.

In marked contrast is the second case — a boy adopted by intelligent people whose interests were chiefly intellectual. They doubtless hoped that he would grow up with congenial tastes, but he was not good at his books. Things meant more to him than ideas. His adopted parents recognized this aptitude and instead of making him feel obliged to succeed in the academic world introduced handwork into his studies and eventually gave him a carpenter's training.

In the first case, the parents were identified with the child, and the idea that he might be other than they hoped never occurred to them; they loved him for what he was — flesh of their flesh — and for what they thought he should become — a fulfillment of their scheme of life. In the second case, the foster parents showed a truer parental feeling. They had a certain detachment, a psychological disidentification. They also loved the boy for what he was and for what he should become, but unlike the first parents they had no preconceived idea to which they attempted to fit the child. Rather, they observed what the nature of the boy was and fostered that nature, subordinating their own wishes and ambitions to the reality.

To be able to act in this way requires a high degree of discipline. This is *redeemed* maternal love, not just the instinctive maternal feeling of the animal and the primitive human mother. The natural maternal instinct is well adapted to fulfill its ends under primitive conditions, but when these conditions cease to exist the maternal instinct in its original nature-form is no longer adapted in any ideal way to the needs of life and of the times. It becomes then, through its all-embracing character, a grave menace.

The woman's ego reaches out and may clutch at her offspring in order to find through them the fulfillment of her ambitions and desire for power and prestige. The children in turn develop to the ego stage of consciousness. Then the bond between parent and child which was at first based on an instinctive mutual love is replaced by a struggle for dominance. This condition of affairs can only be remedied through the development of greater consciousness on the part of both mother and child. It is obviously desirable that the step forward in psychological development should be taken as early as possible so that this false relation shall not arise. This means that the mother must initiate it. If she is successful in releasing herself from her unconscious identification with the child and its consequent possessiveness, as he outgrows the dependence of his infancy she will be able to release him psychologically also. The struggle for power which is so characteristic of the adolescent years will be greatly diminished in violence or even entirely avoided. Some struggle there is likely to be, for the child must win his freedom, it cannot be given to him. But if the mother herself is free from the desire to dominate, the child will have to fight only his own childishness and not the mother's autocracy. As he frees himself, a true psychological relationship will develop between them. This relationship, which is a growing one, often holds much mutual affection. As the years go on and the importance of the age gap between them diminishes, they will meet on a more equal footing, and the relationship will become an increasingly satisfying one.

If, however, the mother remains unconscious of the egotistic and possessive trends which are hidden in her love, there inevitably comes a period of conflict between mother and children. As the boys and girls grow to be young men and women, they reach out naturally enough for greater liberty and for release from the ties which bind them not only to their parents but to their own childishness. A struggle ensues during which the weaknesses of both mother and child are apt to be disclosed. If the mother's love has masked a desire to possess her children and find her own emotional fulfillment through the mutual dependence of mother and child, the struggle for freedom will reveal the "other side," one might say the "under side," of the maternal attitude, aptly called by Jung "the devouring mother." In nature the prototype of this aspect of the mother is seen in the animal which eats her newborn young, and in human life today in the woman who considers her child to be her puppet, her plaything, her unique possession.[1] In extreme cases this "devouring mother" assumes that she has the right to dispose of her daughter's whole time and strength as she sees fit — her daughter is literally her slave. How often do we hear a mother say, "One of my daughters must stay at home to look after her father and *me*," and this without consulting the daughter's own wishes at all. In other instances, the mother considers it her right to make or break her daughter's marriage at will, to make or break her career, or even — as in one flagrant case which came under my notice — to dispose of her daughter's virtue to suit her own convenience. These abuses of the maternal situation actually occur!

The bondage of the daughter comes about more often, however, not through the open dominance of the older woman, but in a far more curious way, seemingly without the direct intervention of the mother and certainly without her conscious intention. The power which determines the daughter's action and hampers her in the living of her own life is not the woman who is her mother but, instead, it is the *imago* of mother which her individual mother carries. The girl seemingly cannot release herself from the childish conviction that her mother is always right and is all powerful, as she was when the child was a helpless infant.

The daughter has her own problem to face in this universal situation.[2] She must find a way to win release from the mother imago. Here, since we are concerned specifically with the other

---

1 In India, a ritual called the Giving Away of the Fruit is practiced as a means of teaching the mother a better attitude toward her child. See Eleanor Bertine's *Human Relationships.*

2 Jung, "The Dual Mother," *Symbols of Transformation.*

side of the quandary, we must ask: How can the *mother* release herself from this imago which has arisen to distort the human reality both of herself and of her child?

The woman who permits the assumption of her perpetual rightness to pass unchallenged plays up to the child's psychological projection of the mother image. She adds her quota to the mother-child dilemma when she assumes that her sons and daughters are and always will be children, needing maternal guidance. The woman who says of her grown sons and daughters, "They will always be children to me," fails to recognize them as separate entities, as individuals apart from herself. In this way she falls into the role of "the Mother," and will have to carry the negative as well as the positive aspect of the archetype, for they are inseparable. If she is to release herself from this necessity, she must be willing to give up her point of vantage which rests simply on the fact that she was a grown woman when they were unconscious infants, and instead base her relation to her children on present reality. In discussing some past action of hers which her son or daughter is questioning, she must not take her stand on the archetype and say, "I am your mother and therefore I know best. Say no more about it." She must say instead, "I did thus and so according to my best judgment *then*. I had to decide for myself and also for you because you were too young to be able to judge. I may have been wrong; if so, I am willing to change my attitude." Saying this, she asserts her real superiority—the age and experience greater than theirs at the time—but she does not shelter herself behind the all-wisdom of the mother imago. This leaves for the youth a place on which to stand. He gains an idea of why decisions are made, of how judgments can change. As he grows older, he can begin to estimate for himself the *raison d'etre* of his mother's decisions, and as he learns to make a responsible judgment the mother can extricate herself from the necessity of thinking for him.

This policy by no means involves an abdication of the authority and responsibility of the mother's position, which must be carried firmly and openly as long as is necessary. Modern theorists who are afraid to exert any discipline for fear of dominating the child's personality have jumped from the frying pan into the fire, for they have removed the solid basis of authority which should mediate the reality of the external world to the child and have placed him instead in a specialized environment adapted to his needs alone. This change does not make the child less dependent but more so, since he cannot function except in an environment where his unadapted or asocial behavior will be condoned. If, however, the authoritative "do this," and "don't do that" are gradually replaced by the equally authoritative commands and prohibitions of the world of fact, the child learns to adapt his personal desires for immediate satisfaction to the conditions of reality which rule in a fashion even more peremptory than the most autocratic parent. Until he has learned to do this he is dependent for warmth, shelter and food—for life itself. The dependence of the child upon the mother is a reality. And the position of dependence involves, inevitably, submission to the authority of the one depended on. That authority can be used rightly or wrongly. It is rightly used if it is carried as a responsibility until the child is able to stand on his own feet. It is abused if, by virtue of the power it confers, the parent assumes some mysterious and permanent superiority.

The mother's release from identification with the good-bad maternal instinct can take place only through a psychological differentiation of herself from her children, by which she grants them the right to live their own lives and die their own deaths— to suffer as well as to enjoy. These are native human rights and no one may with impunity shield another from them. The attitude which says, "I want to make you happy, to make life easy for you. I want to guard you from every breath of hardship and adversity," is terrible. It seems so kind, yet it is really so cruel. It is nothing less than an attempt to play God to the child.

There is another more subtle aspect of the mother-child problem which cannot be overlooked. It depends on the identification between the unconscious of mother and child. This is always present and persists until it is made conscious and is gradually released, either through a development which comes to some people from their life experience or through work on the unconscious which may be voluntarily undertaken by means of psychological analysis. Because of this identification with his mother's unconscious the child is in a conditon of *participation mystique* with her. Whatever lives unrecognized in her unconscious exists also in the psyche of the child, albeit in nebulous form. A recognition of this link is a most powerful incentive to a woman to grapple more seriously than ever before with the problems of her own psychological development. For when she becomes a mother, a woman incurs the deepest obligation to acquaint herself with her unconscious problems, not only for her own sake but also in order to safeguard her child from harm of a most subtle and insidious kind.

When a woman brings a child into the world, she can no longer take the easy road of repressing her emotional and ethical problems. If she lives alone this can be done with harm to none but herself, and she can remain unconscious of all inconvenient or painful facts about herself with relative impunity. Even in a marriage, if it is childless, failure to meet her problems, serious though it will undoubtedly be to her relationship with her husband, will yet affect only those two people.

If she has children, however, the woman's action has far-reaching consequences. To repress her problems will have just as serious effects upon her own development as when she is alone in the world, but the trouble will not stop there. Separation of the child's personality from the mother's takes place only slowly even on the conscious plane; the unconscious union which exists between them is far harder to break. The similarity of children to their parents resulting from identification is a matter of daily observation. Small children, and older as well, take delight in copying their parents' ways and words and gestures. This mimicry is, however, practiced by the child quite instinctively, that is, it springs from an identification of the child with his parent. But we may also see an extraordinary resemblance between child and parent of another kind which is not subject to conscious control as, for instance in facial expression, personal habits of sleeping, digestion and the like, emotional reactions and intellectual aptitudes.

On account of its deep-seated roots, this identity is broken only very slowly. On the level of the unconscious, child and parent seem to have no dividing wall. He reacts to the mother's unspoken thought almost as if he had had the thought himself. A baby will cry if his mother is frightened, for even quite tiny children sense their mother's unexpressed emotion. An older girl once told me she always knew beforehand what her mother was going to say or do and adapted herself accordingly. Doubtless it was exaggeration to say that she "always" knew, but certainly she had an almost uncanny gift for reading her mother's intentions.

This unconscious identification between mother and child can show itself in many most surprising ways. If the mother is a victim, for instance, of some emotional disturbance, the child may have symptoms of physical or nervous illness which are hard to account for. He may develop fears, nightmares, temper tantrums or digestive upsets, asthma or other neurotic manifestations. This is especially likely to occur where unsolved and disregarded problems exist between the parents, especially if the real causes of the difficulty are entirely repressed. The effects of these unworked-out emotional tangles on children have been cited repeatedly. For instance, a little girl who came under my observation had a recurrent nightmare of disaster: either the house was on fire or the Indians were coming and her father was helpless to save them because he was sewed to her mother's work basket. This meant, of course, that unconsciously the child sensed the emotional situation between her parents—that her father was a child, dependent on her mother like a son, psychologically tied to her apron strings.

In another case, a little girl of six years had the most extraordinary dreams at a time when her parents were about to separate, although she naturally had not been told of their difficulties. On one occasion she dreamed *she went into the garden and was assailed by the devil dressed in scarlet, and when she sought to escape from him, she was threatened from the other side by nuns dressed in black. Finding herself in this impasse she jumped up into the air and so escaped.* Here we have the picture of a child caught in a problem beyond her years. The devil and the nuns clearly represent her parents' unsolved sexual problems. The child, unable to tackle this adult conflict, leaves the ground—jumps up into fantasy in order to get away from it. When she was brought to me she was quite unable to adapt herself even to everyday requirements, but lived instead entirely in an unreal world.

Children are in *participation mystique* with their mother, and the illness of her unconscious will also be their illness. [3] If they are not to be harmed, she must keep her problems in consciousness and really struggle with them—then the children will not suffer. But if she remains unaware of something of which she should be conscious the child will be affected unfavorably.

So close is this unconscious bond that it lays on the mother a serious obligation to free herself from repressions. Just as she must keep herself free from infection on the physical plane, so she must keep herself free from contamination with things neglected in the unconscious. If she has a cold she keeps away from her infant in order to protect it; if there is a virus epidemic she will give up her concert ticket rather than risk bringing home the infection. Similarly a mother needs to keep herself psychologically clean. She cannot risk harboring hostile or resentful feelings; if she has a disagreement with her husband, or if a problem arises in their relationship, she must clear it up lest she infect her children. This necessity acts as a powerful motive for summoning

---

3 This subject is discussed at length in my *Parental Image: Its Injury and Reconstruction.*

courage to work on her relation to her husband instead of yielding to the inertia which tempts her with the suggestion, "It is not worth making a fuss about."

The discipline of maternity, then, does not consist only in the outer obligations which it imposes. The external discipline is severe in itself. The disturbed nights, the ever-recurrent duties of bathing, tending, mending, the anxiety which even trivial illness occasions, the sacrifice of intellectual and social recreation through many years, the long-continued submission of personal wishes to childish needs—these things cannot be minimized. Then, when the children reach adolescence, a further discipline is imposed on the parents. For inevitably the young people must go with their own generation. They will discard the attitudes and beliefs for which the parents have suffered and which they cherish as their most valued achievements. Parents must watch their children experimenting with life and running into danger, and they will have to learn the hardest of all lessons—to stand by and not interfere.

But over and beyond all this, for the woman who is aware of the psychical realm, maternity imposes a discipline which reaches below the surface and strikes directly at her most hidden, most secret selfishnesses and egotisms. The child's physical welfare depends upon her, but she has a deeper and more fundamental responsibility than that for his body. She must bestir herself and put her own psychological house in order if she is not to jeopardize his soul.

Not even an altruistic love of the child can solve this problem. Only if she gives her devotion to a value beyond either his personal welfare or her own can she find a way to solve the problems involved in the mother-child relation. She must develop within herself a conscious and mature individuality if she is not to hamper her child with a crippling mother fixation. When she does this, she will be willing to leave her child free to find himself. She will be able, as the Chinese say, "to let go the hand." Thus through the experience of maternity consciously accepted as a *task,* the road to psychological rebirth can be found, justifying, perhaps, the old belief that through his child a parent finds immortality.

7. Off the Beaten Track

No discussion of the emotional life of women would be complete today if limited to questions of friendship and marriage. The problems of love and lovers, old as the human race, present themselves in new and different ways from generation to generation, varying with the prevailing culture and the shifting of psychological emphasis and understanding. As a result of changed and changing attitudes of society toward matters of sexual love and expression, men and women are today compelled to meet certain personal problems in a more direct—a more conscious—manner than formerly when they were governed by social rulings and conventions.

In all epochs, the individual tends to be the puppet, often even the victim of his time. Human problems remain basically the same throughout the ages, but the contemporary form, the fashion, changes. A slow rhythmic movement takes place which is spiral rather than cyclic. The point which represents the "present day" moves around the circle, but it moves also along a line, passing from one level of consciousness to another in an evolutionary "progress"—an apparently straight line which, for all we know, may be but the arc of a large circle. Thus two movements are discernible: first an evolution of human consciousness from the primitive mode through the antique to that of modern man; and second a relatively rapid change in fashion from decade to decade. The first is a long, slow movement. In each generation the moving point seems to stand still, for the change during the lifetime of a generation is infinitesimal. The second movement in comparison is rapid, for its "period" can be reckoned by decades, instead of by thousands of years. In this latter movement the change in one generation is *usually* slight, just sufficient to make the elders regret "the way young people act" or complain that "we don't know what the world is coming to." But every now and then a cultural form changes, suddenly, overnight, with revolutionary violence. Then during the lifetime of one generation a strange phenomenon may be seen. Those values which the parents and grandparents held as their most sacred possession, instead of being modified, are completely overthrown. What the elders cherished is anathema to the children. Such a revolutionary change has taken place in moral and sexual standards in our time.

A liberal-minded mother recently expressed to her daughter the hope that she would not indulge in promiscuous "petting." The girl replied, "Mother, *we* care only what our own generation thinks; it doesn't matter to us in the slightest what your generation thinks of us." This statement of independence is extraordinary, coming from the lips of a girl of fifteen. She and her friends seem to be consciously aware of a complete break in the cultural continuity of the race; as if they felt themselves cut off from the ancestral standpoint. Immigrants from Europe suffer from a similar cutting off, which constitutes one of the basic problems in the Americanization of newcomers. But their problem, large as it is, is small when compared with the problem of modern youth, for today a whole generation is affected by the revolutionary change in cultural form and conventions which govern sexual behavior.

When young people claim to be concerned only with the opinion of their own generation, they do not realize that the attitude of their ancestors is not destroyed or resolved, even within themselves, by a change in the conscious or intellectual point of view. The newly held ideas and ideals take possession of the conscious field and the discarded attitude sinks into the unconscious where it exerts an influence from which no individual can escape. The modern point of view is not an individual achievement which has been won through the assimilation of the old attitude, rather it has arisen by a change in the *collective* standpoint, the result of a *volte face*—a turning around—so that what was formerly esteemed is now disparaged. The conventional "mode" has changed through a rearrangement of the *general* psychic contents of all young people alike. It is a collective change, manifested, however, in each member of the group. Thus the girl who today indulges in petting, or even in free love, may be actuated by a spirit just as conventional as were her aunts or great-aunts who treated young men with the utmost formality.

Indeed, the individual is largely the puppet of his time. In seeking freedom to love as they wish and to express themselves unrestrainedly, many young people launch out like pioneers seeking an El Dorado. Some have won through to a new land. But many who started forth so gallantly were not equipped to be pioneers. The ocean is strewn with frail barks which have not reached the shore of the promised land. Some are nearly swamped, some are hopelessly shipwrecked and others are drifting aimlessly.

These exiles have left the old ways for good and all. The old rules based on authority are no longer applicable to them. What is right and what is wrong under the new conditions must be determined from a deeper level—from a more fundamental understanding of true morality. To go back to the old standard of "authority" would mean inevitable regression. Those who have assumed the task of determining what is right for themselves can never again find "goodness" simply by doing what they are told. Each step forward in experience—in consciousness—makes a further advance inevitable. As Whitman says, "Now understand me well—it is provided in the essence of things that from any fruition of success, no matter what, shall come forth something to make a greater struggle necessary."

The chaos in sexual morality characteristic of the present day is entirely modern. In other ages the code has changed with the passing centuries but as a rule people similarly circumstanced held the same code. For instance, during the Gothic period society was exceedingly unified in its culture. During the Victorian era a similar uniformity held; all thought alike and ideals were identical. But today—certainly in America—there is no centralized ideal of conduct or consciousness, so that what is true for one "class" of people may be entirely false for another. Moreover, these "classes," instead of being self-contained and isolated, are often intertwined; the individuals comprising them rub shoulders indiscriminately. In any group of college students, of office staffs, of teachers, of professional and business women, the most marked diversity of outlook may be found; moreover this diversity is equally marked among women and girls of the leisured and more sheltered classes. Some of these women are naive to the point of childish ignorance, others are sophisticated, disillusioned, hard-boiled in their attitude; many, though free in their intellectual views, are in their emotional reactions still completely bound by convention; others again, though no longer childishly naive, are nevertheless repelled by the hard, almost brutal attitude of the sophisticated, which outrages alike their sense of personal decency and their ideals of love and tenderness. These are all groping for a standpoint.

While the extent of the change in behavior of men and women to each other varies enormously, some alteration has taken place in almost all levels of society and in all localities, both in Europe and in America. The direction of the change is invariably toward a greater freedom, a lessening of restraints, a breaking down of barriers and taboos. Some form of sexual intimacy is almost universally allowed by social custom wherever a boy and girl or a man and woman are attracted to each other. In the majority of cases this doubtless occurs only between friends who are either engaged or have an established relationship. But, in other instances, petting and caressing are indulged in between relative strangers, not as the expression of a recognized involvement and friendship, but because of a passing attraction. In still other cases, this freedom seems to have become almost the mode—"the expected thing"—and if a man should kiss a woman to whom he is but just introduced no one in certain groups of society would be surprised. It is hardly to be wondered at, therefore, that these intimacies, so commonly accepted, should frequently lead to more complete sexual expression.

The readiness with which people today allow themselves to become involved in a sexual relationship depends in no small measure on the widespread knowledge of contraceptive methods which undoubtedly influences both men and women enormously in their social and sexual behavior. For if the sexual act is divorced from the probability of ensuing pregnancy, sexuality ceases to be so specifically a matter of social or collective behavior and becomes more exculsively a personal problem, since fundamentally the concern of society is with the children and not primarily with the actions of the parents.

The consequent release of the individual from the control of the group is viewed by many with grave apprehension. They fear that widespread dissemination of the knowledge of contraceptives will inevitably lead to a great increase in immorality. Two assumptions underlie this fear: first, that sexual expression is necessarily wrong and immoral unless it has been sanctioned by a contract of marriage, and second that people are inherently wicked and refrain from "immoral" acts only because of the possible consequences. It is the old argument that sin is controlled only by the fear of "hell fire."

If sexual expression between a man and a woman were completely divorced from reproduction the intimacy would necessarily come to be recognized as an expression solely of their personal relationship. To the extent to which the fear of pregnancy can be dismissed their attention is focused on the emotional situation between them. But men and women do not necessarily plunge into licentiousness or promiscuity whenever this fear is removed. I have never heard it argued, for instance, that women who have undergone hysterectomy, of whom there must be many in every large community, are especially prone to immorality. Today through the knowledge of contraceptives the biological reasons for sexual restraint have been largely removed, so that a new morality must be sought resting on psychological considerations.

But for many women the question of morality in sexual matters does not depend solely on the possibility of a resultant pregnancy. For them intimacy between men and women is wrong in itself, unless it has been sanctified by marriage. It is a matter of *sanctifying* the relation—making holy what is otherwise wicked. The feeling that intercourse is inherently wrong except when sanctioned by marriage is deeply ingrained in all Christian peoples and has widespread roots among other cultured races, but it is not so universal as some people seem to think. The pagan world, under the Roman Empire, was given over to the exploitation of material and physical resources to such a degree that it was in danger of being lost in an orgy of materialism and licentiousness. Then the Christian doctrine arose with its emphasis on the spiritual, as opposed to the carnal or material, and chastity became a virtue for the many, instead of being an ascetic practice for the few. Gradually, through the centuries, the whole attitude of the Western nations toward sexuality changed. Instead of its being considered a perfectly normal physical function without any particular moral significance, it came to be the main point on which morality and immorality were judged. A "bad woman" meant one who was promiscuous sexually or even one who was known or suspected to have had sexual intercourse outside of marriage. Men were not judged by quite the same standard. Certainly the term, a *bad* man, never had the same significance as a *bad* woman.

But customs change—and sexual customs not least. Even when the Puritan attitude was strongest sexual customs varied enormously in different communities. It is strange that each generation feels so convinced that its sexual customs and morality are God-given—for as a matter of fact these customs are more prone to change than any others of comparable importance.

In certain rural sections both in England and in the United States, it was customary, even during the most repressed days of the Victorian epoch, for a young couple who were "keeping company" to have sexual intercourse and this without social condemnation, provided they married before the arrival of the first child. Indeed, it would have been considered wrong for a couple to wed until it was proved that the union would not be sterile.

In this custom we see a social factor, often overlooked, which is yet very important. It was considered right for the young man and woman to consummate their relationship provided marriage was intended if the girl became pregnant. But it was *not* accepted as right for them to be frivolous in their intentions. They entered into no contract before the community equivalent either to marriage or betrothal, but their seriousness was assumed; promiscuity was not licensed by this custom. Expressions of love between the lovers were their own private concern; but if a family resulted the relationship became a concern of the community. The girl had to ask herself: "Will he marry me if I become pregnant?" It was her business to be sure on this point before she gave herself to him.

In these rural communities, faithlessness on the part of the young man was rare partly because of his own sense of morality and partly because of the pressure of public opinion. A rather similar situation has developed today in urban groups. But the increased freedom for sexual expression does not carry the old sense of individual obligation, nor has it revived the power of the small community to control the actions of individuals. Consequently, a most extraordinary breakdown of the old barriers may be seen — a breakdown which is not safeguarded by the building up of other controls. How widespread this new attitude toward sexuality is, it is impossible to say. In some communities the old customs still hold. Doubtless, in large sections of the country young people are as chaste as their parents — neither more nor less so. But there is unmistakable evidence that in others the old taboos have disappeared and young people who a generation ago would without question have been completely inexperienced in sexual matters are now experimenting in this sphere of life. In many cases the incursions into the realm of love stop short at petting, but the number of young people who go on to complete sexual expression is very large.

When the accustomed barriers and taboos have been overstepped and no dire consequences follow, the sense that sexuality is a forbidden and dread mystery wanes; the whole matter comes to be considered as trivial and unimportant unless a new attitude of seriousness arises to replace the discarded code. A young woman once said to an older friend: "Sexuality is only like cleaning your teeth! Why do you make such a fuss about it?" Taken on this basis sexuality *is* trivial. It is reduced to its lowest denominator, as an animal, a physical manifestation—an instinctive act devoid of meaning—and, if an adequate contraceptive is used, one no more significant than eating a meal. Yet indulgence in sexuality, trivial though they may consider it, seems to these young people somehow obligatory. One girl, hardly more than a child, expressed this idea when she said, "There must be something wrong with me, I don't have sexual affairs." Their actions give the lie to their expressed opinions. Sexuality is not and cannot be trivial—it is important. But the importance formerly expressed in the taboos surrounding the act is now found in the opinion that "there must be something wrong with me if I don't," as though on this criterion rested the child's claim to normality.

The psychological importance of sexuality is naturally to be sought in its significance. But significance was denied by both these young women whose trivial attitudes precluded any possibility of *love.* An emotional experience of any depth was impossible for them, while even a satisfactory physical experience would be unlikely. For if physical sexuality can be taken at any time without check, desire never heaps up, the "potential" is always low and no psychological or cultural achievement can be expected.

If, however, the sexual urge meets a barrier which is real, the potential of desire is raised. An artificial barrier, willfully imposed, does not have the same effect. For instance, if a woman refuses to allow a man to carry his caressing to its logical conclusion, not because of a real moral scruple but from coyness, he may be tantalized into greater ardor or he may turn away in disgust. Whatever the outcome, inasmuch as the barrier depends only on her whim, nothing will be gained. But if she refuses to have intercourse with one whom she dearly loves, not out of coyness but through allegiance to a moral value which is a real value to her, the potential of their love must mount behind the barrier she interposes, and the accumulated energy may enable them to overcome the obstacles to marriage which at first seemed insuperable.

Young people whose love meets a check turn rightly to overcome the obstacles in the external world, for the morality of young people is necessarily a matter of group conscience. With older people under similar circumstances the love energy heaped up by the barrier may turn within instead of to the overcoming of external obstacles. A change is thus brought about in their psychological attitude. Their love impels them to revise their moral standard. Older people who have really accepted and assimilated the collective morality of their group may by the help of this heaped-up potential sometimes achieve a more conscious morality through overcoming the psychological obstacles and inertia within themselves.

This is a difficult task, for the separation of the individual from the dominance of the group is a slow process. In the infancy of the race the group is everything, the individual nothing. Only gradually and very partially throughout the evolution of the human race has individuality been gained. Each human being, too, is in childhood merely a member of a group, with no individual rights or attainments of his own. Gradually, as he grows up he separates himself from the parents and from the group. But this separation is in the majority of cases only partial. His parents can give him independence in certain ways, but in the last analysis a young man has to gain his own independence. For if his parents give it to him he is beholden to them for this gift and so is not independent. Inevitably a time comes when he must take for himself the right to be himself, or must remain forever dependent on the conventional rules and regulations of his family or of society. In particular, the right to possess his own instinct cannot be given to him. He has to take it for himself, and that usually in defiance of the prohibition of his own parents or of society.

Through the sanctioned rite of marriage an attempt to domesticate the sexual instinct has been made so that it may serve the purposes of mankind. The majority of people make their adaptation to the divine fire within them, and to society without, through this rite. But sexuality is an untamable instinct; it works in a perfectly unregenerate fashion, refusing to be domesticated. Sexual love is a spark of the divine fire implanted in man through which he may find his way to heaven and be identified for the moment with the gods or may be damned eternally, scorched by the fire which he has impiously sought to grasp for himself. This "divine fire" has been carefully damped down in marriage to a glow just sufficient to warm the hearth. Perhaps the right to this spark can be *given* the young by their elders, yet in the old days marriage by capture from a hostile tribe was frequently the only possible way of obtaining a bride, and the custom still persists as a marriage form in many tribes even where marriages are arranged between the man and woman or their families—the actual marriage ceremony is an acted abduction. In America this old form is still hinted at in the custom of pursuing the bridal pair when they leave for their honeymoon. Thus even when the torch is passed on to light a new hearth fire, some hint is given in marriage customs that—with all the sanctioning of Church and community, with all the paternal blessing and the "giving" of the bride—something remains which the young people must steal, must take for themselves against the opposition of the community.

Symbolically these customs relate to the psychological necessity of stealing the right to be adult—separate from the group, individual. This is the "necessary crime." It often occurs in the dreams of those who are about to separate themselves from the group and to become individual. For instance, a woman dreamed that *she found her name flower in a public park. She was delighted, gathered the flower, plant and all, and walked off with it. Immediately she saw park guards bearing down upon her. Her first impulse was to hide her trophy, but, taking courage, she held it aloft like a standard and walked triumphantly out, unmolested by the guards.* This dream indicates that she finds *her* flower — her individuality — growing in the public gardens and takes it. Really she steals it, for the flowers in a park belong to the public, not to individuals. But she recognizes it as her own and dares to take it and make it her standard. In her waking life she must take her own individuality, her own nature, as her standard and act in accordance with it, being guided no longer by rules and conventions.

In myths the acquiring of individuality, of personal autonomy, is always represented as a theft, a stealing of something which the gods have reserved for themselves; for to be individual is to be godlike. Thus we have Adam and Eve stealing the knowledge of good and evil — a knowledge in their case closely linked with the stealing of instinct. The story of Prometheus stealing the divine fire and bringing it to earth has the same motif.

Man's experience of sexual love can perhaps most nearly touch this divine fire, can steal from the gods this supreme gift. But in the myths only the hero was capable of this deed. Many people today, feeling the need of renewal, want such an experience, but they want it for their personal satisfaction. The degenerated spirit of democracy abroad today says, "Why not? Everyone may have everything. (Any boy may be president!) Instinct is for our uses. It does not belong to the group, or to the aristocracy or to the parents: it is ours for the taking." In such a spirit of self-seeking the divine fire cannot be found. The gods withdraw. But the pleasure-loving are often as incapable of recognizing this fact as of seeking for anything except their own pleasure. They are not capable of stealing the Promethean fire, the role of hero is beyond them. They are more like bad boys playing with forbidden pleasure, by which they hope at least to have fireworks on the Fourth of July.

Others are less defiant in their determination to secure the best for themselves. They are more law-abiding in their relation to the powers that be. Yet they are no less determined than the former group to get what they *want*. They take an attitude which seems to say, "We ought to be able to have our love affairs where we need them. It is for our good to be free; let society sanction this for us; or let *some* authority sanction it. Let it be made respectable by a 'good word,' such as 'trial' marriage or 'companionate' marriage; or let it be made of very slight importance, so that to take it may be a peccadillo, not a sin; an error, not a crime; a thing of daring to be boasted about in whispers, to be called 'petting' or 'going the limit,' then no one can be very cross at us or take our actions seriously." This attitude belittles the situation and can only result in making the affair trivial and in keeping the offenders children. No freedom is to be gained by it, no renewing experience of instinct or of life will be found. It is not possible to steal the Promethean fire with the gods looking on and acquiescing in the crime with paternal good nature.

Extramarital relations of women differ in their problems and conditioning according to the status of the individual concerned. First there are the quite young women and girls who often meet their first erotic experience while still in their teens and are called on to determine their attitude to this fundamental problem when their knowledge of life is so limited as to afford them practically no guidance—and this too at an age notorious for its emotional susceptibility. Formerly the girl was most carefully guarded at just this age from the consequences of her enthusiasms and inexperience; today she is too frequently left to her own guidance and her own devices.

The conditions of the second group of women are entirely different. These are the married women for whom marriage has not proved a complete and final solution of their emotional and sexual problems. The frequency of remarriage immediately after divorce witnesses to the prevalence of such situations. A few years ago an immediate remarriage would have ostracized a woman from respectable society; now, except in flagrant cases of infidelity, the new marriage is dismissed with a shrug and the woman is accepted as before. Sometimes, however, a woman in such a situation does not seek divorce but remains in the home of her husband although she is in love with another man. Naturally situations of this kind are either disguised or kept entirely secret, but an intimate scrutiny of the life histories of many married couples in America today reveals the fact that such situations are not uncommon. An average, normal woman may be compelled to recognize that in her inmost heart she is not entirely monandrous, but that a man other than her husband can attract her emotionally and physically—a situation which in the most remote past any moral and respectable woman would have striven to hide from herself at all costs.

The third group is made up of women who have chosen work and an independent career, instead of marriage. During the early years of adult life their attention and energies were occupied with mastering a profession. Not until they reach the middle thirties are they free, as a rule, to turn to the emotional side of life, when it is by no means uncommon for a woman of this type to fall in love. Her problem will be quite different from that of either the young girl or the married woman and her way of solving it, also, must be different from theirs.

During the late teens and early twenties, young people usually experience for the first time emotional involvements which stir them more deeply than the friendships of their childhood. They may recognize this deeper stirring as erotic; or it may seem to them entirely idealistic and not sexual at all. Such complete unconsciousness was perhaps the rule forty or fifty years ago; it is still more common than one might suspect from the modern freedoms of this generation. Nevertheless the absence of restraint in behavior has resulted in a widespread awareness, precocious perhaps, of the sexual element in "young love." The freedom to exchange kisses and caresses produces a situation in which awareness of the physical aspect of the emotion can be aroused, and the openness with which such situations are discussed leads to a further breakdown of barriers. As a natural result of all this, many young people see no reason why they should not follow their impulse to experiment with each other quite freely. Having once overstepped the barriers of conventional behavior, they find themselves in deeper water than they had anticipated and the problem arises, "Where shall the line be drawn?"—and this asked by some who are hardly more than children.

Now, in beginning a relation to each other involving caressing and petting they are simply following the mode of their own generation. Many of them are emotionally quite immature, and kissing and hugging really expresses the character of their love more truly than would a specifically sexual embrace, and in many instances Nature herself steps in and determines for them where the line shall be drawn. Take, for example, the story of her love affair which a girl of fifteen confided to me. She and the boy with whom she was in love had gone to a dance together and in a secluded spot began to embrace each other with increasing excitement. He was staying at her home and begged to be allowed to go to her room that night. They each intended to carry the relation through, being convinced that the intensity of their love justified the extreme step. When the house was quiet, the boy went to her. But then Nature asserted herself. The girl was so sleepy that nothing remained for the boy to do but to go back to bed where he also promptly went to sleep. This, I am sure, is the story of many cases. The young lovers themselves are deceived as to the nature of their own emotions. They think their involvement demands complete sexual expression, for that is the prejudice of the day; in reality the true nature of their love is expressed through affection, through kisses and caresses, which completely satisfy their emotional needs.

Others are not so fortunate. Physically they are mature, even in their teens, and the body stirred by the "childish" kissing may insist and may force them, emotionally immature though they be, to carry the physical relation through to the end. Naturally, the physical act of intercourse cannot have for them any very profound emotional significance, and they are disappointed. This particular embrace to which they had pinned their hopes, expecting through it to experience "heaven itself," fell flat in the living and brought about disillusion. The conclusion drawn is that sexuality is not as important as they thought, it seems rather trivial and insignificant. In her more sober moments the girl may even admit to herself that it is a little disgusting, for girls suffer more than boys from this kind of disillusionment. Sexuality for a woman is more closely linked with her feelings; it is more intimately a part of herself than it is for a man. So it follows that separating herself from her own sexuality and treating it as something apart from herself—an unimportant action indulged in for the stimulus and pleasure of the moment only—results in a hardness which is peculiarly destructive to the girl's values. For a boy to take this attitude is also extremely regrettable, but it does not seem to destroy his specifically masculine values in the same way that it destroys the feminine values of the girl.

After such a disillusioning experience, a girl may well lose her sense of the sacredness of love. She feels that sexuality does not mean much either way, but since men want it, why refuse, if by acquiescing she gains and holds their attention. Through such an attitude she inevitably loses touch completely with the deeper side of her own nature. Sexuality can never be trivial to a woman who is in touch with the feminine principle, the Eros, within. Only by repressing and disregarding her emotions can she accept the embrace of a man who does not profoundly stir her, and if she does accept it, she no longer functions as a woman, but takes her sexuality in masculine fashion. The majority of girls, however, who have fallen into this way of acting are really entirely un-awakened—their emotions are sleeping. Young men are, as a rule, more aware of their own instincts, more mature in physical sexuality than girls of the same age, even though they are as unconscious emotionally. Indeed, the man's physical intensity is often a complete mystery to the girl. "Men put so much energy into lovemaking," a girl once said to me, "I can't think how they do it—they are so intense about it. I only wish they would be quick and get through, so that we can attend to something more interesting."

A girl who allows herself to be guided in this way by the man's desire loses touch more and more with herself. Perhaps she yielded at first to an *idea* of what would bring her happiness. She was disillusioned by the event. She thought that she had ex-perienced all that life had to offer in that field. "The novelists were wrong, there was nothing much to it. But," her reflections would continue, "if that is all there is to life why wait for some-thing more satisfactory, better exploit it for all it is worth." With such an attitude a girl readily goes from petting to pro-miscuity, and by the time she reaches twenty, she may well be completely disillusioned, completely bored with life. She has run through the gamut of sensations—what more has life to offer!

The frequency of this attitude among the younger generation is a real menace in certain groups of society. Young women who are utterly worn out, blasé, done with life before they reach the age of thirty, constitute a social problem of some magnitude. The fact that they have never touched the deeper aspects of ex-perience at all does not occur to them. They snatched at hap-piness—life was to them an orange which they sucked dry—and by twenty or twenty-five they are poor, pitiful little "hard-boiled" babes. They submitted to nothing save their own desires and tried to satisfy themselves on the pleasure principle. And even pleasure failed them.

In the past young people were safeguarded from this particular pitfall through the moral control of society. The decree that physical impulses and desires must be held in check until a marriage contract has been entered into raised the whole question from the level of temporary physical satisfaction to a serious undertaking. If there is not to be a regressive movement of society the increased freedom which the individual enjoys today must be accompanied by a greater, not lesser, sense of personal responsibility.

Among human beings sexuality is not merely a means for propagation and the satisfaction of the generative impulse as it is with animals; it has been largely "made over," appropriated to the service of the emotional and psychological life. On account of this change, it has become the most intimate expression of love, of relatedness, between two human beings. But in the transition from the biological to the psychological sphere there is, as always, a pitfall into which man can only too readily fall—the pitfall of the ego, of personal pleasure and satisfaction. The awakening of psychological consciousness and the power to control nature open the door for the selfish exploitation of a realm of life rich in possibilities. Formerly that realm was guarded, first by biological reality, the bearing of children, which imposed an external discipline not to be evaded; and second by social authority with its prohibitions. At the present time, both these external guardians have relaxed their control to a great extent and adventurers seeking freedom, if they are not to fall into pleasure-seeking selfishness with its inevitable disillusion, must find for themselves another no less compelling reality capable of imposing the limits and barriers which alone make possible a further step in development. In the past this reality was masked because men and women were not free and consequently the situation between them had to remain nebulous. But today with the release from external compulsions, they can at last begin to explore the tangled web of emotions and desires which form their relationship. In this way the *nature* of the relationship between them is made conscious and they embark on the new adventure of the spirit.

Those who seek a deeper truth through their love experience

will be guided in their actions by the reality of the actual situation instead of by a desire for a particular kind of physical satisfaction. If the relationship is slight, then intimacies will be correspondingly curbed. If the association is by its very character likely to be of short duration, it is the part of wisdom to avoid indulgence in physical expressions of affection. The younger generation today tends to value physical sexuality as a good in itself. If there is the slightest stirring of erotic feeling, the physical sensations are nursed along — made the most of — the body being forced to function sexually on any and every pretext. Hence the instinctual energy is frittered out. As the Chinese say, "It runs away to the shrimps." This attitude is natural enough in the children of a Puritan ancestry — a compensation perhaps for a code which made sexuality evil in itself.

In other cases a young man and woman may be deeply in love. The intensity of their emotional preoccupation with each other seems to warrant the most intimate physical embrace but before taking this step they would do well to consider most seriously whether their love may not be better expressed through marriage and the formation of a permanent relationship, for this alone can take into account not only the personal aspect of their feeling but also their responsibility as members of society. A scrutiny of the motives which lead to a neglect of this social aspect of the situation will often reveal a sinister *reservatio mentalis* which is like the germ of a fatal disease threatening the security of their love.

If the relationship, important as it is to them emotionally, is lived clandestinely, it will inevitably separate them from their fellows, and lead to an isolation against life itself; for love, when it is anything more than a mutual selfishness on the part of the lovers, brings with it the wish to enter life hand in hand. Hence the strength and depth of their love are best expressed and their permanence most likely to be assured not by snatching at the fulfillment of immediate sexual desire but by seriously attempting to build up a stable relationship. Marriage is the established form for this and it is undoubtedly the ideal toward which young lovers should work. If they do not want to accept the responsibility of marriage, the burden of proof that they have a right to evade it lies on their own shoulders.

In many cases there are external difficulties and obstacles to marriage which seem insuperable. The first romantic love often comes to young people who are still partially or entirely dependent on their parents, for adolescence is prolonged today far beyond the age of physical maturity. If these dependents wish to take upon themselves the privileges of the adult, whether in terms of marriage or in terms of the freedom to carry through a love affair on an adult level, that very desire may become the incentive which enables them to cross the barrier between childhood and maturity and, by facing the difficulties, to win the right to independence. But privileges always involve responsibilities which cannot be shirked with impunity. There is something exceedingly deteriorating to the character in claiming the prerogatives of a state to which one has not grown up. In most primitive tribes the young men are not permitted to marry until they have proved themselves worthy to be considered men, and on this point a civilized society would do well to be guided by the customs of a primitive one.

When the love is genuine there is no need to fear that difficulties will destroy it. On the contrary, an amorphous attraction is often brought to a focus by obstacles, until what was a selfish desire to possess becomes a really heroic power to create. It has frequently happened that a young man who has been willing enough to remain a child and be economically dependent on his father has found through the experience of falling in love the energy to take up the burden of manhood. Thus is love conducive to growth, even as growth increases the capacity to love.

The lovers' own attitude toward the obligations of marriage often gives a clue revealing the true nature of the involvement. The desire for union is the outcome of one of two underlying motives: first an intention, perhaps completely unrecognized, to exploit the situation for pleasure, power and the ego; or second the wish to develop it for values beyond these personal ones. Unfortunately, however, the early signs of these two emotional attitudes are often indistinguishable. For during the "in love" stage, the beloved truly appears as the most coveted prize, the most precious asset, and this enormous value can easily deceive the lovers themselves, their eagerness to seize it appearing as an unselfish aspiration for a spiritual gain even when it is being exploited for pleasure and power. In this latter case the motive is far from being love. It is just at this stage that the lovers' attitude toward the responsibilities of marriage gives the clue to their motive in the relationship; it shows how much they are willing to invest.

Perhaps the greatest advantage of marriage in the case of young people lies in its avowed purpose of permanence. If the lovers live their love through to sexual expression the passion and glamor almost inevitably pass. The urgency arising in this kind of romantic love is nature's way of overcoming the difficulties opposed to physical union; when this is accomplished the urgency recedes. In a state of nature a period of service and discipline follows in the childbearing which usually results. In modern love, if pregnancy is avoided, there is grave danger that the lovers may lose the value of personal development once insured through the discipline of childbearing and rearing. For at the point when the first flush of passion has passed, difficulties arising from differences in temperament usually make their appearance. Personal desires which seemed to coincide during the period of courtship are now found to clash and if there is no external bond between them the lovers may and frequently do part, perhaps in anger, perhaps in an indifference as inexplicable to them as their first infatuation. Each will assert that the other has changed. "He is not the same man I loved." "She is not the woman I thought she was."

This "inexplicable" infatuation and "inexplicable" later indifference witness that the original "falling in love" resulted from a mutual projection of anima and animus onto the loved one. Each was really completely ignorant of the other's true nature, for each saw only the projection of his own soul figure. When the projection was challenged by an assertion of the other's ego, it fell away; the illusion passed and this seemed to be the other's fault. If during this period of disillusion the two were not united by a social bond, there would be nothing to hold them together; the anima and the animus would quite likely be projected immediately to some new object and the search for a magic rightness, for Prince Charming and La Desirée, would begin all over again. The infantile demand for freedom, the wish to remain footloose, would again take possession and the opportunity for development which discipline alone can bring would be lost.

In submitting seriously to marriage, the contracting parties give, as it were, hostages to fate. They are forced to wrestle long and hard with the problems of that stage of disillusion, certain to come, in which the first flare of passion must be transformed into the steady glow of a love based on mutual confidence—a confidence which can be won only by working through difficulties together. To this end they are pledged by openly taken vows and when misunderstandings arise something beyond their own personal inclination holds them together and forces them to struggle for the development of real understanding. They are no longer at liberty to regard temporary disappointment in each other as a reason for throwing over the relationship. They have undertaken a joint enterprise, which everything decent within them demands shall be worked out through a willed determination to make their marriage as satisfactory as possible. If the emotional involvement is serious enough to warrant complete sexual expression between lovers, then the relationship between them must be considered of sufficient importance to be held to and worked on even when the love recedes from consciousness for a time. By *work on the relationship* I do not mean the acceptance of a *conventional* marriage with a mere smoothing over of difficulties, but something far more conscious and active.

Through the complete determination, unswervingly held, to work through difficulties, their anima or animus begins to be disciplined

—a basic necessity for the development of any inner morality. No great psychological development is possible if the love life remains on a casual or cheap level. Development of love cannot take place until the individual is so deeply in earnest that he is willing to invest his full strength in working out to the last possible step the actual relationship in which his sexuality is involved.

The love of young people probably finds its best opportunity to flourish and develop through marriage, but they must choose for themselves. If they decide not to marry or decide to postpone marriage, the decision for or against sexual expression of their love must also be theirs. If they decide for it, the outcome will depend on their own feeling and on their ability to take the responsibility of the decision on their own shoulders. Older people may feel it a pity for the young to experiment in a way which, as the saying is, takes the bloom off their youth and which may leave them hard and disillusioned, but it is not the elders' problem to deal with. The lovers have to decide. There is no judge competent to decide for them, for this whole problem is part of a cultural movement whose final outcome lies obscured in the future. It is so complex, so individual, and the state of morality today is so chaotic that no sweeping generalization can possibly cover the whole case. One fact, however, remains as true today as ever: if an individual's attitude toward his own actions is trivial, he reduces his experience of his personal life to a trivial level and he becomes disillusioned and indifferent. To take life solely on the pleasure principle leads inevitably to satiety and boredom. Man is not just a pleasure-seeking—that is, a degenerate—animal; he is also a living spirit and can find satisfaction in life only through the devotion of all his powers to some end beyond his own personal pleasure. This end beyond themselves is, for young people as for others, to be found through taking their love more, not less, seriously.

The temptation to take emotional involvements lightly is very general, even among the unmarried, and among those who have a previous emotional obligation the temptation is almost overwhelming. When a married woman is attracted to another man, she hopes that an attitude of nonchalance will deprive the situation of its seriousness and minimize any disturbing effects. Both men and women tend instinctively to protect themselves in this way from involvements which they fear may demand more than they are prepared to give, and which, in particular, may upset the *status quo*. The attitude is rather like the proverbial ostrich psychology, which hopes by looking away to keep unpleasant facts in check. But as in the case of the ostrich whose action only exposes him to danger which he might otherwise avoid, so it is also with humans; a deliberate assumption of unconsciousness leaves one vulnerable at every weakest spot. And what, in any case, is the use of such an attitude? If the involvement is really slight, no harm will be done by looking at it squarely. On the contrary, such frankness will bring its reward in release from anxiety and in consequent freedom to act entirely naturally and without restraint. If the affair is serious, no good will be accomplished by pushing it out of sight into the unconscious where its movements, its actions and effects cannot even be observed until they break forth in some compulsive and unadapted fashion. If there is serious mischief afoot, it is just as well to be informed about it.

Ostrich psychology, nevertheless, is very general. It is frequently manifested by unmarried women, while to the married woman who finds herself becoming involved with a man other than her husband, it is an almost irresistible temptation. To conceal from herself the extent of her own emotional involvement is a foolhardy action which a woman of common sense could hardly justify to herself if she were fully aware of what she was doing. But so great is the desire of most people to avoid personal responsibility and throw the onus of their actions onto fate or circumstance that consciousness in such a situation is the exception, not the rule. One cannot but suspect, however, that a woman who remains willfully unconscious is actuated by an unrecognized desire to snatch at a satisfaction in opposition to the moral code she consciously holds and to evade the conflict which awareness of these opposing trends in herself would precipitate. She is pledged to fidelity. The law holds this pledge to refer to her actions, but all old-fashioned women and the more serious-minded of progressive women consider it as applying not only to their overt acts but also to their feelings. Not a few modern people take their marriage vows, it is true, with a secret understanding that if either of them should cease to love the other and fall in love with someone else he would be free to follow his impulses. Yet a marriage contract nonetheless implies an intention toward permanence in the relationship and faithfulness toward the partner.

In many cases, however, where marriage was entered into as a matter of expediency and in some even where there was originally a real emotional involvement, with the passing of the years a sort of blight settles over the couple. The woman had hoped that marriage would make everything right, that she would never be bored again. Yet she finds as time goes on that her husband has lost his glamor, has become an everyday person who is always at hand and whose characteristics, personal and mental, have through their very familiarity ceased to beguile her. Her marriage has become unutterably dull; convention rules at every point. Even the intimate side of the marriage has fallen into a routine in which all spontaneity withers. This is the brief story of many marriages which ultimately end in the divorce courts.

Not uncommonly a woman whose marriage has grown humdrum becomes aware that romance and adventure are calling to her from next door. The man who attracts her may be suffering from a similar eclipse in his marriage. He begins to pay her attentions, to tell her that she is unappreciated, that even though she insists on looking and acting "middle-aged," she is still young and fascinating. At first she is merely flattered and pleased. Then something in her awakens in response to the new interest. She regains her lost good looks and begins to find her dull life growing fresh and interesting. If she is the average woman with a sense of responsibility toward her marriage and her children she generally takes the new situation lightly. At first it probably is light and in many cases undoubtedly remains so — a pleasant interlude causing a few sighs but no broken hearts. But occasionally the emotional tone changes, and the man from next door comes to occupy a larger part of her conscious thoughts and of her daydreams. Most women at this point, becoming aware of danger, attempt to control the situation by an act of will. Certain warnings from within tell them that their involvement threatens to become serious, so, by persuading themselves that it is quite trivial and insignificant, at the most a harmless flirtation, they try to curb the emotional fever before it gets out of hand.

In other cases, a more violent disruption of the *status quo* takes place through the woman's sudden infatuation. She may find herself precipitated into the depths of an emotional upheaval of which she had never dreamed herself capable. The newcomer perhaps awakens in her possibilities of love which her relationship with her husband had left completely untouched. In such a case she *cannot* take lightly the experience of her own nature which has come to her, possibly quite unsought, sweeping her off her feet, or at any rate threatening to do so. The temptation is to give up her marriage at no matter what cost. In the heat of such an infatuation the claims of husband and children lose all perspective and appear as burdens from which she must free herself, regardless of the damage to them. Or, on the contrary, the conflicting claims of the old love which is reinforced by her sense of duty, and of the new one which offers undreamed-of fulfillment, may cause such turmoil and distress that they threaten to break her altogether.

The problem of marriage and divorce and wandering emotional attachments is so difficult and complex that one would much prefer not to speak of it at all. But it is so common that at least an attempt must be made to clarify it. For any woman may find herself caught in the turmoil of these problems of the twentieth century despite her real integrity, when she will be torn by the conflicting claims upon her loyalty and devotion. It is not my place to pronounce on the relative morality of one course of action as over against another. Each woman must solve her life problem in her own way.

Divorce is the most popular expedient resorted to today in such cases. But it is not very unusual for the woman to accept her friend as lover, either with or without the knowledge of her husband. The effect on the impressionable minds of children who are witnesses of these situations in the personal lives of their parents must inevitably be far-reaching. A generation is growing up whose innate sense of the sanctity and permanence of marriage is profoundly modified through their early experience of divorce and of broken families.

The demand that a woman must love, honor and obey her husband all her life is a corollary to the belief in the lifelong permanence of marriage which forms the basis of the old morality. This moral code assumes tacitly that these pledges are entirely within her own power to keep. In many sections of society this assumption is being questioned today, and threatens to be completely overthrown as it becomes more openly recognized that love is by no means entirely under the personal or conscious control of the individual. In the past if the ideal of conjugal love could not be maintained in practice, at least the conventional form was upheld, and the substitution of duty for love and the suppression of any wandering affections were often successfully accomplished. It is not so easy in these present days to repress the errant emotions. The solidarity of the conventional assumption which supported that attitude has been broken into from many directions. Women who hold themselves entirely bound by their marriage vows may not consider a little flirting or even a little philandering with a third party wrong or undesirable, let alone dangerous. But such flirting may, perhaps, prove to be an entering wedge. Repression, to be reliable, has to be complete; a flexible attitude in such matters may well frustrate the attempt to remain unconscious. But if the modern woman indulges in a freedom of action which the old code prohibited while she yet maintains her conscious adherence to the letter of the old morality, a more extensive repression of instinct and the emotions will be necessary to prevent collapse. This repression goes even deeper than the one it replaces, and accounts for the fact that many women who indulge today in a freedom of action which would have been impossible a generation ago do not find themselves stirred by it. The truth is, something within them becomes cold and aloof, for instinct withdraws before an exposure which is not warranted by the emotional situation. This deeper repression may be very marked in young people brought up with ultramodern ideas and habits in regard to sexual matters. If children are taught, by example if not by precept, that modesty or any reserve is necessarily mere prudishness, and if sexual matters are discussed before them and explained in rational terms as if love were merely a matter of anatomy and physiology, they are likely to suffer, when they grow up, from a very severe repression of instinct and emotion. Women brought up in this way may fail to be touched in their deeper natures even when they believe themselves to be in love, and marriage itself may not be able to bridge the gap which divides their rational, materialistic, conscious attitude from instinct and love, which always need a shadowed place for their unfolding and which emerge from the hidden realm of the unconscious only when the conscious attitude is friendly. Such people are protected from conscious conflict by their repressions.

But a married woman who is neither completely out of touch with her own emotions through such a repression nor completely rationalistic and hard-boiled is not protected from the possibility of a severe moral conflict if she departs from the conventional code of honor. If she is not prepared to face this conflict arising from the challenge *within herself* of the old moral code, she had best be careful how she disregards the minutiae of the old conventional rule of behavior. But there are today hundreds of women who want to eat their cake and have it too. They want the security which the old marriage code gave, but they also want the pleasure of excitement which the freer conventions of the day permit. For those whose marriage holds deep and growing emotional satisfaction and for those, also, who have discovered the secret of building conscious relationships, it may be possible to hold these two attitudes simultaneously. Others undoubtedly "get by" through the repression of the more dynamic elements in their natures. There remain, however, a few who do not fall into either of these two groups. For them the desire to obtain what seem the advantages of both epochs proves their undoing. They have tried to straddle the split between two cultural attitudes; they have not held to the safety and restriction of the past, nor have they committed themselves to the uncertainties and promise of the future, and their position becomes increasingly untenable as the new culture pulls away from the old.

The chief emphasis of the new way is on loyalty to the feelings. From every side one hears such dicta as: "Where love is, there is the true marriage," "If love has gone, marriage is no longer binding," and the like. If personal feelings were the *only* consideration, one wonders why have marriage at all? The exclusive emphasis on inclination is as one-sided as the old assumption that the wife could by an act of will give her love where duty said she ought. But marriage has two sides, not one only, and if any deeper and more individual morality is to be worked out in our day to replace the conventional one now tottering to its fall, both aspects must be taken into consideration.

In the past the collective aspect of marriage was emphasized to the exclusion of more personal considerations. Today personal considerations take precedence. Many people even jump to the conclusion that because love has gone the whole marriage is destroyed, forgetting entirely any other obligation. A more responsible attitude to the social aspect of marriage would make the necessity for divorce much rarer than it is at present even where one of the partners has fallen in love with a third party. For marriage is more than a sanction for sexual love; it is a partnership, a joint enterprise, which cannot be abandoned lightly on account of a change of mood, however compelling and significant. The children, if there are any, constitute a liability and responsibility which cannot be lightly discounted. Even if love has gone elsewhere a more serious attitude would perhaps enable husband and wife to pull together until port is reached and their children can then be launched.

A woman in such a position is under a peculiarly binding obligation to try to work out an understanding relation with her husband. For although the deeper love between them may be dead, there still remains the possibility of comradeship and loyalty. Through a recognition of all aspects of the situation they may be able to maintain a working relationship, worthwhile both for themselves and the children. The values of the home will, needless to say, be less than they would if husband and wife were in deeper harmony, but at least by such an arrangement it may be possible to make a place of emotional security for the children. The greatest devotion and self-discipline will, however, be required if they elect to follow such a difficult path.

A woman who tries to carry her emotional life with one hand and her marriage with the other will find herself constantly under the necessity of the most rigid self-discipline if she is to prevent a clash between the two. Her loyalties to husband and lover may well conflict within herself and misunderstandings will always threaten from without. It is a perilous path to tread, and one hardly to be recommended. No woman can possibly help slipping over a precipice unless she can find a means to keep in very close touch with the principle of relatedness within herself and can constantly purify her own motives. For as soon as she puts out her hand to make use of the position of power in which she finds herself, she will inevitably be caught in jealousies and possessiveness. One fact, however, stands out clearly, namely that if she faces the situation with courage and a conscious attempt to do her best she will develop psychologically. Perhaps this is all that life is meant to accomplish.

Marriage fosters and develops the ability to take a responsible attitude toward a willed relationship. This is a very valuable achievement but it has the disadvantage that it tends to over-emphasize the conventional side of relationship, the "shoulds" and the "oughts" of living with a partner. These obligations are in contrast to a "free" relationship. For instance, the wife feels herself under an obligation to bring "good feeling" to the daily happenings; the mistress does not need to do so in the same way. The wife must hide her deeper reactions so as to be cheerful before the children, she is under a necessity to meet her guests with the correct manner, to be interested in the interests of her husband, whether she is really interested or not—every wife could multiply the list of "oughts" indefinitely. The attempt to fulfill these obligations to the exclusion of all else will eventually stultify life, even though the discipline they entail is valuable.

In this way the conventional aspect of marriage curbs the irrational romantic longings which are an essential part of free and spontaneous life. In a relation of obligation it may be im-possible for some people to satisfy the deeper instinctual side of their natures because this necessarily belongs to the unfettered outdoors and so they seek for its satisfaction in a freer relation-ship. Society has recognized that undomesticated desires of this kind are stronger in artistic and creative people than they are in more rational, stable and conventional folk and, in matters of love, judges them by more liberal standards. The artist him-self may recognize that at times his muse comes to him in the guise of love so that in following his love he is also seeking the truth which it is his business to express. But the ordinary individual cannot excuse himself for following his love by urging the claims of creative genius. Perhaps, however, certain men and women, entirely unaware of what they are doing, do become involved in an erotic relation outside of marriage through a similar need to seek for the irrational life-giving spirit. They instinctively feel the need for a relation where the deeper Eros—the principle or spirit of psychic relatedness—shall rule and convention be secondary. But instead of submitting to the laws of Eros they try to overcome the deadening effects of habit by snatching at forbidden pleasures, because they are unaware that the wandering of their erotic interest results from the call of a life urge within themselves.

If a real psychological progress is to be made, a state of culture (and modern marriage represents a high state of culture evolved through many centuries of discipline) may be superseded only by higher culture, which entails further discipline, a discipline applied to a part of the psyche which the former state had not domesticated, had perhaps only enslaved. The new culture must rest on a broader basis than the old. The old culture taught that in marriage the emotions must be servant to the will — "It is a wife's duty to love her husband." The new culture is directed toward domesticating these emotions and disciplining them in order that each man and woman may make an individual relation to the Eros truth, a relation, that is, to the feminine *principle of relatedness* — as deep and binding as is the relation to the Logos truth, the masculine *principle of fact and logic.*

But a married woman who determines to enter on a course of action which involves an emotional relation to a man other than her husband inevitably faces a very difficult task. It is one in which she cannot plan ahead how she will act, what she will do, or what attitude she will take at any given moment. At the best she can only hope to find a way through the tangle by the most complete devotion to the dual truth of love and duty. Egotism and self-seeking can so easily hide under the cloak of high-mindedness that the most unremitting watchfulness is necessary if she is not to be self-deceived as to her own motives. The greatest good will on the part of each of the three people concerned can hardly avoid some of the many pitfalls which inevitably beset them all.

Yet, if the difficulties can be weathered, even out of such a threatened disaster, something of value may be salvaged, some good may come. At the least, the marriage will not die through stagnation; this outcome will be prevented through the very necessity to struggle with the problems created by so fundamental a threat. Protest and rebellion against the old, formalized ways have brought renaissance in many realms of life. Love is no exception. By courageously meeting the threat to their relationship which a new love has brought, men and women have often found that their marriage was more vital, more binding emotionally, than they had conceived possible.

Indeed, there are probably few three-cornered situations which could not be worked through to a satisfactory conclusion provided —and it is a big proviso—that there is a sincere desire on the part of each to find the truth and to give it first place. If a right adjustment is to be reached no fundamental need of any of the three can be disregarded or excluded by egotistic or possessive demands of one of the others. To give *each* what really belongs there, not to snatch something from one to give to the other, these are the fundamental tasks which a divided love and duty impose.

The central person in such a group of three has special problems and difficulties. If this one is the wife, she seems to hold the position of power, with both the men depending on her. This seeming power may easily call down upon her the reproaches and demands of each of the others. She will learn perhaps to her surprise and chagrin that the position of power becomes in actual fact the position of service. "He that is greatest among you let him be servant." Such relations cannot thrive without being a spiritual quest, a religious experience, even while being the fulfillment of love. They must be a sort of religious enterprise or observance of a rite. They ought to be understood as the manifestation of a will beyond the personal that seeks *its* ends.

When we come to examine the extramarital love relations of the self-supporting professional woman, we find again a different set of considerations. A woman of this group, at or nearing middle life, is naturally much freer than either of the other two of whom we have spoken. In matters of personal relationships she is a law unto herself. She owes no obedience to parent or husband in return for financial support for she is self-supporting. She is presumably a responsible human being who is well accustomed to making her own decisions. Her standard of morality is her own concern. If she experiences love at an age when most married women have finished childbearing, and at a time when her own life and career are, perhaps, most exacting, the problem which faces her is necessarily very different from that of a younger woman. She already has many obligations which she cannot, without careful consideration, lay down in order to marry; she is probably established in a home of her own with relationships, perhaps, of years' standing. To marry would mean a tremendous upheaval. Furthermore, if the man she falls in love with is about her own age, he also will hardly have gone so far through life without incurring responsibilities and relationships which do not leave him entirely free either to start a new menage. There are, needless to say, not a few instances where women who are no longer in their first youth do meet suitable men who are free to marry; and this solution, in line with collective custom and opinion, is for many of them the solution of choice, but for others such a relatively easy solution is not available, or does not satisfy the special requirements of the individual case.

The problem which arises is unlike that of the quite young woman and also differs from that of the married woman. The difference in the latter case rests not only on the absence of those social and family obligations which marriage entails, but also on the relation to her own instinct which the unmarried woman has been compelled to develop on account of the absence of sexual expression. A woman who marries young does not know anything of the burden which years of unfulfilled instinct, long years of unbroken chastity, bring. This has been the problem of the unmarried woman.

In former times women, as well as men, have taken vows of celibacy for religious pruposes, their experience of the love of God replacing in their lives the need for human love. But the modern woman has given up love and marriage not for the love of God but for a "cause," namely for the sake of psychological and economic independence. To some women, especially to the pioneers in the feminist movement, the "cause" really took the place of the old religious object, and they were content to devote themselves body and soul to it. Today professional women, many of them, choose that course in life, not at all from religious motives, but as a means of earning their living and finding scope for their abilities. Work undertaken for these reasons cannot satisfy their emotional needs. They do not give themselves "body and soul" to their work, and so both heart and body call out for satisfaction. Many women attempt to solve the problem by repression of their need. In a sense this is the easy way. Personal habit acquired through the years, the pressure of conventional opinion and her own sense of what is morally right, all support the unmarried woman in her attempt to satisfy her life without overstepping the bounds of propriety. Probably the majority of professional women in English-speaking countries still choose this road.

So long as she does not fall in love, it is naturally easier for a woman to continue along this path. If, however, one particular man comes to hold a deep and increasing emotional importance for her, the struggle for repression will become more and more difficult. Looked at from the biological point of view, it is abnormal for either men or woman to pass the whole of their lives in unbroken continence. The effects of continued chastity on the woman's physical and psychological development have been variously estimated by different observers, but there is no doubt that they are profound and far-reaching. Through the process of civilization the sexual instinct has become so closely linked with the emotions that complete sexual abstinence usually implies also the repression of *love*. This is more harmful than the absence of physical sexuality itself. Indeed, to take sexuality without love for the sake of physical relief would be more detrimental psychologically to most women than complete continence.

A deeply buried sense of inferiority and unfulfillment usually haunts the woman who has been preoccupied with her profession and has not given her love to any human being. She seeks to compensate for her feeling of inadequacy in love with achievements in the world, hoping that the recognition she will receive will take the place of the love she has missed. She therefore augments the importance of her work and uses it to increase her own sense of importance and to convince herself that her life is worthwhile. This compulsive devotion gives her work drive, but also tinges it with a partisan quality which is bound to arouse opposition and distrust, increasing in turn the barrier between the woman and any possible love experience. The attempt to meet the problem of sexual repression by work only accentuates the difficulties of her situation.

Instead of repressing her sexual instinct and thrusting it down into the unconscious, the woman may take her lack of fulfillment as a conscious problem, not shirking the pain which it causes. She will then reap the benefit of her struggles in increased psychological development, even though she still remains unfulfilled in her love life.

In the present day a very considerable and perhaps increasing number of women meet this problem by accepting love and sexual relations as a part of their lives, even though they are not married. All these cannot be classed together for their motives and their problems vary enormously. There are, for instance, those who are promiscuous and make their livelihood through the exercise of their charms. Others, by no means promiscuous, who may, indeed, be faithful to one man over a long period, are nevertheless partly or entirely supported by their lovers. The self-supporting women, whose problems I am discussing here, are entirely distinct from these two classes.

The relation between a man and woman who are not married and who are financially independent of each other has an entirely different basis from either marriage or a non-marital relation in which the woman is supported by the man. In either of the latter cases considerations of duty and expediency enter into the relation in a way which inevitably clouds and complicates the situation between them. The woman whose love relation is with a man who is not her husband and from whom she receives neither money nor support has a relationship which is based on the emotional involvement between them and on that alone. The relationship is not enhanced through the advantages, nor hindered through the disadvantages, of the social and conventional bonds of matrimony and money considerations. In such a simple, uncomplicated situation the faithfulness of the two to each other depends solely on the integrity of their feeling and the sense of "aliveness" which they experience through their association. An extramarital relationship—hampered though it is because of its unconventionality, the necessity to sacrifice the desire for children, the discretion and secrecy usually necessary, and the limitation of their time together—can yet, in certain respects, reach a freedom which is often conspicuously absent from the otherwise more complete relation of marriage.

An association of this character is governed by the laws of the feminine principle. The masculine laws of contract, which rule marriage to such a large extent, have been sidestepped. In this kind of relation there is no *obligation* on the part of the woman to perform certain duties, to accede to certain demands from the man, or to tolerate approaches not in accordance with her own desire—just because she is his *wife*.

If money and social position are her own, won by her own efforts, there can be no question of obligation on this score. The relationship is therefore cleared of a good deal which tends to mask the emotional realities in more conventional situations. Sometimes this freedom from limitations is welcomed as an easy way of escaping the responsibilities of marriage and the demands of accepted morality. In such a case love will inevitably degenerate into mere pleasure-seeking. Others, who give their allegiance to the feminine principle, the Eros principle of relatedness which stands above all personal wishes, count the cherishing of love as more important than either the conventional code or their own personal satisfaction. These will develop psychological maturity and refinement, for submission to the Eros law entails discipline just as much as does submission to the conventional code.

The recognition of her own need for such submission, which comes to her through the nature and intensity of her own inner experience, is the chief consideration which makes a woman of high moral character and integrity feel justified in undertaking an extramarital relation. When a woman of this type falls seriously in love, she is compelled to recognize the importance to herself of the emotions aroused within her. This, in turn, forces her to take issue with the conventional code of morals and to attempt to find for herself a way of acting which shall be *right* to her. To deny her love would be tantamount to the murder of part of herself, yet all her ancestral preconceptions warn her of the sinfulness of giving expression to her love, and this in spite of an intellectual opinion that independent women are free to act as they please.

To some the conflict seems to be insoluble. They cannot solve it and so they do nothing about it, which is to say that they continue to *act* as convention dictates, but do not really sacrifice the hope or prevent themselves from dallying with the desire for satisfaction. If a woman acts in this way she destroys a vital spark both in the situation and in herself. She probably becomes neurotic—the fate of all who carry for years an unsolved and unaccepted moral problem—and the relation suffers too. The relationship degenerates into a convulsive attempt to hold the man at all costs; all real love is choked by such an attitude. Strange to relate there are instances where, instead of releasing himself and seeking life elsewhere, the man submits to this treatment. I know of one instance where a woman has kept a man dangling after her for twenty years. She is now hopelessly neurotic, while he still doggedly follows her with attentions and gifts. He is no nearer the fulfillment of his hopes than he was in the beginning when she admitted that she loved him, but for some moral scruple would not marry him nor, also for moral reasons, enter into an extramarital relation with him. They are still suspended in a state of indecision which keeps them remote from life.

Other women with greater inner integrity realize that they cannot hold the issue in suspension indefinitely without suffering from a psychic split which necessarily brings neurosis. They feel it is essential to resolve the conflict. Some realize that for them obedience to the moral law is more important than their love. If this decision is reached after a really profound self-examination, the woman will perhaps be able to sacrifice this particular love and reassimilate it—a very different matter from repression. This course of action will bring pain, for she cannot avoid the suffering arising from her voluntary renunciation, but she will not break down psychologically and become neurotic as a result of her sacrifice. Indeed, the psychological effect which the decision has is most valuable as evidence of the motives which led to her choice of action. The insight obtainable from the outcome can be utilized as a guide to action if the decision can, at first, be made tentatively or temporarily. For example, a woman with such a problem before her may make a choice according to her best judgment, and then, instead of doing anything final or irrevocable, go forward cautiously in line with the decision she feels to be right. If she then finds that she is falling into neurosis (that her love for the man cannot be reassimilated after she chooses to follow the moral ruling; or that she is filled with misgivings and remorse upon deciding to overstep the conventions) she will be compelled to recognize either that her decision was contrary to the laws of her being or that her motives were not what she thought them. If her decision is based upon an unconscious complex, she will not escape the penalty of living according to ideas which do not express her real or essential nature. Indeed, one of the chief values which can be derived from such a fundamental conflict in life is that it challenges the basic assumptions on which an individual's character and conduct are built.

The majority of my readers probably concede, in theory at

least, that women who are self-supporting are at liberty to run their private lives as they please, provided that they injure no one and preserve an outward aspect of respectability. This concession implies that if they behave decorously in public, do not obtrude their love affairs in an objectionable fashion, safeguard themselves adequately both from scandal and from pregnancy, the rest is their own affair; the exact degree of intimacy between themselves and their men friends is no one's business.

A woman who is actuated by such a standard usually finds that she makes a direct relation to men in a way which undercuts those social reserves which make an almost complete barrier around more conventional women and the men they meet. If she has really freed herself from the bonds and restrictions of the old social order, not only in her intellectual opinions but in a deeper way, she will find she possesses a talisman which enables her in all the simplest contacts of daily life to touch the real man behind the social mask. This unmasking of the human being opens the way for a deeper, more vital, more dynamic reality to come to light. The door has been opened and life may well come in. Life, however, tends to be an embarrassing visitor in a well-organized, thoroughly domesticated and controlled existence, in which Routine and Efficiency may have ruled unchallenged for years.

Thus, for the woman who has discarded the conventional way of guiding herself in emotional situations, the problem of what new guide shall be hers will arise almost immediately. If she attempts to let the affair "run along" and guide itself, she will soon find herself in difficulties, for her own desires and the man's can hardly be expected to tally at every point. Some standard, some impersonal principle to which they can both consent to subordinate their personal wishes, must be found if they are not to become involved in a struggle for domination.

If she is deeply in love, the acceptance and expression of her love feelings will be of very great importance to the woman. Accepting her feelings, however, is by no means so simple and easy as it sounds, for their acceptance will probably demand from her considerable changes in her whole attitude to life and to her own work. Her love will take more of her time than she could have anticipated; she will not only spend many hours with her lover, but an even larger share of her time will be occupied with musings and dreams and emotions which, before she fell in love, she would unhesitatingly have condemned as idleness and a waste of time. In compensation for this, she is likely to find that her energy, both physical and mental, increases almost proportionately with the development of her emotional life. Although her energies increase she may find, however, that her desire for work and her interest in her career have not remained as absorbing as before. A subtle change may well come over the whole cast of her personality. In a hardly perceptible fashion, the emphasis on life's value has shifted. The change is one against which she may struggle vainly. To her conscious, rational, intellectual attitude, it is absurd that her personal love life should interfere with her work. It does not affect a man in that way, why should it affect her? It is not that she works less efficiently; she may, indeed, work better in one sense, but in some strange fashion she has lost drive, she cannot go at things with the old vehemence and passion. It is probably that her colleagues like her all the better for the softness, the more feminine grace, which begin to replace the old keenness and hardness, but to herself she may seem to be suffering a grave loss. Why should her love for a man rob her of her own ambition? If she were getting the advantages of marriage it might be possible to accept the change in herself with good grace, because then she would have certain obvious advantages to set against her losses; furthermore, she would have a husband to fight for her the battles she can no longer fight in the old way for herself. Yet, there is hardly a woman but will admit that she would not go back for anything in the world. Life has gained too much from the warmth which has come not only into the relation to the one man, but into all her relationships.

In addition to this change in her professional attitude, the woman who accepts love has other burdens to carry. In the old days she was free. Now she is bound by an invisible thread to a man over whom she herself exerts no control; his comings and goings affect her in her most vulnerable place, but he is bound to her by no tie which the world recognizes. If he is seriously ill, she may not go to him. If he leaves her in anger, she cannot follow to be reconciled with him. These limitations are constantly in the background of her mind. They have an unseen influence on many of her reactions. They may make her soft, so that she spoils him, humors him, tries to keep him in a good temper. If she is a more conscious person, the knowledge of her dependence urges her on to establish a bond of *real* understanding and acceptance, each of the other, which may hold firm in case of difficulty and which will be strong enough to act as an adequate substitute for the duty and *bond* of matrimony. But all the same, anxieties and emotional preoccupations of this kind are necessarily often in the background of her mind. There is also another anxiety which she cannot entirely escape. However careful she may be in her use of contraceptives she can never be entirely free from the haunting dread of pregnancy, a dread which is harder to bear because one part of her nature longs for that which she is nonetheless compelled to fear. She has been obliged to renounce by a conscious decision the fulfillment of motherhood; yet there is hardly to be found a woman who does not long to bear children for the man whom she loves. She may realize that it is impossible, she may recognize the necessity to carry her own burdens and not to complicate life by seeking fulfillment for herself in bringing into the world a child whose existence would be shadowed from its beginning. She may recognize all these things and give them conscious assent, and still find herself haunted by thoughts and dreams of a child which should be hers and his. This desire will have to be sacrificed over and over again, for it has its roots in her biological nature. The desire for children is closely related to another insistent desire whose denial often causes her repeated battles with herself. This is the desire to make of her love and her relation to her lover an open and accepted social situation. The necessity to keep secret a matter of great emotional importance has an isolating effect which is hard to bear. The married woman speaks of her husband whenever the conversation requires it. She neither obtrudes him into talk nor is she obliged to exclude his name. In contrast to this, the unmarried woman must be ever on her guard not to give away to society in general the secret of her liaison. She is lucky if she can allow her immediate circle to guess at her intimacy, even if she does not take them specifically into her confidence, for complete silence on the subject means an isolation of the relationship from all contact with the rest of her environment, resulting in a certain quality of unreality. It is lived so exclusively, is touched so little by other realities, that it becomes almost like a dream life lived in an enchanted castle. This, at least, is the danger of having to guard it too closely from contact with everyday concerns.

All these matters make a love relation carried on outside of the conventional mode a serious undertaking. To be sure, it is not always regarded in this way. Some women are unable to face the problems involved in a serious relationship and prefer to shut their eyes to these considerations. They try to take their emotion lightly and to hide from themselves the deeper issues which are involved. Their attitude is one of pleasure-seeking. They hope by evading the responsibilities of marriage and by ignoring any others to be able to gain the satisfaction and emoluments of love without paying the price which life exacts. If the woman does not take her end of the affair seriously she cannot expect the man to do so, and the relation is not likely to go very deep or to last very long. In this way life, regardless of her attempt to escape without paying, exacts its price, either in heartache and regret or in the gradual deterioration of personality which overcomes any woman who has to seek one affair after another, each a little less vital, a little more sordid than the last one.

If the woman is more serious-minded and less preoccupied with immediate pleasure satisfaction, she will summon courage to face the problems and difficulties of her relationship. When she does this she will be obliged first of all to ask herself again whether her love feelings are of sufficient intensity and importance to warrant the sacrifices which their indulgence will demand. She may be willing to undertake even the burdens of an extramarital relationship, great though they undoubtedly are, if she really loves deeply. The next problem she will have to face consists in keeping the relation to the man clear and direct. He too must submit to his own feeling, and this allegiance she may have to demand from him, for he cannot be allowed to take merely for pleasurable satisfaction what, potentially at least, costs her dear. If his attitude in this matter of allegiance to feeling-truth is irresponsible, it will inevitably break up the relationship.

In a marriage the man's contribution to the cost of the love relation is in terms of his support of the home and in his care for those things which have to do with the man's world; he puts at the woman's disposal his physical strength, his knowledge of business, his ability to judge in many matters, and his sworn allegiance. But in a liaison he cannot offer these services. The service that *is* required of him is in terms of understanding. Here he has to learn the laws of relationship — how to act in accordance with the requirements of feeling instead of in accordance only with thought. These things are hard for the man to grant. For instance, he cherishes his freedom and hates to be bound. If he is unexpectedly rushed at business, he resents the woman's demand to let her know that he cannot come to her at the appointed hour. He much prefers just to stay away and to come back when he has more leisure. It never occurs to him that if she is expecting him and he does not come she will be not only disappointed but sick with anxiety before the evening is over—more especially if the social situation is such that it is inadvisable to telephone and ask what has detained him.

If the man persists in doing such things, the woman is compelled to make an issue of it, for unless he gives his allegiance to the feeling-relation she cannot go on. The relationship between them, created through their love for each other, is almost like a separate entity with its own rights and obligations which cannot be disregarded except at the risk of destroying their love. It is very valuable to think of the relationship in this way, as an entity in itself. To do so helps to differentiate between personal or egotistic demands and the needs and requirements of the relationship itself, for these two considerations are not the same. In marriage, *the marriage* and *the home* have largely attained to the position of a value *per se;* there it is an institution which holds supreme place as object of allegiance. In an extramarital relation there is no equivalent "institution"; *psychological relatedness* is the paramount value whose reality must be progressively delimited and before whose claims all personal considerations must be set aside.

But because their relationship is not a social one, that is, one which is recognized by society and upheld by external forms and customs, because it has not, as it were, a material form such as is made by "the home" with all that implies, the emphasis falls on the reality of their *feeling*. It is to this feeling or love aspect of their relation that their unflinching loyalty must be given. This belongs to the principle of Eros.

From the foregoing discussion it becomes clear that the opportunity arises in extramarital relations, perhaps more than in any others, for developing a relationship between a man and a woman based purely on Eros. The discipline such relations impose is not the discipline of external laws or happenings. It is the discipline of the voluntary sacrifice of personal desires—whether for security or children or social approval—and the submission of these most human wishes to the exigencies of love and to the feeling realities based on love.

Through this sort of experience a woman can outgrow the childish morality dependent on blind obedience to an authoritative code and find instead a no less compelling law gradually developing within her to which she must give her unflinching adherence. This law, which is based on the validity of Eros truth or feeling reality, subserves the transformation of blind instinctive attraction into a conscious realization of life and love. It may seem to the onlooker that the woman is interpreting the Eros law quite arbitrarily in any given situation. The skeptic may say that she manipulates it to her own advantage. But this is not necessarily the case, for if her conduct and motives are observed more closely, it may be found that she regulates her life by loyalty to a new morality which is no less binding in its demands than the old. If it allows of, indeed compels, individual interpretation appropriate to the individual case, it is binding in a way that the old was not. Under the old law many people found that they could, by observing the letter, evade its more fundamental implications, but never can a woman who has given her allegiance to the new morality avoid the utmost implication of its dictates; the outer written law has been replaced by an inner spiritual one. Whoever thinks this inner law easy let him keep its dictates one day!

Under the old moral order a woman could give apparent obedience and beyond that steal whatever satisfaction she might, but under the law of the new morality she cannot so easily evade her moral conflict. The gap between the old order and the new — between her obligation to convention and her loyalty to the living experience of her love — must be bridged by a personal, more fundamental contact with the principles of love and truth, Eros and Logos, which govern her from within. A woman of no great integrity who can readily assume the liberty which the present day allows in the behavior of men and women toward each other may be able to remain blind to the whole significance of this transition through taking love and sexuality lightly with a trivial or frivolous attitude. A slender tightrope may suffice to carry a lightweight over a difficulty. A more considerable person would need to build a more substantial bridge.

Through an analysis of the unconscious some women have found a means to reconcile the opposing loyalties to the moral code and to love. But this reconciliation is necessarily individual. Each must seek her own reconciliations; there is no formula which points out a general way of solution. The problems are general in that they are very frequently to be met with among the more sophisticated groups of society today and, indeed, are not unknown in many simpler circles also. But the solution is still a matter of individual experiment. Each woman is compelled to take her own problem and to seek to reconcile in her life the warring loyalties and claims—a reconciliation which is no longer only a theoretical question but a burning necessity. She has to find her individual way through or be destroyed by the conflict. In the last analysis no theory will serve for a woman of deep integrity. She craves for and must find a practical way of life. She may not be able to *see* her way at all, she may feel herself to be quite blind. All she can do is to be loyal to the life within her, to safeguard as far as possible the interests of others and beyond that to decide each incident as she can, giving due weight with the best of her ability to all the factors concerned. It is quite possible that she will find herself utterly helpless to safeguard adequately the interests of others. If she is married the interests of her husband and children cannot be completely protected; and in any case the interest of her lover, the possibility of offspring and the demands of conventional morality form conflicting obligations which cannot all be met in any *entirely* satisfactory way. Yet if she does not meet her obligations she naturally feels guilty. It is of no use for her to throw off her responsibility and say, "I could not help it, life was too difficult for me." These obligations are fundamental ones, and if any one of them is disregarded, she fails in her duty. This from one point of view is sin. Quite aside from a moral judgment, it is *blackness*. The realization of this fact is a burden which she herself must carry, and for which she must be prepared to pay. Indeed, she may find as life goes on that the price exacted is more than she can pay alone; others, and those her nearest and dearest, may also have to pay. Yet this impasse is not of her own making, it is part of life. By taking the alternative course she would not have escaped a perhaps deeper blackness and a still heavier penalty both for herself and those close to her. The alternative ways are in stark opposition, but if she works patiently through her difficulties, trusting herself to life, living each day as fully and as truly as possible, seeking through sincerity of *living* to solve the problem of their opposition, she may perhaps find a way to a reconciliation.

Certain women who have attempted in this simple and sincere fashion to live their lives to the best of their ability see on looking back over the period of perplexity and blindness how each step which they took fitted into a whole, invisible at the time, but making at the end a complete and amazingly apt solution of what seemed at the time to be an impasse. The end result, had it been consciously worked out, might have been called *clever*. Inasmuch as it evolved of itself out of a facing of the difficulties, it can only be called clever in the same sense as can a vine which finds its way through a stone wall into the light. The solution which grows up from the unconscious in this way has just that kind of cleverness which the vine shows in finding its way to sunlight. The human being, by a sincere and unconditional facing of the situation, develops psychologically and gradually overgrows the barrier. In his commentary on *The Secret of the Golden Flower*, Jung writes, ". . .all the. . .most important problems of life are fundamentally insoluble. They must be so, because they express the necessary polarity inherent in every self-regulating system. They can never be solved, but only outgrown." [1] The difficulties of a moral problem such as the one we have been considering in this chapter do not disappear, the

---

1 *Alchemical Studies*, par. 18.

opposing claims for allegiance remain, but the woman herself grows, and perhaps outgrows the obstacle, through the development of her own relation to the Eros and the Logos within herself. As a result, her relation to others involved with her grows and deepens also and a new level of mutual confidence is attained in which a degree of harmony, even among the opposing loyalties, at last becomes possible.

A solution of this character must inevitably be individual, unique, it cannot be used as a precedent by others. The time has not yet come, and for all we know it may never come, when a rule of conduct can be promulgated to guide men and women through the intricacies of extramarital love relations. Such affairs are and must remain the personal responsibility of each man and woman who essays them. The dangers both psychological and social are necessary safeguards to prevent mankind from recklessly leaving the trodden path and perhaps slipping back into an animal-like indulgence in instinct, wherein would be lost that specifically human achievement—the capacity to love with the heart and the soul, as well as with the body.

8. Autumn and Winter

After the harvest and the fruits of the summer's work have been garnered there comes to nature in the late autumn one last brilliant flare of beauty in a generous outpouring of color and vividness. The leaves do not just fade and wither and fall. Their death and decay are inevitable, but before they pass and are swept away into winter and death, they put on their most gorgeous dress in a final riot of life. In the lives of men and women a similar transformation is sometimes seen. The springtime of promise has been left behind with the early thirties; the heat and burden of the day which characterized the middle period of life have been laid aside; and as the first forewarnings of coming winter make themselves felt, an autumn of brilliance and beauty may be ushered in. The psychological energies which in earlier life were fully occupied with the inner and the outer adaptation are released from that arduous task and shine forth in pure beauty. This is the period of culture—the time of the beginning of wisdom.

The beauty of autumn and the acceptance of winter are possible in the vegetable world because plants follow their own natural laws completely, fulfilling their destiny in accordance with the changing seasons. But through the partial control of nature which man has achieved this complete following of natural law has been interfered with among human beings. And so the natural law of "downgoing," which inevitably follows every building up, overtakes many people unprepared. Old age and death can be warded off, perhaps for years, but in the long run even the strongest must meet them. For some this experience spells frustration, the gradual decay of all they have built up, with inescapable defeat as the end. For others, however, later middle life and old age do not spell defeat, but instead bring the opportunity for gathering in and enjoying the fruits of a life well spent. This outcome can only be achieved by those who have passed, at least in some measure, through the three stages of psychological development previously discussed.

The peasant woman, in the naive stage, accepts old age as a part of the natural course of life. When the time comes to resign her duties to her daughter she withdraws to the chimney corner and accepts the inevitable with the stoic patience of unconsciousness. She labored throughout her life because work was there to be done; she bore her children and cared for her man, because that is the way of nature for woman. Then when old age comes she leaves the tasks, which have grown too heavy for her feeble strength, to others who replace her. Such a woman has very little sense of a personal ego. Life is the great reality and life goes on; its tasks must be accomplished regardless of who lives or dies.

A sophisticated woman, more conscious than a peasant, is aware of *herself* as an entity separate from the collective life of family and community which goes on regardless of the individual lives of each generation. Her consciousness of a personal ego brings new problems in regard to old age and death. The woman who is aware of *herself*, who has lived under the guidance of the ego principle, seeking consciously to gain power over nature and the external world and to satisfy her personal desires, cannot accept old age in the simple matter-of-fact way which is so characteristic of unsophisticated folk. For her the inevitable downgoing can be little else than a tragedy.

The Chinese say that when the moon is nearly full, at her brightest, at that moment the power of darkness is strongest within her—the dark power is most heaped up. Darkness over-comes not the crescent, in whom the light power seems weak, but the full moon in whom it appears to be strong. So, many a woman who has lived fully and well and has found success and satisfaction in life feels the "light" to be entirely dominant within her. She has learned to exploit and control herself and her environment through the exercise and discipline of her ego; she is considered by her world an established and well-balanced person. Her management of her life—her whole life philosophy— appears to have vindicated itself; the success it has brought seems to show that her attitude was the right one to take. Yet in the moment when she reaches the zenith of her power, the shadow appears on the wall—*Mene, mene!*—strength, power, dominance are doomed; the time of the shadow and of the downgoing has come. If her life is not to sink in tragedy and defeat, some new guide or principle whose very nature shall be different from the old is needed for the coming phase of life whose opening is heralded in this sinister way.

The coming of autumn brings to light in pitiless fashion the weakness and deficiency of life lived under the rule of the ego. A woman who has developed to a stage of greater consciousness will welcome this phase of experience as gladly as any of the preceding ones. But one who has neglected this culture of her psyche and developed only ego values must inevitably view old age as a period of defeat and will be at a loss how to meet it.

Most people, if they allow themselves to think about the subject at all, look forward to this period with fear and appre-hension. The curtailments of activity and of the natural powers seem to hold no prospects but those of frustration and failure. The increasing limitations arising from loss of physical strength and the failing powers of the body, the slowing up of the mental processes, the waning of sexuality, the loss of friends—these things loom up in the future like a series of battles with defeat as their outcome.

No wonder that the majority of people put all their effort

into warding off old age as long as possible. By "keeping young," and binding themselves to their children and to their work activities, they hope to hold on to life as they have known it during the years of their strength. Defeat will certainly come in the end, "but," they argue, "perhaps the period of ignominious submission to old age can be curtailed, perhaps death may even release us before the dreaded time of helplessness overtakes us." But in trying to keep up with the times and with the younger generation, they really lag behind their own generation, they fail to keep up with their own time.

Surely this is the attitude of an adolescent people. In the childhood of humanity, and among some primitive peoples today, there is to be found a method, shocking to us, of solving this problem. The old, when they can no longer bear children, work or go to war are quietly put out of the way, and this is a fate which overtakes them while they are still young in years, for primitive people age early. Thus the problem of old age is very largely avoided. Among modern western peoples it is evaded as far as possible by the prolongation of youth. But up to the beginning of the twentieth century, old people had a recognized place in the family circle. Today this is no longer so. Each individual man and woman must now face old age, with its difficulties and necessary adjustments, for himself.

In the Gothic period later life was reserved for religious developments; after the heat and struggle of the day were over, men and women turned their attention to making their peace with God through prayer and meditation. Culture of the inner life was recognized as the specific task of the old, more especially if their active years had been passed entirely in secular occupations. For instance, Roger de Montgomery, cousin of William the Conqueror and First Lord of the Marches, consolidated Norman rule in Western England, created and maintained an armed frontier between Britain and Wales, organized the building of castles and forts along the Welsh border, and acted as baron or overlord of the surrounding country. When he began to grow old and his thoughts turned to the future, he realized that the time had come for him to leave the scene of his worldly activities and make his peace with heaven. He surrendered his duties to a successor and himself built an abbey and monastery which he entered as a monk. There he passed the evening of his days in cultivating the inner values for whose nurture he had found scant time in his youth.

Among Oriental peoples, older in culture than Western races, the period of old age is looked upon as the age of wisdom and the old are revered in a way quite foreign to us. To them the attainment of old age and its values is an aim toward which the best men and women direct their energies even while they are still young. It is not unusual for a statesman or a man of affairs to give up his worldly position at the height of his power in order to follow the disciplined life of the yogi. Such men believe that only after the strenuous periods of youth and middle life have been lived to the uttermost can an individual acquire the wisdom of the inner life through which the whole meaning of his existence can be realized. In the Orient these values are naturally couched in religious terms, as they were in Europe during the Gothic period. For us the culture of the inner life is no less of the spirit even though we choose to express the values and significances which it carries not in religious but in psychological terms.

Here Jung is again the pioneer and leader. The psychoanalytic schools of Freud and Adler help the individual to the adaptation of youth whereby he may satisfy his needs for power and instinct gratification. The middle-aged or elderly applicant for analysis is discouraged by these schools because he has already passed the period of life in which an extension of activity in the outer world could be expected to solve his problem. Jung, however in studying the problems of older people, followed the movement of the psyche as it pursues its course of retrenchment in matters of the outer world and found that to the individual this is far from being pure loss but, on the contrary, is the necessary condition of bringing to birth a spiritual creation, no less important than the creations belonging to the earlier periods of life. He writes: "The afternoon of life is just as full of meaning as the morning; only, its meaning and purpose are different. Man has two aims: the first is the natural aim, the begetting of children and the business of protecting the brood; to this belongs the acquisition of money and social position. When this aim has been reached a new phase begins: the cultural aim." [1]

Old age can no longer be considered a tribal problem, no longer a family problem, no longer a religious problem taken into account by society at large through the maintenance of retreats and monasteries. The problem of old age is today principally a personal one which each individual must solve for himself and its solution is hardly to be hoped for if preparation for it is delayed too long.

"Man masters these changes in nature by noting their regularity and marking off the passage of time accordingly. In this way order and clarity appear in the apparently chaotic changes of the seasons, and man is able to adjust himself in advance to the demands of the different times." [2] So wrote a Chinese sage some three thousand years ago. The changes of the seasons we have learned to recognize and to prepare for. The farmer sows his corn in expectation of the warm weather which will be coming. The householder lays in his winter's supply of coal before the heat of the summer has gone. We recognize the sequence of the year and adapt ourselves to its demands *beforehand*. The changes of the seasons which represent a life cycle are less generally recognized and many people fail to make adequate preparation for them in advance. Yet "the moving finger writes and having writ moves on"; the downgoing is inevitable. Each individual wishes to avoid being overwhelmed by the power of this inex-

---

1 *Two Essays on Analytical Psychology*, par. 114.

2 *I Ching*, p. 202.

orable fate; his ability to do so is almost exactly proportionate to the preparation which he has made. "The man who has contemplated death for a long while," runs an old Latin aphorism, "is the one who will meet it without fear."

In certain respects the need for preparation is recognized rather generally. The necessity, for instance, of saving for old age is an acknowledged one. But with certain people there appears to be a curious blind spot in regard to old age. They do not seem to recognize that their days of strength and power to work are limited. They cannot visualize themselves as old. So they continue to live up to, or even beyond, their incomes, being caught by the salesman's slogan "everyone must have," as if they did not realize that more than physical comfort will depend upon the material preparation made for the later years. Serious poverty in old age will almost inevitably frustrate any attempt to achieve the inner developments which should be the chief concern of the autumn of life; and dependence, whether upon children or other members of the family, distorts a relationship which should be increasingly free.

A more conscious realization is needed of the extent to which psychological freedom in old age is dependent on financial independence. If the woman's attitude has been irresponsible and pleasure-seeking, payment will be exacted in her old age in terms of irksome dependence. If, however, the failure to save has not been due to selfishness but has been a risk voluntarily taken in full awareness of the danger it involves, it may not have the devastating results which self-seeking inevitably brings. For instance, if a woman has sacrificed the independence of her old age in order to give her children a better education, a better start in life, and has done it openly, having talked it all over with them and reached an agreement about it, then in her old age she can perhaps accept support from them, as the payment of their debt, without all the emotional involvements and power demands which so often embitter the relation between aged parents and their children.

But all this is only outer preparation to meet the external conditions. An inner preparation is also needed to meet certain other aspects of age. As time goes on, for example, the older woman will find that the body demands more and more care and attention if she is to keep well. When she was younger she could put considerable strain on her physical resources and recover her strength in twenty-four hours. After reaching the age of fifty-five or sixty years this is no longer possible. When she is tired she must rest or pay a disproportionate price in prolonged fatigue. If she is not to be ill, small physical ailments must be taken more seriously than formerly. These facts to be properly met need an inner adjustment as well as an outer one. This readjustment will need to take into account not only the actual disabilities of the moment but the progressive physical deterioration of which they are but the forerunners. They are messengers of death and warn of the coming of the end.

To most people there comes a time as later life approaches when they are compelled to pause and take stock, looking back to estimate their accomplishments and forward to calculate what possibilities still remain. This period is particularly apt to occur at a time when the demands of life suddenly ease up. For the mother it comes when her children leave home to go out into the world, either to college or to homes of their own. It confronts the professional woman when the question of retiring is raised or, in more tragic cases, when she loses her job on account of her age, because a younger and more vigorous woman is wanted in her place.

At such a time the woman, whether professional or domestic, may find herself confronting a blank wall. She looks back on what she has accomplished. The professional woman says to herself, "If only I had put my energy into a marriage, into making for myself a place in the hearts of husband and children, I should not be facing such a cold, meaningless old age!" From the married woman a very similar complaint is heard: "If only

I had not given myself so completely to the children but had put some of my energy into my individual life, I should have something to show for the years—friends and interests to turn to now that the children need me no more and indeed repudiate me as if I were in the way!''

To many a woman, coming to consciousness of her dual nature only at the age of fifty or more, it seems utterly impossible to create anything of value from the years that remain. The sense of having come to the end of the road, the sense of irreparable failure, may be so terrifying and obsessing, so intense and imminent that she can give her attention to nothing else. Depression and insomnia fall upon her. Nothing holds value or significance. It is as though she drops into a bottomless pit. The fact that the rest of the world goes on with its business, apparently blind to the precipice over which all things have fallen for her, only aggravates her condition.

She has come to the period of downgoing and she does not know how to meet it. Western philosophy, based almost exclusively on the idea of progress, has nothing to offer in these circumstances. Any life accomplishment, no matter *what* it may be, however valuable, however complete, loses all its significance when the first poignant realization that all will be swallowed up in extinction and death forces its way into consciousness. For there is no *external* achievement which *by itself* justifies the expenditure of the life energy. Man possesses a spirit as well as a body and because of this no work which is merely temporal can satisfy his conscience. Unless during his life span on earth he has created something which shall transcend time his effort has been in vain.

Most people, however, facing the threat of old age, strive to keep on in the old way as long as possible. They do not revise their attitude, do not change the direction of their effort. Their achievement in the world has not been as great as their intention, and they struggle desperately in the later years to make up its deficiency. A woman whose lifework seems meagre to her (as it always must seem to any but the most self-deceived, especially when compared with the large range of youth's dream) may begin some new undertaking and once again flourish in the glow of expectation. This may go on into extreme old age and death may find her in no more than the "state of promise," with nothing made actual either in the external world or—what is more pathetic—within herself. She is still an adolescent girl, looking forward to accomplishing at some future time that which shall justify her existence.

Some women remain all their lives unconscious that the law of devolution—of downgoing—applies to them. They go on to the end, apparently in complete unawareness of the approach of death. Some of these are women who have passed beyond the state of promise and have actually accomplished something in the world of reality. Their work, which may well be of real value, occupies the whole of their attention, to the exclusion of all considerations of a philosophic nature. They never question the value and importance of their work. It is as if the period of middle life were prolonged indefinitely. The challenge to pause and take stock is never heard by them. When actually old in years, they are still apparently in the full vigor of middle life. They die in harness. I have known at least two women physicians who continued in active practice until the middle eighties, working up to the day of their death as hard as they did at sixty. The period of middle life has been indefinitely prolonged: they never experienced old age. But old age is a part of life, with its own characteristic task—the development of inner or spiritual values.

The woman who has looked exclusively to her motherhood for giving significance to her life is not exempt from a problem similar to that of the professional woman. She too tries to ward off the inevitable termination of a phase which she has erroneously taken as the whole of life by keeping a close hold on her children, seeking year after year, even after they have grown to be adults no longer needing her care, to find her own satisfaction in *their* lives and interests. Under this treatment they either become resentful or lose all capacity for initiative, for this type of mother steals the life opportunity of the younger generation. Her ability to ignore the flight of time is simply amazing. I remember hearing one elderly lady commenting on the marriage of her daughter's friend, on how lovely it was that this "girl," in order to care for her mother, had postponed her marriage for fourteen years, and that now, after the mother's death, the "dear girl" was to be married. When reminded that the "girl" was nearly fifty years old, with the possibility of motherhood gone forever, the old lady replied, "Well, she will always be a girl to me," implying that, since *she* did not think of the younger woman as aging, time must have stood still for her also. By this attitude she had barricaded herself against the necessity of adapting to the passage of time; by considering her daughters and their friends as "only girls," she exonerated herself from recognizing that they were being denied the right to live their lives fully, and justified both herself and the whole generation of "the mothers" in demanding the exclusive service and attention of the daughters.

In other cases the maternal role may be carried on into old age in a rather different fashion. As grandmother the older woman may again find an outlet for her maternal feelings. Many children have a relation of deep affection and close understanding with their grandmothers. Among American Indians and often in India and China also, the grandmothers are the recognized teachers. The older woman plays the part of the "Wise One" who imparts, not factual knowledge but the wisdom of the race embodied in custom, dealing particularly with religious observance and with the relations of human beings.

If a woman is to attain to full psychological development, she needs to experience, at least in some measure, many phases of life. It is not sufficient that she develop one side of her psyche, whether this be the love aspect or the work aspect. The whole range of her psychical potentialities must be experienced if she is to come to anything approaching full consciousness. Thus for the all-around development of her capacities for growth, a woman must live on both the Eros side and the Logos side of life.

In actual practice, however, most women find that they are compelled to give themselves almost exclusively to that experience which they have chosen as their *metier*. The woman whose best — or at all events active — years are devoted to a love relationship with a man and to the bearing and rearing of a family experiences life as wife and as mother. With few exceptions, such a woman cannot, no matter how talented she may be, at the same time devote herself to practicing a profession. Her relations with women, too, are in most cases left in an exceedingly undifferentiated state. Her chief concern is relationship with her husband; her friends are secondary. The professional woman, on the other hand, gives her attention and her energy not only to following her individual bent, creating directly in the world, but also to developing the ability to stand alone and to rely on herself in all the ordinary emergencies of life. To her, women friends are exceedingly important and she probably devotes a good deal of thought and care to cultivating her relationships with them. But her relations to men remain undeveloped; she does not learn how to function as woman to a man, and the maternal side of her nature has only a vicarious play in relation to someone else's children or to her subordinates in work. Consequently, when a woman reaches the age of forty-five or fifty she is very apt to become aware of a lack in herself, corresponding to the lack in her too one-sided life.

In other cases consciousness of her one-sidedness is forced upon her through the natural termination of her chosen adaptation. The mother, when her children grow up and leave her, is heard to lament, "No one needs me any more." With no consciousness of any value in life than in being needed by someone else, she may well find herself on the edge of a precipice. She sorely needs to develop individual values and her relation to the Logos. The business woman who has devoted her life to those values which have been neglected by the married woman, having reached the peak of her achievement, also finds that life has grown stale. No longer can she nourish herself on success. Some experience is needed which will give her emotional satisfaction and a chance to develop her Eros values.

Even among naive middle-aged women who are exceedingly unconscious of what is happening to them and not at all aware of the significance of their own actions, these life needs may be seen to be working themselves out. It is by no means rare for a woman whose children have grown up to engage herself, either from choice or necessity, in some kind of work in the world. Sometimes these women succeed; more often they find themselves unable to compete successfully with younger, more enterprising and better trained women. If they could recognize the subjective aspect of their adventure they would be content with a very modest external success, for their chief interest would then quite rightly be turned to the under side where the cultural effect of their undertaking upon themselves would become apparent. In the same way middle-aged professional women may seek a romantic adventure because of their own sense of need and loss, or may be forced into one through an unexpected attraction to a man. With them too the subjective aspect is more important than the objective one. Marriage at such an age is quite unlike the typical marriage of young people and indeed may be excluded by the circumstances of the case, and the bearing of children is either out of the question or may be considered inadvisable. But as *subjective experience* such a love affair, late though it is, is of the utmost value and importance, for through it the professional woman may establish an entirely new contact with the feminine values within herself, may experience the joy and the pain of loving another more than herself and of submitting to a law of her own nature which goes its way entirely regardless of the ego values she has spent her life in building up.

Thus there is opened to her a second life, lived in miniature as it were, but capable nonetheless of carrying the opportunity for psychological growth which she missed through her former one-sidedness. A woman who has in this way experienced both sides of her own nature shows, as old age approaches, a warmth and maturity resembling the red and gold of autumn. Her experience of love makes her humanly accessible, while the discipline she has undergone through work in the world gives strength to her character and balance to her judgments.

Around the age of sixty or thereabouts it not infrequently happens that thoughts turn involuntarily to the past, and memories of situations of long ago arise of themselves with surprising vividness, compelling attention. It is almost as if one is driven against one's will to relive the past. When about to fall asleep, perhaps, the older woman (the same is true of men) finds herself back in her youth in some situation in which, she now realizes, she acted in a very unadapted way. She spoke unkindly without realizing the effect of her words, though now it is only too clear how cruel they were. Or she acted impulsively or egotistically with most unfortunate results. These memories come with all the vividness of unconscious fantasy and may repeat themselves at intervals until she finally manages to lay the ghost by repression, or perhaps by penitence. But then another similar incident comes forward out of the shadows and confronts her, and again she tries to lay the ghost, only to find that this painful memory is replaced by a third or fourth incident of similar nature, until she begins to feel herself hounded by her long forgotten misdeeds. If now instead of trying to get rid of these importunate ghosts she could summon the courage to face them and explore what these incidents had in common, it is probable that she would find that they actually do have a common denominator. It may be that in each case she unconsciously spoke or acted without realizing that she was hurting another's feelings; or possibly her motive was the need to dominate, or she was jealous; or possibly a hidden dishonesty lurked beneath her action which she never realized was more than a chance incident of no account. But now when she is obliged to realize that such chance incidents were frequently repeated, she must recognize that she *was* fundamentally lacking in honesty or concern for another's rights or feelings, probably because she wanted her own way at whatever cost to others. And so the review of her life forced upon her by her unwilled fantasies will bring her face to face with her dark side, her shadow, and now at last in her old age she will be in a position to deal with the problem fundamentally instead of merely trying to excuse or repent of the separate incidents which are only symptoms of the underlying problem. In this way, even though she is in her sixties, an opportunity for psychological growth is offered to her.

A woman who was dying of cancer once said to me: "What shall I do about my sins?" She was evidently greatly distressed over just such happenings as we have been considering. I replied "Accept them." Then seeing that she did not understand I went on, "Have you learned more from your sins or more from your good deeds?" She thought for along time and then said, "From my sins." Is this perhaps a hint at least of one meaning of evil? Evil that is not redeemed by understanding, by consciousness, is of course only evil, but perhaps the old saying, "Good may be the final end of ill," is not just the sentimental optimism of a Pollyanna. If the recognition of one's failures leads one to the assimilation of the shadow, and to acceptance of that dark other self who lurks in the background, one may thereby come nearer to becoming a whole person, a true individuality.

The approach of old age brings with it a gradual deterioration of the body itself. A woman must face the loss of many of the characteristics of youth which have been among her chief assets. Not only will her strength and elasticity diminish as the years go by, but her complexion and figure will lose their youthful beauty. Because of the great value set on feminine beauty, this aspect of the loss of youth is of far greater moment to women than to men. A man may be seriously hampered by losing his youthful vigor, but few men are seriously concerned when the color of their complexion changes or wrinkles replace the smooth contours of youth.

It has been said that in youth a woman's good looks depend on her natural charms, but that after she passes forty it is her own fault if she is not beautiful, for after forty a woman's beauty depends much less than formerly on physical features and far more on her character and disposition. She is beautiful or ugly according to the kind of spirit that looks out of her eyes; she attracts or repels by the kindliness or bad temper which are expressed by the lines round her mouth. In other words it is her essential "being" that counts rather than the accidents of her physical makeup.

The dark principle, as the Chinese call it, gains the balance of power at the turning point of middle life, and claims recognition not only from the one-sided, but also from those who have sought to give due weight to both sides of life. These more balanced people too must find a way of adapting to the limitations imposed by age. For them, however, the emphasis has already been shifted from the outer to the inner world, on account of their increased *self*-consciousness, so that they cannot be dismayed to the same extent by external changes and limitations. In certain respects the unavoidable physical changes hold considerable compensations, the release from the pressure of outer necessity giving freedom for occupation with the inner world. For instance, the loss of her moon-cycle relieves a woman of a recurrent problem in adaptation which the unevenness of her temperament during the sexual period imposed upon her. Again, release from the urgency of youth leaves her free to sense life in a more introverted fashion. She has shot her bolt and success or failure no longer matters to her with the same intensity as it did when she was still in the arena of life. She is content to leave others to try out their strength, while she occupies herself with the problems which are the special concern of her own epoch.

This sense of the increasing freedom of older life does not always develop spontaneously. It needs to be consciously sought. There comes to most people, for instance, a day when they are forcibly reminded that their tenure of possession is transitory. Possessions, whether land, money or other valuables, must pass on to the next generation. "Things," material objects, have a duration in time which is so long in comparison to the life of man that the impermanence of human life cannot fail, at some hour, to come before every thinking person with startling effect. Life and death! The one so temporary, the other so long in duration! The recognition of this basic fact of life makes possible a very different attitude, not only in relation to material possessions but also to emotional and psychological values, whether these are one's own or other people's. One cannot live through a long life without catching a glimpse of the inevitability of change, even in those things which at the time of their flowering gave the most complete illusion of permanence. For example, an intellectual conviction which seemed, at the time it held sway, eternal in its rightness soon faded and was replaced by another; the emotional conviction of permanence born of being in love also faded quickly or slowly and was in its turn supplanted by realization of such things an understanding of the impermanence of human nature in the *psychological* realm no less than in the physical may be reached.

Yet something forbids us to stop there! Much that once seemed permanent proves to be impermanent. The very qualities by which we have reassured ourselves of our immortality are often the most transitory. And yet even so the idea of a life which shall pass beyond death remains firmly planted in human speculation. Whether this belief is an illusion or the premonition of a truth, we do not know. All we can say is that the life energy which came out of the unknown expands during youth and middle age, then draws together once more and during old age gradually withdraws itself from the outer world, finally sinking again beyond our ken.

This indrawing of attention is very characteristic of old age. The period of strength passes. The period of service goes by. In middle life the woman is needed, her energy and resourcefulness are drawn upon by those around her. But when she grows old, she is no longer needed. The recognition of this fact gradually forces itself upon her. She needs other people now more than they need her. The tables are turned; whereas formerly she was strong, now she is weak. The recognition of her own powerlessness to serve may well leave a sense of emptiness which makes life seem no longer worth living. Some means must be found for traversing this empty space in the midst of which she asks herself anew, "What is the goal of life?"

We have spoken already of the medieval baron who became a monk, of the Oriental statesman who becomes a yogi. These men follow a "rule," they enter an established school, they do as many others are doing. They seek for inner values by a recognized road, through an accepted religious practice. In our day no such school exists, no such custom is established among us, even the necessity of developing the inner life during the declining years is not generally recognized. If individual men and women are to seek for inner values which shall bring them to a conscious understanding and acceptance of the significance of life in its downgoing as well as in its expansion, they must tread a lonely path, must function as pioneers—and that at a time of life when pioneering initiative is at its lowest ebb.

As people grow older, their contact with the primary realities of life tends to become more and more remote. Especially is this the case with the well-to-do. Their food is prepared for them, their only task is to eat it; their homes are kept by someone else, even their clothes and personal belongings are under the care of a trusted servant or devoted daughter.

All this means that the elderly depend increasingly on other people for interest and amusement. Much of the satisfaction available to younger people through actual contact with what may be called the *primary* duties of life is denied older people, either through their real physical helplessness or, a condition perhaps commoner, through their own lack of understanding of their needs. For many older people relegate to others the routine of daily life which they are quite capable of performing for themselves. "But," they say, "why should I do this when I can well afford to pay to have it done by someone else?" This argument would be valid if there were something of greater value which they could do in their all-too-leisure time.

If freedom from domestic duties leaves the elderly free only to sit in bored idleness until the next mealtime comes around, the value of this release is at best questionable. Even menial tasks performed in the service of life are capable of giving a sense of satisfaction entirely unknown to those who have been waited upon all their lives. The duties of daily living, relegated to others at a time when they themselves were occupied in more strenuous and exacting work, would serve in the leisure of old age to save them from falling into a kind of vacuum. But it does not always occur to them that to be occupied even with simple tasks would be better than to remain idle.

Another factor in the situation which older people rarely appreciate is that their own idleness throws a burden onto those on whom they depend for their entertainment and occupation, as well as for all vital contact with life, even though they may be financially independent and have a home of their own. For instance if Grandma is asked to her daughter's house, the party begins for the older woman only when she actually arrives, while the daughter has had to fit into her busy life all the additional preparation which may be necessary. The younger woman with her many duties does not need anything more to fill her time, but seemingly must carry the larger share of work; the older woman, whose day is empty except for the bright spot of the evening's visit, too often must wait for the "party," instead of sharing in the preparations which might occupy and interest her. The daughter naturally feels diffident about asking an older woman to do for her small services which perhaps she as a child did for her mother. The older woman on her part hesitates to offer help, realizing that as she grows older she cannot do as much as formerly for she tires more easily and any task takes her a much longer time to perform. Discrepancies of this kind are to a certain extent inevitable. But perhaps the inequalities might be reduced if they were recognized more consciously.

The amount of work an older woman undertakes will have to be gradually diminished, but there is no reason why she need be burdened with hours upon hours of utter idleness. As age advances longer periods will be needed for rest and in extreme old age strength may fail for any but the directly personal tasks of caring for herself and taking sufficient daily exercise. But in the period preceding this final stage, there may well be years when life's work is over and yet some measure of strength and a need for occupation and interest remain. During this period a woman will be far happier if she can make for herself a routine of small tasks to give interest and occupation for several hours every day. Through the simple hand-tasks needed for daily life, some degree of the peasant's close contact with nature may be regained even by those who through education and culture have cut themselves off from the primitive realities of life.

Today a call "back to nature" is heard. This call can be followed in a right way or in a wrong way. [3] If in the heyday of life we drop our culture with its complexities and responsibilities and retire to a lonely place to rusticate we almost inevitably lose our conscious values. The experiment has been tried more than once in America, as at Brook Farm and in the current hippie communes; but the problems of the world cannot be solved by leaving the world. However, in the later years of life the situation is changed. The external world with its insistent demand for adaptation no longer claims so large a share of attention; the moral problems which clamored for solution in earlier years lose something of their urgency. Instead death makes

---

3 Cf. Jung, *Two Essays on Analytical Psychology*, pars. 258-259.

its presence felt. The increasing strength of the powers of the earth — darkness, decay and downgoing — force themselves upon the old. At such a time a return to the simple realities ·which every peasant knows may bring, even to the more sophisticated, an understanding of the meaning of life not to be found in books.

For the light of the conscious personality grows up from the depths of the unconscious animal, the bodily existence. The light of consciousness will at death pass from our ken by that same road on which it arose. At times the spark of the spirit seems to have departed even before death from the very old, leaving the body to continue an almost exclusively vegetative life. Always as age advances attention is progressively withdrawn from the outer world. The field of consciousness narrows down little by little until for an old woman only those things which are close at hand retain any power to catch her attention. In earlier life a similar withdrawal of attention from the world is sometimes experienced during a serious illness. To the onlookers the patient seems to be unconscious. But should she recover she can perhaps tell of experiences so vivid and intense that they blotted out the outer world. It may even be that during her stupor she resented the simplest demands for adaptation because of the interruption to the subjective happening which was claiming at the moment her exclusive attention.

The old rarely come back to tell us of their experiences during the period of withdrawal from the world. But I knew one case where an old lady passed through a long period of senile melancholia in which she was quite apathetic. During this time she seemed to onlookers to have passed into a state of blank forgetfulness as if her mind, indeed her psyche, were undergoing a slow process of decay. But this was not the case; she recovered her faculties before her death; her mind became clear and she explained that during the period of withdrawal from the external world she had been going through a prolonged subjective experience which resulted in a fundamental change in her attitude to the world. Her world philosophy had been re-created.

This case is unusual because we have an account of the subjective happening. I am not sure that it is unusual as an occurrence. It is quite possible that during the long periods of helplessness or even the pronounced apathy of the old, some profound inner change may be taking place which, if we could but be aware of it, would justify in our eyes the months or years of extreme old age which we are too ready to consider as nothing but a burden and loss. For the value of the last fifteen or twenty years of life lies in the opportunity they give to acquire a more subjective attitude. Only through such inturning of the attention is it possible to assimilate the experiences of the earlier years and gain a release from the activities and demands of the world.

In the case cited above, this change of attitude came about without any conscious intention on the woman's part. The moral problems resulting from the divergence between her ideals and the actual experiences presented to her by life had not been consciously grappled with. She had identified herself with her ideals, repressing all other facts, and had thus left the conflict unsolved. Then the indrawing of the life forces occurring in the course of nature brought about a change which occurred in this case without the cooperation of the individual. The period of later life can, however, be deliberately planned for and utilized in an endeavor to meet and solve problems and conflicts for which the activities of earlier life left little time. Through such a willed attempt, each individual man and woman today can seek for himself the development of his inner life which in other ages was supplied through religious retreats. By turning his attention away from the world, he can consciously participate in the movement of the life energy within himself. If his task is truly accomplished, he is ready to die when the time comes. Viewed from the outside this is all we know. The man who has prepared for death by living fully, both in the objective world and on the subjective plane, dies without struggle and without regret.

We spoke above of the recognition which comes to most people in face of death of the futility of any external accomplishment whatsoever. All creations in the world will pass—they cannot endure—and even before they crumble away, their human creator has gone we know not where. But when in later life the attention is withdrawn from the external world it may be that the life-energy gathers itself together for its last and most significant creative act. The human being *himself* becomes the recipient of his own life energy. He is liberated from identification with the outer world. He is free, as Whitman sings, "with the delicious near-by freedom of death" and like a free man can devote himself to the final task of his life which is—to use Jung's phrase—the *achievement* of Death.

9. Psychological Relationship

In each successive generation, while some are seeking worldly success, others are concerned with the problem of *inner* culture and *inner* development. These men seek for a value by which they may be lifted from the level of ego and body desires to a more fully human and spiritual plane.

As far back as we can trace the history of what men have thought and felt, the sense of a value above personal considerations can be perceived to be acting as a powerful motive in man's life. This suprapersonal value is the subject of many of the ancient books which have survived the centuries, and the images and pictographs of gods and pre-gods left by the earliest man are evidences of its influence. Whenever this value has been differentiated, man has tended to express it in a symbol or in a god — which is also in a certain sense a symbol, for those inner forces which we sense only, without either knowing or comprehending them, are generally concretized. This is so even in the present day. The idea of the "ether" was just such a concretization. Until as late as the beginning of the present century, it was believed that a hypothetical substance of a very tenuous nature, "a pure air, a pure element," permeated the whole of space. This concept was really a symbol. Naive man, less aware than the modern scientist of what he was doing, created, or perhaps we should say *perceived*, gods—symbols of the psychological and physical laws revealed through his experiences. Through his experiments in the outer world, man came upon the symbol of the ether; through his inner experience he perceived the symbol of God. But just as the concept of the ether held more of truth than was at first realized, so the symbol of God held truth greater than any living man knew. It has been essential to man's psychological development and we make a mistake to discard it prematurely. But we, like the scientists, should keep always before us that essential "as if" which alone protects the user of a symbol from falling into superstition. The scientist said, "It is 'as if' there were an invisible substance—ether." The psychologist would say, "It is 'as if' there were gods and demons and ghosts."

Every man who consciously strives to relate himself to God brings about a development in the concept of God. A gradual evolution of God may be traced through the centuries, taking place side by side with the evolution of human culture and civilization. It is apparent in the Old Testament where the jealous and terrible Jahweh changes to the more spiritual God revealed in the writings of the later prophets. With the Greeks the primitive animal gods gradually became the cultured Olympians whose animal origin was still evidenced by the emblems they bore. For Zeus was once "that old one-foot" the serpent; Athena, the owl; Dionysus, the bull.

In history, especially that of the Jews and the Greeks, may be seen the change which occurs when a whole culture is developed in relation to the suprapersonal value which God represents. But when a generation arises which does not relate itself to God, then God retrogresses. Many scientists today, for example, hold a concept of God far more concrete and less psychologically evolved than that of the wise men of old, less evolved even than that of the wise men of such primitive tribes as the North American Indians—for the God they deny is still their concept of God, to whom they refuse the grace of their hypothetical "as if." Indeed, the idea of God is so generally linked to superstitious and almost anthropomorphic concepts that it fails to convey to most people the meaning of a psychological value, which is perhaps better expressed by the term suprapersonal value.

Whenever men have sought above all else for such a value they have gained an inner maturity and development which others of their generation entirely lacked. They have become wise men, seers. In the Orient these wise men are greatly respected and are frequently chosen as the leaders of public affairs. In the Occident the choice falls more often on men who have achieved worldly success. Western countries gain by this in efficiency, but too often sadly lose in wisdom.

Each generation has its own peculiar way of seeking inner values. The ways of the fathers are apt to seem bigoted and narrow-minded to the sons who fail to recognize that their modern culture, their ideas, their ideals even, are only possible because of the psychological development the fathers attained through their striving.

Our immediate ancestors sought their suprapersonal value, conceived as "the Will of God," through their relation to the *moral law*. The great majority considered that a relation to the moral law involved external obedience only; some even substituted an appearance of conformity for obedience. Take, for instance, the general attitude to the moral law which regarded sexuality as wrong except when sanctioned by marriage. Adultery and divorce were to them equally immoral. The majority of good men and women accepted this ruling and obeyed the law. Married people remained together even when the bond of love was hopelessly broken. Misunderstandings, quarrels, a terrible atmosphere of resistance, rivalry, even hate might develop, but the moral law was kept unquestioningly. Others merely appeared to conform; they kept the law on the surface, but in secret they found a way out. This outer conformity and secret nullification occurred chiefly among men; but women agreed to the practice by persistently shutting their eyes to the facts, and by casting the blame on the "other woman." That these effects of the moral law are bad, we all today agree, as they are inimical to our own attitude to life. We are apt to conclude that nothing good can possibly come out of a philosophy of life based on conformity to a moral code.

But we must not forget that others, who really lived in submission to this same moral law—the will of God they would have called it—sought for a deeper meaning of life. When such a one found himself involved in a marriage where love and passion had grown cold, he did not seek to escape his fate through the bypaths of divorce or secret adultery, nor did he submit sullenly to his bondage. For him there was another way. He believed that the moral law should rule him *within* and control his motives, feelings and thoughts as well as his actions. He took the external form of his life—his unhappy marriage— as the limits within which his soul must develop. He strove to be really acquiescent; through repentance he gradually assimilated his resentments and frustrated longings and through self-discipline he controlled them. The man who *really* did this, who did not fool himself by disregarding his negative feeling and thrusting it into the unconscious, was doubtless rare. But those who struggled with their inner problems attained a depth and sweetness, a strength and maturity which men of all ages admire.

But to us in this twentieth century the older way is a closed book. Submission to the moral law meant repression in the majority of cases and we have swung away from repression toward a greater acceptance of life. We demand release of energy and desire and the freedom to work out our own lives in accordance with the promptings of our own natures. This attitude has resulted—again, I take the sexual side of life for my illustration, though illustrations in plenty could be drawn from other spheres—in an enormous increase both in extramarital relations and in divorce. If difficulties arise in a marriage, the first impulse is toward a separation. "Let us not be bound," is the great cry of the day. "Let us not pretend." "Let us be conscious of our desires and our feelings — of our resentments and jealousies, as well as of our loves."

The quest for consciousness and a deeper appreciation of reality stands today as a guiding principle, replacing the discarded "submission to moral law." But modern men and women in their quest for consciousness are not all motivated alike. By far the majority are controlled entirely by the desire for personal and ego satisfaction, although others do seek a relation to a suprapersonal value which transcends these.

Where the personal desires are the ruling factor, the quest for consciousness does not lead to development, but only to a breakdown of the moral law, permitting young people to experiment widely and wildly — a state of affairs which seems to the older generation nothing short of unbridled license. We cannot, however, assert that this is necessarily worse than the general and complete repression of fifty years ago. But I believe we *can* say that whether the natural instincts and desires are repressed or are taken as a guide and freely expressed, so long as an individual's action is in relation to *personal* and ego ends no development of the psyche will take place. Only when a relation to a value beyond the personal wishes and desires has been established can any real development and maturity result.

In a marriage of the old school, where obedience to the moral law was taken as guide, and submission to a suprapersonal value furnished the motive power by which the primitive instincts were held in check, development of the individual's personal character could and often did take place. But development of the "relationship," with the increased consciousness it alone could bring, was not sought and so only rarely resulted.

Let us examine a marriage in which the partners seek sincerely for individual development, but do not recognize the quest for relationship as of equal importance. Such marriages occur today as well as yesterday. A young man and woman marry. They love each other and for a time all goes well. But sooner or later some situation arises in which both are amazed and hurt. The woman, believing it a part of her "wifely duty" to make her husband happy and his home a place of peace and freedom from worry, represses the hurt and greets him with the usual smile. He, on his part, seeing her smiling face, thinks the difficulty cannot be so bad after all, and, more unconscious of the feeling situation than the woman, takes his cue from her and also represses the hurt. The trouble blows over; each thinks of it as the other's fault or as "my bad temper." As they have made no effort to arrive at the root of the difficulty, they can have no constructive understanding of its cause. In the course of time the same trouble recurs and is again repressed. Through this they may learn real self-control and the ability to assume an air of serenity in troubled hours. If they continue to love each other, they will grow in tolerance for the other's weaknesses and peculiarities of character, but at the end of a long life together they will still be fundamentally strangers to each other and to themselves. They have gained in personal development, but the relationship between them cannot grow under such conditions.

To many it seems but the part of all cultured and kindly people to overlook in this way differences and disagreements with their loved ones, and to disregard all the lesser faults of character or behavior which would otherwise mar the peace and happiness of their home life. These people are cultured and disciplined. In difficult situations they act not selfishly but according to a code; "a good sport," "a lady," "a Christian" would do so-and-so, and so they do. They are the highest type of those who act from an adapted persona. Their motives are "personal" ones. They want personal goodness, personal happiness, for others as well as for themselves; everything not in accordance with the standards of good behavior must be excluded from action and if possible also from consciousness.

Not everyone, however, is satisfied by this way of behaving. More sensitive people, and weaker ones also, whose wishes are apt to be overridden under such a regime, are more acutely aware of disharmony. They are less able, perhaps, to exclude unpleasant things from consciousness, either because they are more aware of the unacceptable elements, or because their desire for truth is not satisfied by this rather blind attitude. Thus many people today are not content to take *personal* happiness and harmony as their aim. They have to seek out the *real truth* of the matter and base their relationship on this. If the actions or words of their friends disturb them, they have to speak about it and find what is the underlying reality. For they seek consciousness even at the expense of present peace. Truth is for them a value above personal happiness and a harmony which may be based only on illusion.

To the other generation this process of aiming at "understanding" would appear very like bickering and quarreling and, indeed, if the aim—consciousness—is lost sight of, it may degenerate into just such futility. Moreover in all this discussion there is a definite danger of losing touch with the emotional situation through intellectual analysis. Only a deep sincerity of purpose can avoid these pitfalls. There must be no attempt at self-justification to save one's face, no patronizing or impertinent dissection of the partner's character and psychology, no wandering from the actual incident into easy generalities. Truth may be served only if each one holds loyally to his purpose of discovering his *own* hidden motives through an understanding of this bit of life. If the discussion is carried on in order to gain a realization of the unconscious elements of the incident, then the very difficulties which inevitably arise between two people serve to tear down the veil of unconsciousness in which many of their motives are masked from themselves. In this way a relationship unlike any other may be built up.

To undertake to talk over the problems of relationship in this fundamental way is no easy task. Misunderstandings between two people who love each other are practically always due to unrecognized ego desires or to dark unknown shadowy things lurking in the hinterland of consciousness. The difficulty often touches the weakest spot, the most intimate inferiority. It is connected with things hardly admitted to oneself; the deepest instinct of self-preservation hides them even from the nearest and dearest friend. To talk about such problems is difficult for everyone, but especially difficult, I think, for a man. It is peculiarly distasteful to him to have to work on problems of human relationship, and he is assailed by a great pullback to unconsciousness when confronted with them.

For the woman, whose principle is Eros, or relatedness, the task is not so difficult. She meets her greatest inertia when the need is to become conscious of discrimination, of accurate definition—not when dealing with relations. How often has a woman exasperated her husband by interrupting him when he is painstakingly differentiating two similar things by saying, "It does not matter, it is all the same anyway." Here she is his inferior. But when it is a question of relationship the woman has an advantage over the man, for it is this which particularly interests her. She is willing to take the discrimination for granted, to override it or accept it on authority, but the relatedness is something over which she naturally spends time and energy.

This quality in women is one which men rather dread, for women make things concrete—relate theories instantly to practice. This is well illustrated in the story of a young scientist. He had been trying to isolate a certain vitamin which controls the growth of young animals. One evening he announced triumphantly to his wife that he had at last succeeded. "I'm so glad, my dear," she said, "how clever you are! What does it mean I should give Johnny for his supper?" She immediately and quite automatically *related* the new fact first to her feeling for him and then to her daily life without stopping to question what the substance was which he had just discovered, or what the proof of its efficacy, or how it worked, or, indeed, any of the questions a man would ask.

Psychological development for Western people, whether men or women, cannot progress very far, however, apart from relationship. We have not the ability to go deeply into self-knowledge through introversion uncontrolled by close contact with another human being. In the Orient many well-elaborated systems of self-culture as, for instance, the various yoga systems, have been developed; these are based on solitary introversion though even there the disciple is usually in close relation to a teacher who guides and controls the work. But for us in the Occident, something beyond analysis of the psyche through introversion is needed for real inner development. Introversion is, of course, enormously valuable, especially when it is guided and checked by one experienced in these things—here we call such a one an analyst. But the resulting development must be tested against a reality of its own kind—in other words, a psychological relationship is absolutely necessary for psychological development.

What, however, do we mean by *psychological* relationship? And how does it differ from any other kind?

The word "relationship" is used in ordinary language to describe many different forms of human association, but most commonly to denote connection by blood. This does not preclude psychological relationship, but the two conditions are not identical.

Two people closely related by blood may never have met each other. In such a case, blood-relationship persists, but no psychological relationship is possible. In other instances, the contact between the different members of a family may be close and constant. To the world they will present the appearance of a "very united family," and yet, if you inquire a little further, you may find perhaps that they are all complete strangers to each other, or that one member may be isolated within the group, living his real life apart in the seclusion of his own thoughts. As a woman once expressed it, "There may be a deal of family life and very little relationship!"

The various members of such a family are often extraordinarily alike, so that it is difficult for them not to be identified. Blood relationship implies a common, or partly common, inheritance and also, if the family is closely united in this way, a common environment. From these factors family resemblances develop which extend beyond the physical into the psychological realm. For instance, two sisters from such a family may look alike, have the same voice inflection, the same gestures, the same ideas; furthermore, the resemblance may be increased in matters which one would think were open to free choice, such as going to the same hairdresser, taking up the same studies, and belonging to the same club. They may even change their religion or their politics simultaneously—a unanimity which may occur against their will and possibly to their mutual annoyance. Their psychological condition approaches complete identity even in ways which are ordinarily considered to be determined by chance. They seem to share a similar *fate*.

Sisters who are in this way identified with each other often fall in love with men who are alike, perhaps even with the same man, and that without knowing of the other's involvement. Or they may marry men who do not appear to be alike but whose subsequent history is similar; for example, the sisters both marry men who turn out in later years to be drunkards. In such cases the identification reaches into the unconscious, as is witnessed by the striking similarity often to be found in their dreams. The members of such a united family usually attempt to differentiate themselves from one another by emphasizing certain external differences; but the identification, reaching as it does into the unconscious, will remain nonetheless a binding fact. In certain families each sister takes a clearly defined role— one will be the pretty and social sister, one the domestic one, one the clever one, and so on. This discrimination is felt by them to be a differentiation, but in reality it is a further evidence of identification—else why should not each sister be free to function on any or all sides of life? The answer is that in this case she is not a whole individual, but only a part of the family; she is identified with the other sisters, who together with herself make up a completed whole. In such cases no psychological relationship is possible, for relationship implies separateness; things that are identical cannot be related.

For this reason it is essential for human relationships to be tested in a way which will bring to light identifications which otherwise nullify their psychological values. This can only be accomplished by expressing the real feelings and not repressing them. It is of course easy to recognize and admit that much enters into our social and business relationships which is an adaptation and not the expression of our actual feeling. But this form of unreality does not disturb us; our "society manners" do not allow us to express what we are really thinking and feeling, and the expediency of a business situation compels us to wear a professional mask, a persona. Adaptations of this sort are more or less conscious; the mask is more or less voluntarily assumed for a particular purpose. In extreme instances, however, certain people so persistently and continuously act the role they have chosen to assume before the world that we begin to wonder whether there is a real human being inside the mask or not. Such a person has become identical with his persona; the "good hostess" who greets everyone with a gracious smile, even those she heartily dislikes, or the minister who utters pious sentiments on all occasions though he may have his moments of bitterness and irritation like most other men, furnish outstanding examples. In a relationship with such people no reality, in the psychological meaning of the word, is possible. For they only accept their conventional mask and do not recognize their own disagreeable feelings and reactions.

The search for consciousness does not of course mean that a woman must cease being polite to people whom she does not like. A persona is as necessary to a conscious woman as to an unconscious one—only instead of being a mask of conventional design which is mechanically worn, it must be developed as a living function relating the human being in a purposive way to the outer world. Above all it must have complete flexibility, so that it never conceals the individual from herself nor prevents her from appearing to others exactly as she feels whenever she wishes to do so.

In dreams the persona is often represented by clothing, and the symbol is an apt one, for clothes signify much. For instance, our clothes must be in general accord with the style of the day, for we are the children of our own historical time, psychologically as well as culturally; they must be suitable for the occasion on which they are worn, and must also be adapted to the wearer. We feel it to be ridiculous for an elderly woman to wear clothes suitable for a girl of eighteen (it argues a certain infantility and unreality in the wearer) and we feel it to be almost tragic for a young woman to be dressed as though she were already done with life. Or clothing may reveal a contradiction: If a girl sets out to give the impression that she is sober and studious, frivolous clothes will give the lie to her intentions.

The persona must agree closely with the inner reality, but this obligation does not mean that a woman can take the liberty in every situation of expressing the whole of her thought entirely unclothed, as it were. She would not walk into a drawing room clad only in her night clothes — much less nude. (Yet how many people have had just such a nightmare!) So also if she reveals her inner self naked before a group of people, she must not expect to be understood. Thoughts and feelings must always be mediated by an appropriate mask of manner and word, so that they may be adapted to the situation and comprehensible to the audience. Fully as many people fail to make satisfactory relationships through lack of a persona as through too much persona — a fact that few realize. Women especially are apt to be sinners in this respect. They expect the world to be tolerant of them if only they are true to themselves. But they forget that one person's truth may be contrary to another's, may indeed be quite destructive to it. For truth is a powerful and a dangerous commodity and needs to be adequately guarded. It should be clothed for the occasion, and not indiscriminately exposed. A new *Sartor Resartus* might be written in terms of analytical psychology. In the street

—that is, with strangers and crowds—we are most guarded and most conventional; we wear coats and gloves. For the house we have working clothes and social clothes. We may wear a bathing suit on the beach but must have an evening dress for a party, and only under the most intimate circumstances do we don a negligee. These things are allegories. To put on business clothes means that we are summoning up our determined effort to face the difficulties of our work in a businesslike and impersonal way. Much of the criticism directed against women in business refers to a lack of the proper persona which allows personal considerations and feelings to obtrude themselves into a situation which should be entirely impersonal.

The same problem of the proper persona should be deliberately taken into account in social situations. To dress outwardly in an appropriate manner is not enough. A woman must attire herself inwardly as well, by collecting all her resources beforehand as contribution to the general gaiety. If the man she loves is coming to dine with her, merely to dress with care and provide delicious food will not do—she must prepare subtle psychological food for the relationship as well. Many people seem to think that the fact of love is enough—that the situation can be left to take care of itself. They do not take this careless attitude toward material food—the dinner, they know, must be well chosen and served. Why is it that the same careful attention is so seldom given to psychological food of which the heart and mind must eat or go hungry?

The inner preparation to meet a situation involves, however, more than the persona. For instance, a man puts aside his business worries in order to take part in an intimate social evening. This is a persona adaptation; but a time may come when to omit all mention that he is worried would amount almost to a deception. For if he shows himself to his friend as something other than he is, illusion inevitably creeps into the friendship. If, for instance, he always plays the role of the "good sport," his friends and intimates may well identify him with his persona and come to think of him as rather hard, needing neither pity nor help in difficult places; whereas in reality, inside his persona, he may be like a quite unadapted child, shrinking in a very human way from suffering and hardship. Misunderstandings of this sort may undermine even the most intimate relationships of life where it is of the greatest importance to build on a firm foundation of reality. Many people, if they were to examine the basis of their relationships, would find that illusions, assumptions and projections have entered in to an alarming extent. The solid ground of the friendship begins to shift beneath their feet and they do not know where they are; in any problematical situation they cannot interpret words or actions, for there is no standard to go by.

If the whole realm of human relationships is not to be left in this nebulous state in which each must muddle along guided only by a homemade empiricism, some standard of psychological reality must be found which shall be generally valid. In testing any reality we compare it with something of a like quality. If we wish, for instance, to estimate the hardness of an object, we test it with a solid — our hand or a hammer. We compare color with color, length with length, and so forth.

If a man wishes to test the validity of an idea, he puts away his hammer and foot-rule and compares the new and untried idea with well-tested old ones. Similarly, if a woman wishes to test the validity of another's feeling, she must bring her own feeling into play with it and not try to estimate it by thinking. But the feelings she brings must be her true feelings or they will not form a true standard by which to measure and she will remain ignorant of the other's reality. It is the same in testing motives: if a woman does not act clearly, if she confuses the comparison by camouflaging her own motives, then the motives and acts of the other will be unclear to her also. She may have many theories and opinions but she cannot be sure that her conclusions are true of the object; they may well be but the reflection of her own inner lack of clarity.

We are obliged in everyday life to deal with the surface — the mask of the person is worn by us ourselves no less than by others. We do not know what is behind that mask. If we are good judges of character, we may be able to guess something of what lies behind, but such knowledge does not necessarily make for relatedness. Only conscious people can be related in the psychological sense of the term, for they alone can reveal themselves intentionally. Conscious relationship demands not only that A know what is behind B's mask, but that B shall know too, and shall be willing for A to know. And the same must be true of A and his mask in relation to B. One is reminded of the old rhyme:

> I saw Esau kissing Kate,
> The fact is, we all three saw,
> For I saw Esau, he saw me,
> And she saw I saw Esau.

But apparently in this case (since the incident was tattled to the world) nothing was said about it between them; it remained, as it were, clandestine, ministering not to relationship but to suspicion. Had Kate and Esau frankly talked it over with the observer and engaged either his sympathy or met his objections, the incident could have cemented the relationship between all three. As it was he could only guess at the situation; and Kate and Esau must always feel embarrassed when they meet him! Most important of all, the fact that their privacy had been invaded made it imperative that Esau and Kate clarify their own situation. Up to now affairs had progressed, let us say, in a state of dreamy bliss but once their lovemaking is known to another, they must ask themselves what it all means and where they are drifting. Life has challenged their unconsciousness; life is demanding from them a new phase of consciousness. Whether they know it or not, their lovemaking can never be quite the same again. They must either go on to betrothal with marriage as the goal, or their relationship becomes one of intentional secrecy. Society knows this from the accumulated wisdom of life and has expressed it in conventional laws which psychologically are quite right. What can be done in innocence cannot continue to be done except as a conscious deception, once awareness has entered in. So long as the act is purely instinctive—that is, without consciousness—it is neither evil nor good. But when consciousness enters the field, then a decision has to be made; the situation must be clarified and a course of action must be definitely chosen. This will be either evil or good. In terms of the conventional morality of a generation ago, there was but one choice for the man. "If a gentleman is found kissing a girl he is immediately under the obligation of declaring himself and his intentions." We use different standards today, but there is an underlying morality all the same. As I said above, Esau and Kate and the bystander need to come to an understanding. The subsequent history of Esau and Kate will depend on what is the basis of their relationship. They may make a Victorian marriage, where unruffled happiness and a pleasant association are the ideals—but where no real relatedness between husband and wife are to be looked for. Or they may base their marriage on another principle, seeking for consciousness and development instead of mere harmony.

Details of the old type of marriage were rarely recorded; folk tales, fairy stories and, until quite recent years, most novels and plays came to their end with a trite, "And they lived happily ever after," which underscored the peal of wedding bells. Until recent years contemporary interest was satisfied when the problems and difficulties between a young man and woman were so far overcome that the biological aim of life could be satisfied within the moral and conventional law. It was assumed that when the barriers to a conventional, "moral" sexual relation were surmounted, the problems of relationship ceased. From that point it was taken for granted that their conduct would be guided entirely by custom, that married people think, feel and act in the same way; hence their life after marriage held no interest for the tellers of tales.

This point of view belongs to a state of society where the animus and anima are still completely unconscious and, therefore, autonomous, found only when projected onto a man or a woman. In such a stage of consciousness the concern—as in the case of Tristan and Isolde—is with this mutual projection. A new state of consciousness and a new relation to the anima and animus is needed before the ideal of a more conscious relationship can dawn on the minds of men and women even as a possibility.

A step in this direction has been taken through the rebellion of women against the anima role imposed upon them. In the Victorian type of marriage the man felt little compulsion to adapt himself to the projection of the woman's animus, or, indeed, he felt it no burden to play the part of god in the household. We hear much more complaint from men, today, of the burden of this role. The woman, however, was called upon to mold herself far more to fit the conventional pattern of the man's anima, and must have suffered considerably from the hampering self-restraint involved. If we read the Victorian novelists, Dickens for instance, we see that his heroines are exact representations of the man's anima—child wives, gentle, tractable, acquiescing, characterless. To the modern woman it is a marvel that any man should look at the living models twice. Yet, strange to relate, in most cases the modern woman holds for man just the same kind of charm as a Dora or an Agnes. We can only conclude that the man sees in her not what is actually there but the reflection of something deep in his own unconscious, which is to him infinitely alluring.

Where the bond between two people in love consists in this way in the involvement with their own anima or animus, projected onto the loved object, the psychological aim of the life energy is fulfilled when the two are united. It is as though through such a union a life cycle is completed, on one plane. But this at-one-ness cannot be a permanent condition, for it is based on an illusion. If the woman were in truth the incarnation of the man's anima and were nothing else, and he, similarly, the incarnation of her animus and nothing else, then a marriage between them might offer a permanent solution of their life problems, for all the psychological affinities would be so satisfied in each other that no energy would be left free to disturb the situation by seeking restlessly for further satisfaction. Such a miracle naturally never really happens. The illusion of completion in the marriage may persist for a period, but eventually that part of the personality which was excluded in playing the anima or animus role will begin to stir in its prison and rebel. There will come a rift in the complete veil of their happiness. There will be a struggle which will end either in readjustment or in the death of their love. Or this may eventually happen: the terrible sense of disloyalty to the partner of years of married life will compel the other to repress again the disturbing element and to force it back further into its prison. A period may come during which a lost happiness is partly refound. But always there will be present a haunting sense of its insecurity; its joy will ring a little hollow. Then an uprising of the suppressed elements will occur again. This time, if the repressive attitude is persisted in, health may break down and a neurosis develop.

So long as his inner value is projected into the outer world, a man may seek it there for years, before he comes to realize that he is pursuing a mirage—that he has failed to find his anima, his soul, outside himself and has only wasted the time which should have been spent in seeking it within. He is a disappointed and a disillusioned man; he has gained nothing in development, and his love, rooted so insecurely in a fantasy, wilts and perishes in his hands. This is the inevitable result of the lived-happily-ever-after attitude to the problems of wedded life.

The simple fact that the modern novel no longer ends with wedding bells is an indication that the stage of relationship represented by the projection of anima and animus no longer contents us; it is an indication that our field of consciousness is widening, so that a young couple can begin their association with a different aim. They will seek not merely to fulfill each the ideal of the other, not merely to make a "success" of their marriage, not merely to live according to the conventional idea of what constitutes a good husband, a good wife and mother, but instead will take truth as their goal and the extension of consciousness as the means of attaining it. In such a case their marriage will result in a relationship quite different from one based on illusion. "All association on the basis of common interests," said an Old Chinese sage (and the finding of the anima and the animus in a mutual projection is such a "common interest"), "holds only up to a certain point. Where the community of interest ceases, the holding together ceases also, and the closest friendship often changes into hate. Only when the bond is based on what is right, on steadfastness, will it remain so firm that it triumphs over everything."[1]

The man and woman beginning their relationship on this basis of truth have many difficulties ahead of them. They do not know themselves and they cannot know each other. But an understanding of fundamental human problems may stand them in good stead when difficulties arise. For most problems of relationship depend on one of a small number of basic psychological "complexes," or blind spots. This discussion is based on the assumption that the man and woman concerned really love each other, and that they are well-meaning people who wish to make their relationship as true and lasting as possible. Problems arising from flagrant selfishness and bad temper or other breaches of the ordinary standards of considerate behavior will not be considered here. Something more than good will and consideration is necessary, however, if a conscious or psychological relationship is to be built up between two people. For the roots of action often lie below the levels to which conscious introspection can penetrate and conscious discipline and culture be applied. If such problems of relationship are to be solved, the unconscious roots of the difficulties must be systematically sought out and brought to consciousness where they can be dealt with.

---

1 *I Ching*, p. 251.

Difficulties in relationship, however small, usually lead to profound problems. They may be "little" in their manifestations, but they are not little in their psychological significance. This explains why such "little" difficulties, if they are not dealt with, have the power to wreck a seemingly sound relationship. Indeed it is not too much to say that most broken friendships really have "little" troubles to blame for their breakup. But if the roots of the difficulty are sought out an opportunity arises for love to exercise its humanizing power at a deeper level of the character than is ordinarily available. An intimate relationship is for this reason of inestimable value in the development of the individual.

Certain psychological roots or complexes are responsible for such a large proportion of difficulties in relationship as to merit special mention. First is the demand for personal satisfaction and fulfillment from the partner, which, legitimate though it may seem, nevertheless can produce a bitter clash of wills. Another lies in the sense of inferiority from which most people suffer, and which can cause endless resentments and hurt feelings. A third cause of misunderstanding results from a lack of development on one side of the psyche with a consequent inability to handle certain problems of relationship wisely, and a fourth is due to the intrusion of the animus and anima into the relationship, resulting in misunderstandings based on the subjective and illusory character of the whole situation.

A surprisingly large number of the difficulties between any two people are likely to arise from the first source, namely unconscious power demands and unrecognized possessive attitudes on the part of one or both. One of the great services close relationship can render the individual is to bring to light these slumbering ego attitudes. If the recurrent difficulties are to be overcome the power attitude must be recognized and foresworn, but if the difficulty is not to recur, something more than repentance for the particular incident is needed. Each incident serves to bring the power attitude to notice; but the demand is a manifestation of a deeper lying problem which can rarely be unearthed through a scrutiny of conscious motives. In order to find its roots it will be necessary to explore the unconscious aspect of the situation. Sometimes these roots lie fairly close at hand in the individual's infantile past, more often they have a deeper origin in the ancestral past. When through a far-reaching exploration of the unconscious a man or woman begins to bring to light these ancient and buried factors, the first thing demanded of him is a recognition that *there IS evil.* I wish to make this statement with great emphasis because many people today deny its existence. They say that action is the result of inherited tendencies or of conditioned reflexes or of the natural instincts and that the old idea of good and evil and of man's responsibility are outgrown. To them God is dead; there is no God and therefore there can be no moral responsibility; there is no evil. Others say that God is all powerful, suffusing all his works and as God is good there can be no evil. These attitudes lead to the belief that human problems can be solved by simply disregarding the *fact* of evil. Anyone who, with truth as his one criterion, has delved at all into the unconscious, must have become convinced of the existence and power of evil. But mere acknowledgment of the fact is not sufficient; more is needed if a solution is to be found for the problems it brings in its train. Such a solution is not found easily; it is not discovered by anyone unless, like the heroes of old who fought and slew the dragons personifying the evils of their day, he also is prepared to risk life and limb in the fight against the monsters in the unconscious.

Let us take an example. Supposing some action of the wife's seemed to her husband domineering, so that his reaction made it necessary to discuss the matter. She may protest that she was quite unaware of any egotism in her motives. She may, indeed, have thought herself cooperative, willing to give him and his wishes room, she may even have thought that she had acted altruistically "for his good." But at his protest she would be compelled to search for the unconscious motives of her action. Then she might find that far from being civilized and kindly, they were quite primitive, the expressions of the "natural man" hidden in the unconscious. This primitive being within her wants to dominate, wants always to be first; he "wants what he wants" fiercely, and will stop at nothing, not even murder, to get it. He is primitive man entirely unregenerate! She may well be dismayed.

Yet if she looks a little further she will find, coming also from the unconscious, an entirely different attitude and an entirely different set of desires, something compensatory to the egotism and dominance of the "natural man," for instance, she may find a willingness to be sacrificed. These attitudes are a pair of opposites, when one comes up the other goes down. It is an automatic mechanism. If an individual, having become aware of this dualism, identifies herself consciously with the more adapted attitude, she will "cleave to the good and repress the evil," and excuse her bad behavior by saying, "I didn't mean to be dominating, I was a little out of temper;" or, "You must try not to be touchy about my tone of voice, it does not mean anything." In this way, however, she only lays up trouble both for herself and her friend. For whatever is pushed last into the unconscious will be first to come up.

The evil is merely stored up in the unconscious; it cannot be made to disappear in that way. A persistent identification with the "good," resulting in a continuous repression of the "evil" is an attitude fostered by our Western culture and morality. Not only has it been practiced by individuals but for several generations it has represented the ideal of behavior for the whole of society. If progress is to be made in development, however, the under side, the "evil," has sooner or later to be brought to consciousness and assimilated. An individual who refuses entirely to face the problem of his own a-moral desires may, it is true, die in the "odor of sanctity," but that is not the end of the story. His children, sharing as they do in the unconscious of the parents, have to take up the problem and either live out what he repressed or assimilate it in some other way. The fate of the clergyman's son is proverbial. This law is illustrated in our day on a large scale by the almost complete overthrow of the code of sexual behavior which for the last few generations represented the very kernel of the moral law. The repressions of the fathers make up the conscious attitude of the children; or, as the old saying has it, "The sins of the fathers shall be visited upon the children unto the third and fourth generation." For the sake of the next generation if not for our own it behooves us to find some way of assimilating the evil in our own unconscious.

But if identification with the good and repression of the evil effect no real change of character what further can be done? Awareness of the balance of good and evil in the unconscious seems to have led us no further in our quest for a more human and developed relationship. It is obviously no use for a man to identify himself with the unconscious and let the moods come as they will, now an evil one and now a good, each following the other like the waves of the sea, while he himself takes no responsibility for their occurrence. It may, perhaps, be asked, "Is he, then, responsible for the moods in his unconscious?" and we must answer, "No, he is not directly responsible." For the unconscious is part of nature, and is beyond his control; he is no more responsible for its moods than the mariner is responsible for the waves of the sea. The mariner cannot direct these, but he can direct his ship in relation to them; he can take an attitude toward them instead of merely drifting with them. In the same way the attitude which a man takes toward the moods of the unconscious determines the direction in which he moves.

The unconscious mirrors or portrays the facts viewed as it were from "the other side," and so is compensatory to the conscious appearance. If in the conscious the woman takes a moral attitude toward her action, the unconscious will respond. By *moral attitude* I do not at all mean one based on conventional morality, but on a far deeper loyalty to truth necessitated by the effort to achieve a conscious relationship. Accordingly she has to assume the responsibility not only for the conscious part of her action, but also for the unconscious part unexpectedly brought to light for which at that time she was not directly responsible. Through the discussion of the incident which her husband's protest brought about, however, she was made aware of something previously unknown to her. She has had a taste of the fruit of the tree of knowledge, she is no longer unaware and can no longer claim complete innocence. Her newly acquired consciousness throws fresh light on her action and she must take up the responsibility for it as though she had been conscious when she did it. She must accept the *evil* shown in that action as her conscious burden and problem. By this acceptance her unconscious is relieved of the evil and is left free to manifest the complementary attitude. In the instance we are considering, the evil in the attitude was a power or egotistic demand, ready to override all other considerations to get what it wanted. The complementary attitude is a willingness to sacrifice the personal wishes, even to sacrifice the ego itself, rather than override another. To accept the responsibility for the natural man's desires and power demands is a sort of eating or assimilating of the evil—a very different thing from repressing it or denying its existence.

Let us turn to the second group of relationship difficulties, namely those dependent on feelings of inferiority. Every woman has (as also indeed has every man) certain sensitive spots in her psyche about which she has a sense of inferiority out of proportion to the actual conscious situation. These spots are, as a rule, carefully guarded and concealed, but sooner or later during the course of a close relationship they are almost inevitably rubbed against unwittingly and become inflamed. Let us suppose that the wife has a sensitive spot in regard to her personal appearance. Although normally good-looking, she always fears that she is unattractive or perhaps even physically repellent. To any criticism of her appearance, either actual or implied, she reacts violently with self-justification or anger or perhaps with a high-handedness which is a compensation for her own feeling of inadequacy and humiliation. This is naturally a protective mechanism, but her husband, knowing nothing of the underlying situation, does not see the weakness she so carefully conceals. As he is probably not exempt from inferiorities of his own, he may well be hurt by her sharpness and a slight estrangement may result which they will have to talk over if they are seeking for a conscious relationship. Then the sense of inferiority underlying her sharpness will come to light. This is only a preliminary step, however. To discover that she has a sense of inferiority and to learn what it is attached to and what situations bring it into action is an important piece of self-knowledge. But it is only the beginning; the question remains: What is it that makes her feel inferior?

Sometimes the feeling of inferiority is itself a compensation for a more deeply unconscious demand for power. If the woman is unduly sensitive about her appearance possibly the truth is that unconsciously she expects to be perfect and so cannot accept herself as an ordinary human being with faults and weaknesses like the rest of humanity. A fantasy of being a princess often lurks under such a sense of inadequacy. In her own unrecognized opinon of herself she is all-perfect and all-admired, perhaps still papa's little darling. If through her husband's challenge of her attitude, she discovers in her unconscious this kind of "perfection fantasy" with its accompanying demand that he admire her under all circumstances, the problem resolves itself again into the need to "assimilate the evil," and recognize herself as the ordinary human being that she is.

But perhaps she feels inferior because some other woman of their circle is better looking than she. A sense of inferiority, however, does not arise simply because of a recognized and consciously accepted difference, but only if there is rivalry and a desire, conscious or unconscious, to excel. If she wishes to be first, then admiration given to another woman will seem like a threat to her position, and she will feel inferior.

In other cases the inferiority feelings may depend on an unresolved family bond. When you ask such a woman why she feels inferior, she may perhaps tell you that she was an unwanted child

or that her older sister domineered over her. Adler has emphasized these family conditions in his theory of power psychology.
The sense of inferiority may, indeed, have originated in some such
condition, but one must still ask, Why do they persist into adult
life? Is it merely a question of habit functioning? Or is it not
rather that a certain quantum of libido, of interest, is still fixated
on the parents or elder sister, and so is held unseen and unrecognized in the unconscious? If the woman is to become a complete and rounded-out personality this energy must be freed from
the unconscious and applied to her conscious development. In
other words she does not today feel inferior because years ago
in her schoolroom days her sister was bigger than she was; she
feels inferior *today* because part of her psyche has remained undeveloped. She has as it were, a flattened place on the circle of
her individuality which can only be rounded out and developed
through the redemption of the energy held in the unconscious
by the image of an elder sister more successful than herself.

The libido or psychical energy tied up with the father or the
mother may produce similar results. Indeed this parent fixation
is more prolific of inferiorities than the tie to the elder brother
or sister. Perhaps the woman may say, "I feel inferior because
my mother did not like me. She always misunderstood me and
put me in the wrong." Her life may be made miserable by the
effects of her mother's attitude, even though her mother may
have died years before. For as long as the daughter lives in a
psychic world dominated by the Mother, her own mother occupies
the place of Queen Regent in that little world and can continue
to put her daughter "in the wrong." Or perhaps she may say,
"I could not bear to hurt dear Mama," having in consciousness
the positive side of her fixation; or "Yes, Mother is exacting but
dear Papa always said we must not cross her." While she takes
this attitude she is bound, not by her mother, but by her fixation
to the Mother. Only when she dares to break free can she begin
to live by some other law, some other standard than that imposed
by her own mother. But strange to relate, this is something of

a vicious circle: only when she beings to live by some other law, some other standard, can she dare to break free. So deep is the bond to the Mother, guarded as it is by the most sacred ties of religion and custom, that nothing less than a suprapersonal aim or value can impel her to break it. An object above and beyond her personal desires, sought for and served with religious devotion, is the one thing that can wean her from the Mother. In many religions the figure of the Mother holds a central place. Through devotion to her, men have found release from the infantile bondage to their own mothers. But this statement also must be put the other way round. Christ said, "If any man come to me and hate not his father and mother . . . he cannot be my disciple," and only as a man succeeds in freeing himself from the tie to the human mother by a real sacrifice of the longing to be comforted and protected by his mother can he serve with devotion the Mother who thus comes to hold for him a suprapersonal value.

The third cause of difficulty in relationship to be discussed here depends upon the lack of development of one of the psychic functions. We will take as an example lack of development of the feeling function. Perhaps some misunderstanding occurs between a man and woman, but when they talk it over they find no power problem or dark shadowy motive. The misunderstanding appears to have no basis in fact. What one did in all good faith and friendliness simply is, to the other, the reverse of a friendly and loyal act. This unresolvable sort of misunderstanding usually comes from ignorance of the laws of feeling with a consequent disregard of some essential need in the relationship.

For instance, a young man telephones to the girl with whom he is in love, to ask when he can see her. She answers the telephone in a room filled with guests, and unable in her embarrassment to talk with him freely she makes some evasive reply and cuts the conversation short. The young man, knowing nothing of her predicament, is left wondering whatever he can have done or said to make her so reserved; perhaps he goes off in a huff. She for her part is quite unaware that anything she has said or done could have hurt him, and is herself hurt, when next she meets him, to find him distant and cold.

This situation seems to be so utterly trivial that it is hard to understand how any serious difficulty could arise. In real life, however, it is just such an insignificant episode which most frequently lies at the bottom of a serious misunderstanding. The two individuals, in our illustration, were probably entirely unaware of the cause of their estrangement and, indeed, if an inner voice should suggest the telephone conversation as the starting point of the difficulty it would be immediately dismissed as too small to warrant attention, or if the inner conviction should grow that this was the cause of the trouble few would be brave enough to pocket their dignity and avow it.

It is, however, somewhat misleading to say that such trivial incidents are the cause of misunderstandings. They are the occasion only, and if they were solitary incidents they could be dismissed without danger. But when such things occur not once but many times, a deeper problem must be sought, just as one spot on the skin can be dismissed as probably a gnat bite but many spots indicate a constitutional disease, like measles.

A constitutional disease of the psyche—in this case a lack of development of the feeling function—must be recognized in this trivial beginning of a misunderstanding which does not seem to be the fault of either party. It arose from a disregard of one of the basic laws of feeling expression, namely that in any situation involving two people there are at least two feeling trends or strands which must be kept separate and be given separate expression. These two considerations are the feeling for the person and the situation. The girl should have said, "How nice of you to call. I am sorry I can't talk with you now, I have friends with me." But the young man, too, failed on the feeling side. When he heard her cold tone of voice he might have asked, "Is there anything the matter, or is it that you are not alone?"

The need to pay attention not only to the feeling for the person, but also for the situation, seems so simple a requirement as not to need mention; yet I have repeatedly seen it disregarded in life in a way resulting in serious misunderstanding. The conventions of formal behavior take cognizance of it, but in throwing off formality the collective wisdom it incorporates is sometimes lost. It is impolite, for instance to write in reply to a friend's invitation to dinner, simply, "I can't come." Convention requires instead: "How kind of you to ask me" (feeling for the hostess), "but I have another engagement" (feeling for, or recognition of, the reality of the situation).

In talking of feeling, we must bear in mind that feeling is not always kind, positive feeling. It may just as frequently be feeling against as feeling toward—it may be "I dislike," not "I like." This, because it tends to withdraw from the object, is called negative feeling. When it arises toward a loved one for whom the main current of feeling is positive, it always produces a conflict or even a sense of confusion or chaos. To express dislike of any characteristic seems to contradict the very fact of love. This confusion can be cleared up if the nature of feeling is more clearly recognized.

Feeling is not something solid, static; it is fluid, dynamic. It flows back and forth like the sea; it has depth, and that depth, like the sea's, is at a certain point fairly constant; it has currents flowing from one person toward another, to one the attachment grows stronger, to another weaker. Like the sea it has tides; between a man and a woman, the tide of love rises or falls, diurnally or in a longer monthly cycle. It has waves too—a continuous up and down movement of the feeling reactions between two people. One of them may have to say, "I love you deeply, but I dislike this thing you have done." If he is careful to phrase his reaction in somewhat that form, she will understand that the depth of his love remains, and will not fear that the wave of negative feeling may have obliterated it.

This reassertion of the positive side of the relationship, in opposition to the negative feeling, is a most important point to bear in mind when differences and divergences are under discussion, otherwise one of the friends may be left in doubt as to how serious the estrangement is. The value of this rule is recognized conventionally. Surely we should not be less careful in dealing with our friends.

The fourth source of difficulty that may arise results from the intrusion of the woman's animus or the man's anima into the situation. This is practically unavoidable as it is one of the main factors in the phenomenon of falling in love. Naturally it is the positive aspect of this projection which arouses love. There is, however, a negative side also to the anima and animus, and when this negative side becomes constellated between a man and woman, it arouses what is ordinarily called *animosity* — bad feeling. Very serious difficulties may result which are hard to clear up because the projection of the anima or animus takes place unseen and unknown. The subjective origin of the negative material is not for a moment suspected; the man or woman reacts to it as though it has originated in the partner.

The woman's animus generally takes the form of thinking judgments and opinions, leading her to make assumptions which are extremely exasperating to the masculine mind. Her great resource and standby is, "Oh, I see what you mean!" and this often before he has expressed his thought. Or she will, in her turn, recount an incident, burdening it with unnecessary details or insisting on some irrelevant point until she, as the saying goes, "drives him nearly crazy." This kind of thinking is always associated with a certain *noli me tangere* attitude which, if he loves the woman, arouses all that is dominating in him; if he does not love her, it drives him away. It was this kind of attitude which made a man once say, "I can't talk to a woman until I've slept with her." In this somewhat crude jest he was trying to express a truth he had discovered; namely that animus thinking of this kind gives way if he can reach her real feminine nature, for then her psychological center of gravity leaves her head, as it were, and finds its proper place in the center of her being. She can function once again as a real woman.

The man's anima leads him to make assumptions about feeling. If his own feeling is not clear, he is very apt to assume negative feeling in the woman. He will act then as though she were vexed with him and become so grouchy as to induce real vexation in her—a result which naturally justifies him in his first impression. Much patience is required in dealing with this kind of difficulty. If the woman can keep clear of his projection and remain in contact with her own feelings she may be able to help him discover the trouble. If she senses, for instance, that he is in "one of his moods," it may be possible for her to take the initiative immediately and to ask him what the trouble is, instead of waiting for him to accuse her of some imagined unfriendly action.

Or in other cases his anima may lead him to project to her, instead of negative feeling, a certain positive feeling which is not true at all. He may, for instance, continually take it for granted that no matter what he says or does she will always understand and will continue to love him. This is, of course, a projection of the Mother onto her, for only a mother continues to love a man regardless of what he does. If he fails, for instance, to give her any explanation of his actions, secure in the assumption that she is interested only in his welfare, he may be amazed at her reaction. The ordinary woman, if a man leaves her suddenly without explanation, first wonders where he is, then begins to search her memory for a clue to the trouble, and finally is filled with anger at his neglect. He, coming back in his own good time and expecting to be met with open arms, feels injured to find her angry and hurt, and in his turn becomes angry. It may be that she "learns her lesson" and never shows him anger again. But if she does "learn" the lesson after this fashion, it is the beginning of the end as far as any relationship is concerned. To attain a real, conscious relationship they will have to face the difficulty; he must attempt to find some way by which he can release himself from his childish self-absorption, to the end that, counting no longer on the maternal indulgence of his wife, he will no longer fall under the Mother's dominance within.

When difficulties, no matter what their nature, arise in the relationship between lovers the temptation to withdraw temporarily from the intimacy and to fly somewhere else inevitably obtrudes itself on consciousness. The woman longs to carry her troubles to her nearest woman friend for sympathy and comfort because her great need is on the feeling side and it takes an act of conscious determination to stay and work on the problem with her husband. The man is tempted to fling off and seek out another woman in order to find his sexual satisfaction in a temporary affair where the conditions are not so difficult, but where his obligation can be met by some material gift and where, above all, no intolerable demand is made to talk things over and to understand.

A close association between two individuals almost always causes friction of this character at some point. But if they are truly in love with each other, the relationship between them has one great asset to set over against the disintegrating effect of the friction, namely their mutual sexual involvement. If the instinctual bond between them is really deep and is deeply accepted, they are obliged to come back to each other however difficult their life together has been. This instinctual bond is like a compulsive force, it works between two people who have experienced profoundly together in their realm of life, even where the question of a conscious relationship and of love do not enter in. For instance, a woman will take back a "brute of a husband" again and again if she has found contact with the instinctual life forces with him, in spite of the fact that he may spend all her money, ill-treat her physically and seek his pleasure elsewhere during her pregnancies. DuBose Heyward showed such a situation in his play *Porgy*. The girl loved Porgy, all her tenderness and feeling both of love and of gratitude flowed out to him freely, but when her criminal husband returned and, as she says, "put his hot hand on me," she followed him to inevitable degradation and misery. A man for his part will give up business and family, will often surrender even his honor, to pursue a woman of doubtful reputation with whom he has had a deeply satisfying experience. This contact with the life force will hold him as no self-interest can hold him to a wife with whom sexuality had been perhaps little more than a marital duty.

This matter of instinctual rapport is a very important one if a deep psychological relationship is to be developed between a man and a woman. For men and women are exceedingly incomprehensible to each other. All women, in spite of the fact that modern education has tended to mask the fundamental differences between the sexes, still have a similar standpoint in their assumptions and instinctual attitudes to life's problems. If the surface of any woman, even a feminist, is scratched, beneath it will be found reactions which are unmistakably feminine, but the masculine outlook, inherent in all men, differs markedly from the feminine one.

On account of this fundamental difference in point of view, it would seem that a conscious relationship between a man and a woman could never in the world be attained were it not for the compulsion of sex instinct which reaches deep into the roots of the psyche — roots whose beginnings penetrate below our personal consciousness, below even the racial, the human origins, into the dark abysses of our being. A relationship which stirs these unconscious forces within a man and woman can lead them far in the quest for greater consciousness and psychological development.

In talking of a deeply significant instinctual rapport between a man and a woman, we have to bear in mind that the experience of sexuality is not the same for men as for women, but is, indeed, exceedingly different; and we must remember further that the role which sexuality plays in relationship is also a different one for them. These facts are not, I think, sufficiently realized. Few people have the courage to talk frankly to each other about such intimate and deeply personal matters, or they talk simply from the head, theoretically, which does more harm than good. Usually each one assumes that his partner in a significant and much-prized experience lives through exactly the same emotional and physical stages as he himself does. But this is a pure assumption which is rarely put to the test of a conscious discussion, and so it persists unchecked in a way which may later lead to serious misunderstanding.

For the man sexuality is the chief power or force which can bridge the gap between himself and the woman he loves; it is not so at all for the woman. When there is a difficulty or misunderstanding between them, *he* feels that if only they could come together sexually all would be put right. But *she* feels that under such circumstances a sexual approach is almost a violation. She *must* have the difficulty straightened out and the rapport on the feeling side reestablished before she can give herself to him again in any real sense. If, however, he overrides her reluctance, their union is likely to be unsatisfactory emotionally and perhaps physically as well.

The sense of satisfaction or of frustration resulting from the sexual act may even be an indicator or test of the state of rapport between two people. For men, and women too, are often exceedingly unconscious of the nature of their own feeling states; they may not be aware at all of how they feel toward each other. Perhaps there has been a difficulty which has blown over. They think that everything is all right between them and they attempt to come together sexually. Then the lack of deep sexual harmony informs them of what they should have known before, namely that there are still resistances between them which have not been worked out.

Cultured people have been taught for many generations that if they act pleasantly nothing further is required. As a result a thick wall of unconsciousness has been built up (or perhaps has not yet been broken down) in regard to their own true feelings. This wall of unconsciousness is thickest in regard to the loved object. For the loved one is almost always idealized so that it is hardest there to become aware of the negative pullbacks from good feeling. Each one is most anxious that all should be right between himself and his beloved, and so the temptation to disregard the tiny warnings of danger is very great. Those warnings come from deep within, but it is much easier to repress than to heed them. To bring out into the open those *little* resistances—those so unadapted hurt feelings—would make the man or woman feel soiled, or inferior. They hope against hope that by disregarding them, the hurts and resistances can be made to disappear. So they make love as they have been accustomed to do and come together in the sexual act, but if they are pretending, playing a part to each other, possibly also even to themselves, they will not find mutual satisfaction. The tendency then is to avoid talk about the experience—how can they talk about such an experience when the rapport is not exactly right! Instead each, as a rule, generalizes about the situation in ways usually derogatory to the other. Each feels that "perhaps, after all, the glamor of love cannot be expected to last forever" or that "life is like that anyway." If instead of contenting themselves with such cynical assumptions the partners were to take this experience as a warning, they would be able to take a step toward building up a conscious relationship; the knowledge of their lack of harmony would then compel them to go back and discover what they had left undone, or where the unresolved difficulty lay which had robbed them of their real union. So slender, however, is the relationship and confidence which most men and women have built up in their marriage, and so fundamental and age-old is the suspicion between men and women, that only rarely can a pair be found who are willing to risk all for the sake of consciousness and talk out such a problem.

The sexual rapport is sometimes threatened in another way. If the man has failed to free himself from his childish attitude that regards his own needs as paramount and the woman as responsible for their satisfaction, he may force his wife to play the role of mother to him. The almost universal custom that a man should bring gifts to the woman he loves is perhaps intended to counteract this insidious tendency. We find instances of this widespread custom among civilized man and savages alike.

Malinowski in *The Sexual Life of Savages* states that if a man, or even a quite young boy, among the Trobrianders goes to his friend for sexual purposes, he always takes her a gift, a flower perhaps, or a fruit. This is an interesting primitive custom, for it is never doubted that the girl gets as much pleasure and satisfaction as the boy; and as the relation of paternity is not recognized in the tribe, the gift cannot be considered a compensation for her risk of pregnancy. It must have some other meaning.

This other meaning is perhaps related to the temptation, so prevalent among men, to seek for the satisfaction of their sexual needs in much the same spirit as the small boy who demands from his mother the satisfaction of his physical needs—as a right —"I need it, give it to me." This attitude has a tremendous hold on every man; as evidence we need but mention the large place which the Oedipus complex has taken in the literature of psychology. If he is to free himself from it and gain his own manhood, he needs to remind himself each time he approaches his loved one that the motive must not be his own personal satisfaction, but rather the desire that the instinctual, procreative life force may live through them. If he is to be released from his infantile bondage to the Mother, he must bring a gift not to the woman he loves, for he does not need to pay her off, but to Womanhood who must be paid in order that the hold which woman has on him may be loosed—in order that the gift may release him from Woman—that he may release himself through the gift. It is the Goddess of Instinct that he pays, the Great Mother within himself who otherwise would not let him go. The gift could be taken as well—as once, indeed, it was taken—to the temple of Aphrodite, or Hecate, or Ishtar.

But why must the man give a gift and not the woman also? The answer lies in the different parts that men and women play in procreation. It takes but a small proportion of a man's time and energy; from the woman it demands the sacrifice of her whole life, at least temporarily. In every act of sexual intercourse, the woman implicitly accepts her role as servant in the Temple of

Life. For her all is not finished when the night is over. For the night may be to her but the beginning of a long service not to be completed until her child can fend for itself. Every act of intercourse is not, to be sure, followed by pregnancy; but any one may be so followed, contraceptives notwithstanding, and every time a woman gives herself to the man she loves, she asserts again her willingness to pay, not with a gift, but with her body, her energy, even with her life, for the privilege of participating in that creative moment.

In the recognition that man does not live for himself alone even in his most individual and personal acts—not even in his relation to the one person in all the world whom he loves—in this recognition the truly religious spirit is born. The most precious things of life do not belong to us personally. In our most intimate acts, our most secret moments, we are *lived* by Life. Again and again we are reminded that in the daily contact with one we love our little personal egos must be surpassed; only so can we take our place in the stream of life and submit ourselves to that suprapersonal value which alone can give significance and dignity to the individual. For when two people experience each other unmasked—in stark reality—emotional energy which has had its counterpart in the past only in religious experience is in modern times released and made available for human development.

In these chapters the psychological problems of woman have unfolded themselves as they occur in the various phases of her fate. Through facing the daily reality of her life a gradual growth and deepening of consciousness is achieved. Her personal and egotistic desires recede before a more fundamental aim and are replaced by a suprapersonal value which is related to the deeper principles of life. Out of this development woman finds for herself a spirituality based on the principle of Eros, which is expressed in life by a new kind of human relationship.

As we have followed woman through the various vicissitudes of her life, the myth of womanhood, shrouded by the illusion of man's anima which he has projected upon her and which she has carried uncomplainingly through all the years of her unconsciousness, has faded, and the real woman as she is in *herself* has emerged. In so defining her personality she has released herself from the anima projection of the man; she has stripped herself as far as possible of the garment of glamor with which he has clothed her and has dared to reveal herself in her weakness and in her strength. Man's illusion painted her in colors superhuman both in their brilliance and in their sombre tones. To him she has seemed divinely fair and demonically ugly. When she steps out into the light, she both loses and gains by the change. Formerly the effects she produced arose from the unconscious, either her own or the man's, and she could have little or no control over them. Now for the first time she is humanly responsible for her own qualities. If she sins she can repent; if she does well it is her own doing. It is, indeed, unquestionably a gain in psychological evolution, for by revealing herself as she is she has become a self-conscious individuality.

Bibliography

BERTINE, Eleanor. *Human Relationships*. New York: David McKay Co., 1958.

BOAS, Louise Schutz. *Elizabeth Barrett Browning*. London: Longmans, Green & Co., 1930.

DICKINSON, Emily. *Final Harvest: Emily Dickinson's Poems*. Boston: Little, Brown & Co., 1961.

ENGLISH REVIEW. June 1923.

EVANS-WENTZ. W.Y., ed. *Tibet's Great Yogi Milarepa*. London: Oxford University Press, 1928.

HARDING, M. Esther. *The Parental Image*. New York: C. G. Jung Foundation, 1965.

I CHING or BOOK OF CHANGES, translated by R. Wilhelm and C. F. Baynes. Princeton: Princeton University Press (Bollingen Series XIX), 1967.

JUNG, C. G. *Alchemical Studies*. Vol. 13 of the Collected Works. Princeton: Princeton University Press (Bollingen Series XX), 1967.

-----. *The Archetypes and the Collective Unconscious*. Vol. 9 (1) of the Collected Works. Princeton: Princeton University Press (Bollingen Series XX), 1959.

-----. *Civilization in Transition*. Vol. 10 of the Collected Works. Princeton University Press (Bollingen Series XX), 1964.

-----. *Psychological Types*. London: Routledge & Kegan Paul, Ltd., 1964.

-----. *Two Essays on Analytical Psychology*. Vol. 7 of the Collected Works. Princeton: Princeton University Press (Bollingen Series XX), 1953.

MAITLAND, Edward. *The Life of Anna Kingsford*. London: John Watkins, 1913.

MEAD, G. R. S. *Fragments of a Faith Forgotten*. New York: University Books, 1960.

Index

7 50

MARKETING

and

DEVELOPMENT

The Thailand Experience

MARKETING
and
DEVELOPMENT

The Thailand Experience

by

DOLE A. ANDERSON

Professor of Business Administration
Graduate School of Business Administration
Michigan State University

1970

MSU International Business
and Economic Studies

Institute for International Business
and Economic Development Studies
Division of Research
Graduate School of Business Administration
Michigan State University, East Lansing

Library of Congress Catalog Card Number: 78-631957
© *1970 by the Board of Trustees of Michigan State University*
East Lansing, Michigan

PRINTED IN THE UNITED STATES OF AMERICA

Dedicated
to the memory of my mother

Contents

Tables

xi

Appendix Tables

Preface

This study began when I was collecting materials for teaching a course in Marketing at the National Institute of Development Administration in Bangkok in 1967. Subsequently, the focus was broadened because of the feeling that it might have interest for a wider audience than two dozen Thai graduate students in Business Administration. I thought this was so for three reasons. First, the process of marketing development is of crucial importance in the larger problem of economic and social development of a nation, in which there is widespread interest and concern in the West. Second, the tragic years of western involvement on the Indochina Peninsula have meant an enormous investment in men, materiel, and emotions. In consequence, there is special interest in the modernization of Thailand, which has the largest population and the longest sovereignty in the peninsula. While the issue of the political future of Thailand and its capacity to remain independent is not the object of this study, it will probably not be resolved in isolation from the background of the economic and social development of the nation, of which this study is an aspect.

Finally, the subject of comparative marketing has received increasing attention in recent years. Multinational firms are interested in evaluating the prospects and problems of overseas markets and academics are probing the process of marketing in economies at various stages of development. Much of what has been written is criticized for its failure to relate the marketing system to the total environment of the society. I was attracted by the possibility of presenting Thai marketing in the form proposed by Bartels (1963) for the comparative analysis of national marketing systems. Thus, the first part of the study describes the ecological matrix of marketing through a brief review of the history and geography of the nation, characteristics of the society including its social institutions such as the family, religion, education and government, and an examination of the recent development of the economy. In the second part, the marketing structure for consumer goods is examined, and its functioning explored. An appendix provides statistical data on the society, the economy, and the marketing system which are intended not only to illumine the discussion in the text but also to provide information useful to students of either the case of Thailand or of comparative marketing in general. The rapid build-up of the heavy American military presence in 1968 and 1969 has obviously inflicted heavy distortions on the Thai society and economy; neither the statistical data nor the text discussion significantly reflect this distortion, however, since they bring the story up to the 1965-67 period with only occasional references to the later period. Similarly, there is little distortion through the main period of the study from change in the internal or external value of the baht, which is used throughout at the rate of twenty to the U.S. dollar.

Studies of developing societies generally carry a caveat on the quality of statistical data and this one is no exception. It is of obvious interest to quantify the socioeconomic dimensions of the market in a study of marketing development, and use has been made of most of the statistical data encountered which seemed relevant. Nearly always, this has been done with a certain uneasiness, however, and with modifications, partial rejection, and warnings. The capitals of developing countries give an illusion of modernity, and the outsider may forget that it is very much easier to import, install, and operate a computer (with the technical assistance of the manufacturer) than to carry out a nationwide census or sample survey which inspires confidence.

The uniqueness of the Thai society has attracted the interest of a number of western scholars, especially political scientists, anthropologists and some economists; their analyses have greatly simplified the work of later students. I acknowledge here my debt to these scholars collectively, and individually throughout the text in citations to their published work.

I am indebted also to a number of informants in private business and in government who have shared their information and experiences with me; out of respect for the confidentiality of their information in many cases and because of the length of the list, they will have to remain unnamed. A number of individuals have read parts or all of the manuscript and it has benefited greatly from their criticism and suggestions. In particular, I have imposed unconscionably on two Thai scholars of long experience—William J. Siffin, at Indiana University, and Frank J. Moore, now at Stanford University. At Michigan State University, Stanley C. Hollander and Kasum Nair have been most helpful on the problems of marketing and modernization respectively, and in Bangkok I am especially indebted to Frederic L. Ayer, Hermann Hatzfeldt, and to Barbara and C. Hart Schaaf. I acknowledge the friendship and help of my students and my colleagues on the faculty at the National Institute of Development Administration, and especially to Drs. Amara Raksasataya and Phaichitr Uathavikul. I must be held responsible, of course, for the errors of fact and of interpretation which remain.

A grant from the Midwest Universities Consortium for International Activities, Inc. made possible a period of research and writing upon return from my Thailand assignment, for which I am deeply grateful. Mrs. Esther Waite performed the editorial surgery with great skill.

Introduction

One of the crucial problems of our time is the acceleration of the process of nation building—that unifying or integrating into a viable organization of the people who reside within a country's boundaries. While this integrating process has political and social dimensions of great importance, our interest is in economic integration as manifested by the spread in the use of money and in the exchange of goods across the nation's land area. The development of a national market is at the very center of the process of economic development.

Marketing, however, is a relatively neglected aspect of the process of economic development. Whether from the view that it is a passive, self-adjusting mechanism in the economic system which can safely be ignored in a nation's somewhat frantic efforts to raise the level of well-being of its citizens, or from the view that the marketing system is so complex and so intertwined in the private lives of every citizen that it is better left alone, the fact is that development plans and strategies have typically left change in the marketing structure until later. Yet it is probably true that the development of marketing "makes possible economic integration and the fullest utilization of whatever assets and productive capacity an economy already possesses" (Drucker 1958, p. 253).

If national income accounting had been practiced in the seventeenth century and international comparisons of per capita income had been available, it is likely that Thailand, then Siam, would have ranked among the more developed nations of the world. All we have from that period, however, are the reports of European traders expressing their amazement at the splendor of this Oriental kingdom. It was not only the extravagance of the gilded palaces and opulent courts that impressed them; the peasantry in this soft and pleasant land were living comfortably in comparison with their starving ragged counterparts in Europe. Today, three centuries later, revolution has pushed the European peasant far ahead of his Asian counterpart. No longer is a condition of mere survival with relative ease considered sufficient for a citizen of the modern world, and Thailand's per capita income ranks her among the least developed nations.*

A study of marketing in Thailand goes beyond the relationship with the process of economic development, however. Only a scant century ago, Thailand began the traumatic experience of modernization, breaking out of the relative isolation of a kingdom dating from the thirteenth century into a modern nation in accommodation with the West. The Thai people have had a long history of accommodation to other cultures; wars, migrations, and trade have made them acquainted with change since their origins in the seventh century. From their neighbors came their religion and their alphabet; their art and literature and political organization show the imprint of others. Out of this history came an independence, and an adroitness, that left them the only nation of the Indochina Peninsula which was not subjugated to western colonialism during the last century. Instead, the two great kings, Mongkut (1851-68) and Chulalongkorn (1868-1910), examined the display of western wares—education, government, materialism, and economic development—and choices were made which, it was hoped, were consistent with the national character. Modernization and economic development have occurred, although

---

* Other measures than national income confirm the relatively low level of economic development, but it is nevertheless the case that Thailand and others suffer in international comparisons by the nature of national income accounting, as Usher's (1968) recent study has shown. His introductory paragraph merits quotation:
"My interest in the meaning of national income statistics began when I was working with the United Nations in Bangkok. In Thailand I saw a people not prosperous by European standards but obviously enjoying a standard of living well above the bare requirements of subsistence. Many village communities seemed to have attained a standard of material comfort at least as high as that of slum dwellers in England or America. But at my desk I computed statistics of real national income showing people of underdeveloped countries including Thailand to be desperately if not impossibly poor. The contrast between what I saw and what I measured was so great that I came to believe that there must be some large and fundamental bias in the way income statistics are compiled."

there is debate over how extensive has been the change in either aspect. Limited westernization, on the surface at least, is a good description of what has happened in Thailand in its recent history.

NATION-BUILDING AND INTEGRATION

Although the land area of Thailand has been occupied for centuries, integration into a nation has been slow; one author has described the nation as "the territory over which the Bangkok monarchy has been able to maintain its authority" (Silcock 1967, p. 1). Contrary to popular impression, Thailand is not small: among 151 nations, only 18 had larger populations in 1965.* But Thailand's is an ethnically diverse and geographically dispersed, and until recently, isolated population. An examination of the development of marketing, particularly of consumer goods as this study emphasizes, is inevitably concerned with the occupancy of space. A concept of Friedman's (1967), establishes an important dimension of this study:

> What are the major functional relations between the spatial distribution of activities and nation-building? The master concept here is integration. The reference is to integration of the national territory with respect to certain political, social, and economic variables. Corresponding to each variable is a space with respect to which integration occurs. We are thus able to speak of political, social, and economic spaces. National development is achieved through the political, social, and economic integration, at progressively higher levels, of the effectively settled territory of a nation.

The development of a national market for consumer goods is of obvious relevance to the growth of marketing in Thailand. The availability of goods and the sophistication of marketing for the 3 million people of the Bangkok Metropolitan Area must somehow be expanded to include more of the other 27 million people of Thailand. Again, the theme of dualism—the coexistence of the modern and the traditional which is found in developing societies—repeats itself in the two Thailands.

One of the theses of this study is that the creation of a road system

---

* Thailand is approximately the size of Spain in area and population, or of California and Florida together, although a third larger in population than those two states (United Nations, January 1967).

during the decade of the 1960s, which was largely motivated by considerations of national security rather than economic development, has revolutionized transportation and communications within the nation and has constituted an enormous step upward toward the integration of the economic space—that is, toward creating a national market —in Thailand. As recently as 1941 a reporter observed that:

> To this day, Siam is virtually a roadless land. For years the only roads that existed were confined to the capital and were built mostly for the pleasure of the wealthier Siamese. The transportation of the country's produce was and is still carried chiefly by river and on a network of canals throughout the country (Thompson 1967).

Since then, and particularly during the present decade, the construction of a road system with the financial and technical assistance of the United States and other nations has created an outlet for surplus products of the hitherto self-sufficient agricultural sector, expanded the reach of the money and exchange economy, and spread a variety of consumer goods throughout the nation.

THEMES IN COMPARATIVE MARKETING

Beyond the recent mobility revolution, which demonstrates the relationship between transportation and the extent of the market, a number of issues in comparative marketing are illustrated by the Thai case. The most basic issue is, of course, whether each nation is *sui generis*, so that there are no observed tendencies in common; while there is much uniqueness in Thai society and culture, as we shall see in the first two chapters, the last two chapters indicate many instances where Thai experience parallels marketing development in other nations. Among these instances are evidence of the role of incentive goods in commercialization and diversification of agriculture, of the coexistence of peasant, itinerant, and fixed-location marketing in rural areas, and the evidence that the marketing system reflects the society and economy it serves and changes with development of the society and the economy as exemplified in the impact of import-substitute industrialization on marketing channels. Finally, the Thai case illustrates the role of expatriate minorities in the commercial sector and Thailand's accommodation to the Chinese and to the West.

Part One:

The Ecological

Matrix of Marketing

I
The Thai Nation
and
Its Economic History

Our interest in the development of the marketing system of Thailand inevitably forces us to view the development of the economy, of which marketing is one aspect. And the economy and its development is of course one aspect of the Thai society and its development. Thus before we can go forward to the specifics of the marketing system, we must go back to the general, the ecological matrix of the society. By this we refer to the population and its characteristics, the resource endowment of the space which that population occupies, the economic and social organization which these people have developed, and the technology which they apply in relating their resources and institutions to their objectives as individuals and as a nation.

Since these matters are background for our principal interest, we must select for mention only those topics which seem of relevance to the marketing development of Thailand; hopefully this brief and generalized treatment will not distort or misrepresent reality, the essence of which is always complexity and nuance.

THAILAND AMONG THE NATIONS
OF THE INDOCHINA PENINSULA

The color and the tragedy in the early history of the lands now occupied by Thailand and her neighbors are well described in the following:

From the earliest times the great peninsula which lies between India and China and is now generally known as Farther India, has been peculiarly subject to foreign intrusion. Successive waves of Mongolian humanity have broken over it from the north, Dravidians from India have colonized it, Buddhist missions from Ceylon have penetrated it and buccaneers from the islands in the south have invaded it. Race has fought against race, tribe against tribe, and clan against clan. Predominant powers have arisen and declined. Civilizations have grown up, flourished and faded. Thus out of many diverse elements a group of nations have been evolved, the individuals of which . . . fundamentally much alike but differing in many externals, have striven during centuries for mastery over each other and incidentally over the countless minor tribes and clans which maintained a precarious existence in their midst (Graham 1912, p. 1).

The first kingdom of the Thai was founded in the mid-seventh century at Nanchao in the Yunnan province of China; from there the Thai migrated southward down the Menam River through the center of present-day Thailand. From the same origins and through similar southward-flowing river systems, the peoples of the other ethnic groups arrived at their present-day homes in the peninsula. Despite common origins, a common religion among the four contiguous Theravada Buddhist countries (Burma, Thailand, Cambodia, and Laos), and a common cultural heritage, their histories have been dominated mainly by common hostilities (Cady 1966, pp. 4-7). Even before the Kingdom of Nanchao had fallen to Kublai Khan, migrating Thai had reached a Cambodian garrison town of Sukhothai, conquered it, and established the first kingdom in the north-central region of present-day Thailand. After little more than a century, this empire disintegrated from within and a new capital was established in 1350 farther south at Ayutthaya in former Cambodian territory. The expanding Thai kingdom had the Cambodians on the defensive; a Thai raid on the Cambodian capital of Angkor in 1393 yielded ninety thousand prisoners who were transported back to Ayutthaya (Blanchard 1958, p. 29) and in 1431, Angkor had to be abandoned as the capital. But in the mid-sixteenth century Burma began a series of wars with Ayutthaya which lasted for two hundred years. The toll suffered by both realms was enormous—in a decline in population, production, and foreign trade. Finally, in 1767, Ayutthaya fell after a fourteen-month siege and was completely laid waste; the Burmese destruction of a city of over a million inhabitants, the center of a kingdom which had ruled much of the peninsula, seemed complete. Yet within the year a guerrilla leader of Thai-Chinese parentage who had escaped the Burmese and the ruins of Ayutthaya with a small band of followers succeeded in establishing a new capital farther south at Bangkok. Thus was formed the heritage of hostility which colors the current relations of Thailand with its neighbors, particularly Burma and Cambodia. As Cady (1966, p. 6) notes, "the striking similarities of religion, social organization, and governmental institutions which characterize the Theravada Buddhist states finds no counterpart in traditions of commercial or political cooperation."

Concurrent with this warfare among the nations of the peninsula were foreign intrusions from the colonial powers of the West. From the sixteenth century, Portugal, Holland, France, and England had jostled each other over the peninsula. By the beginning of the present century, Thailand was accepted as an independent buffer between the French interests to the East (now Cambodia, Laos, and Vietnam) and the British interests to the West and South (now Burma, Malaysia, and Singapore). As will be noted later, Thailand's "independence" cost her in many ways beyond the loss of territory; however, we may note here that during the period 1893-1909, she ceded (while French gunboats rode in the river at Bangkok) what is presently the country of Laos together with territory in Cambodia to France, a total of approximately one-third of Thailand's land area. Other grants included surrender to Britain of tenuous suzerain claims to four Malay sultanates in exchange for a railway loan (Cady 1966, p. 111).

The dimensions of the nations making up the Indochina Peninsula today are indicated in the following table; while the land areas are approximately as established early in this century, only Thailand was an independent nation until the post-World War II period when the other seven became nations:

Nation	Land Area (thous. sq. miles)	Population[1] Absolute (millions)	Density (per sq. mile)
Thailand	200.1	30.6	150
Burma	261.8	24.7	95
Cambodia	88.8	6.2	69
Laos	91.0	3.0	33
Malaysia (excl. Sabah and Sarawak)	50.6	8.1	160
Singapore	0.2	1.9	8,500
South Vietnam	65.0	16.1	250
North Vietnam	62.0	16.2	260

[1] Roughly for the period 1962-1965, based on latest census or U.N. estimates.

While these data on the area and population of the Indochina nations help us to characterize them, comparisons among the nations on certain other socioeconomic variables will be especially useful.

SOME MEASURES
OF PRESENT DEVELOPMENT

Our purpose is twofold in presenting the data of Table 1.1, which rank Thailand and the nations of the region on 19 variables; first, to confirm the level of economic development achieved by Thailand and its neighbors, and second, to indicate the character and quality of the *infrastructure of marketing.* The table shows the decile rank of each nation in the region and Japan among the approximately one hundred nations of the world which were analyzed in Norton Ginsburg's *Atlas of Economic Development.**

After more than two decades of concern with development, one of the few issues on which opinion is near unanimous is the imprecision of measures of development. And the weakest reed of all is the use in internation comparisons of that single best measure of development—per capita income. Table 1.1 shows that among 92 countries, Thailand ranked in the ninth decile, or next to the lowest group, on GNP per capita. Malaya ranks in the fifth decile, and Japan a bit lower, in the sixth. (We have included this example from outside the Indochina Peninsula because Japan is the dominant Asian economy, the most highly developed nation in the region despite this ranking on per capita GNP, and is increasingly the pacesetter and model for others like Thailand. Interestingly, commentators in the mid-nineteenth century felt that Thailand had a better chance than Japan to achieve a high level of economic development.) In terms of total gross national products, the nations of the region typically improve their rank because they are more populous than most nations. We have included this measure because sheer magnitude of the output of an economy has significance in marketing. However, both measures of the level of development are highly suspect. Myrdal's massive study of Asian development questioned whether national income figures for the region

---

* For the 19 indicators we have selected from those examined by Ginsburg, his number of countries varies from 92 to 139. We have, therefore, divided the rank of each of the countries in the region by the number of countries ranked on that factor and converted the resulting percentile into tenths where the highest rank 1 comprises the quotients 0-9.9 and the lowest rank 10, the quotients 90.0 and above.

Table 1.1 — Decile Rankings among Nations of the World on Income and Levels of Living: Indochina Peninsula Nations and Japan

Measures of Levels of Living[1]	Thailand	Burma	Cambodia	Laos	Vietnam[2]	Malaya (incl. Singapore)	Japan
1. Per capita income	9	10	n.a.	n.a.	8[b]	5	6
2. Total income	5	7	n.a.	n.a.	6[b]	5	1
3. Infant mortality	4[3]	10	n.a.	n.a.	n.a.	6	3
4. Medical care	6	7	10	10	10[b,c]	6	2
5. Food supply	9	10	9	10	n.a.	5	8
6. Youthfulness of population	10	5	9	7	9[a]	10	5
7. Concentration in agriculture	10	n.a.	9	10	n.a.	5	8
8. Urbanization	7	7	6	8	n.a.	4	2
9. Literacy	5	4	7	7	8[b]	6	2
10. Newspaper circulation	9	8	9	10	9[b]	5	1
11. Primary school enrollment	4	9	9	10	10[a]	6	4
12. Post-primary enrollment	4	5	9	10	7[b],9[c]	5	1
13. Railway use	8	8	10	—	10	8	3
14. Motor vehicle density	9	9	n.a.	10	n.a.	4	7
15. Energy consumption	9	9	10	10	10[b,c]	5	4
16. Steel consumption	8	9	10	n.a.	9[b,c]	4	3
17. Fertilizer consumption	8	10	9	n.a.	7[a]	5	1
18. International mail flow	9	10	9	9	7[a]	3	9
19. International trade turnover	8	9	10	10	10[b]	2	7

SOURCE: Ginsburg 1961.

Notes: 1 Details of the measures, and in parenthesis, the number of countries ranked are: 1. per capita gross national product (92), 2. total gross national product (96), 3. infant death rates per 1,000 live births (96), 4. physicians and dentists per 100,000 population (122), 5. calories per person per day (93), 6. percentage of population in ages 5-14 (115), 7. percentage of active population in agriculture (97), 8. percentage of population in cities of 20,000 or more (128), 9. percentage of adults literate (136), 10. daily circulation per 1,000 population (112), 11. percentage of children 5-14 in primary school (113), 12. percentage of total population in secondary and higher education (134), 13. million ton-kilometers per 100,000 population (89), 14. vehicles per 1,000 population (117), 15. megawatt-hours per capita (124), 16. tons per 1,000 population (108), 17. kilos of commercial fertilizer per hectare of cultivated land (100), 18. pieces dispatched per 1,000 population (111), 19. imports and exports per capita (123).

2 a. North and South Vietnam together
  b. South Vietnam only
  c. North Vietnam only

3 Other data suggest a ranking in the eighth decile is more probable, as discussed on page 9.

deserved to be published at all, in view of the conceptual problems and the weaknesses in the data which underlie the estimates. His decision was to publish the data, partly to call attention to their weaknesses and to the dangers of applying western concepts to the alien Asian situation, but also because there was the "possibility" that the evidence "may have some rough relationship to reality and in a very crude way have some meaning" (Myrdal 1968, pp. 482-83). It is significant, however, that Myrdal's group recalculated the per capita income estimates as published by the United Nations with the result that Thailand moved from sixth from the highest among nine Asian nations to third highest (Myrdal 1968, pp. 2165 ff.). On the new ranking, the Indochina Peninsula nations which he used showed Malaya first, Thailand third, South Vietnam fifth, and Burma sixth.

The eighteen measures of level of living shown in Table 1.1 can of course be considered as corroborative of the rough GNP estimates and hence of the level of general economic development. But they may also be viewed as evidences of the character and quality of the infrastructure which is available in the society to support marketing development. The most obvious illustration of this infrastructure is found in the four measures related to education and circulation of ideas—literacy, primary and post-primary school enrollments, and newspaper circulation. Thailand's rank, well above the median nation of the world on literacy and education, both attests to the high value placed on education in the society and suggests a necessary though not sufficient condition for a high circulation and receptivity of ideas and innovations. On the other hand, the rankings of all Indochina Peninsula nations on daily newspaper circulation are roughly consistent with their income levels and with other measures of their development, suggesting that newspapers are not yet prime vehicles for communication in these societies. The striking exception of Japan, with 397 copies of daily newspapers per thousand population compared with four per thousand for Thailand, is notable.*

Another group of factors concerns the physical quality of the people—infant mortality, number of physicians and dentists, and the food

---

* International Research Associates (1966, p. 24) reporting on a survey of consumers in seven Asian cities, showed that newspapers were read during the preceding twenty-four hours by 68 percent of the people interviewed in Bangkok, which was lower than all other cities except Manila with 52 percent. Tokyo and Hong Kong showed 93 percent and 90 percent respectively and Singapore 76 percent. No other Indochina Peninsula city was included in the survey.

supply. The assumption is that the lower the number of infant deaths, the larger the number of doctors and the larger the number of calories consumed daily per person, the healthier the population is, and therefore the better producers and consumers the people are. It should be noted that Thailand's very low infant mortality rate, ranking it in the fourth decile of 96 nations, attracted Ginsburg's suspicion and perhaps reflects noncomparability in the data. Myrdal (1968, p. 1404) cites ECAFE data which are calculated by demographic techniques rather than relying on official statistics and which suggest that a decile ranking of perhaps eight would be much more reasonable.* Another factor describing the population is the proportion of persons in the age range of five to fourteen years; for the nations of the world, this factor appears to be inversely related to wealth, as was infant mortality. And from a marketing point of view, the large proportion of the young in Thailand and its neighbors constitutes a burden in that they produce little if anything and consume less than adults.

The way the people are organized economically is indicated by the degree of concentration in agriculture; the assumption, of course, is that a high proportion of the population in agriculture is associated with a low level of development. Indeed, there are no examples of high income countries that contradict the assumption, and the Soviet Union is the extreme case of a "developed" country with half of its population in agriculture. Thailand with 85 percent in agriculture and Laos with 90 percent are at the very top of the scale,† and, except for Malaya, which includes Singapore with its *entrepot* activities, the peninsula is heavily agricultural.

A more refined measure of underdevelopment than the total agricultural population is the proportion of the population in subsistence agriculture which lies outside the reach of markets and money. Adelman and Morris (1967, pp. 19-22) use a variety of sources of information and estimates to classify the 74 underdeveloped countries of their study into four broad groups on the basis of the percentage

---

* This example illustrates Ginsburg's view (p. 24) that perhaps less is known about the demographic characteristics of a people than of any other set of facts about them. This is hardly surprising since to the peasant the process of registering births and deaths may be extremely burdensome and one's life simpler and more flexible without a birth certificate and its rigid date of birth. Other problems of demographic data are referred to in the article of Ayer, "Quantifying Thai Opinions," reproduced as Appendix C.

† Myrdal (1968, p. 494) offers estimates of 70 percent for Burma and 82 percent for South Vietnam.

of the population which was in "traditional" agriculture where the marketing of crops was relatively unimportant. Of the Indochina Peninsula nations, five were among the group of 74; Laos was among seventeen nations (mostly sub-Saharan) with 80 percent or more of their populations in subsistence agriculture, and Thailand, along with Burma, Cambodia, and South Vietnam fell in the next highest category of twenty-two nations with from 55 to 79 percent. Clearly Thailand and its neighbors were, about 1960, among the best examples of traditional subsistence agricultural nations in the underdeveloped world.

A corollary to high "agriculturalization" would be low urbanization of the population; while the data are arrayed in inverted order (that is, from low to high and high to low, respectively) the higher deciles signify the "less developed" condition here as throughout the table. All of the peninsula nations except Malaya again show lower urbanization rates than the mean for the world, with obvious implications for the marketing structures in these societies.*

Two factors in Table 1.1 relate to the mobility of goods and people within the nations: ton-kilometers of rail service and motor vehicles, both in relation to population. Since nearly one-fifth of the nations of the world have no railroads (Laos is one such nation), we have ranked only those having this service available. A characteristic of railroad systems in many less developed areas is their orientation to the transportation of raw materials for export rather than to the needs of the domestic economy. Hence the development of the highway system and motor vehicle density is probably a more essential infrastructure for marketing development; Chapter IV will explore this matter in the Thai case in great detail. At this point, we may note the relative underdevelopment of all peninsula nations, and that a nation's rank on this factor could improve rapidly in a few years of highway construction and high growth rates in the economy, as has characterized Thailand in the decade since these data were compiled.

Three measures of the consumption of critical items for development are shown next. It has been argued that the consumption of energy (here the estimate is for all forms except animal and human)

---

* Another factor, concentration of population in the primate city, will be discussed in detail in Chapter II. We may note, however, that all of the peninsula nations, along with other low-urbanization, low-income, recent-colonial-status nations, show heavy concentrations in a single great city, and that Thailand shows the highest ratio among 104 nations.

is the best single indicator of the level of development. The rankings of the peninsula nations on this factor and on the per capita consumption of steel and the use of commercial fertilizer per hectare of cultivated land are generally confirmatory of the relative levels of development.

Finally, two factors measure a nation's relationships with the rest of the world. A high per capita outflow of international mail in general correlates with the prosperous and highly industrialized and commercialized nations of the world. Similarly, the sum of the value of imports and exports, on a per capita basis, resembles the pattern of per capita income. However, there are exceptions, of which Malaya is a good example. Its very high ranking on trade and on mail flow is, of course, related to its position as the world's principal producer and exporter of tin and rubber and to Singapore's historic position as a center for international trade.

Table 1.2 summarizes the average ranking of the peninsula nations on the measures of the level of living (excluding the GNP rankings) with the income rankings.

Table 1.2 — Some Comparisons of Indochina Peninsula Nations

Country	Average Decile Ranking from Table 1.1	Per Capita Income Ranking	Percentage of Chinese in Total Population[1]		International Flights of Commercial Airlines, Weekly Arrivals[2]
			Singapore	75.2	191
Malaya	5.2	1	Malaysia	41.4	29
Thailand	7.6	3		12.0	161
Burma	8.1	4		1.6	79
Vietnam	8.7	2	South	9.4	38
			North	0.8	n.a.
Cambodia	9.0	n.a.		5.4	29
Laos	9.3	n.a.		1.5	9

[1] Estimates for 1966 from Liu (1967, p. 3).
[2] Number of weekly scheduled flights into the national capital, in November 1967, from Official Airline Guide. It should be noted that 54 weekly flights arriving at Kuala Lumpur are from Singapore, and vice versa; before the separation of Singapore from Malaya in 1965, these would have been classed as domestic flights. Perhaps a more indicative measure is the number of flights arriving whose last stop was outside the peninsula; by this measure, Bangkok had 127 flights weekly, Singapore 49, and Kuala Lumpur 14.

The last two columns contain data of special significance in interpreting Thailand's position today in relation to her peninsula neighbors. The overseas Chinese have played a prominent part in the modernization of these societies by reason of their interests and competencies in trade and industrialization. Thus it is not coincidental that the most advanced nations, Malaya and Thailand, should have the largest concentrations of Chinese in their populations. Another fortuitous circumstance for Thai development and marketing is the geography of air transportation. Bangkok's ideal location for routes which were forced to skirt the southern edge of the China land mass gave an initial advantage in the prejet era which persists today in the great disequality shown in Table 1.2.

From this brief consideration of the position of Thailand in the Indochina Peninsula, we turn now to an examination of the nation's economic history in order to identify the roots of its marketing system.

A SUMMARY OF THE HISTORY

We have briefly referred to the rise and fall of kingdoms in the Indochina Peninsula and the emergence of the Thai nation out of this background of continuous struggle. A very important thread in Thailand's subsequent history concerns the development of trade, which in turn is the story of the society's accommodation with the Chinese and of struggle and accommodation with the West.*

By the time the migrating Thai reached the delta of the Chao Phraya and the Malay Peninsula in the thirteenth century, Chinese traders had probably already established themselves in ports and markets around the Gulf of Siam. And soon after the first distinct Thai kingdom was established at Sukhothai in 1238, the Mongol power in China attempted to enroll the kingdom as a tributary state. By the end of the fourteenth century, when Ayutthaya replaced Sukhothai as the center of the kingdom, frequent missions carried tribute to China and brought back Chinese goods for which the Thai rulers had acquired a taste. As the power of the Thai kingdom grew during the next three centuries, tribute declined and private trading increased. There were periods of vicissitude of course. One Thai king developed close relations with Japan and for a brief period (the

---

* Any brief treatment of these subjects is inevitably a distillation from the work of two careful scholars—Ingram (1955) on the economic history of Thailand, and Skinner (1957 and 1958) on the Chinese problem.

1620s), Thai trade with that country was greater than with all others combined; Chinese traders had a substantial part of the trade, however. The next king inaugurated royal trade monopolies in 1629 which required the Chinese to get permits from the king and to deliver tin and lead, which they had been mining for centuries in the south of Thailand, to the king's warehouse in Ayutthaya before export. But even this innovation was soon turned to the advantage of the Chinese who, as the most competent and experienced traders available, were entrusted with these activities on behalf of the king and at a good profit to themselves.

The origins of these commercial activities lay in the geographic position of Thailand—a bridge between China and the East and India and the West. Collis (1936, p. 46) describes the wonderment of the European traders of the sevententh century who came upon Ayutthaya, "a mart of the fabulous Orient, with an extravagant atmosphere of it own." Each measured it against the drab West of his own experience. East India Company directors found it "as great a city as London." The French found it "larger than Paris with poor houses (very shabby-looking outside but . . . clean within. We entered one of them prepared to see the peasants in rags, but all was spick and span, the floor covered with mats, Japanese coffers and screens everywhere. Hardly inside the door, they offered us tea in porcelain cups), magnificent pagodas, an admirable river (three times the size of the Seine, flowing around the strong great inland city), a huge population and with countless boats." A Dutchman marvelled at the king's palace, "like a town apart, great and magnificent, many of its buildings and towers being entirely gilded." What they were seeing was, in the words of Collis (1936, pp. 47-49)

> the distributed dividend of the coast [within the East, not East-West] trade. The Chinese and Japanese brought to Ayudhya silk, tea, porcelain, quicksilver and copper-bronze vessels, taking in exchange such articles as scented woods, pepper, hides and bird's nests. The far-eastern products were largely sold to dealers for transport via Mergui [on the Bay of Bengal] to Golconda [India] and the Persian Gulf. The enterprise of Mahomedan merchants had made Ayudhya a great center for the exchange of goods between China and India. They had also found a market for the Siamese home products. As a result, even the common people were comfortably off, far better provided than the ragged starving peasantry of Europe.

In such a heady atmosphere for westerners, the attractions were great. The cordiality of contacts with the West, which had begun with the first treaty with Portugal and an exchange of ambassadors in the early sixteenth century, were intensified by King Narai (1657-1688). Since both imports and exports came under royal monopoly, foreign traders had to vie for favor with the king and his court while trying to frustrate similar plans of their competitors. The king was in need of military aid; Louis XIV sent a mission in 1683, but to convert him to Catholicism. Instead the mission had to settle for a treaty assuring France of 90 percent of the pepper produced in Siam. Western adventurers and agents of the East India Company acting on their own behalf came to positions of control in the royal trade. One such, a Greek named Constance Phaulkon, had been made a Thai noble and administrator of all Siam's foreign trade. In 1688, Phaulkon was executed by the aristocracy on the charge of having brought French troops to Siam with the intent of staging a coup d'etat. King Narai was overthrown, ruthless persecution of foreigners followed, and for the next century and a half Thailand was in effect closed to the West.

The departure of the westerners left the trade of Siam in Chinese hands, where it had been before; as Skinner puts it (1957, p. 11) the Chinese "fared well for the simple reason that they were never considered foreigners by the Thai." The royal trading monopoly, which lasted until the Bowring Treaty in 1855, provided the Chinese with profitable jobs as factors, warehousemen, accountants, and seamen as well as opportunities for private trade, and the migration of Chinese to Siam was encouraged.

Chinese immigration to Thailand is a fact of enormous importance in the nation's economic history and in present-day marketing. Thus we must not only briefly examine the "Chinese problem," as it is commonly referred to, as a part of the national history but return to it in the next chapter on the Thai society, and in Chapter III on the marketing structure. Not surprisingly, the dimensions of Chinese immigration before the present century are largely conjecture; however, the broad terms are sufficient for our purposes.

As early as the seventeenth century, between four and five thousand Chinese were emigrating to Thailand annually, according to one estimate (Blanchard 1958, p. 55); another estimate for the latter half of that century finds a minimum of ten thousand Chinese residing in the country, or less than 1 percent of the total population at that time (Skinner 1957, p. 13).* For most of the eighteenth century, China placed various restrictions on emigration and invented lures to return, largely in an attempt to break up the colonies of overseas Chinese which were centers of opposition to the regime. After the fall of Ayutthaya to the Burmese in 1767, the accession of King Toksin began a period of favorable treatment by a monarch who was himself half Chinese, and immigration continued to be stimulated until the imposition of restrictions by the Thai in the present century. Of course, the flow varied from year to year as economic conditions in the two countries increased the "push" from South China and the "pull" to Thailand.

A crucial question in marketing development obviously is the size and the degree of assimilation of a minority group such as the Chinese, as well as the extent of the difference and distinctness in the value systems of the two societies. The latter question will be dealt with in the next chapter. Since the closing of immigration from mainland China, the question of assimilation concerns the ethnic Chinese—that is, of those who while born in Thailand and are therefore automatically Thai citizens nevertheless identify with the Chinese way of life.†

According to Skinner's carefully made estimates, the ethnic Chinese population rose from about 5 percent of the total population of Thailand in 1825 to a peak of about 12 percent during the period 1927-1947, and has since begun a slow decline; current estimates would put the ethnic Chinese at about 10 percent. The proportion of the China-born Chinese in Thailand is of course much smaller; according to Skinner's model (1957, pp. 79, 183) these Chinese accounted for about 2 percent of the population in 1825 with the figure rising to a peak of over 5 percent at the end of the 1920s, and declining to 3.4 percent by 1955. These proportions vastly understate

---

* The two estimates are not necessarily inconsistent; many Chinese returned to their birthplaces after making their fortune, or at life's end. Skinner's analysis of the statistics available from 1882 on shows annual departures of Chinese from Thailand equal to over half of the arrivals, and in the period 1906-1917, as high as 78 percent (p. 61).

† Skinner (1957, p. 184) defines "local-born Chinese" as those born of a Chinese or half Chinese (*lukjin*, i.e., one born of a Chinese father and Thai mother) father, who speaks a Chinese language (although he usually also speaks Thai), and who identifies in most social situations with Chinese rather than Thai. Business Research, Ltd. (1966) defines ethnic Chinese households as those in which Chinese is spoken at home by two or more members of the household.

the importance of the Chinese, however. For one reason, the Chinese were concentrated in the nation's capital. When Bangkok became the capital in 1782 with the beginning of the still-ruling Chakkri dynasty, the Chinese market of that day had to be moved bodily outside the royal city to make room for the palace. But the Chinese remained very much in evidence. In fact, there were more Chinese than Thai in the capital city during the first half of the nineteenth century, and even today a market research survey finds 37 percent of the households in the metropolitan area ethnically Chinese (see footnote below and Table 2.3). Thus there was a substantial multiplier effect from the concentration of the Chinese presence at the center of power and innovation of the nation. Similarly, the attitude that the Thai did not consider the Chinese as foreigners reflects the high degree of inter-marriage which occurred in the earlier periods when Chinese immi-gration consisted largely of males. This assimilation occurred even in the royal family; not only was the king before the beginning of the present dynasty half Chinese, but down to the present century the Chi-nese strain was continuously reinforced so that the sixth and seventh monarchs similarly were at least one-half Chinese by ancestry (Skinner 1957, pp. 26-27). Thus, in this respect also, the actual Chinese influ-ence on the society was greater than the very minor share of the total population would suggest. Finally, the Chinese were important be-yond their numbers by reason of the economic role they played.

The earlier reference to the Chinese not being considered foreign should not be construed to mean that they were an integral part of Thai society. From the beginning, Thailand has been a nation of rulers and ruled: the rulers were the king and his retinue of princes and officials of high and low status; the ruled were the Thai com-moners, either slaves or freemen.* Many slaves had voluntarily in-dentured themselves in exchange for the assumption of their debts by an elite family. At the same time, freemen could become attached to a patron family to satisfy their *corvée* obligation. The essence of both conditions was protection or support at the cost of substantial or full-

---

* By the fifteenth century, a highly elaborated hierarchial system existed which assigned "dignity marks" (*sakdi na*) to each individual in the realm. Originally related to the amount of land over which an individual had nominal or actual jurisdiction (the marks ran from the low of 25, signifying the 25 *rai* of land or 10 acres of the commoner, to 10,000 marks or 4,000 acres associated with the head of an important department (Siffin 1966, pp. 18-19), the marks came to signify relative position in the hierarchy. Designations by this point system were abolished only in 1932 when the absolute monarchy was ended.

time service; the freeman was not really free nor was the slave really oppressed. But neither had geographic mobility nor incentive to develop personal skills, which might make him more indispensible to his patron or owner and thus even less free. The Chinese, on the other hand, was outside of this system since he was exempt from the *corvée* obligation, from slavery and the patronage relationship and from restrictions on his geographic mobility; in the nineteenth century, his obligation was limited to the payment of a head tax which was "large enough to be a sizable source of revenue but not so large as to discourage immigration" (Skinner 1957, p. 97). The tax levied on the Chinese was only one-third that levied against a Thai (Ingram 1955, p. 211). This special position of the Chinese within the Thai society from the earliest times was an important element in the economic specialization along ethnic lines which became of crucial importance in the economic history of Thailand in the nineteenth century.

One other subject—the so-called revenue or tax farms—merits brief attention before we reach the great turning point of Thai history in the mid-nineteenth century. During the reign of Rama II (1809-1824) the government adopted the practice of farming out the collection of various taxes to private entrepreneurs. The right to collect a particular tax in a specified area was put up for bid annually by the government agency concerned. Such concessions were highly profitable, at least in the hands of the Chinese entrepreneurial class, and the government realized revenues it was not yet well enough developed administratively to collect directly. The introduction of free trade in 1855 eliminated the royal trading monopolies, and as the government was forced to turn increasingly to revenue farms, the stakes rose for the Chinese leaders, who had to pool resources to bid for these monopolies and to pay the high amounts required by Thai officials for their influence. As we shall see later, the economic growth of the period was made possible by the immigration of Chinese laborers; they brought with them their love of opium, spirits, the lottery, and other forms of gambling and the Thai government obliged by creating monopoly farms for these vices which provided it with between 40-50 percent of its total revenues during most of the second half of the century. Another characteristic of the period was the growth of Chinese secret societies, organized on speech-group lines (some half-dozen mutually unintelligible Chinese dialects were represented in the immigrants) to protect the occupational interests of the group; since the societies cut a vertical swath through the economic and social classes, the thugs at the bottom were available to "protect" the revenue flow to the leaders at the top who had bought the revenue farms. Finally, the Thai government legitimized these Chinese leaders, who were supplying the state with its revenues, by ennobling them; the result was to foster assimilation and neutralize power which might have otherwise undermined the state. So much for accommodation to the Chinese. We turn now to the developments which opened Thailand once again to the West and brought the nation into the modern world.

MODERNIZATION IN
THE NINETEENTH CENTURY

The revolution which brought enormous change to Thailand centers around a treaty with Great Britain in 1855 and the reigns of two kings—Mongkut (1851-1868), the subject of *The King and I*, and his son Chulalongkorn (1868-1910).

From the point of view of marketing development, the signing of the Bowring Treaty in 1855 was certainly one of the most important events in the nation's history. The treaty opened Thailand to the West by the imposition of a regime of free trade, both internally and externally. It fixed import duties at 3 percent ad valorem on all articles and set export duties on most of the products of any significance. With such provisions, Thailand not only opened the way for western imports and for the exportation of her primary products but also in effect gave up control over her own fiscal affairs (which she did not regain until 1926), since changes in revenues from trade became the subject of treaty negotiation. British subjects were given the right to trade freely and directly with individual Siamese at all seaports, to travel freely throughout the interior, and to enjoy extraterritoriality. The treaty became a pattern for similar negotiations with other nations during the latter half of the century. The effects of the Bowring Treaty were immediate and dramatic.* Western trading houses opened offices to develop import and export opportunities. Ingram's study (1955, p. 36) of economic growth in the one hundred years from 1850 has carefully documented the major trends resulting

---

* A limited amount of trade with the West had begun as a result of the Burney Treaty of 1826 with Britain and subsequent treaties with the United States. However, duties and tonnage charges on foreign ships were onerous and only the Chinese were exempt from them and free to travel within the country, own property, and so forth.

from the increase in foreign trade. The volume of rice exports increased twenty-five times by 1930 as the Thai population specialized more and more in the production of rice and a few other minor primary products. During the same period the population merely doubled in size. Imports of a variety of manufactured goods increased roughly proportionately. Local industry and household crafts were inhibited, and cotton acreage was abandoned or switched to the cultivation of rice to earn money to buy British textiles. The history of the destruction of the Indian textile crafts (Myrdal 1968, p. 455) was repeated in Thailand; it was "the natural outcome of the unequal struggle between an old and a new technology . . . helped and hastened by protection in England against Indian products combined with free entry into India of English products." The cases are different, of course; Thailand had never had India's advanced industrial and commercial methods, the equal of those of any other part of the world up to the eighteenth century. But the similarity in the end results are striking for Thailand—the only country in Southeast Asia which was never "colonized" and which has maintained its "independence" throughout the last two centuries.

The market for consumer goods in Thailand after the Bowring Treaty is picturesquely described in the following, published in 1912:

> In the almost complete absence of local manufacturers, the whole nation depends altogether upon imported goods for the supplying of all its wants other than foodstuffs. In the village market-places throughout the kingdom, the trade marks of Manchester cotton-sellers, the familiar legends on the tins of English-made biscuits, German dyes and Swiss milk, and the flash advertisements of British and American tobacco dealers meet the eye. The peasant goes clad in English or Indian calico, wears on his head an Austrian straw hat, makes his tea in an Austrian enamelled iron kettle and pours it into a thick, stoneware cup, gilded with what he takes to be words of foreign magic, though these are in fact no more than the invocation "Forget me not," or the dedication "For a good child" (Graham 1912, p. 395).

This description, for the beginning of this century, suggests that monetization of the economy had spread over the entire kingdom, which was hardly the case. In Chapter IV, a discussion of the growth of the transportation system will show how slowly the nation's land area has been integrated into Bangkok and the Central Plain, which historically has been the heartland as well as the principal rice-growing area.

An indirect measure of monetization (Appendix Table 12) shows that 65 of the 71 provinces of Thailand had no commercial bank offices in 1940, and by 1955, 42 provinces or 60 percent of the total still had no banks; by 1967, however, all provinces had at least one bank.

The negotiating of the Bowring Treaty was one of a series of responses of an extremely able monarch to a threatening environment. The air was heavy and the skies over the Orient dark. The end of the Opium War in 1842 saw the British force open five Chinese port cities to trade, and in 1854, Perry and the American fleet achieved similar aims in Japan. The reign of Mongkut opened with the British taking control of all of southern Burma on Thailand's western frontier, and closed with the ceding of Cambodia to France on the east. Thailand was caught in the middle; Mongkut described the dilemma in a letter to his embassy in Paris as "whether to swim up-river to make friends with the crocodile or to swim out to sea and hang on to the whale."*

It would be erroneous, however, to view Mongkut and Chulalongkorn as merely defenders of the traditional Thai way, reluctantly retreating before the onslaught of western culture backed by superior force. Rather, they were true modernizers, trying as Riggs (1966, p. 371) puts it "in some way to harmonize alien values and practices with their own history."

We may summarize briefly those achievements of the modernizing kings which had special significance for economic, or for marketing development. While the task of "harmonizing alien values and practices with their own history" had to fall to the Thai, the display of western "wares" was not left to chance contact. The use of foreign advisors in the government was begun by Mongkut, who invited eighty-four Europeans to serve as military officers, technicians, and, of course, as palace tutor for the children of the royal family, including

---

* Cited in Moffat (1961, p. 124). The same letter observed that "the British and the French can entertain no other feeling for each other than mutual esteem as fellow human beings, whereas the likes of us who are wild and savage, can only be regarded by them as animals. We have no means of knowing whether or in what way they have contrived beforehand to divide our country among themselves" (p. 119).

the future king;* during Chulalongkorn's reign, 549 foreigners provided thousands of man-years of advice and technical assistance (Siffin 1966, pp. 50, 96). Some of these westerners served as advisors directly to the king and his ministers and obviously exerted great influence over policy. They tended to be selected along national lines so that the Financial Advisor was always British, the Legislative Advisor always French, and the General Advisor an American (Siffin 1966, p. 95). Most of the foreigners worked in top- and middle-level administrative and technical positions in the ministries, however, and effectively provided the expertise lacking in the developing bureaucracy and the on-the-job training of the Thai who ultimately took over the functions. Western education for the Thai began when Chulalongkorn sent his son abroad; four reigns later, the present king was born in Cambridge, Massachusetts, where his father was studying public health. As we shall see in the next chapter, western education has become standard for the elite and a modernizing force of great significance.

Two other developments during the reigns of the modernizing kings had far-reaching effects on the developing economy. The systems of *corvée* and slavery were viewed as inconsistent with the aims of the developing nation. By 1850, the obligation of *corvée* labor had been modified by accepting payments in money or goods in lieu of the service requirement; Mongkut decreed that wage labor should be substituted for *corvée* in public works projects where possible. Similarly, slavery was gradually reduced during his and his son's reigns and was finally abolished in 1905. Two results ensued—Thai peasants were free to devote themselves exclusively to the clearing of new land and the growing of rice, and at the same time, the demand for wage labor at high wages stimulated new waves of Chinese immigration. Thus the racial specialization of labor which had begun centuries earlier was strengthened and expanded. The Thai wanted to grow rice and to enjoy the village way of life. The Chinese, on the other hand, wanted to make money, since most intended to return to their families in China with their accumulated savings, which would enable them to escape the grinding poverty of the homeland. Many settled in

---

* The practice of polygamy, together with systematic attention to the male children's education, provided competence and loyalty in the bureaucracy which Mongkut was trying to develop. He fathered 94 children over a period of 45 years and when his son, Chulalongkorn died, 20 of Mongkut's other children were still alive, including four cabinet ministers (Siffin 1966, p. 94).

Thailand instead. Rapid upward mobility was possible in the second half of the nineteenth century as a result of the Chinese willingness to work hard at the high-paying jobs and consume little. It was said of the most common Chinese day laborer in Bangkok in the 1870s that he could save two-thirds of his earnings. And the spreading monetization of the economy offered opportunities in the new towns of the interior. The railroad system was built, beginning at the end of the century, almost exclusively with Chinese unskilled labor, many of whom afterward settled into small trading in the area opened up by the transport line.

The other development during modernization was the creation of a government structure to administer the nation, largely achieved during Chulalongkorn's reign. Our interest centers on those government activities concerned with revenue and with attempts to unify or integrate the national territory. The larger story of the development of the Thai bureaucracy has captured the interest and attention of a number of western scholars, most recently and in greatest detail by Riggs (1966) and by Siffin (1966).

We have seen how, in the absence of administrative machinery, the government was forced to "farm out" the collection of taxes, including those on opium and gambling, and the handling of the state trading monopoly to private individuals, largely Chinese. The elimination of trading monopolies by the Bowring Treaty and of freedom of the government to tax foreign trade, together with abuses under the tax farms, made revenues a critical problem for the government. The introduction of direct collection by the government in 1892 increased tax collections threefold in a decade and without the imposition of new taxes, but the Chinese entrepreneurial class was forced to shift its base of revenues and activities.

The continuous threat of the British and the French to Thai sovereignty made perfectly clear to the Bangkok government the need to integrate the nation by building a transportation and communications system and this effort began in Chulalongkorn's reign. This of course was of crucial importance in developing a national market and in Chapter IV we will show in some detail the achievement of this national integration in very recent times.

The change and economic growth triggered by the introduction of free trade forced the Chinese to adapt to the new rules; at this they had shown themselves very adept, however. Skinner (1957, p. 100) has listed the special advantages the Chinese had built up over the years as their knowledge of the Thai market, their connections with other Chinese retailers throughout the country, their willingness as importers to go directly to the consumer with however small quantities the latter could afford, their experience in dealing with Thai officials for centuries, the discrimination in their favor such as low duties assessed on their cargoes and their ships, their freedom to engage in foreign trade with the king's rather than their own capital, their right to buy real estate, and to travel freely throughout the country. But, as Bowring himself observed of his achievement: "Though a small number of the Chinese profited by the [now outlawed monopoly] farms, the enormous majority expressed their great delight at the emancipation which the treaty provided" (quoted in Skinner 1957, p. 101).

The fact is that the Chinese had for centuries applied their proclivities to an excellent opportunity with the encouragement of society. Not surprisingly, attempts to equalize with western trading interests, as in 1855, or to purposely stifle the Chinese, as in the outright discrimination during a period of nationalistic fervor in the 1930s, were largely ineffectual. The Chinese advantage was noted in the following description by a first-hand observer in 1855:

> The greater activity of the Chinese and their roving and adventurous spirit have made them the principal channels of trading operations in all parts of the country. There are no districts too remote to be explored by them, no object of traffic too small to escape their notice. They are awake to everything which is to leave lucre in their hands; they are masters of the art of exploring and exploiting . . . there is no class of settlers who . . . are so likely to be useful. . . . The very quality, the passion for acquiring wealth, which leads them to dare all danger and difficulty, is a most valuable recommendation (quoted in Blanchard 1958, p. 338).

It is pertinent to explore the Chinese response to the advent of free trade for it demonstrates the adaptability of the most important entrepreneurial class in Thailand. The quotation cited above describes their control over internal trade at the time that Thai markets were opened to western firms. Seventy-five years later, observers commented on the fact that 85 to 90 percent of the country's trade was concentrated in their hands. At the retail level, which is most visible to the layman, this was probably true; at the wholesale and importers level, the Chinese and the westerners were in competition, although the western trading houses were probably importing the greater volume of goods, which they passed on to Chinese wholesalers/retailers.* The crucial point (and we shall return to it in greater detail in the discussion of the marketing structure in Chapter III) is that the Chinese were interposed between the western producer and the Thai consumer.

Coughlin (1960, p. 4) has described the relationship between the Chinese merchants and western trading firms as symbiotic. The trading houses had access to manufacturers in the West, together with financing, shipping, and insurance facilities, which the Chinese could not hope to match. The Chinese, for their part, were the final link with the consumer, whether in Bangkok or the remote countryside. The Chinese collection and distribution network and the western importing and exporting firms were indeed two dissimilar organisms living together to the advantage of each, and, for imported consumer goods, the marriage prevailed from the mid-nineteenth century generally until the post-World War II period when western manufacturers began local assembly and more direct marketing.

The Chinese did not accept the relationship passively, however, and the western retreat beginning in the latter part of the last century was into a changing mix of activities. An example of Chinese challenge and western response is in the mechanization of rice milling, cited by Skinner (1957, p. 104). Prior to the great increase in rice exports which resulted from the Bowring Treaty in 1855, milling had been by hand in small Chinese mills. In 1858, an American company built the first steam mill and ten years later there were five such mills, all western owned. The superiority of steam milling was obvious and the Chinese began buying small mills, together with the services of western engineers; by 1912, nearly all steam mills were in Chinese hands. The key to the Chinese success was vertical integration on ethnic lines; Chinese itinerant middlemen upcountry bought paddy

---

* Coughlin (1960, pp. 3-4) has cautioned against exaggerating the economic importance of the Chinese. He cites Landon, who examined the ethnic affiliations of trading firms listed in business directories in 1933 and 1940 and concluded that of 235 firms in the former year, 48 percent were western and 26 percent Chinese; by 1940 western firms had declined to 35 percent and Chinese increased to 33 percent of 299 listed trading firms. Coughlin queried a British bank officer in Bangkok regarding the nationality of the owners of the 50 leading commercial firms, according to the bank's confidential information, and reported that 29 were western-owned, 4 Chinese, and 17 were of other nationalities, principally Indian and Near-Eastern.

from the rice farmer, thus securing the source for the Chinese mills and freezing out the westerners. Since the chief market overseas was in areas where the Chinese controlled importing (Singapore, Hong Kong, and South China) the ethnic chain was complete. In Skinner's words: "Thus did the Westerners lose to the Chinese the biggest prize of all in Siam. The Thai declined to compete." In other areas such as rubber exporting, banking, and insurance, Chinese power increased, not always at the expense of western interests. Of course, individual Chinese were widely employed by western firms and the institution of the *comprador,* or native (in this case, Chinese) manager of western interests had many applications in Thailand. Even today, western firms advertising for sales personnel frequently require a command of three languages—English, Thai, and Taechew, the latter being the Chinese dialect most common in commerce.

The Thai response to the growing power of the Chinese in the economy constitutes an important thread in the history of the nation's development and the basis for a second symbiotic relationship which emerged. In 1932, the absolute monarchy was ended by a coup engineered by an alliance of civilian government officials and army officers. Since then, the political history has been characterized by frequent shifts of power among cliques, some coups with bloodshed, a number of constitutions, occasional elections, and other evidences of the trauma of moderization, including a strain of nationalism. Beginning in the 1930s, a number of laws were passed which attempted to restrict the Chinese power over the economy. One form of this Thaification movement has been to require the employment of minimum proportions of Thai citizens in certain activities, such as 50 percent in rice mills and 75 percent on Thai ships. In other cases, aliens were excluded from such specified occupations as rice cultivation, salt-making, production and distribution of charcoal, taxi-driving, barbering, manufacture of ice and soft drinks, and others. In some instances, the prohibited activities appear to be related to national security or the essentiality of certain goods; in other cases, the logic is elusive. In any event, the net effect of such controls has been minimal since enforcement has not been carried to the point of disrupting the functioning of an industry. Probably the greatest effect of these laws has been to spur assimilation, since by becoming a Thai citizen, a Chinese avoids the exclusion.

Another form of pressure on Chinese power has been through the creation of state-owned enterprises to provide competition to the private sector, to assure supplies of essential goods not capable of interdiction by aliens in a national emergency, and to provide employment opportunities to Thai nationals. One example of this policy was the creation, in the immediate post-World War II years, of state-owned trading companies (actually, retail stores selling food, appliances, hardware, and the like) in every province. Many of these stores have been managed by Chinese in the absence of interested and capable Thai. While Thaification of the economy was often involved in the justification for the creation of these enterprises, other factors flowing out of the disruptions of the war and Japanese occupation were important, such as the need to supplement the inflation-eroded incomes of officials and the military.* Once created, however, they increasingly came to be viewed as sources of income and patronage to the ministries to which they were attached and to the officials who managed them. We shall return to consider other aspects of the problem of state enterprises later; suffice it to say that by the decade of the 1960s, this form of pressure on Chinese economic power had given way to a new form of assimilation.

The new symbiotic relationship in business activity is between the Chinese business leaders and the Thai political leaders—what Riggs (1966, p. 251) has described as "pariah entrepreneurship," a phenomenon arising out of the economic growth and industrial development beginning in the 1950s. Piecemeal purchase of protection by the Chinese businessman against arbitrary acts of government officials became expensive and uncertain, and the possibilities of harassment were limitless.† On the other side, the Thai official needed wealth commensurate with his power, his government salary was inadequate and participation in the management of state enterprises offered only limited relief. Since the culture had no inhibiting concept like the western "conflict of interest," prominent Thai officials were invited to become directors of Chinese businesses.‡ Even among the less prominent bureaucrats, a variety of opportunities to participate in the growing business sector were available.

---

* The subject of state enterprises has been discussed in detail in Artamonoff (1965), and Silcock (1967, pp. 258-77), in addition to Muscat.
† "Where communism is a crime . . . who is to say whether or not a Chinese businessman harbors dangerous thoughts, especially with the growth of power in neighboring Communist China" (Riggs 1966, p. 253).
‡ See Riggs' (1966, pp. 254 ff, 270) discussion of cabinet ministers' participation on business boards.

In this latest example of Thai adroitness in adapting to an external threat the rationale of the bureaucracy is that it is fostering Thaification of the economy and the further assimilation of the Chinese.

THE ERA OF DEVELOPMENT

The two western economists who have examined Thailand's growth in greatest detail, Ingram (1955) and Muscat (1966), have both been intrigued by the question of why more development did not occur. As a result of his study, Ingram found

> many changes in the economy of Thailand in the last hundred years, but not much "progress" in the sense of an increase in the per capita income, and not much "development" in the sense of the utilization of more capital, relative to labor, and of new techniques. The principal changes have been the spread of the use of money, increased specialization and exchange based chiefly on world markets, and the growth of a racial division of labor (p. 216).

Indeed, the great gap betwen Thailand and Japan in their economic development is especially dramatic when viewed in the light of their approximately equal start a century ago and of the expectation of some commentators of that day that Thailand offered the better prospects for growth.* The consensus seems to be that development did not occur because the government failed to take the steps which might have stimulated development. Ingram speculates on what Thailand might have become had the government adopted a program of incentives to growth: limiting immigration of the Chinese, restricting imports to protect infant industries, and relaxing the very conservative monetary and fiscal policies in order to provide an infrastructure in transportation, power supply, irrigation, and education.† However, he

---

* Ingram's conclusion (1955, p. 215) was that "Thailand remained virtually static except for quantitative changes in traditional lines of production, while Japan entered a period of rapid technological and economic change. The actions Japan took were just the ones Thailand could not take. This, of course, does not mean that Thailand could have matched the Japanese record, but a sharp contrast nevertheless appears when we observe that in Thailand, unlike Japan, virtually no new products and no new methods emerged in the last century. Economic changes were in volume rather than in kind."
† In Chapter IV we shall examine in greater detail the adverse effect on the integration of a national market of the government's failure to develop a transportation system.

acknowledges that the limitations on Thailand's sovereignty, such as the Bowring Treaty obligation to permit free trade and the conservative financial policy imposed by the British advisors, made a different course of action than that taken somewhat unlikely.

Muscat's answer to the question of why the nation is still under-developed is in the same vein, noting the unusually passive attitude of the government:

> The absence of conditions producing great social cleavages and tensions, the existence of religious and social behavior patterns conducive to reducing and repressing what tensions did arise, the lack of a harsh environment that would call for vigorous economic and technical activity and improvement for reaching some minimum of comfort, and the extraordinarily adept ruling class which clearly saw the limitations on Thailand's freedom of action and the need for an adaptive foreign policy—all these factors operated to raise stability to the first place among economic goals, and to militate against adoption of growth as a major goal of domestic economic policy. Under these circumstances it is meaningless to inquire what should have been done to stimulate economic growth since growth was not recognized to be (and was not) one of the problems confronting Thai society (pp. 29-30).

By 1950, economic development *was* a problem and the government became heavily involved in growth and change, as the chronology of the decade shows:

1950—National Economic Council formed, supplanted in 1959 by the National Economic Development Board

1951—first aid agreement with the United States

1952—first national income estimates, prepared by an American financial advisor

1954—Act to Promote Private Industry, initial legislation later superceded in 1959 by law creating Board of Investment

1959—World Bank Mission, which proposed increased emphasis on development and suggested administrative reforms

1959—Industrial Finance Corporation of Thailand established to lend to private industry

1961—First National Economic Plan

The growing interest in economic development reflects the influence of a number of factors. Certainly of great importance was the demonstration effect in planning, infrastructure building with foreign loans and grants, and technical assistance. Short of withdrawing from the community of nations, it would have been hard for any less developed country to maintain a passive attitude toward economic growth in the postwar period. And it was not only the visits of foreign missions that carried the message; Thai sent abroad for formal education or training programs in the West returned with an exposure to the goals and the techniques of development. Finally, the political threat and war in the region gave an immediacy to the need for economic and social development; the collapse of French power at Dien Bien Phu in 1954 occurred less than two hundred miles from Thai soil, and at their closest, North Vietnam and Communist China are only about sixty and seventy miles away, respectively.

Growth during the six years 1961-1966 actually exceeded the expectations of the First National Economic Plan. The average annual increase in real gross domestic product was about 7 percent and in real per capita output about 4 percent. Targets for the Second Plan period, 1967-1971, are slightly higher than the achieved rates for the First Plan period. Obviously only a small part of this high growth rate can be directly attributed to the plans themselves; good crops and favorable markets and the side effects of the Vietnam war, including external assistance in infrastructure building, were more important. Since the economy is basically agricultural and with private ownership and enterprise, the plans consist of long-range *budgets* for government expenditures which are related to economic development, and of *forecasts* of anticipated growth in the various sectors (Trescott 1967).

Significant structural changes in the economy are taking place, as Appendix Table 3 shows in the percentage distribution by industrial origin. Although agriculture continues as the dominant sector, its contribution to the GDP declines from 37 percent in 1957 to an anticipated 26 percent in 1971. Wholesale and retail trade, the next most important sector, was expected to decline slightly over the period from 19.1 percent to 18.6 percent. The two sectors registering the greatest growth during the Plan periods were electricity and water supply, and banking, insurance, and real estate.

Regional disequalities in development are a significant obstacle to creating a national market system, as well as to the growth of the whole economy and, of course, to the control of terrorist activities in the more isolated and impoverished areas. The Second Plan took cognizance of this problem in a chapter devoted to regional and local development and provided for the creation and coordination of five regional development committees. Data in Appendix Table 5 show the inequality in the contributions of the various regions to the national product and may be summarized as follows:

Percentage Distribution of
Shares of Area, Population, and Domestic Product

Region	Area	Pop. 1960	Total Gross Domestic Product (1963)	1963 GPD Originating in:			
				Agricul- ture	Manuf.	Trade	Banking, Insurance, Real Estate
Central	20	32	54	36	67	62	92
Northeast	33	34	18	26	13	15	2
North	33	22	14	20	11	11	3
South	14	12	14	18	9	12	3
Total	100	100	100	100	100	100	100

The situation of the problem area of the nation—the impoverished Northeast, with one-third of the area and population of Thailand—is clearly evident in these data. In Chapter IV, we shall examine the spread of the transportation infrastructure into the disadvantaged regions, which is a force tending to reduce regional disparities in the future.

Industrialization

Little industrialization occurred prior to the beginning of promotional efforts in the late 1950s. Ingram (1955, p. 113) found that industrial production declined both relatively and absolutely as the export and import trade increased after 1850; only about the time of World War I did domestic industry begin to revive. Production of textiles in the home for family consumption only has continued even when monetization made alternatives available to the rural family.*

The character of the industrial sector, while changing slowly, still shows the importance of small-scale processing in the home of raw

---

* The *Household Expenditure Survey* revealed that as recently as 1962, nearly 49 percent of the rural families in the Northeast possessed looms, although elsewhere the figure was less than 10 percent of the households.

materials originating in the agricultural sector. Appendix Table 4 shows that as late as 1960, 60 percent of value added by the manufacturing sector was in the food and beverage industries, tobacco, and textiles; Plan targets anticipate this concentration dropping to 50 percent by 1971 as the industrial base broadens. The Industrial Census of 1964 showed that home industry, i.e., activities carried out in living quarters by family members and with no paid employees, accounted for over half the employment in industry and 3.6 percent of industrial sales. At the other extreme, 239 establishments employing 100 or more persons accounted for 15 percent of the employment and 52.7 percent of total industrial sales.*

Government actions and attitudes prior to the beginning of effective promotion in 1959 were actually contrary to the development of the private industrial sector. We have referred above to the view that the government failed to take those actions which might have stimulated development, such as providing infrastructure, and protection against free importation; this posture of inaction has been corrected during the decade of the sixties. Secondly, the creation of state enterprises, beginning with textiles, paper, and sugar during the period prior to the World War II and their continued operation by the government in the face of inefficiencies, inept management, and financial losses in the majority of cases, did not encourage a private sector. (A significant exception to the generally poor showing of the public sector is the highly profitable Thai Tobacco Monopoly which was created in 1941 by nationalizing the very successful British-American Tobacco Company.) This deterrent has been recognized by the government and corrected, at least ostensibly. In the First Plan, the government announced it would not compete with private industrial interests and in the Second Plan (p. 110) stated:

> The Government will operate only those state enterprises which are considered public utilities, which contribute to Government revenue, or which are essential to the security of the nation. The Government will not establish new state enterprises, except those which will be of unquestionable benefit to the public and will not conflict with the policy of promoting private enterprise.

---

* Recent growth in large establishments is indicated by comparison with earlier surveys; in 1949 there were about 100 plants employing 50 or more (Blanchard 1958, p. 330) and in 1957, 307 establishments with 50 or more employees (IBRD 1959, p. 89).

We have seen above that the state enterprise is only one form of bureaucratic involvement in the economy. Indeed, Muscat (1966, p. 250) has argued that the greatest deterrent to industrial investment in Thailand is the "uncalculable potential increase in costs, loss of markets, or outright loss of capital" facing the entrepreneur who is unable to secure protection from the direct competition of the bureaucratic elite.* He further observes that, of all the sources of entrepreneurial talent, the Thai middle class is, ironically, most exposed to this risk; the large foreign firm has easy access to protection and the Chinese has found his accommodation through the "pariah" relationship described above.

A significant start has been made toward industrialization. In most developing societies, import substitute industrialization has been forced by shortages of foreign exchange. Such is not the case for Thailand, but rather the contrary; its reserves have increased substantially in spite of expenditures for development and have continued to exceed the equivalent of a year's imports.†

The aims of the government in promoting industrialization have been to reduce the relative importance of agriculture in the economy, to utilize local raw materials, and to develop employment opportunities for the rapidly growing population. Promotion has consisted of granting tax exemptions and reducing duties on the importation of machinery and raw materials for a five-year period. Import controls on finished products have been used sparingly so that local manufactures

---

* Informative on this problem is the *Monthly Review* (August 1967, p. 260) of the Bangkok Bank, the largest and perhaps most influential commercial bank, whose chairman of the board was the Deputy Prime Minister, also Minister of Interior, and with the Minister of Finance as a board member. After noting that the government had time and again failed to adhere to its stated policy of not competing with the private sector, it observed: "In banking, industry, and other commercial activities, the government or government officials have, either directly or through some deceptive screen, come into competition with private enterprises. This is most unfair, not only because the government failed to abide by the policy as laid down, but also by its misuse of the tax-payers' money in undertakings competitive to those of the tax-payers themselves. It would, therefore, be wise for the government to make no further attempt to interfere with private enterprises through either competition or partnership."

† In a tabulation of the number of months each of thirty-two countries, both developed and developing, could finance imports with their reserves, Thailand in January 1967 led all others by far with fifteen months, while the nearest challenger had nine months' reserves. Ironically, last on the list was the United Kingdom, from which Thailand learned its lessons of fiscal conservatism (Bangkok Bank Ltd., Annual Report 1966, p. 50).

generally compete with similar imported products. By the end of 1967, promoted industries in operation had a total investment of the equivalent of U.S. $282 million. Twenty percent of this investment was in an oil refinery and a cement company; of the remainder, 38 percent was in consumer goods industries including foods and textiles, 14 percent in services, mainly hotels, and about 28 percent in non-consumer goods including construction materials, chemicals, and intermediate metal processing.*

Clearly, a significant start has been made toward industrialization. However, it is still too early to say whether this industrialization will develop goods, except for foodstuffs and textiles, which are adapted to local needs, at lower prices than the imported equivalent, and with adaptations to use local raw materials; as yet, this has not occurred to a significant degree. Employment in industry has been created and substantial foreign capital attracted by the promotion program. By the end of 1967, the investment of all enterprises granted promotion certificates, including those not yet operational, totalled nearly U.S. $700 million and were estimated to provide employment for 69,000 Thai, the equivalent of 45 percent of the persons engaged in "Large Industry" (10 persons or more) as reported in the Industrial Census of 1964. The majority of enterprises are joint ventures with twenty-four nations represented; in terms of registered capital, Thai investors account for 68 percent, Japan, 11 percent, and the United States and Nationalist China about 5 percent each of the total registered capital (Investment Board 1968).

Some indication of the characteristics of the largest business firms operating in Thailand would be useful in rounding out our picture of the industrial structure with which marketing is concerned. While the data are a rough approximation only, it has been estimated that 34 business and industrial enterprises (excluding banks and public utilities) had gross revenues in 1967 of U.S. $10 million or more. Of these

---

* Tabulated from listings of promoted firms in operation, as reported by the Board of Investment, Bangkok 1968, mimeographed. A tabulation covering the period through 1966 (NEDB 1967, p. 64) by *number* of promoted enterprises, not investment, showed 57 percent in agricultural processing and refining of mineral resources, 13 percent in machinery and electrical equipment, 9 percent in services, 5 percent in chemical products and 2 percent in other fields. It should be noted that promotion certificates were available for expansion of existing, as well as initiation of new industries. The cement company referred to above is the Siam Cement Company, the largest private industrial enterprise in the country, which was founded in 1913.

34 enterprises, 18 were primarily trading firms and 16 primarily industrial. All were privately owned except for the Thai Tobacco Monopoly. The industrial firms consisted of the following:

five firms in petroleum refining and distribution, of which one is Thai, one British, and three are American owned,

two firms in beverages, both Thai owned,

two firms in soaps, detergents, etc., one wholly owned American, one British-Thai joint venture,

one firm in each of the following:
Thai, auto assembly, with general trading,
Thai, cement,
Thai, tobacco,
American-Thai, tin refining,
American-Thai, tires,
Japanese-Thai, glass,
Japanese-Thai, steel.

Of the trading firms:

two were wholly locally owned,

seven were Japanese, including three of Japan's five largest trading companies,

three were British owned,

two were American owned, including one joint venture,

one each, were wholly owned by Danish, Dutch, Swiss, and German-Swiss interests.

The predominance of trading firms among the list of largest business firms in the country reflects the historical foreign trade orientation of the commercial sector of the economy. The exportation of rice, teak, rubber, and tin and the importation of consumer goods has dictated the character of marketing institutions as well as the banking and transportation structures. Almost all of the foreign trade leaves and enters through Bangkok. Commercial banking has developed to finance this trade and has concentrated in the capital. The map of the transportation system on page 113 and the discussion in Chapter IV shows that the waterway, railroad, and much of the highway patterns center on Bangkok; only very recently have intra- and interregional roads been laid out across the traditional grain of the national space. The growth of industrial activities and the spread of banking and transport facilities have initiated a process of adaptation of the traditional marketing system toward more emphasis on the needs of the domestic market as will be described in subsequent chapters.

II
The Thai Society

Marketing in Thailand, as elsewhere, reflects the society it serves. Our purpose, in this chapter, is to describe those characteristics of the society which seem essential for an understanding of the evolution and present nature of the marketing system.

Some characteristics of the society are already clear from the discussion in the preceding chapter of the history of the nation and of its economy. Although Thailand has the longest history as an independent nation of all its neighbors, it has not lived in isolation behind a protective wall. Its frontiers include the Mekong River and the Gulf of Siam, which serve more as bridges than as moats. Elsewhere, the border runs through jungle; the wars on the peninsula of the past two decades have demonstrated how easy it is for a man to walk across a line on a map, and it has always been so. There are obvious similarities between Thailand and its neighbors, but the differences are more important. Certainly, Thailand's history of accommodation to the Chinese influence from the East and the European influence from the West and its two periods of modernization—first under the westernizing kings of the last century and now under the impact of the Vietnam wars—set it off as a quite unique society. In this chapter we shall examine the characteristics of the population, urbanization, the developing social classes, religion, the family and the role of women, and education. Throughout, we will be concerned only with those aspects which have a direct bearing on the marketing problem.

Before proceeding to an examination of particular Thai institutions, it is pertinent to examine the profile of the Thai society which emerges from some of the recent multination comparative analyses of socioeconomic data. In the preceding chapter the position of Thailand, and its Indochina Peninsula neighbors, among the nations of the world was examined on a variety of socioeconomic factors. A number of studies in recent years have followed this approach in attempting to identify the critical factors or processes associated with the economic and social development of nations. Two may be cited which are of special interest here.

Sherbini (1967, p. 135), in his study of methods of classifying countries for purposes of international marketing efforts, proposed an Index of Internal Stability and Cohesion to measure the presence of conditions conducive to business operations, long-range planning, and marketing coordination. On this index, among seventy-five developed and developing nations, Thailand ranked among a group of twelve countries with maximum scores, along with the United Kingdom, France, the Scandinavian countries, and one other developing country—Turkey. A maximum score on this composite index was achieved by those nations with (*a*) less than five deaths from domestic group violence annually, per 100,000 population, (*b*) racial homogeneity, where 90 percent or more of the people were of one of the three major racial stocks, (*c*) linguistic homogeneity, where 85 percent or more speak a common language, (*d*) religious homogeneity, where 75 percent of the population identify with one major religion, and (*e*) duration of national identity, where the nation has been sovereign since before 1800. In addition to this index, Sherbini presented another composite index consisting of twenty-one indicators of economic development, education, and health; on this scaling, Thailand ranked fifty-first among the seventy-five nations. This type of multinational comparative analysis is based on the availability of published statistical data; it is therefore limited to those variables which are quantifiable and is subject to the many known and unknown biases in the data.

In their recent study of seventy-four countries, all underdeveloped, Adelman and Morris (1967) included the available statistical data but also went beyond to variables where the judgment of experts formed the basis for ranking. The position of Thailand as of about 1960 on some indicators of development which have special relevance for marketing was as follows:

Rank of Thailand among Seventy-four Developing Nations*	*Indicators of Development*
28th	*Social mobility,* as measured by access to education, opportunity to enter middle-class occupations, and the absence of cultural ethnic barriers to upward mobility.
42nd	*Importance of an indigenous middle class,* with Thailand grouped among those nations where "expatriate entrepreneurial, commercial, administrative, and technical groups dominated the middle class but in which a growing, though still small, indigenous middle class also existed" (p. 32).
50th	*Extent of mass communication,* based on a composite index of daily newspaper circulation and number of radio receivers.
58th	*Degree of modernization of outlook,* based on judgment of the degree to which the outlook of the urban educated population is modernized ("the adoption of Western or modern styles of living had gone considerably farther than external forms and dress, and had entailed the evolution of at least some important modern forms of social and political participation such as voluntary associations" p. 50), and whether programs of political, social, and economic modernization have gained significant support among the urban and some of the rural population.
58th	*Strength of democratic institutions* in the period 1957-62, measured by the presence of competitive political parties, freedom to oppose the government, stability of the political party system, and experience in national elections. (It should be noted that oligarchic may be more effective than democratic structures in fostering growth in the short run and at certain levels of development.)

---

* For each indicator, Adelman and Morris grouped the countries into three to five classes (A-C, A-E), qualifying further with plus and minus designations within some classes. In our ranking of Thailand, we have counted all countries in superior classes and subclasses and have considered Thailand at the midpoint of the group of nations with identical ratings.

| 46th | *Administrative efficiency of the government bureaucracy*—a highly subjective judgmental measure of the degree of permanence and training of administrators, of the extent to which corruption, inefficiency, and incompetence in the bureaucracy and instability in top policy hamper efficiency. |
| 25th | *Leadership commitment to economic development* measured by judgment of attitudes of those participating in the decisions which guide the economy and their willingness to attempt to achieve institutional change. |

With this positioning of the Thai nation among other developing nations on some key aspects of development and among the other nations of the region as presented in the data in Chapter I, we now turn to examine in greater detail the present-day Thai society.

CHARACTERISTICS OF THE POPULATION

A number of characteristics of Thailand's population are important in describing the marketing system as it exists today and in extrapolating its probable future evolution; principal among these are the youthfulness of the people, the high growth rate, and the distribution of people over space and among the various economic activities.

The familiar pattern of developing societies—high growth rates resulting from falling death rates due to medical advances, while birth rates remain high—is also characteristic of Thailand. Historically, disease rather than hunger has been the limiting factor in population growth. For at least a generation prior to World War II, the growth rate averaged about 2 percent annually and since then, over 3 percent. Improvements in medical care and hygiene have dramatically increased the *quantity* of life for the average Thai; infant mortality has probably been cut in half in the postwar period and life expectancy increased from thirty-five years in 1937 to fifty-four years in 1960 and to a projected sixty-seven years by 1980 (Caldwell 1967, p. 39).

The youthfulness of the population is apparent in the data shown in Appendix Table 1. Approximately 46 percent of the population in 1966 was fourteen years or younger (compared with 31 percent in the United States); by 1981, this is projected to about 42 percent as the average age rises. It should be noted that the population may even be somewhat more youthful than these figures show because of under-enumeration of children.

The young are important in the marketing system in eroding traditional values and implanting the new. With their minimal commitment to the past, they are among the most effective carriers of modernization. Lerner's study of change in the Middle East (1964, p. 195) describes a Lebanese traditional—an old shoemaker—who finds intolerable "the young people's search for the opposite—their fascination by the strange and new and foreign." Opinion leadership in rural Lebanon was passing from the old traditionals to the young villagers as a result of their mobility, literacy, and media exposure. The story in Thailand is not different, although the strength of traditional deference to authority may facilitate communication across the generation gap. Moerman (1968, p. 107) found a greater gulf between the experiences of the young and old than ever before in the history of the tiny Northern village he studied. "Only men younger than thirty-five have worked as soldiers, policemen, or teachers for the national state; only women younger than thirty have gone to school; only girls younger than twenty regard a milling machine as a normal convenience of daily life. In their dress, dialect, deportment, and dreams, the young are devoted to things their elders never knew" (p. 108). The gap between under- and over-thirty extends to consumption patterns; the wristwatch, white shirts, tight trousers, and fountain pen of the young are foolish extravagances to the village elders.

The location of the population and particularly the urban-rural dichotomy is of course of great importance in a description of the marketing system. The growth since World War II in rural and urban population, including that of the dominant Bangkok Metropolitan Area (the municipalities of Bangkok and adjoining Thonburi) is shown in Table 2.1.*

---

* The first census of 1911-1912 was conceived as an essential element in the development of public administration of the modernizing state and thus went beyond a mere enumeration of population to include items useful in tax administration, such as the number of vehicles, beasts of burden, and weapons. According to Siffin (1966, p. 84) the admittedly incomplete 1912 census indicated, in addition to 8.3 million people, "the existence of 6,500 elephants, almost 87,000 horses, more than 2 million water buffalo—and 24 cars. Peace-loving, tranquil Thai admitted to the ownership of 421,688 guns of various types, an average of about one weapon for each eighteen persons covered." Data for 1947 and 1960 are from the fifth and sixth censuses and for 1965 from an intercensus sample survey.

Table 2.1 — Rural and Urban Population of Thailand, 1947-1965
(*in thousands*)

	1947	1960	1965
Kingdom total	17,443	26,258	30,561
Rural—absolute	15,708	22,984	26,246
percent of total	90.1	87.5	85.9
Urban[1]—absolute	1,735	3,274	4,314
percent of total	9.9	12.5	14.1
Bangkok—absolute	762	1,703	2,308
percent of urban	43.9	52.0	53.5
percent of kingdom	4.4	6.5	7.6

[1] 117 municipalities in 1947, 120 in 1960 and 1965.

The definitions of urban and rural are related to local government administration rather than strict socioeconomic criteria. There are 120 municipalities in Thailand, set up by royal decree, and it is the total of their populations which constitute "urban" in Table 2.1 and throughout Thai demographic data. The kingdom is divided into seventy-one provinces (*changwats*), each of which has a principal municipality where provincial government activities are located and may have other municipalities when population density, tax revenues and other factors make such appropriate.* All persons residing outside of municipal areas are considered rural and nearly all reside in villages, of which there are 41,100; the typical spatial organization has been a cluster of houses surrounded by fields which the residents own and work.† The isolated homestead is a recent development, found mainly around Bangkok and related to the development of commercial agriculture (Wijeyewardene 1967, pp. 69-70).

The urban sector of Thailand has grown during the postwar period from 9.9 percent of the total population to 14.1 percent, but Bangkok has grown even faster and in 1965 the metropolitan area contained 53.5 percent of the Thai urban population. The predominance of Bangkok is a fact of such relevance in marketing development that this characteristic of the Thai society merits examination in closer detail.

---

* A description of the various levels of local government is in Ministry of National Development (1966, pp. 8-10).
† Throughout the text we shall use the words *rural* and *village* interchangeably.

42 MARKETING AND DEVELOPMENT

The Primate City Phenomenon

The importance of Bangkok early in this century has been described by Graham (1912, p. 22) thus:

> Up to a few years ago Bangkok resembled nothing so much as a huge wen which had been growing steadily for a century and a quarter, absorbing the life and the substance of the country, taking the revenue of its outlying provinces to pay for its own embellishment, and the best blood of the peasantry to fill the households of its nobles, and to rot in the insanitary barracks of its naval and military establishments. At the present day, however, this is no longer the case. With the abolition of slavery the nobles have disbanded the greater part of their following; new laws have immensely improved the conditions of military service, while a policy of partial decentralization of government, and above all of railway extension, has brought the outlying parts of the country into a prominence not formerly imaginable, and is teaching the upper and the official classes that life may be made endurable elsewhere than in the beloved capital.

Graham went on to describe Bangkok as containing one-ninth of Siam's population, noting that except for London, no other capital in the world had so large a population in relation to the rest of the country. Whether it indeed held 11 percent of the nation's population then is open to question,* but in 1965, it held 7.6 percent. And in relation to other cities of the nation, the Thai case is certainly unique. Ginsburg (1961, p. 36) measures primacy by the population of the largest city as a percentage of the total population of the four largest cities and finds Thailand the most extreme case (94.2 percent) among 104 nations, both developed and underdeveloped. The 1960 census data for populations of municipalities ranked by decreasing size show the rapid drop-off: after Bangkok/Thonburi with 1.7 million in 1960 come Chiengmai, the principal Northern city, with 66,000, followed by Korat, the principal city of the Northeast, with 42,200, and eight cities ranging from 36,500 down to 30,400. Since 1960, some of these cities have grown rapidly, particularly those benefiting from American military activity in the area, but the extreme case of primacy persists. The following data, from special tabulations of the National Statistical Office made available to the author, show the regional distribution of urbanization in 1965, excluding the Bangkok Metropolitan Area:

---

* Graham cites a population of about 630,000 for Bangkok, or about 8 percent of the total population according to the 1912 census, which was incomplete.

Population by Regions, 1965
(*excluding Bangkok Metropolitan Area, in thousands*)

		Rural			Urban	
			Percentage	*Number*		*Percentage*
			of Regional	*of Muni-*		*of Regional*
Regions	*Total*	*Absolute*	*Total*	*cipalities*	*Pop.*	*Total*
Central	7,081.5	6,312.8	89.1	48	768.7	10.9
Northeast	10,217.3	9,815.3	96.1	21	402.0	3.9
Northern	6,605.7	6,179.7	93.6	24	426.1	6.4
Southern	3,760.0	3,349.9	89.1	25	410.1	10.9

The least urbanized region, with only 4 percent of its population so classified, is the relatively underdeveloped Northeast and the most urbanized, the Central and Southern regions, with 10.9 percent of their population residing in municipalities. However, urban places are rather evenly spaced over the nation, except for the Central region provinces around Bangkok, and are uniformly small, averaging between sixteen and nineteen thousand in the four regions. Thus a marketing effort aimed at reaching the urban population must cover a large part of the national territory.

Rural-Urban Contrasts

It is commonplace that the quality of life varies substantially between the urban and rural populations of a society. Some evidence of the differences in 1962-1963 between the typical family in Bangkok, in the other 118 municipalities, and in the rural areas of the nation are shown in Table 2.2. The extreme cases on each characteristic are, of course, Bangkok and rural families, with the values for town families lying in between. Thus the average monthly money income of rural families was 480 baht (U.S. $24) or less than one-half of the incomes in towns (1,048 baht) and less than one-third of Bangkok incomes (1,519 baht). Rural families are only slightly larger in size but more family members are economically active, mostly as unpaid family workers in farming. Ninety-five percent of the heads of families in rural areas had only a primary education or less, of which 38.3 percent had no formal education at all; in Bangkok, the comparable figures were 71.9 percent and 32.1 percent (not separately shown in the table). Home-ownership predominates among rural families while tenancy is more common in Bangkok; in modern facilities and appliances, rural homes are poorly supplied.

Table 2.2 — Some Characteristics of Urban and Rural Households, 1963

	Bangkok	Towns	Rural
Family characteristics			
Average monthly money			
income (baht)	1,519	1,048	480
Number of members	5.5	5.3	5.6
Average number of eco-			
nomically active persons	1.8	1.9	2.7
Percentage of households with 3			
or more employed members	22.1	21.8	43.2
Heads of family: percentage			
which are self-employed	33.2	50.5	77.3
with primary education or less	71.9	77.1	95.0
with university degree or more	3.0	1.1	0.1
Family housing: percentage			
of families owning home	38.7	55.2	94.6
of houses with electricity	93.6	62.1	2.8
of houses with running water	69.5	21.5	0.1
of houses with treated			
drinking water available	99.0	59.2	17.8
Ownership of durable consumer goods			
Percentage of families owning[1]			
radio	60.3	32.6-56.8	4.9-39.5
television	17.2	0- 6.1	0- 0.8
refrigerator	11.1	0.3- 3.1	0- 0.6
electric fan	33.0	3.1-15.8	0- 1.7
air conditioner	0.9	0- 0.3	0- 0.3
washing machine	1.3	0- 0.7	0.1- 0.3
sewing machine	33.5	15.0-30.1	3.7- 7.8
automobile	8.5	0.6- 3.9	0- 1.5
motorcycle	5.0	2.9- 5.5	1.0- 2.5
bicycle	8.7	28.4-51.3	9.7-47.4
boat	2.9	2.8-17.3	1.6-49.0
loom	0	0- 7.9	0-48.6

SOURCE: National Statistical Office, 1963, *Household Expenditure Survey, Whole Kingdom.* The survey defined an "economic" family as either a group who lived and ate together, pooling income and spending from the pool, or a single individual who was financially independent. In urban areas, the not uncommon situation where daughter and son-in-law live with the parents gives rise to two "economic" families but only one household. In rural areas, almost all households consist of one "economic" family (p. 34).

[1]For towns and rural, the values shown are the extremes among the five regions: Northeast, North, East, Central, and South.

The rural-urban dichotomy, however, extends far beyond differences in the way people earn their living or in the quality of life as measured by income and possessions. Rural society in Thailand is essentially classless, while in Bangkok and the larger towns a class structure is rapidly developing. Since rural people are in the main farming their own small land holdings, they are earning similar incomes. Also, as we shall see later, a significant part of windfall gains such as those from unusual harvests or gambling wins may be contributed to the temple to acquire merit for the hereafter, with further income leveling effects. In consequence, the dispersion around the typical values shown in Table 2.2 would be quite narrow for rural areas and broad for urban areas, especially for Bangkok. Stifel (1967, p. 128), reworking the data of the *Household Expenditure Survey*, finds that the universal tendency in both developed and less-developed societies for the income distribution to be more equal for rural than for urban areas is confirmed in Thailand:

	Percentage Distribution of Households by Income		
Annual Income Class	*Bangkok*	*Towns*	*Villages*
Under baht 6,000 (U.S. $300)	20	36	78
Baht 6,000-12,000	32	34	16
Baht 12,000-24,000	28	20	5
Over baht 24,000	20	10	1
	100	100	100

These data cover money income only; non-money income (principally, rice produced on the farm) accounts for a larger part of total income in rural areas (26.2 percent) than in towns (5.5 percent) or in Bangkok (2.7 percent) so that the difference between rural and urban income levels is not as great as would appear. A corollary of this is of substantial importance to marketers of consumer goods. While rural money incomes are small in absolute terms, much of this income is available for such purchases so that the market is better than it looks.

Parenthetically, it should also be noted that Stifel found the total income distribution of Thailand less equal than that of developed countries but more equal than other less developed countries of Latin America and Africa. Thailand's income distribution is roughly comparable to that of presently developed countries four or five decades ago; for example, the top 20 percent of Thai households accounted for 54.5 percent of the income in 1963, compared to 59 percent of the income in the United Kingdom and Sweden in 1913 and the United States with 54 percent in 1929.

Life in rural Thailand retains the traditional attitudes and values that reflect a people's adaptation to the soft climate and easy harvests of their land. Wit (1968, p. 39) describes the most important results to be: the belief that rice cultivation is the most worthwhile and en-nobling form of labor (and conversely, a disinterest in commerce and permanent urban living), a sense of self-reliance, personal dignity, economic independence, and a psychological and cultural sense of well-being. From Buddhism come other essential values for the Thai: conformance to the Buddhist moral code, which provides rules for every ethical situation but also allows substantial individual freedom in interpretation and application; for the male, the opportunity to enter a temple as a monk for a few months or longer; and for all, the chance to earn merit for the hereafter by gifts to monks and to the temples and by other meritorious acts.

We may list some additional characteristics, attested to both by the Thai and their foreign observers, which have significant effects on their economic and marketing behavior:

1) The Thai possess a natural inclination toward leisure, recrea-tion, and having a good time. Rice cultivation involves only limited periods of intense activity, and while a number of other kinds of work fill up the year (see Klausner 1966), village social life, which is centered on the *wat* or temple grounds, is highly developed.

2) In contrast to many Asian peoples, Thai have a propensity to travel. "One of the most frequently heard terms in a Thai village, *pai thiao* (literally, 'to go around'), has many meanings, all of which suggest that . . . to travel, to see new things, to wander at leisure—is to have fun. . . . It is difficult to determine exactly how far the spatial horizons of the average Thai go, although they certainly include his province and region, and to a degree the nation as a whole. One thing is quite certain: the Thai does not think of himself as a member of an isolated, self-sufficient little community" (Blanchard 1958, pp. 429-30).

3) They have a love of gambling. The national lottery is highly popular throughout the country; according to the Household Expendi-ture Survey, nearly 1 percent of average monthly family expenditures went for the purchase of lottery tickets up-country and nearly 2 per-cent in Bangkok. In addition to the national lottery, a wide variety of

other forms of gambling is available everywhere. Beyond the recreational aspects of gambling is the opportunity to improve the family financial situation; increasingly and especially for the urban family, the widening gap between income and the standard of living the family feels it must have is a problem for which gambling appears an ideal solution. "Husband-wife conflicts about money matters are most frequently fought out on the battleground of gambling, usually the husband's gambling, but often the wife's" (Graham and Graham 1957, p. 44).

Any description of the Thai national character or style of living inevitably reflects the behavior and attitudes of the heavily predominant rural population. However, these traditional values are being eroded by modernization, which arrives in Bangkok and spreads to other urban areas and over the countryside. The rapidly developing class society is a case in point and of great importance in marketing development because of the role of the elite groups in the spread of materialistic values.

Urban Classes

In connection with his studies of the Chinese in Thailand and based on his observations of this very important minority, Skinner (1957, pp. 18-19) described the general lines of the urban class system which was then developing. More recently, a market research study by Business Research, Ltd., *Bangkok Profile* (1966), provides confirmation and quantification of characteristics of the class system, based on a prelisted, randomly drawn sample of over seventy-seven hundred households in the Bangkok-Thonburi Metropolitan Area. Results of this survey are summarized in Tables 2.3, 2.4 and 2.5.

Bangkok is highly atypical in the ethnic composition of its population; only 53.5 percent of the households are ethnic Thai, while 37.1 percent are ethnic Chinese (defined as households in which the Chinese language is spoken at home by two or more household members). In the preceding chapter, we have noted that there were more Chinese than Thai in the capital city during the first half of the last century and that ethnic Chinese probably constitute about 10 percent of the total population of Thailand today. *Farang*, the Thai designation for foreigners from Europe and North America, comprise 3.6 percent of the Bangkok population and an additional 1.1 percent are of other

Table 2.3 — Socioeconomic Status of Ethnic Groups in Bangkok, 1966

A. *Percentage Distribution of Status by Ethnic Group:*

Ethnic group	Upper	Upper Middle	Lower Middle	Upper Lower	Lower Lower	Total
Thai	22	65	64	53	50	53
Chinese[1]	2	8	33	47	49	37
Farang[2]	68	24	1	*	—	4
Other	8	3	2	—	1	1
	100	100	100	100	100	95
				Not ascertained (361)		5
(Base no. of households)	(170)	(546)	(2361)	(3178)	(1102)	(7723)

B. *Percentage Distribution of Ethnic Group, by Status:*

Thai	1	9	36	41	13	100
Chinese[1]	*	2	27	52	19	100
Farang[2]	41	47	12	*	—	100
Other	16	21	47	12	4	100

SOURCE: Business Research, Ltd., 1966, *Bangkok Profile. Selected Characteristics of Households in Bangkok and Thonburi*, Table III.

Notes: Data in A have been rounded, and in B recalculated from the source and are thus approximations only. The sample consisted of 7,723 households of which details were not ascertained in 361 cases and five were monks; confidence limits where the base was at least 400 households were within ± 5 percent at the 95 percent level of probability, and less than ± 3 percent where the number of households exceeded 1,000. The asterisk in the table signifies less than 0.1 percent.

[1] Households in which the Chinese language is spoken at home by two or more members of the household.

[2] *Farang* is an imprecisely defined term denoting foreigners who are generally white and from Europe and North America; other Asians such as Indians or Japanese are classified "Other."

[3] The classification system reflects four factors: (a) economic, or the relative distance of the household from subsistence living, (b) social, or degree of acceptance by other members of the population (whether members of the subject household "pay respect" to others, and to whom, or "respect is paid" to them) (c) occupational level of head of household, and (d) educational level of head. See Tables 2.4 and 2.5 for details on occupations and possession of durable goods by class.

ethnic groups, with the remaining 4.7 percent of the households not identified. Table 2.3 relates these ethnic groups to the socioeconomic status they occupy. Not surprisingly, 41 percent of the *farang* are classed as upper and 47 percent as upper-middle class on a classification system which reflects the four factors of economic situation, social status, occupation, and education of the head of the household. On

Table 2.4 — Selected Occupations of Heads of Households in Bangkok, 1966

	Executive and Managerial	Military and Police	Professional Worker	Sales Worker	Clerical Worker	Skilled Labor	Unskilled Labor	Other	Total	Base No. of Households
A. By socioeconomic status										
Upper	35	22	7	4	9	2	—	16	100	170
Upper middle	32	15	13	14	8	3	—	15	100	546
Lower middle	8	5	2	41	16	11	1	16	100	2361
Upper lower	0.1	6	0.1	32	7	33	5	17	100	3178
Lower lower	—	0.4	—	31	2	10	32	25	100	1102
Total	5	6	2	31	9	19	7	21	100	7723
B. By ethnic group										
Thai	7	8	2	20	13	18	7	25	100	4139
Chinese	1	+	0.1	53	3	24	9	10	100	2862
Farang	30	25	4	5	14	3	—	19	100	277
Other	24	4	5	38	12	2	—	15	100	84

SOURCES and *Notes*: See Table 2.3.

Note: The category "Executive and Managerial" consists of those who manage, execute, and issue orders and ranges from prime minister and ministers of the cabinet to provincial and district governors, their deputies, and business executives including department heads. "Professional" covers those occupations for which a specific educational background is necessary, such as engineer, lawyer, physician, dentist, or accountant. "Sales Worker" includes retail, wholesale, and brokerage occupations ranging from shop personnel and door-to-door sales to real estate and insurance but excluding hawkers and vendors, who are classified as unskilled labor. The seven occupations shown here are the most important; "other" includes six additional occupational categories.

The following are some typical monthly cash incomes for these occupational groups in U.S. dollars (salaries exclude perquisites): "Executive, Managerial, Military," manager of a large factory or office—$750, manager of a small factory or office—$350, cabinet minister —$450, general—$415, colonel—$200; "Professional," engineer—$250, medical doctor—$500; "Sales," small shopkeeper—$50; "Clerical," government or business office clerk—$50, beginning typist—$30; "Unskilled Labor," factory worker—$14, farm worker—$4 (unpublished data supplied by Business Research, Ltd., 1966).

49

Table 2.5 — Possession of Durable Goods by Class and Ethnic Group, Bangkok Households, 1966

	Percentage of Households Owning			
	Radio	TV	Automobile	Motorcycle/ Scooter
A. Distribution by socioeconomic status				
Upper	87.1	52.4	66.8	2.4
Upper middle	92.1	82.8	85.9	5.5
Lower middle	91.6	67.2	29.1	9.0
Upper lower	77.4	29.8	3.4	4.0
Lower lower	53.9	6.2	0.9	0.9
All classes	76.0	40.7	18.0	5.0
B. Distribution by ethnic group				
Thai	84.1	48.1	20.7	4.6
Chinese	73.3	33.6	9.6	6.2
Farang	81.2	53.8	76.9	2.5
Other	83.3	52.4	57.1	10.7

SOURCES and *Notes:* See Table 2.3.

the other hand, Thai and ethnic Chinese are predominantly (77 percent in each case) in the lower-middle and upper-lower classes. A comparison of these data with those of Table 2.4, where the occupations of the heads of households are correlated with socioeconomic status and with ethnic group, adds meaning to the class designations. In this table, the columns for selected occupations have been arranged from left to right so that the modal group for each occupation descends along the socioeconomic scale. Thus, the occupations of the upper and upper-middle classes are predominantly executive and managerial (which includes cabinet ministers and business executives) and military, police, and professionals; of the lower-middle class, predominantly sales and clerical workers; of the upper-lower class, mainly skilled labor, and the lower-lower class principally unskilled labor.

Skinner's observations on the urban class structure are generally confirmed by these data. At the top of society Skinner found two elite groups. The traditional elite, consisting of the royal aristocracy and old-time noble families, enjoys high prestige, with its wealth based primarily on real estate. The new elite consists of government and military officials, businessmen, and a small group of professionals, and commands respect because it holds political and economic power. While the traditional elite is limited to ethnic Thai, the new elite includes growing numbers of ethnic Chinese as the business class increases in prominence. In the middle class, Skinner found two groups: ethnic Thai who are upper-level government employees, small business people, and lesser professionals, and the ethnic Chinese—which would correspond to the sales occupations in the *Bangkok Profile* data and account for over half of the heads of ethnic Chinese households in Bangkok. In the Skinner scheme, an artisan class, the great majority of whom were ethnic Chinese and who identified with the Chinese middle class although lacking its prestige, came between the middle and lowest class. This artisan class, corresponding to the skilled labor group in the *Profile* data, is predominately Chinese although not by a wide margin (24 percent, versus 18 percent Thai). Finally, Skinner identified a lower class of unskilled individuals; of this group, he observed that the ethnic Chinese were steadily decreasing because of the momentum of upward mobility and the closing of immigration which cut off entrants at this entering step of the ladder of Thai society. On the other hand, the ethnic Thai predominated and were increasing in importance, fed by rural emigration and protected in the lower-class occupations by the government's anti-Chinese legislation. *Profile* data do not confirm Skinner's observation of the predominance of ethnic Thai in the lowest class, however; Table 2.3 shows Thai and Chinese about equal in the lower-lower class, with 50 percent and 49 percent respectively.

While we do not have information on the spending patterns of urban households by ethnic and by socioeconomic characteristics, *Profile* data do include ownership of four durable goods, as shown in Table 2.5. Not surprisingly, it is the upper-middle class rather than the upper class that shows the highest saturation of radios, television sets, and automobiles. In general, ownership declines as one proceeds down the scale of socioeconomic classes, and the decline is more rapid, the more expensive the item. Thus radios are owned by 92 percent of upper-middle class households and by 54 percent of lower-lower class households; automobile ownership for these two classes drops, however, from 86 percent to less than 1 percent respectively. The ownership of motorcycles or scooters is most prevalent in the lower-middle class, reflecting the fact that it is the minimum-investment powered vehicle available to the urban resident.

The distribution of ownership of these goods by ethnic groups reflects both the class position of the group as well as its life style. The affluence and the life style of the *farang* is clearly evident in the fact that over three-quarters of these households own automobiles. At the other extreme, the frugality of the Chinese is also evident; their ownership of all these goods is lower than that of any other ethnic group, except for the motorcycle, which for a Chinese commercial household is a combined producer's and consumer's good. It should also be remembered that for many who are living and working in the Chinese sections of the city, geographic mobility is neither necessary nor desired.

Bangkok among Other Asian Cities

Despite the hazards of cross-cultural comparisons, data which have been uniformly collected for similar societies can be suggestive in highlighting those elements of a national style which bear particularly on modernization and marketing development. Market research teams affiliated with that which produced the *Bangkok Profile* data described above replicated a survey of the populations in seven Southeast Asian capital cities—Tokyo, Manila, Singapore, Hong Kong, Taipei, Seoul and Bangkok (International Research Associates 1966). Table 14 in the Appendix compares the Bangkok population with the remainder of the group. In terms of home ownership and durable consumer goods, Bangkok households rank about in the middle of the group of seven cities, except for automobiles where it led all cities in the percentage of households with two or more cars. On the other hand, the ownership of financial assets—bank accounts, life insurance, and securities—was relatively low. The high value placed on education in Thailand, to be discussed in detail below, and of overseas travel, especially for educational purposes is apparent in Bangkok's top ranking in the group. Finally, attitudes toward their own national image confirm the more impressionistic characterizations of foreign observers. Thus, the words *pleasure-loving, lazy, excitable,* and *frivolous* were used more frequently by the people of Bangkok to describe their own countrymen than was the case for any other city. It must, of course, be noted that the respondents may be merely reflecting a well-known national stereotype. However, the low opinion held by the Thai of locally-made products is confirmed by buyer preference for imported goods, although this attitude appears to be slowly changing.

RELIGION

We now examine a social institution which has great potential impact on both economic development and marketing development. In the Thai society, Buddhism has two principal effects: one is the possible reduction of the interest in, and drive toward, materialism, the other is the diversion of discretionary income from acquiring consumer goods and services to buying "merit." The former effect, whether rooted in religion or elsewhere in the value system, has been widely discussed in the literature of economic development as an obstacle to agricultural diversification or to increased productivity through innovations in methods, seeds, and fertilizers throughout the world. The latter effect is of more limited importance in Thailand or at least the Oriental world.

Since Buddhism is the religion of 94 percent of all Thai, its influence in the society cannot be doubted. Blanchard (1958, p. 491), commenting on the great emotional attachment of the Thai to the doctrines and rites of the Buddhist Order, observes that it "is constantly woven into their thoughts and actions. The *wat* [or temple] is the religious and social center of the Thai community; the average Thai, both rural and urban, accepts unquestioningly the importance of its spiritual-emotional role in his daily life and supports it through his contributions and labor."

Central to the Buddhist goal is a renunciation of "things of the flesh"; since life is sorrow, and sorrow is the result of desire, the suppression of all desire is essential to the achievement of nirvana. But this is the counsel of perfection and perhaps not more binding on the Thai Buddhist than is the asceticism of Jesus on the western Christian. The goal of the modern Thai is more of the things of this world than achievement of the ideal of nirvana; reincarnation in a lower heaven with the pleasure of uncounted wives, or rebirth in this world in a powerful or wealthy position are examples cited by Blanchard as possible goals. The illustration of the powerful and wealthy calls attention again to the individualistic emphasis of the society and of the religion. Evil and good acts produce evil and good consequences for the individual, either misfortune or prosperity in this or in the future life. Thus the powerful and wealthy demonstrate to some extent their accumulated balance of merit over demerit and hence their moral excellence.

The following quotation from Blanchard (p. 491) indicates what seems to be the concensus of western observers on the Thai attitude toward materialism:*

---

* Other observers who would seem to find the Thai attitude toward materialism one of neutrality, if not disinterest, are Sutton (1962, p. 7), Wijeyewardene (1967, p. 81), and Kirsch (1962).

The greater part of the population are less concerned with the acquisition of material possessions and objects than with the development of their spiritual life and the attainment of merit—though they have no objection to material comforts if these do not seriously affect their balance of religious merit. Enjoyment of life is not considered prejudicial to merit (contrary, that is, to their moral code) if it is accompanied by moderation. The acquisition of merit is an essential part of life, and a great amount of time and energy is expended for this purpose.

However, a contrary view is found in Phillips' (1965, pp. 196-99) study of the Thai peasant personality. In applying the sentence completion technique to a group of adults in a small village outside of Bangkok, this researcher was impressed by the insignificance of responses reflecting religious considerations and merit accumulation in the peasant's statements of his ambitions, what he considered the most important thing in life, and what he wished he were. In all instances, the possession of money or its surrogates and material status heavily predominated over merit acquisition or other non-material values. Thus the statement "the most important thing in life is . . ." was completed by 57 percent of the respondents with "money," "earning a living," and similar answers, while only 10 percent mentioned religion and merit, another 10 percent family, and the remainder distributed over a variety of opinions including happiness and death. To the more fanciful question of what the individual wished he had most, 77 percent responded with money or wealth and only 8 percent with merit.

Two comments may be made on the view which assigns materialism a secondary role to merit acquisition. One is that the Thai peasant reacted materialistically to the development of an export market for rice in the last half of the nineteenth century and again for other products since World War II. As we have seen in the preceding chapter, the peasant was induced, after the Bowring Treaty, to give up leisure and other activities, working longer hours each day and more days during the year, to produce more rice for sale and to use part of the incremental money income to purchase consumer goods. However, as Ingram has made clear, the acquisition of consumer goods was closely related to the availability of discretionary income; in periods of poor harvests and lowered export earnings, imports quickly retracted. The peasant has for long been interested in, but not a slave to the passion for, material possessions. But this attitude of neutrality may better characterize the traditional rural view than the modern urban view. Also, it is possible that the male is more neutral toward materialism than the woman; later in this section we shall examine the dichotomy of the "other-worldly" concerns of men and the "this-worldly" concerns of women.

The second comment recognizes Myrdal's (1968, p. 16) caution against the western "beam in our eyes." There has been much discussion in the literature of economic development of whether other-worldly religious values, as in the case of India, explain her underdevelopment and constitute an obstacle to development and change. It is possible, however, as Kunkel (1965, p. 269) has suggested, that we have been misled by some western scholars' reading of eastern scriptures much as eastern scholars would have found in our New Testament a misleading description of western attitudes toward materialism. A better understanding of the Thai attitude toward materialism and change is suggested by Myrdal's (1968, p. 112) criticism:

> It is completely contrary to scientific principles to follow the easy, speculative approach for explaining the peculiarities in attitudes, institutions, and modes of living and working by reference to broad concepts of Hinduism, Buddhism or Islam, or to personality or cultural traits such as abstention, spiritualism, lack of materialism, and other allegedly "Asian values." And it is not accidental that these broad generalizations can so easily be shown to be unrealistic. It should rather be an hypothesis for further study that people in this region are not inherently different from people elsewhere, but that they live and have lived for a long time under conditions very different from those in the Western world, and that this has left its mark upon their bodies and minds.

An observer in Thailand today, whether in Bangkok or in many upcountry locations, would find it difficult to detect any deficiency in materialistic drive. However, the Thai does want to be sure that what he is getting is worth what he is giving up. In the case of his behavior as a producer, this means careful consideration of alternatives before undertaking change. Muscat (1966, pp. 87-96) describes the decision-making process in the partially commercialized rural economy and quotes a study of a Northern village (p. 161): "If something will bring profit it will be done, and conversely, if the villager sees no immediate return on his investment of time, labor, or money, he will be reluctant to undertake a particular task." The most recent example of response to new alternatives, with enormous implications for the future, is of course to the new service jobs created by the presence in 1969 of some 49,000 American military at upcountry bases and in Bangkok. It has been estimated that approximately 150,000 Thai, many of them from rural areas, were employed in activities related to this military presence and at much higher compensation than they had hitherto experienced. In his behavior as a consumer, it appears that the substantial evidence of peasant sophistication found elsewhere in the world (for example, as reported in Bauer and Yamey 1957, pp. 91-101) is confirmed in Thailand. Incentive goods must be attractive, inexpensive, and of reasonable quality, as will be discussed further in Chapter IV.

One final point regarding materialism and religious values must be noted. In an essay entitled "Western Culture and the Thai Way of Life," Moerman (1964) properly notes the transformations which occur to western customs and ideas when they are introduced into the Thai society. In making his point that items from the West took on new meaning in the tiny, isolated Northern village in which he lived from 1959-1961, he observed that although every household from time to time bought packs of cigarettes (Thai factory-made with paper wrappers as distinct from the traditional rural cigarette of tobacco wrapped in banana leaves) and imported cans of condensed milk, hardly any household consumed these items. Instead, they were purchased to be given as gifts to the monks. Certainly this buyer behavior may have been widespread in the past and would tend to persist longest in the most isolated areas. But it cannot be considered the rule in rural Thailand today; for example, the annual output of factory-made cigarettes by the Thai Tobacco Monopoly is of such magnitude that it could hardly be consumed by the urban population and the monks, without substantial participation by rural consumers. In any event, the use of western goods in non-western ways is probably a transitional case and not contradictory to the expected typical behavior by the rural population of increasing purchases of western-type goods for their own consumption as disposable income increases. Another example offered by Moerman of the use of Coca-Cola in rural areas would seem to confirm rather than deny the cultural similarities: "only in Thailand can a minor official, by drinking it, signal the fact that he is more progressive than the simple villager who drinks only water yet less exalted than the district officer who can afford beer" (p. 32). In the West, status symbols merely carry higher price tags.

The conflict between acquiring material possessions and merit, mentioned in the quotation from Blanchard above, brings us to the second adverse effect of religion on economic and marketing development. We have seen that the temple is the religious and social center of the community. Its construction and maintenance as well as the support of the monks in residence* depend on the voluntary contributions of money, labor, and food by the populace. The magnitude of this burden is difficult to gauge. Feeding the monks who canvass door to door in the residential areas at daybreak is a privilege, an opportunity to gain merit; the food contribution by a rural household to the *wats* and the monks is probably equivalent to the feeding of one additional person in the family. Beyond this rather fixed cost, however, the evidence of the burden of additional forms of contribution is conflicting. Blanchard quotes one survey which found that cash outlays for merit making in rural areas ranged from 7 percent to 84 percent of the total cash expenditures of a family, with the average around 25 percent. However, the Ministry of Agriculture Farm Survey of 1953 found an average of 8 percent of total cash income spent on ceremonials, weddings, cremations, and gifts to the *wat*, exclusive of food contributions and volunteer labor. A comparison of family expenditures for charity and entertainment in Bangkok and in Northeastern towns and villages may be made from the Household Expenditure Survey of 1962 as shown in Table 2.6.

These data are suggestive of a decline in the proportion of expenditures for acquiring merit as urbanization, development, and higher income levels spread the quantity and variety of goods and services over the nation. Finally, we do not have evidence of the extent to which contributions to the *wats* represent a form of tithing and hence a fixed cost or are a form of sharing windfall gains. Probably they are a mixture of the two; daily food to the monks would represent a fixed expenditure, while Wijeyewardene (1967, p. 82) suggests that a significant proportion of all merit-making comes from windfalls, especially from lottery wins.

---

* Evers and Silcock (1967, p. 99) estimate that during the retreat period of Buddhist Lent, which coincides with the rainy season when farm labor demands are lowest, more than 250,000 men will typically be in residence in the *wats*, or about 3 percent of the adult male population. During the rest of the year, the permanent monastery population is smaller.

Table 2.6 — Expenditures for Charity and Entertainment, 1962

Item	Percentage of Average Monthly Family Expenditures		
	Bangkok Met. Area	Northeast Towns	Region Villages
Charity			
Food and offerings to monks	0.5	0.9	1.7
Weddings and other ceremonies	1.7	0.9	3.4
Funeral expenses	0.3	—	—
Cash contributions to organizations	2.0	2.2	3.1
Total	4.5	4.0	8.2
Entertainment			
Movie admissions	0.9	0.7	0.1
Other entertainment	0.5	1.2	0.7
Lottery tickets	1.8	0.9	0.8
Total	3.2	2.8	1.6

THE FAMILY AND
THE ROLE OF WOMEN

Characteristics of the family and the economic role and position of women have substantial significance in the marketing system of any society. In Thailand, these institutions and values form a picture not greatly different from that of the United States, except for the vestiges of polygamy which survive among a very small percentage of the upper classes in the form of second or minor wives or mistresses. Also, of course, the woman is inherently inferior because she cannot enter the priesthood and thus enjoy that avenue to merit.

The Thai family, whether rural or urban, is typically nuclear—husband and wife and unmarried children. As the children marry, they split away and form another household although they may live in a house in the parents' compound temporarily until they get established.* The extended family or kin group such as has traditionally

---

*According to the 1960 census, half of the males have been married by age twenty-four and half of the females by age twenty-one for the country as a whole. In Bangkok, the comparable figures are about two years older for both. Ultimately, almost everyone marries; aversion to celibacy, except for those in the Buddhist Order is strong, and family pressures to marry off all the children are irresistible (Sonakul 1967, IV). The extreme sex ratios which interfere with the formation and maintenance of stable families in other developing societies (such as 50-75 percent

characterized the Chinese does not exist among the Thai, nor indeed do they have a sense of ancestry or family extending back for generations. Even the use of family names was not common until early in this century when it was required by government decree for purposes of bureaucratic identification. Blanchard (1958, p. 422) observes that a spatially extended family group does exist, much as in the United States, in the sense that those children who grew up together and have since left home function as a unit to celebrate birth, marriage, and death and to provide economic aid to a member in difficulty.

Thailand has achieved a substantial equality of the sexes, and descriptions of the typical day of both the farm and the urban family (as in Blanchard 1958, pp. 424-42) read much like the togetherness of American families. The basis for this is in the economic role of women as producers in the society. Nearly 42 percent of the female population was in the labor force (fifteen years of age and over) in 1966, according to the Second National Development Plan. Of course, the predominance of the agricultural sector goes far to explain this, since the typical farming unit is the family, consisting of the husband with the wife and unmarried elder children as unpaid family workers. Soon after marriage a son acquires his own farm and his wife joins him in the farm work. But even in the urban labor force, women are important despite the difficulties of child care in cities. According to the 1963 Labor Force Survey, 44 percent of all females eleven years old and over residing in the urban areas of the kingdom were in the labor force, compared with 68 percent of all males. Of those women not in the labor force, about one-half were engaged in housework and nearly one-third were students; among males over eleven and outside the labor force, three-quarters were students. Not surprisingly, women in the urban labor force are principally involved as sales workers—40 percent of them are so engaged—and about 20 percent as craftsmen, production-process workers, and general unskilled laborers. The principal category of employment for males, on the other hand, is as craftsmen, production-process workers, and general labor (28 percent), and secondarily as sales workers (20 percent).

The degree of equality between the sexes varies among the differ-

more males than females in some principal Indian cities and in places in Africa [Hoselitz 1955, p. 179]) has not been characteristic of Thailand, where, according to the 1960 census, the almost exact equality in number of males and females in the nation is distorted to only 5 percent more males than females in Bangkok.

ent areas or types of activity. At the one extreme of inequality, religion is a preserve of the male, while at the other, commercial functions, especially in rural areas, are almost exclusively a female activity among the ethnic Thai. In education, equalization is proceeding rapidly. Appendix Table 2 shows that the gap between the sexes in literacy is closing, although in 1960, 61 percent of the females were literate, compared with about 81 percent of the males. University enrollments, however, reflect the recent rapid rate of westernization in urban areas (nearly 70 percent of entering university students in 1967 came from an urban environment. Kraft 1968, p. 18). In 1967, 42.5 percent of the students in the seven principal Thai universities were women, whereas as recently as 1961, women accounted for only 26 percent of the enrollment. Even more surprising is that 45 percent of the full-time faculty members are women (Raksasataya 1968, p. 89).

Government is another area traditionally reserved for the male. Thus only 20 percent of Thai civil servants (excluding teachers, judges, police, and military) are women, but this participation rate drops to 16 percent for supervisory and higher civil service positions. A few women have been elected to parliament, but none has ever achieved the level of cabinet minister (Raksasataya 1968, pp. 88-89).

We have noted above the important role of women as producers in the Thai economy; we now expand this to the more general possibility of a dichotomy between the "other-wordly" male and the "this-worldly" female. Kirsch (1962, p. 13) has observed that "the allocation of 'this-worldly' concerns in particular economic roles to women, has allowed men to maximize their specializations in terms of merit-mobility and 'other-worldly' concerns." This argument, as stated by Kraft (1968, p. 9), is that women in the traditional Buddhist system are limited in their "merit-mobility" (i.e., ability to move up a ladder of increasing merit by good acts in order to achieve rebirth in a higher position in the next life) to such slow and indirect means as raising a son who could enter the monastery, supporting the family during temporary sojourns of the men as monks, and, in general, specializing in the satisfaction of the material needs of her family, including its money contributions to the *wat*. The result is a division of labor with the woman free to be "this-worldly" and concerned with the family's economic mobility, while the man concentrates on spiritual mobility, for which useful activities include growing rice (part of the crop is given as food to monks), acquiring political power (a person high in merit has power or influence, and vice versa) and, of course, retreats into the monastery. Sharp (1968) carried the argument further and cast the Chinese in a similar role to the Thai women; with their interests and capabilities in such economic activities as commerce and industry, they and the Thai women together have made possible the economic development of the nation without despiritualizing the Thai male.

Unfortunately, we have no data which would quantify the importance of women in the national economy beyond the labor force statistics cited above, which showed their principal activity to be as sales workers.* However, the impression is widespread, based on well-known cases of individuals, that women are important as business owners or investors and to a lesser degree as managers in substantial enterprises. The Thailand Management Association roster shows fifteen women in a membership of 283 and has had women on its executive board. Other evidence which may be cited is that one branch bank in Bangkok, highly successful since its opening five years ago, is staffed solely by women.

Woman's freedom to be materialistic results in her exercising more than an equal share in the control of family finances. Blanchard (1957, p. 436) notes that in rural areas it is her marketing activities which provide much of the family cash income, and she usually both holds the money and controls its expenditure.† However, in the areas of commercialized agriculture where large amounts of cash income are brought in from the sale of rice, the farmer becomes more of a businessman and apparently retains financial control. In urban areas, the ideal seems to be of marriage as a business partnership, clearly reflecting the western influence. Hanks and Hanks (1963, pp. 436-37) describe it thus:

> Almost all social relationships in Thai society define a superior and an inferior. In marriage, on the contrary, the relationship between husband and wife is a partnership between equals. Their authority over

---

* The 1963 Labor Force Survey showed 20,400 males in the Bangkok-Thonburi area occupied as administrative, executive, and managerial workers, and 3,150 females. Of these, 54 percent of the males and 52 percent of the females were classified as government employees and 24 percent and 19 percent respectively as employees of private firms. Three percent of the males and no females were classed as employers with the remainder counted as own account workers.

† A survey of rural credit in the 1930s (Andrews 1935, p. 332) noted that the Thai farmer and especially his wife were more interested in money-lending to other families at high interest rate than were the Chinese.

household, children, or other matters of common concern outside the household is equal. Though the work divides into areas of special interest, consultation is necessary, particularly in the poorer families, in order to allocate funds, arrange working schedules, share work and render needed assistance. . . . Some of the strengths and weaknesses of Thai marriage may be due to the fact that it is the only equal relationship which exists in Thai society.

If this business partnership is the ideal, then it also suggests problems of family income management as the area of major marital conflict. Indeed, Graham and Graham (1957, p. 43) find that the principal cause of difficulty is the minor wife problem (but in its economic aspects of the expenditures on the second wife or mistress rather than infidelity and dilution of affection), followed by problems of the adequacy and the control of family income. These observations are probably biased toward the behavior of the more westernized Thai families, however.* The only survey evidence of how family buying occurs is from the National Statistical Office's 1966 *Survey of Buying and Shopping Habits*, which is described in more detail below at page 79. This meagre and somewhat defective evidence suggests that approximately 60 to 70 percent of all buying trips were made by women. In the case of food items, 85 to 90 percent of the purchases were made by women and only in the case of durable goods such as electrical appliances and furniture did the buying trips involve men and women in equal proportions.

In summary, the status of women in Thai society must be regarded as a favorable factor not only for economic and marketing development but for the general process of modernization as well. In his introduction to Lerner's (1964) study of change in Middle Eastern societies, David Reisman has called attention to the importance of equality of the sexes in the process of modernization. The lack of sex discrimination in the Thai society assures that all members can be fully utilized as producers, exercise their influence as consumers, and receive the stimuli to change.

---

* In response to the question of who handled the money in the average Thai family, a group of graduate students who were studying English with the author's wife in 1967 in Bangkok indicated that the more traditional "this-worldly woman" role was to some extent still operative, with the observations that in some families the man "honors" his wife by letting her handle the money, since he either doesn't care about money or doesn't trust himself to not spend it carelessly.

EDUCATION

We may accept as adequately documented the high correlation (although Myrdal 1968, p. 1667 argues, not the direction of causation) between literacy and education on the one hand and the level of economic and marketing development on the other.*

Certainly, literacy and beyond is essential for an individual's effective performance as a producer and as a consumer. The examples in the literature of comparative marketing of illiterate consumers who are nevertheless keen and discerning buyers (see Bauer and Yamey 1957, p. 94) does not necessarily constitute an exception since they are sophisticated only with respect to articles with which they are familiar. It is, of course, the individual's ability to evaluate the new and unknown which is crucial in transforming economies and societies. However, it must be recognized that there are a variety of substitutes for literacy. A study of acceptance of agricultural innovations among rice farmers near Bangkok found that those adopters who were illiterate tended to have higher exposure to radio and movies, more direct observation of urban ways through travel, and wider social contacts within their village than adopters who were literate (Goldsen and Ralis 1957, pp. 20-27).

The educational situation in Thailand is generally favorable for the spread of a monetized market of national dimensions, as we saw in the discussion in Chapter I of the relative position of the nations of the world. Appendix Table 2 compares the literacy rate for 1947 and 1960 by sex. Among the developing societies there is a bias toward overstating literacy, since in this modern Olympiad, countries gain points for low illiteracy as well as for high and rising per capita income. Even discounting some overstatement, however, the Thai average is high and is increasing at a substantial rate as indicated by the comparison between the two years and by the much higher literacy of the younger segments of the population. Free public compulsory primary education has been in existence *de jure* for nearly fifty years in Thailand; at present the requirement is four years, although extension to seven years is contemplated under the so-called Karachi

---

* In Sherbini's comparative study (1967, p. 146) of marketing systems of various countries, experts in comparative marketing were queried on the most significant indicators of the character of a nation's system. The percentage of literate adults ranked very high in the number of times mentioned by these experts; secondary school and university enrollments, however, ranked rather low in their judgment.

Plan pledge of Southeast Asian countries.* Enrollments for the first seven years of schooling (ages seven-thirteen) during 1960-61 equalled 84 percent of the school-age population, somewhat better than the Southeast Asian regional average of 79 percent. For the secondary level, ages fourteen-eighteen, however, enrollments in academic and vocational schools were 12 percent of the population in that age bracket— somewhat below the regional eight-country average of 13.3 percent (Hayden 1967, pp. 45-46).

Education is highly valued in the Thai society as a producers' good, which pays off in higher income to the holder of a diploma, more than to the possessor of knowledge or skills, it must be added. The development of the educational system of Thailand was initiated as a part of the modernization begun in the middle of the last century by King Mongkut, himself outstanding for the breadth of his education. Education was important to prepare the administrators of the bureaucracy; in this respect, Thailand without colonialism came out with the same goals as those areas of Asia and Africa which were subject to colonial rule (see Myrdal 1968, p. 1641 and Andreski 1968, p. 205). Later emphasis on education of the broad mass of the population still left higher education, whether secured at home (the oldest university in Thailand is fifty years old) or abroad, as the door giving access to the most prestigious career in the society—government service. We have seen above that a career in the government bureaucracy is considered consistent with the Buddhist philosophy, and at the upper levels it provides all the rewards which this life can offer. In the open Thai society, entrance into government service has been available to all in the modern period, without regard to family, social position, or income. It is no wonder that the appeal of government service has been so strong. Nor is it surprising that educational attainment, as represented by a diploma, should have become the selection device for screening the enormous number of aspirants and for determining the civil service level at which an individual will enter. Two aspects of this institutionalizing in the civil service system of selection and promotion by education are dysfunctional for national development; one is the tendency to select only on the basis of possession of a degree,

---

* (Hayden 1967, p. 41.) A number of recent excellent studies of education in Thailand exist. In addition to such regional studies as Hayden and Myrdal (1968), there are a series of studies under the general title *Education in Thailand* jointly conducted by the Thai government and the Institute for International Studies in Education of Michigan State University and published in 1967-1969.

without regard to the subject matter of the degree or its relevance to the job performed. The other dysfunctional aspect is that a foreign degree earns its holder a higher salary than a comparable degree from a local university, obviously with adverse effects on the development of local institutions,* although some but not all students abroad were probably getting better educations than they could have at home. Of course, studying abroad is possible only at great sacrifice for the family unless it be rich or if the candidate can win a government scholarship (for which there may be a thousand applicants for one-hundred vacancies) or the support of foreign governments or foundations. Even for admission to a Thai university the competition is severe—some twenty-six thousand applicants in 1968 for nine thousand freshman class openings.

The traditional appeal of government service as a career and of a diploma as the entrance fee seems to be weakening as careers in private business have become more attractive in recent years. A study by the Ministry of Education (cited in Kraft 1968, p. 6) of career plans of university entrants in the period 1962-1966 found 48 percent with government service as their goal and 20 percent preferring business; certainly the interest in business would have been much lower a decade earlier.†

---

* Soonthornsima (1959, p. 107) states that the cost of maintaining the 2,000 students studying abroad in 1957 was estimated at $1¾ million, roughly twice the annual operating costs of Thailand's oldest and best university during that year.

† Unpublished data of the Institute of International Education office in Bangkok suggest that the percentage of students majoring in business among Thai beginning programs of study in the United States in 1957-58 was about 30 percent but that ten years later it was about 60 percent.

The percentage distribution by major field of the 32,700 students enrolled in the eight principal universities in Thailand in 1966-67 were: business—22 percent, education—16 percent, medicine, dentistry, and public health—14 percent, law—10 percent, engineering—7 percent, and agriculture—6 percent. Government was the major field of 3 percent, ranking tenth among all fields (Shaw and Buasri 1968, p. 77). Of course, as was noted above, it is not inconsistent to major in business and anticipate entering the civil service. Riggs (1966, pp. 339-40) makes the point that "in a bureacratic polity, the most relevant skill is capacity to exercise influence," for which the finest academic institution is hardly useful. He cites the case of an official who as manager of a government enterprise was unable to exert effective control and avoid losses because of having to appoint the protégés of others to key positions. Only by exercising influence to secure government subsidy grants was he able to cover the losses. Yet he had an excellent reputation as being effective and knowledgeable in the field and, in fact, on the side, and sub rosa, ran a private firm in the same field, where he made substantial profits.

Part Two:

Marketing

and

Development

III
The Marketing Structure

The institutional arrangements or the system by which goods pass from producer to consumer in the Thai society is the subject of our attention in this chapter. To speak of the marketing structure is to invoke a western concept and western terminology, particularly that of the "channel" through which goods pass and of the intermediaries or "middlemen" stationed along the channel who collectively perform the various functions involved in distribution. Even more basically, the concept of distribution as intermediate between production and consumption assumes a level of specialization which characterizes the West but which may be only rudimentary in developing societies. In the pure case of self-sufficiency, producer and consumer are one and distribution is no more than the transfer from a man's left hand to his right. Where four-fifths of the people are engaged in agricultural employment as in the Thai case and where the principal crop is the nation's staff of life, then economic activity signifies feeding a family and trading any surplus. Even for many of those engaged in manufacturing activities, factory and retail outlet and home are merely different floors in a two or three-story row house with every member of the family alternating in the various jobs to be done; in such a case, so prevalent in the East, the western distinction between production and distribution becomes blurred.

This is not to say that distribution is unimportant in these cultures but rather the opposite. It is the pervasiveness of trading in the Thai society, in the sense of the widespread searching out of opportunities

69

to buy cheap and sell dear which makes the indiscriminate application of western concepts and terminology dangerous. Western observers (such as Usher 1967, p. 230, and Mayer 1962, p.
14) have
noted a fuzziness in the distinction between wholesale and retail trade
in Thailand with the same firms and individuals acting at both levels;
this corroborates Hirsch's (1961, p. 287) finding of a blurring of
distributive functions among Indian middlemen and elsewhere in
other underdeveloped countries.

One further complication in the analysis of the marketing structure
should be noted—the two (or more) Thailands to which we have
alluded earlier. Any conception of the stages of marketing development must accommodate the very unequal levels of development
between regions and between sectors of an economy.

Two examples of retailing in Thailand illumine both the similarities and dissimilarities with western distribution and the stage concept
of the development of marketing.

TWO RETAILING EXAMPLES

The Central Department Store in Bangkok serves the sophisticated
market of upper-income Thai and foreigners; the small store in the
isolated village in the Northeastern province serves the nearly self-
sufficient peasants who are still only on the fringe of the modern
world. The product lines of the two retail operations portray two
worlds, much farther apart than the 350 miles that separate them.

In April 1968, the fourth store in the Central Department Store
chain opened in a nine-story, one- and one-quarter million dollar
structure containing $2 million worth of merchandise on broad Silom
Road, where a dozen similar-sized new office buildings and hotels have
recently mushroomed above the line of one- and two-story shops and
showrooms extending for over a mile. The founder and sole owner of
the firm had begun business twenty-one years before with a small shop
consisting of about 500 square feet of space; today the firm employs
400 persons and is managed by the founder's twenty-six children,
assisted by a number of "brilliant" daughters-in-law.* The eldest son

---

* Special supplements (in English) of the *Bangkok Post*—and the *Bangkok World*—of
12 April 1968, commemorating the opening of the Silom branch store of the Central
Department Store. We have frequently used the phraseology of these advertising
pieces, in quotation marks, to preserve the flavor of the statements of company
policy.

is the general manager of the company and he is assisted by four brothers and four sisters. "Each member of the family is given the responsibility of a department, which they run in competition with each other." Other children act as buyers, and the three youngest are studying in England and the United States in preparation for their joining the firm.

Many retail outlets in Thailand use the name department store or supermarket despite their small size and narrow lines. The Central Department Store, however, is organized along department lines and carries a wide variety of merchandise, almost all of it imported. (One of its departments is the Wholesale Department, supplying merchandise to other Bangkok stores.) Its policy is to sell only top-quality products imported from the United States, Europe, and Japan and to "immediately exchange items which are of doubtful quality." In addition to quality, it stresses the newest products; "at all times of the year there is at least one member of the family somewhere in the world to grab up the latest products for Bangkok," thus assuring that it "offers shoppers here no stale products." Central advertises that despite the quality and newness of its lines, it sells at lower prices than other stores in the city because of its bulk buying ("Central is able even to sell sunglasses at cheaper rates than sidewalk peddlers"). In addition, the store points out that it retails the goods of foreign manufacturers "at prices agreed upon by the manufacturers, all calculated to push sales with no unauthorized marking up, a practice often resorted to by less reputable stores."

The diversity of lines and their disposition throughout the five split-level shopping floors (the building includes covered parking space for 200 cars) is shown in the following:

First level: cosmetics (including exclusive distribution for Joy, F. Millot, Lancome, Worth-Je Reviens, Helena Rubenstein), jewelry, watches, pens, Smoke Shop.

Second level: men's shirts, Baby Department, Fair Lady Shop (lingerie), Young Ladies' Corner, ladies' dresses and shoes.

Third level: photographic equipment, hi-fi, television (e.g., 21″ Zenith black and white at the equivalent of U.S. $550 and a 21″ Norde Mende [German] color television at U.S. $1,250), home appliances.

Fourth level: Playland (toys), auto accessories, luggage, men's wear and shoes, Young Men's Shop, sports equipment, musical instruments, Bed and Bath Shop.

Fifth level: records, stationery, books, Coffee Shop.

In another world 350 miles away, retailing is a much simpler matter, corresponding to the simplicity of peasant life. From Appendix Table 15 we may summarize the typical product line from a sample of ten general stores in isolated villages in the Northeast provinces:

Flour, sugar, condensed milk, biscuits were carried in all stores; in some, cigarettes and soft drinks (with a typical inventory of two or three cases).

Weaving and sewing items, underwear, hats, and shoes.

Bath soap, toothpaste, hair cream and hair dye, combs, face powder, and headache remedies.

Flashlights and batteries (also used in transistor radios) and kerosene were carried in all stores and oil lamps in some.

Matches, laundry soap, dishes, and spoons were carried in all, and in some stores floor mats (the peasant's bed), blankets, pails and brooms, mirrors.

Pencils, paper and rulers, and temple ceremonial items—joss sticks (incense) and candles, were all carried in all stores.

Rope, nails, and wire were carried in all, and in some stores, fertilizer, and oxen and buffalo bells.

Although we do not have detailed profiles of the five villages in which the ten stores surveyed are found, we know that until recently they were without road connections and their citizens largely self-sufficient farmers with limited money income. Although the items in the product line of the typical village store are now either manufactured in Thailand or packaged locally from imported raw materials, this is a development of the past two or three decades. Finally, it is of interest to note that of the ten salesmen interviewed, only two reported selling as their sole occupation; for six of the ten, farming was their major activity and selling only secondary.

The differences between the Central Department Store and its customers, on the one hand, and the isolated village store near the Laotian border and its consumers, on the other, are enormous and evident. Both stores, however, exemplify the last link or middleman in a channel which runs across space and through time from the producer to the ultimate consumer of a good.

RETAILING IN RURAL AREAS

In addition to the trade in goods imported from outside the region and sold at a fixed-location store in the village just described, two other kinds of retail trading take place in the rural area: the trading of local produce in the village market and of goods produced outside the region and retailed by itinerant traders.

We have seen in Chapter I that the principal activity of most Thai is in growing rice, and that the farmer consumes about one-half of what he produces with the remainder being exported, traded to the nonfarmers in the town and cities, or given to the monks. But the farmer does a good deal more than simply grow rice for a few months of the year and relax the remainder. Some of these activities, such as farm and home maintenance and improvement, yield no immediate cash income, while others, such as manual labor on government-financed dams or roads or clerking in the village store yield some cash return. In addition, a variety of activities by members of the farm family yield products which are bartered or sold for cash in the permanent markets of the village or town; examples are surplus vegetables from the family garden, chickens and eggs, and cotton cloth woven from either home-grown or purchased thread. Klausner (1966, p. 6), studying a rural area in the Northeast, found specialization by villages reflecting either their resource endowments or merely custom, and with barter or sale in the markets of other villages or the nearer towns; such was the case of processing salt from the salty topsoil, or gathering snails to make lime, which is used in the chewing of betel-nut, or of fermenting fish for a staple dish of the region.

The general structure of peasant marketing has been described in detail for Java in a classic study by Alice Dewey (1962); in addition, she found confirmation of similar trading patterns in the descriptions by other scholars for Malaya, West Africa, and Guatemala. Although no comparable study in depth has been made for Thailand, fragmentary evidence all points to general similarity in the trading patterns in Java and Malaya.* In describing Thailand's rural marketing, it is helpful to borrow Dewey's distinction between goods produced and consumed within the peasant economy and goods imported from outside the economy, whether these have been produced in cities within the region, elsewhere in the nation, or imported from foreign countries. In the former case, small-scale, part-time indigenous traders predominate, with little capital, low opportunity costs, and hence low profits. In the latter case, distribution down to the final stage at the small village is handled by specialist traders, generally non-indigenous (Chinese in both Java and Malaya), with some capital and market knowledge.

In rural Thailand, households exchange their surpluses by sending a woman of the family to a centrally-located market to barter or sell for cash. On the basis of his observations principally in 1948-49, de Young (1955, p. 12) reported that the regular morning market would be found in a larger village strategically located to serve a group of smaller villages. He observed that in the commune he studied, consisting of eleven villages and a total population of 4,000, women did not go to the market every day but "in the course of a week or ten days every household with an able-bodied woman was represented at the market" (p. 104). Undoubtedly substantial quantities of goods change hands among rural households throughout the kingdom, although it is not a matter of particular interest to us in marketing development even though the exchanges increasingly are for money. The traders are Thai women; it is unspecialized and part time (women trade between six and eight o'clock and are back in the home by nine in the morning) and consists essentially of adjusting household stocks by exchanging surplus items for goods in short supply. Persistence of this trading is not inconsistent with progress in the development of a market economy; much of it is probably similar to a housewife's borrowing a cup of flour from her next-door neighbor.

---

* Much of the evidence is found in the work of anthropologists interested in matters other than the marketing or economic structure of the villages they studied. It is interesting to note that one of Dewey's purposes in making her study was to counteract the overemphasis she felt her fellow anthropologists have given to the economic isolation of the small communities which they prefer to study. Her approach was to focus instead on markets and the activity of economic exchange as a major mechanism which in fact binds together various villages.

Itinerant Trading

The limited demands of individual households in rural areas are summed by the itinerant trader into a market of sufficient size to justify his specialization in full-time trading. In addition, he adds the convenience of delivery which, for isolated villages at all times and for all villages during the busy seasons of rice planting and harvesting, is a service for which some premium will be paid. The most important is the itinerant Chinese notions peddler who, in de Young's description (1963, pp. 105-106)

> regularly makes his village rounds, by small boat in central Thailand, on foot or by bicycle or bus in the rest of the country. A typical traveling vendor carries two trays made of soap boxes suspended from ropes on a carrying pole; these are stocked with needles, thread, buttons, soap, matches, belts, plastic bags, powder, hair pomade, and many other small drygoods. . . . The improved roads and increased bus lines have cut into his business but at the same time they have enabled him to extend his range of vending so that much of what he has lost in quantity of sales to a given customer has been compensated for by his being able to reach an ever greater number of customers. That itinerant peddling is still profitable is attested to by the fact that even remote villages are plied by the soapbox merchants. On a good day in the planting season a peddler can sell about 80 *ticals* (US $4) worth of goods in the course of visiting several villages (the average in 1948 given by several peddlers who regularly ply the San Pong commune). Vendors are reluctant to discuss their profits, but it is obvious from the difference in retail and wholesale prices that at least half of each sale is clear profit. Vendors of more special items such as cloth and lottery tickets visit the villages during the dry season.

The stock of the itinerant Chinese peddler is so limited in comparison with that of even the small village store described earlier that it is doubtful that de Young's optimistic view of the peddler's ability to compete against the villager's increased mobility from improved transportation could prevail for long. Even if the peddler should switch to a motorized van which would enable him to carry a variety of goods equal to that of the fixed location store, the peasant would probably prefer the other attractions of the village and the excitement of the social contact there, except during the short periods of heavy farm work. It should also be noted that de Young's observation that half or more of the retail price is "clear profit" fails to take into account a necessarily high premium for home delivery over a very dispersed population; his observation should not be considered as contradicting the consensus view that retailing profits are probably quite small.

Another example of itinerant peddling of imported goods is the distribution of kerosene and charcoal. Because of their unpleasant odor or disagreeable handling qualities, shoppers wish to keep them separate from food purchases and even in urban areas, distribution is by specialist peddler. Still another form of peddling prevalent in both rural and urban areas is in prepared foods, which are consumed either as snacks or as parts of a meal, and for which the purchaser values the convenience. Finally, a form of itinerant trading of substantial interest in marketing development is by wholesalers or manufacturers of consumer goods using water and land vehicles and combining sales at wholesale to stores and at retail to peasants, often with entertainment added to attract attention. Of the pharmaceutical suppliers who have blanketed the rural areas for years, de Young (p. 106) reports that the mobile units play recorded music over amplifiers to sell aspirin, quinine, aralen, sulfa, and local and imported patent medicines to both peasants and village doctors. More recently, the method has been adopted by a variety of consumer goods manufacturers and wholesalers from Bangkok; sales are made to up-country retail stores and stocks of popular items supplied by salesmen traveling in van-type trucks for extended periods through the rural areas. One manufacturer, for example, divides the nation, outside the Bangkok area, into four regions, with a truck and two-man crew moving through each territory on a three-month long pre-established itinerary. In addition, a specially fitted boat is used to serve wholesalers and retail stores located on the Central Plains waterway system and which are often accessible only by water. A common practice is for such traveling salesmen to replenish the truck from stocks maintained in the custody of friendly hotelkeepers throughout the territory and to reorder from the Bangkok plant or warehouse by common-carrier truck delivery to the hotel ahead of arrival. In the case of a manufacturer of dry cell batteries, the truck which is selling and stocking small retailers is also fitted for showing a free program of movies in the evening in those towns and villages which have no theatre. The program is shown in the open air on the grounds of the temple, which is the center of social activities in such communities, and crowds are drawn from substantial distances away. Between reels in the film, flashlight or transistor batteries are sold at retail from the side of the truck to the spectators. There is nothing peculiarly Thai in this distribution method, of course. Omana (1965, pp. 138-39) has noted that the sound truck, often fitted also with a movie projector, is by far the most important advertising media in Sub-Sahara Africa, and compares the operation to the roving medicine man shows of the past century in the United States.

The diversity of the trading carried out by individuals without fixed locations is extremely broad but probably not significantly different from what the itinerant vendor has done all over the world, or from what he was doing centuries ago in Thailand. The basis for this type of retailing is the relative immobility of the rural family and its limited financial resources which restrict its needs and inhibit its impulses. Under these circumstances, retailers who bring to the home one or a few products for sale in very small quantities provide a valuable convenience. By the same token, the process now going on in Thailand, and described in detail in the next chapter, by which the rural family's mobility and its disposable income are both increasing significantly must inevitably reduce the importance of the itinerant vendor.

URBAN RETAILING

Just as the small village store is not the whole of trading in rural areas, so the Central Department Store is only a part of trading in Bangkok and quite atypical. One other department store, Japanese operated and retailing a full range of articles largely imported from Japan, is less luxurious than Central but thoroughly modern, and well patronized by the upper and upper-middle income classes. Most of the retailing in Bangkok is of course done in very different circumstances than these stores exemplify, however. We have referred earlier to the fact that just as there are "two Thailands," so there are a number of Bangkoks; the diversity of retailing within the city illustrates well these "different cities." The patterns of commercial land use in the city of Bangkok reflect ethnic and socio-economic groupings of the population. The ethnic grouping is most evident in the large Chinese section of the city; this is a high-density, low-income area with each building mixing commercial, small industrial, and residential use and which is clearly delineated by the use of Chinese characters alone or along with Thai lettering in shop signs. At the other extreme are those shopping areas catering to westerners and the upper socio-economic classes of Orientals, where the shop signs are in English, or in Thai and English. Except for these Chinese and western commercial sections, the rest of the shopping areas cater to the Thai population of the city. (Even here, English may be attempted in the signs, often with amusing or confusing results such as "Luckily Limited Partnership," or "Scandia Furniture Co., Touch Your Feeling Cover Luxurious Interior Decoration.")

Such consumer characteristics as frequent purchases of small quantities of food, because of limited income and refrigeration, and immobility from limited automobile ownership, congested streets, and inadequate public transportation have fostered the development of a large number of food market areas throughout the city. Clustered in the streets around these public markets with their small stalls, often numbering in the hundreds, are small shops handling general merchandise and hard goods. A listing of the types of stores encountered in consecutive order on one side of the street as one walks away from a food market area (Pratunam) is illustrative: housewares, largely pots and pans, men's women's and children's shoes, tailor for men, dishes and glassware, hardware, photo studio, toy store, photo studio, and two tailor shops, side by side. A quarter of a mile farther away from the food market area and approaching a cluster of large movie houses, the shops become larger and thoroughly modern in display and lighting, clearly aiming at the upper middle-class consumer and an occasional foreigner. In less than a thousand feet of street frontage, there are fifteen shoe stores (mostly women's, with purses and belts), two tailors, three boutiques, and one store each with silk yard goods, toys, souvenirs, records, and an auto agency. At this point on this main thoroughfare, bus transportation is good but parking for private cars very difficult. Growing automobile ownership is reflected in the development of the "strip" shopping area as well as in the Gaysorn district of six square blocks of shops catering to the upper class and foreigner trade. In the "strip" shopping area the main road is often solidly developed with shops on the ground level, and with the proprietor's apartment above or in the rear. Narrow dead-end streets branch off the main artery giving access in the rear to the residential areas of predominantly single-family homes of the upper-middle and upper classes. It is along these arteries that a number of "supermarkets" have developed in recent years; while only the name was widely appropriated by many food stores (Wigglesworth and Brotan

1966, p. 45), nearly a dozen today could be considered American-type (self-service, complete with basket carts, plastic-packaged meats and vegetables, and a wide assortment of imported foods in single or a few brands, housewares, paperback books and liquor) but on a compact scale, and with no parking. A 1967 survey by the office of the U.S. commercial attaché found the customers of supermarkets to be predominantly American and European (70 percent) and only 30 percent from the upper-income Thais.

Consumer Buying Habits

Some evidence of the shopping habits of households in a middle- and lower-middle class area in Bangkok is available from a survey conducted in April 1966 (National Statistical Office, *Survey of Buying and Shopping Habits** 1966). The survey covered a random sample of 176 households in an eleven-block area containing 1,200 households; the area could be characterized as mixed commercial and small or cottage industry with the apartment over a store or shop, predominating over single-family residences. Within a radius of one and one-half miles are three other similar areas, each with its own market or commercial complex. Residents of the survey area reported they did 50 percent of their shopping in their own area and an additional 36 percent in these three nearby areas, with the remainder in other areas of the city, the most distant of which is about three and one-half miles away. The shopping explored by the survey covered food, clothing, drugs, household articles, electrical appliances and furniture, and services such as restaurants, personal care, and medical and dental treatment.

Of the reasons for selecting the shopping place, 51 percent gave proximity and 12 percent indicated ease of transport. The variety of goods available, quality, and price were cited by 11 percent, 8 percent and 7 percent respectively. Finally, 5 percent and 4 percent indicated

---

* The survey was undertaken by the National Statistical Office with partial financial support from the Rotary Club of Bangkok. The report describes the study as a pilot survey and acknowledges its weaknesses, such as in the small sample and in interviewing techniques used. The purpose of the survey was to measure customer satisfaction with the retail trades and to elicit suggestions for improvement. The level of satisfaction which was revealed was high. Interestingly, 4 percent of the respondents suggested the desirability of price reductions and 2 percent expressed the wish that "prices of commodities be fixed and exposed to customers so that no bargaining would be needed" (p. 11).

their place of shopping was from habit or friendship with the proprietor.

THE STRUCTURE OF TRADE

Descriptions of the structure of trade in Thailand have been, and must continue to be, highly impressionistic. We have already referred to the pervasiveness of trading in the society; with much trading subordinated to other activities and thus not flowing through the specialist middlemen, understatement of unknown proportions seems inevitable. There are other reasons for imprecision in the description of the structure of trade; the near complete control over commerce by the Chinese, who are feared and discriminated against by the government, and the normal secretiveness of any small businessman who fears that his competitors, customers, suppliers, or the government could easily dislodge him from his precarious perch in the economy, if they knew more about him. Finally, until recently, there have been no census data on commerce. The first *Census of Business Trade or Services, 1966* (actually covering trade *and* service for the calendar year or year-end of 1965, preliminary reports of which began to be published in early 1968) provides data which overcome some of the impressionism of earlier discussions of the structure of trade, although the other reasons persist and, of course, color the census results.

The magnitudes of the trading structure are indicated by the following data for wholesaling and retailing in both urban and rural areas.*

	Receipts (million baht)
Wholesale only	15,176
Retail only	9,885
Wholesale and retail	17,851
	42,912 (or U.S. $2.1 billion)

---

* Appendix Table 9 includes data on five other types of activity which were covered by the census: producing and retail, services only, wholesale trade and services, retail trade and services, and wholesale, retail and services. Since all four of the "mixed" types of activity contain wholesale and/or retail receipts, the total of 42.9 billion baht shown above is understated by an unknown amount. A principal purpose of the census was to improve national income accounting and many concepts reflect this orientation: "receipts" is defined as sales of goods purchased, plus brokerage fees or commissions, plus change in inventory.

The relatively small size of retail sales deserves comment since the selling price of an article normally increases as it moves through the channel. A number of reasons for the larger size of wholesale sales can be posited:*

1) A particular article may be sold more than once at the wholesale level (with multiple reporting of value) but only once at retail by the customary definition which was used in the census and which covers sale to the *ultimate* consumer.

2) Goods for export to ultimate consumers abroad would be reported only at the wholesale level, such as agricultural products (for example, the 4.3 million baht in rice exported in 1965).

3) Understatement of retail sales seems inevitable for a number of reasons. For one, the scope of the census excludes mobile vendors who are clearly of greater importance in retailing than wholesaling. To the extent that barter exists in the villages, or where the open account system prevails with the rice middleman supplying the farmer with goods between harvests against payment of the debt being made partially or wholly in rice at harvest time, retail sales reported to the census are biased. Indeed, when to these reasons is added the very small scale of commercial activity at the village level and the opportunities for underreporting, we may be sure we have only a partial view of trading activity at this point in the channel.

The Census of Business Trade or Services was conducted in two parts—a complete enumeration of the 120 municipal areas in Thailand, and a sample of 650 villages (expanded to produce an estimate for the total of over 41,000 villages in the nation) for the areas outside of the municipalities, which are called rural areas. The following tabulation distinguishes between the commercial activity in urban and in rural areas and shows, in addition to sales, the number of establishments and number of persons employed (including working proprietors and unpaid family workers if they work at least 20 hours a week).

This breakdown highlights the great importance of the urban sector. Although the 120 municipalities contain only 14 percent of the nation's population, they account for 80 percent of retail sales, 92 percent of wholesale sales, and 82 percent of the total sales of all three categories. Even in the case of the number of establishments, 40 per-

---

* Data for other countries show the same relationship but to a lesser degree.

Type of Activity	Number of Establishments	Number of Persons Employed	Receipts (million baht)
Wholesale only	4,970	28,992	15,176
Urban areas	2,395	20,261	13,902
Rural areas	2,575	8,731	1,274
Retail only	128,165	318,302	9,885
Urban areas	51,859	123,965	7,832
Rural areas	76,306	194,337	2,053
Wholesale and retail	7,466	51,399	17,851
Urban areas	5,238	40,748	13,455
Rural Areas	2,228	10,651	4,396

cent of all retail establishments are in urban areas, as are 48 percent of all wholesale establishments.

In relation to population, there were approximately 240 persons per retail store for the entire nation in 1965.* Urban areas were of course better served, with 84 persons per store, while in rural areas, the figure was about 340 persons. However, rural data exclude the myriad mobile vendors who blanket the countryside and whose merchandise lines in total probably equal the diversity in stocks in the fixed-location village stores.

A final summary tabulation from the data in Appendix Tables 10 and 11 presents two measures of size: average number of employees and average receipts per establishment. In addition to the data for the 120 urban areas, the Bangkok Metropolitan Area (the municipalities of Bangkok and Thonburi) are shown separately.

Certain characteristics of the distribution system are evident from the ratio analysis that follows. One is the large scale of firms in the Bangkok Metropolitan Area, related to other municipalities and to rural areas. Another is the large size of wholesale establishments in comparison with retailing, with the mixed activity wholesaling-retailing occupying an intermediate position. The average annual sales of the equivalent of nearly half a million U.S. dollars for the 1,300 wholesale-only establishments in the Bangkok area are indeed large and reflect the concentration of the export and import trade there for the entire nation.

---

* This figure may be compared to the 74 persons in Japan, cited in Dunn (1964, p. 620).

Type of Activity	Employees per Establishment	Receipts per Establishment (thousand baht)
Wholesale only		
Bangkok met. area	11.4	8,872 (U.S. $443,600)
All municipalities	8.5	5,805
Rural areas	3.4	495
Retail only		
Bangkok met. area	2.5	201 (U.S. $10,500)
All municipalities	2.4	151
Rural areas	2.5	27 (U.S. $1,350)
Wholesale and retail		
Bangkok met. area	9.4	3,885
All municipalities	7.8	2,569
Rural areas	4.8	1,980

Having examined the available data on the size of the two broad types of middlemen in Thailand, we turn now to some evidence on the flow of goods through distribution channels.

CHANNELS OF DISTRIBUTION

Channels in Industry

Some evidence on the flow of goods from producer to consumer is available from the 1964 *Industrial Census* (Table 7 in the Appendix presents summary data and definitions from the census). A question in the census requested the percentage of the value of the firm's goods which were distributed to other industrial establishments, to wholesalers, to retailers, and directly to consumers.*

Unfortunately, the responses were not weighted by the volume of sales, and the results can be ambiguous. For example, the industry category "Manufacture of Machine Equipment and Parts," consisting of three "large" firms, shows equal thirds of the value of industry

---

* One objective of the business censuses conducted during this decade is the improvement in the quality of the national accounts. We may presume the purpose of this question was to improve on the earlier procedure which had been used for calculating value added in the commercial sector and which was described thus: "it is determined arbitrarily whether each group of products has to pass through one or two levels of middlemen before reaching the final consumers (for example one level for commercial crops and most manufactured products and two levels for rice, fruit, and vegetables" (Prot Panitpakdi 1967, p. 115).

sales distributed to industrial establishments, through wholesalers, and direct to consumers. This could mean either that all three firms distributed one-third of their product to each channel member or that each firm distributed all of its product to one of the categories; since we have no knowledge of the relative sizes of the three firms, the flow of the industry product could be very different than the apparent equal shares. In some cases, the meaning is clear: where there is one manufacturer only, or where all or none of the industry sales value went to a single channel member. Despite the ambiguity the data in Table 3.1 for selected consumer goods products are of interest (*large* and *small* refer to establishments with ten or more persons engaged, or less than ten, respectively).

It will be noted in Table 3.1 that the smaller industrial firms uniformly sell less of their output to wholesalers and more to retailers or directly to consumers than do the larger firms. This tendency would confirm the theory of stages or a cycle in channel development, according to which the expansion of markets, increased output, and increased specialization bring about first a lengthening of channels by the insertion of new intermediaries between producer and con- sumer and later a shortening of channels. We have verified this tendency by examining the entire list of 107 industries (including the eight shown above) which had both large and small establishments operating in 1963 but with not more than 50 percent of industry output going to other industrial establishments. The results were as follows: (*a*) the proportion of output distributed *to wholesalers* was smaller for the small firms than for the large in 81 out of 107 indus- tries, or in 76 percent of the cases; (*b*) correspondingly, more of the output of small firms than of the large was distributed *to retailers* (66 industries out of 107 or 62 percent and directly *to consumers* (78 out of 107 or 73 percent). These data would appear to confirm the lengthening stage in development, with the larger firm, which is characterized by a geographically larger market and greater output, making more use of specialized middlemen in the distribution of its product. However, we shall note below a tendency for the largest manufacturers, and especially the foreign firms, to circumvent the wholesaler and distribute directly to retailers.

Channels in Agriculture

In agriculture, the channel begins with the farmer as the producer and carries his goods across space and through time to the consumer

Table 3.1 — Manufacturers' Sales to Channel Members of Selected
Consumer Goods Products

No. of Establishments	Product	Percentage of Output Sold by Manufacturers to		
		Wholesalers	*Retailers*	*Consumers*
	Ice cream			
3	Large	60	12	28
43	Small	28	54	17
	Rice mills			
643	Large	70	15	14
3,756	Small	12	14	73
	Meat and meat products, preparation and preserving			
3	Large	50	27	23
23	Small	10	41	49
	Soy Sauce			
6	Large	60	32	8
16	Small	45	43	12
	Medicine and pharmaceuticals			
45	Large	61	34	5
25	Small	42	39	15
	Toilet preparations			
18	Large	68	29	1
33	Small	64	28	8
	Ready-made outerwear and underwear			
38	Large	28	31	41
2,737	Small	3	12	83
	Cotton textiles			
112	Large	80	14	3
113	Small	63	24	12

Note: Failure to add to 100 percent is explained by small amount of sales to other industrial establishments.

in Thailand or to the port of export. While our interest is more in the flow of what the farmer consumes than in what he produces, the two are related; in fact, the same middleman who buys the farmer's surplus produce often sells him the goods he needs, through barter, for cash, or on open account. Therefore, it is of interest to summarize briefly the characteristics of these channels.*

The first transaction in the agricultural channel occurs on the farm or in the village (it will be recalled from Chapter II that the peasant lives in the village and walks to the fields he owns or works, although he may live in a makeshift field house for several months of the year [Klausner 1966]). The farmer does not transport his crop to market, but, rather, the middleman seeks out the farmer and purchases from him. There are a number of reasons for the middleman performing this collection function: not every farmer has a surplus of rice† and what he has of the cash crops is small in quantity. In addition, transportation is difficult for the farmer who has, at most, a cart and bullock. Thus the first middleman collects the small quantities from individual farmers and transports them to the district or provincial centers where he sells to the second middleman or to the processing mill. The following diagram shows the percentage distribution of the flow of rice from eight Northeastern provinces (Ministry of Agriculture, 1964).

It will be seen that this portion of the channel accounts for 77 percent of the rice originating on the farm; the remainder is accounted for by local milling and direct sale from farm to consumer. The farmer is confronted by three types of purchasers; in order of importance by this survey, they are the local merchant, the merchants from district towns or provincial centers or their agents, and mills in the towns or centers and their agents. The channels vary somewhat among the products studied, particularly where no processing is involved between producer and consumer (chickens, tamarind, and watermelon) but in all cases the local merchant is important as the

---

* A number of descriptions, largely impressionistic, are available and they coincide in the rough outlines of this trade. We have relied heavily on Blanchard (1958), on Usher's study of *The Thai Rice Trade* (1967) based on an unspecified number of interviews with farmers, traders, and officials, and on the Ministry of Agriculture (1964) study of marketing margins and channels of major agricultural products and livestock in eight Northeastern provinces, based on interviews with 144 middlemen and a number of processing plant and transportation company managers.
† Blanchard (1958, p. 345) observed that less than half the farmers have surplus paddy and for those who do, the average is less than three tons per farmer. Usher (1967, p. 210) points out that the middleman's willingness to buy small quantities of rice enables the farmer to sell his rice bit by bit as he needs cash.

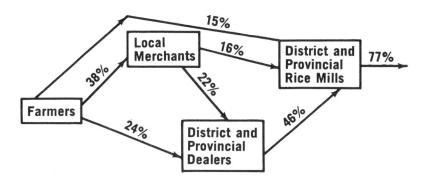

first middleman, although he is not the sole bidder for the farmers' produce.*

Another consequence of the small size of the individual farmer's sales is in the diversification of activities of the local merchant.† In addition to this trading and transporting of agricultural products, he typically owns the small store described earlier and is the money-lender in the village.

To complete the channel diagram of the flow of rice from the Northeast, the 77 percent of the farm output which passed through the rice mills in the marketing centers of the region was destined about equally to Thai consumers (31 percent), and through Bangkok for export abroad (33 percent), with 13 percent going north across the border to Laos:

---

* The percentage of farm output purchased by the local merchant for the other products, to compare with the 38 percent for rice was: swine—40 percent, buffalo—64 percent, cattle—63 percent, chickens—51 percent, kenaf—28 percent (decentralized baling plants were most important), kapok—74 percent, sticklac (shellac)—47 percent, tamarind—62 percent, watermelon—56 percent.

† With regard to the lack of specialization, the Ministry of Agriculture study found that except for rice, the local and provincial dealer typically traded in a number of agricultural commodities; 21 percent handled one commodity only, while 48 percent handled five or more commodities. The typical dealer had been operating less than five years, reflecting the recent development of surpluses and cash crops for trading (Ministry of Agriculture 1964, pp. 10-11).

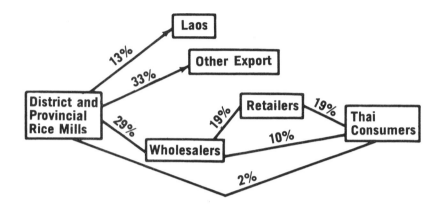

It will be seen that the majority of the flow to Thai consumers passed through two levels of middlemen but with a third of what the wholesaler received being shunted around the retailer and direct to the consumer.

In view of the importance of rice in the nation's economy, it is not surprising that a folklore has built up regarding the predatory and exploitative middleman. To what extent this is the traditional view that questions the productivity of the trader in any society, or a reflection of the animosity toward, or fear of the Chinese who control all commerce in Thailand, is not clear. Perhaps the juxtaposition of the theme of nationalism and exploitation in a statement of government aims from *The Second National Economic and Social Development Plan (1967-1971)*, is not coincidental:

> (iv) Encourage Thai nationals to participate more effectively in commerce through the provision of educational facilities in business administration and marketing advisory services.
>
> (v) Improve the marketing system so as to give agricultural producers a fair share of the retail price paid by the consumers (p. 246).

The role of the Chinese in marketing will be described in greater detail below; some observations are in order at this point on the problem of the agricultural producers' "fair share."

The argument of exploitation of the rice farmer is based on his lack of knowledge of market conditions and prices, his inability to transport his surplus to a market place where he could seek out potential buyers, and his being tied to his creditors by the pledge of his produce to moneylenders or to his open account at the village store. The evidence does not support these allegations, however.*

On the question of the efficiency of the marketing structure for agriculture, much further research is required. The Ministry of Agriculture 1964 study concluded that marketing costs are too high, to the detriment of the agricultural producers. The argument is that an excessive number of middlemen are required because deficiencies in transportation necessitate the collection of small lots of produce for transfer to the district or provincial assembly points. To evidence excessive marketing costs, the following estimates of the Northeastern farmer's share in the final retail price were offered:†

	Percentage		Percentage
Pork	48	Kenaf	68
Beef	47	Rice	47
Buffalo	49	Watermelon	28
Chicken	48	Kapok	26

---

* The following quotation verbatim from the conclusions and recommendations section of the Ministry of Agriculture report (1964, p. 119) is interesting in its reasoning as well as its evidence:

"The trading of most agricultural products, such as rice, kenaf, sticklac, kapok, tamarind and watermelon is conducted at random by the local dealers who trade under free market conditions with a maximum of competition. There appears to be some areas where rice-mill ownership is to a slight degree monopsony which may influence paddy prices. There should be improved control over the number of dealers in business. When the prices of the products increase there is an increase in the number of dealers and vice versa. This not only affects the orderly marketing of farm products but results in lower tax revenues for the government. In addition to rice marketing, other products which must be processed are subject to influence by processors in spite of an otherwise free market. Most of the capital which supports kenaf baling plants, lac processors and large rice-mills is derived from Bangkok sources. Many of the factories in different provinces appear to be under the direct or indirect control of parent firms in Bangkok. This results in the possibility of price fixing at certain times or combining to restrict prices in certain areas. Most of the owners of agricultural processing businesses are Chinese who have numerous trade contracts with other Chinese in Bangkok. Thus they are able to move very quickly as market changes take place and are able to continuously outsmart the ill informed farmers." Also on the competitiveness of sales at the farm, see Usher (1967, p. 211), Silcock (1967, p. 234), and Muscat, (1966) and the studies of Thai economists cited therein (pp. 96-101). On credit as a device of exploration, Pathum Thisyamondol (1965), and Rozental's unpublished paper, "Financing of Rural Households in Thailand," June 1966.

† Unfortunately, the study does not make clear whether retail price was to consumers in the same terminal market for all products, that is, whether the transportation component in marketing costs was for a uniform distance.

An opposite conclusion—that marketing costs in Thailand are very low—was reached by Usher in his study of the rice trade. His calculations for rice grown in the Central Plain and milled about 30 kilometers from Bangkok showed that the farmer got 79 percent of the Bangkok retail price.* In his view, "distribution in America costs three times as much as distribution in Thailand when costs are measured as percentage deductions from the retail price of rice and comparable items" (p. 222). The reason is that rice distribution combines retailing, at which the Thai (or Chinese) have a substantial comparative advantage, and trucking, at which they are not disadvantaged in relation to the United States (p. 224).

While it is not conclusive, of course, the fact that it is the government which protests the exploitation by the marketing system rather than the producers who are assumed to be suffering undermines the argument. Attempts to develop a government-sponsored marketing organization and to foster the cooperative movement in Thailand have been less than successful. And even a private attempt whereby the East Asiatic Company, a Danish trading house which operated rice mills, developed an organization to buy paddy directly from the rice farmer and to lend him money on land as security at low interest rates ran into violent objections from the government and was abandoned.†

THE WESTERN TRADING HOUSES

We have seen in Chapter I how the rivalry of the old East India companies of the British, French, and Dutch, and the excesses of agents of those companies led to the closing of the doors of Siam to the West from 1688 down to the mid-nineteenth century. It was the Bowring Treaty of 1855 which reopened the doors, enabling western trading houses to establish themselves once again in Siam. For more than a century, then, these foreign firms have occupied

---

* However, the price paid the farmer was equal to only 46 percent of the f.o.b. price for rice to be exported. The difference, 42 percent of the export price, is in the much-discussed rice premium, an export tax criticized for its depressant effect on rural purchasing power to the benefit of the urban, including bureaucratic, population. Cf. Corden (1967, p. 169) and Silcock (1967, pp. 231 ff.).

† (Blanchard 1958, p. 345.) According to this author, "the government was not averse to seeing Chinese middlemen replaced—but not by other foreigners who might obtain possession of large amounts of rice land through foreclosure."

important positions in Thai marketing. Although no quantitative measures of their importance exist, it is evident that a significant part of the imports of Thailand enter the country through these firms to begin their movement down the distribution channels. In addition, their organizations and methods have influenced non-western establishments.

One of the oldest large trading firms operating in Thailand is the Borneo Company, Ltd., a British firm organized in London in 1856 and with its Far Eastern base at Singapore (Longhurst 1956). The company's first representative took up residence in Bangkok as the accredited Lloyds agent and began to explore the trading opportunities, along with a number of other western firms which had rushed in upon the conclusion of the Bowring Treaty. The development of the product lines of these trading houses is illustrated by the Borneo case, although with more glamour than most, for it was to the company's Singapore manager that King Mongkut of Siam had written a famous letter in 1862, requesting a reorder of cough lozenges, inquiring about a small cannon which was being shipped from London, and outlining the duties of a governess the king wished to employ for the children in the royal household. (By odd coincidence, twenty years after the Borneo Company had introduced Anna to the King of Siam, her son was in the company's employ, and twenty-three years later still, he had founded a similar trading firm, Louis T. Leonowens, Ltd., which is now a principal competitor of Borneo; Leonowens describes its product line today as "from toothpaste to tractors, textiles to toilet tissues and flashlights to frozen food.") During the first two decades of its operation in Thailand, the Borneo Company's activities centered on the operation of steam-powered rice and saw mills, a steam towboat and coastwise passenger and freight service, pepper exporting, and representing three British banks as well as the Lloyd's agency. Beginning in the 1870s the teak trade became all-important for the western firms operating in Thailand; it consisted of their holding of leases to timber lands as concessionaires of the government, ownership and operation of saw mills, and the exportation of teak, often in ships owned or chartered by the companies. The end of World War II marked a shift in the government policy regarding foreign participation in concessions, and the western trading firms were forced to turn more and more to general trading, that is, to the importation and wholesale distribution throughout the country of manufactured goods, with perhaps a small amount of exporting of Thai agricultural produce and raw materials. Finally, the developments in the economy of the past ten years, which have been described in Chapter I, principally industrialization and the construction boom, have imposed further drastic changes in the operations of the trading houses, at the same time that new non-western firms have come into being which are competitive in at least certain areas with the traditional firms. All of this change reveals the real nature of the western trading houses as *general business* enterprises (including manufacturing, trade, and transportation) which are committed to a country or region and interested in any activity that can be carried out with profit by reason of their knowledge, contacts, and organization within the underdeveloped country and in their home country and throughout the world.

Two examples of trading houses may be cited to illustrate the diversity of more recent entrants to the field pioneered by firms like the Borneo Company, Leonowens, or the Danish-owned East Asiatic Company:

1) The International Engineering Co., Ltd, was founded in 1923 by an American engineer to participate as contractor in the building of a railroad line to the Cambodia border. Upon the termination of this construction four years later, the company began to import American goods for sale in Thailand—Crisco, Proctor and Gamble products, and Westinghouse and International Harvester equipment. Wiped out by the Japanese occupation of Thailand, the company was built up again to its present size of 600 employees, annual sales of the equivalent of U.S. $21.5 million, with the products of 70 American firms handled in four departments—electronics, communications, Caterpillar tractors, and general merchandise. A wholly owned retailing subsidiary handles household appliances, office equipment, and precision tools. The American founder has now retired and distributed most of his shares in the company to Thai employees.

2) The Bangkok United Mechanical Company was organized in 1960 by a group of Thai businessmen who were interested in getting into the importing and exporting business, starting with the agency for Mitsubishi heavy construction equipment. In its second year the firm added a contract heavy-load trucking operation and in its fourth year, assembly of low-bed trailers. In its fifth year, it created a coastwise shipping line to handle petroleum products on contract, and a year later became the agent for a Japanese truck manufacturer and opened a tire retreading plant. The following year, the company

entered the construction field, first in buildings and later in highway construction. In 1967, it launched the first ship from its new yard for constructing steel vessels and began a charter air service.

Finally, it is pertinent to note the importance of Japanese trading houses, which are relatively recent in the market. In Chapter I, we saw that of the eighteen large trading firms with probable gross sales in 1967 of U.S. $10 million or more, seven are Japanese. In the next chapter, the growing importance of imports from Japan in Thailand's foreign trade will be examined—from one-fifth in the early 1950s to over one-third in the mid-1960s. Although no substantiating data are available, it is clear that the Japanese trading houses have played a significant role in this increasing share in Thailand's rapidly growing imports.

IMPACT OF
INDUSTRIALIZATION ON DISTRIBUTION

Much recent industrialization has been accounted for by foreign manufacturers whose products have been imported over the years and have gained acceptance in the local market. This import-substitute industrialization by the firm has also been stimulated by the growth of the Thai market to the point where local production could be justified, especially with the incentives available through the government's industrial promotion program.*

It is not surprising that foreign manufacturers should continue to use the distribution network of the trading house even after they begin local production; usually, it has been the same house which distributed the imported product in the past. Prospective manufacturers have been advised to follow this policy, as the following quotation from a report on the feasibility of manufacturing electrical appliance shows:

> Many foreign companies which have established manufacturing facilities in Thailand have entered into joint ventures, with varying degrees of local participation. Frequently the local investors have been the firms which previously represented the manufacturer in this country. Local capital is available in Thailand for sound business ventures of

---

* Among the western manufacturers granted promotion certificates for building or expanding plants up to the end of 1967 are such firms as Bata, Dumont, Electric Storage Battery, Eveready, Firestone, Foremost Dairies, Hoechst Pharmaceutical, Kimberly-Clark, Merck, Sharp & Dohme, National Lead, and Singer.

this kind. Where the local participants are an established, successful organization with a knowledge of local markets and a going sales and distributor organization, such an arrangement is likely to be highly desirable and beneficial to the enterprise. Without this, a new firm would probably be faced, initially at least, with considerably greater expense in achieving market penetration (Ebasco Services 1963, p. 20).

In a guide for prospective American exporters to Thailand (Mayer 1962, pp. 41-42), the advice has been similar: in that instance, selling directly through the manufacturer's own sales organization was recommended for "goods where sales depend on a highly specialized sales apparatus, such as petroleum products" or for "goods with a very high mark-up, such as perfume, where factory-trained travelers will energetically work on a few customers and book small-volume but lucrative direct business." Except for those cases, and the special situation of selling raw materials such as cotton and tobacco to one or a few end-users through agents, the advice was to "sell to a distributor, who would use his own organization for distribution in Thailand."

The inherent conflict between manufacturer and resellers which is widely acknowledged in the literature on marketing channels is clearly apparent in Thai distribution practices. Soon after the foreign manufacturer begins local production, his distribution problems become apparent as his preoccupation with brand performance clashes head-on with the resellers' brand and item indifference. The recommendation cited above that a joint venture be formed with local capital providing distribution facilities has been used to a limited extent; more common, however, is that the manufacturer begins to develop his own distribution system. A business case on the problems of a western manufacturer of soaps and detergents, reproduced in Boyd et al. (1965, pp. 398-406), is sufficiently representative of the difficulties facing other manufacturers to merit brief summary.

A western trading firm had been the sole distributor for the manufacturer's products since 1954 when they were introduced in the Thai market; by 1960, the manufacturer decided in favor of local production because of the growing domestic market, uncertainty over the future tariff policy on imported detergents, and the government's industrial promotion program. Local production began in 1962 and a year later the manufacturer was considering severing his distribution contract with the trading firm; since the latter years of the 1950s, the manufacturer's local manager had been preoccupied with the inadequacies of distribution and had been steadily increasing his involvement, expenditures, and control over the marketing of his product.

Perhaps the most troublesome aspect of the original arrangement was the role of the *kongsi*, a twenty-one-member cartel formed specifically to handle the detergent by the sixteen largest Chinese wholesalers of soap and toilet articles and five smaller Chinese wholesale-retail firms. The *kongsi* members were obliged to take a specific quantity of detergent monthly or on arrival of the shipment, at a specified price. They picked up the arriving shipments at the dock and distributed to other wholesalers and retailers throughout the country; although they refused to reveal their outlets, apparently only about 10 percent of sales were outside of Bangkok during 1954-57. Upcountry prices were higher by the amount of their freight cost. The trading house gave the *kongsi* members sixty-day credit, while they in turn usually extended seven-day credit to their customers; this "gold-coasting" (from the West African practice; see Bauer 1963, p. 17), which in this case provided a very attractive fifty-three-day interest-free loan, has not been uncommon in Thailand. The manufacturer was convinced that *kongsi* members did not properly exploit the potential for his product; they understocked stores they supplied, did not attempt to reach smaller stores, and got rid of their monthly quota with the minimum selling effort. The manufacturer forced a number of modifications in the arrangements on the trading house, principally the creation of a small direct sales force to develop upcountry sales which was carried on the staff of the trading house but with the manufacturer sharing in their cost. Also, he prevailed on the trading house to grant an upcountry freight differential to the *kongsi* so that a uniform retail price could be charged nationwide. However, when the *kongsi* members pocketed the differential and continued the higher upcountry prices, company salesmen were able to take over the *kongsi's* customers. Pressure was applied on the *kongsi* in other ways, such as reducing the quantity discount on large volume purchases, and by the early 1960s the cartel had broken down, with seven members remaining, who accounted for only 20 percent of the manufacturer's sales in Thailand. By that time, approximately 60 percent of sales were upcountry and 40 percent in Bangkok, compared with only 10 percent upcountry less than a decade earlier. While this manufacturer had the largest share of the market throughout the period, his principal competitors—two other western manufacturers—were going through similar experiences with the trading house-*kongsi* relationship and similarly moved toward more control over their own distribution.

In generalizing from this and similar examples, we must distinguish between the manufacturer's problems with the trading house, whether western or local, and with the Chinese wholesaler and retailer. When nearly all consumer goods were imported except for the products of local cottage industries, the small size of the market made the lack of direct contact between manufacturer and final consumer both unavoidable and relatively unimportant. Under these conditions, the trading house could be reasonably effective. Contributing to this was the complementarity in the import and export trades; the regions and the people producing for export through the trading houses constituted the monetized sector and consequently were the principal market for goods which the trading houses imported. As the market grew and spread, direct contact between the trading house and the ultimate consumer became less common, except in the case of industrial goods where there were relatively few customers. Retailing by the trading houses has been a somewhat limited part of their activity; at most they have maintained a retail outlet as a part of their main offices in Bangkok and in half a dozen of the principal provincial cities. Thus, they have not contributed to the development of a national market to the degree that European trading firms did in West African trade, according to Bauer's (1954) description. There, the absence of an indigenous trader class with capital encouraged greater vertical integration of the trading firms. Finally, the growth of competition among brands and of concern with market shares has exposed the inherent weakness of the trading house as distributor of a broad line of consumer goods.* However, where the trading house in Thailand limits itself to a few carefully selected products, and especially where it enters joint-venture arrangements for local manufacture and distribution, it transforms itself from the traditional trading house activity and is capable of continued survival.

The manufacturer's problems with wholesalers and retailers remain, however, even if he bypasses the trading house. He quite naturally views the wholesaler and retailer as sellers of his product, if not as individuals who divine and then satisfy the needs and desires of cus-

---

* In a recent discussion of Japanese trading houses, Wilson (1969, p. 80) observes that all five of the principal postwar Japanese industrial successes have by-passed trading houses and assaulted world markets themselves by direct selling.

tomers by promoting his products' virtues. A more realistic view is of individuals who discover and exploit opportunities for profit—the trading function of buying cheap and selling dear rather than the distribution function.* Actions by the wholesaler such as gold-coasting and tying inferior products with a western manufacturer's quality product into a package which is then forced on the retailer are consistent with this view, although not less reprehensible to the manufacturer. A number of western manufacturers now by-pass the wholesaler and distribute directly to retailers.

The examples of shortening of channels which have been cited raise the question whether the "law" of the channel development cycle (Moyer 1965, p. 36) is confirmed in Thailand. According to this law, primitive economies are characterized by short channels, exemplified in barter among producers, or the household which both produces and distributes its product. As development proceeds, the geographic spreading of markets and the increased flow of goods justify specialization by full-time intermediaries and channels thus tend to lengthen. Finally, the growing importance of differentiated goods requires greater control over distribution by the producer, at the same time that his increasing financial resources make possible his absorbing more of the distribution function, thus shortening the channel again. It will be recalled that the data of the Census of Industry suggested that "small" industry used more direct marketing than "large" industry, which distributed more through intermediaries. If we assume that the firms classed as small are characteristic of the *predevelopment* stage in the cycle and the larger firms of the *developing* stage, then the data would tend to confirm the law. At the same time, the tendency of the foreign manufacturing firms (which are among the largest of the "large" and represent the *developed* stage) to move from the use of trading houses and Chinese wholesalers toward more direct marketing would also suggest confirmation. The fact that illustrations of all three channel cycle stages of predevelopment, developing, and developed may be found in Thailand today is a counterpart

---

* Bauer (1954, p. 57) has called attention to the lack of specialization in West African trading which results from the narrowness of markets: "In narrow and dispersed markets opportunities for profit in trade occur frequently and unpredictably and there is thus a premium on readiness and ability to recognize a new opportunity and to take advantage of it. In these circumstances there is less incentive for traders to specialize on a limited range of merchandise or even in a particular locality."

of industrial dualism—the coexistence of modern and traditional sectors in the same developing economy.

It is interesting to note the high incidence of perception of marketing problems by the owners or managers of Thai industrial establishments. The 1964 Industrial Census inquired whether the enumerated firms were confronted by one or more specified problems or difficulties in carrying out their operations; Table 8 in the Appendix summarizes the responses. Marketing difficulties were second only to shortages of raw materials as a problem facing "large" (10 or more engaged persons) industry and they were the leading problem cited by small industry. It is tempting to speculate on the characteristics of industry revealed by the relative importance of the different problems and the differences between larger and smaller establishments but the data are probably not "hard" enough to be more than suggestive. The ranking in last place of "lack of good management" as a perceived problem is no surprise, however, and puts Thai managers in the good company of their colleagues the world over.

ANCILLARY MARKETING
INSTITUTIONS AND SERVICES

A description of the marketing structure of a society is hardly complete if it is limited to those who buy and subsequently resell, that is, to those who stand in the direct line between producer and ultimate consumer. In this section we explore briefly the various institutions and services that exist in Thailand which are the source of external economies to the marketing specialists and the basis for the degree of sophistication they can achieve. We shall limit our consideration to the marketing system's needs for information, advertising services, credit, and human resources, leaving for the next chapter the special case of the supply of transportation as it is related to marketing development.

A thesis of this study is that transportation development has been one of the most crucial elements in national economic integration in Thailand in recent years. In another respect, transportation services are a special case and merit separate consideration. Demand for the transportation of goods to consumers did not spark the creation of the supply, at least in the quantities of transport investment which have been made in the past two decades in Thailand. Rather, this investment in all-weather roads has been the government's response to the threat of guerrilla infiltration and the communist thrust at that sector of the population which is most isolated and hence "forgotten" by the central government.* On the other hand, the dramatic increases in the private motor vehicle fleet, which followed on the highway development program, do represent the creation of a supply of transportation services as the demand became manifest. This example highlights the more general problem of the supply and demand for ancillary services. Moyer and Hollander (1968, pp. 230-31) have underscored the difficulties arising from "the severe undersupply of ancillary marketing institutions and services in the developing countries" and suggested a vicious circle where the marketing system cannot grow to the level which would support these services precisely because of their absence. They do observe, however, that some ancillary services are responsive to the market mechanism so that supply is forthcoming when demand becomes apparent, while other services are not similarly responsive. In the Thai case, the informational needs of marketing would illustrate the distinction, with the difference in response depending on whether the service is provided by the public or the private sector.

Informational Needs

In this and the preceding chapter we have examined a variety of statistical data published by the government which have great value in the marketing activity of the firm, such as the censuses of population, industry and commerce, labor force and household expenditure surveys, and the national accounts. The motivation in these data collection efforts is of course the bureaucracy's need to know in order to administer more effectively; in addition, there is a demonstration effect and the stimulus to standardization provided by United Nations agencies and technical assistance efforts such as AID. Thus the first census in Thailand was related to the need to improve tax collection and the conscription of soldiers. More recently, the household expenditure survey was related to the need for a cost of living index and the census of business trade to the need for refining the national income accounting methods. Hence it is to be expected that the

---

* Interestingly, the argument has been made in government circles that paved roads make it that much easier for terrorists from beyond the frontiers to reach Bangkok. This is reminiscent of the policy of choosing a railroad gauge for a nation which is different than that of its contiguous neighbors.

private business sector would be somewhat unhappy over what data are collected, how they are presented and how long they take to be published. For their part, the government officials responsible for data collection feel the informational needs of the private sector are definitely secondary to their primary responsibility to other branches of the government. However, business firms have often found it possible to secure official statistics collected by the government, such as import data from customs prior to publication or in greater detail than is normally published, through the use of informants within the collecting agency. Although the government's disinterest in the needs of the private sector disadvantages the marketing system, the problem is of course not distinctive to Thailand.

In part, the gap between the informational needs and what the government supplies is filled by private data collection, illustrating the case of supply of ancillary services being provided when the demand is apparent. We have cited above the data on the market from the *Bangkok Profile* continuing survey since 1966 of over seven thousand households by a private research firm which complements and goes beyond the government's 1962-63 Household Expenditure Survey of nearly one thousand households in Bangkok-Thonburi. There is no evidence of private firms being unable to secure consulting and market research services when the need is felt. This is not to say, of course, that more and better government data would not be useful to and used by some firms in their market evaluation, thus reducing their present costs of data collection and reducing the risk of bad decisions made with inadequate knowledge. It is our impression, however, that disinterest is far more prevalent than dissatisfaction with the information available, an attitude obviously more acute in local than in multinational firms and in smaller than in larger firms. An example of the supply of information responding to, but actually going beyond, apparent demand is in the television audience survey service which had to be abandoned for lack of business subscribers. The article "Quantifying Thai Opinions," which is reproduced as Appendix C, offers further evidence on this attitude of the businessman that he won't believe research which shows him to have been wrong and sees no reason to pay for research which shows he was right.

The multinational firm is certainly the leading force in the development of more and better information about the market. For example, it is reported that only five companies in Thailand—all western multinational firms—have undertaken any research on market potential beyond mere extrapolation of past sales. One of these has gone as far as experimenting with sales quotas for each province based on an analysis of twenty factors and is a confirmed user of the data-processing facilities of a local computer service bureau. Although these efforts yield unpublished data for internal use, the message of such an approach by large, well-managed and apparently profitable firms is not lost on the young Thai who participate in the data collection and processing.

Advertising

The availability of media and of specialized agencies for the preparation of the message are ancillary services to the marketing system which are recent supply responses to the apparent demand. Data available on this development are the roughest of estimates and should be considered as merely suggestive of what probably has occurred. The following table shows two estimates, for 1960 and for 1966-1967, of expenditures on advertising by the different media presently in use:

Distribution of Advertising Expenditures

	1960		1966-67	
Medium	*Baht (millions)*	*Percentage*	*Baht (millions)*	*Percentage*
Radio	30.0	25	65.0	27
Television	17.5	15	50.0	21
Newspapers	36.0	31	50.0	21
Magazines	11.5	10	20.0	8
Cinema	5	4	12.0	5
Outdoor	18.0	15	35.0	15
Transit (bus and shelters)	–	–	3.0	1
Direct mail	–	–	3.0	1
Miscellaneous	–	–	2.0	1
Total	118.0	100	240.0	100

SOURCES: For 1960, from Dunn (1964, p. 767); for 1966-67 from Perera (1966-67, G. 99).

It seems reasonable to expect a rapid growth in advertising in recent years, paralleling the growth in the mass market, which is described in the next chapter. If advertising expenditures indeed doubled during this period as the table suggests, it would be a relatively high growth rate; during the same period, personal consumption expenditures rose about 53 percent and national income about 66 percent according to estimates of the National Economic Development Board. Although rising rapidly, advertising expenditures do not seem excessive in comparison with other countries.* However, advertising is highly visible. In 1965, the Ministry of National Development complained that "the 'excessive' use of advertising was becoming a 'nuisance' and contributed to increased prices of consumer goods" (Perera 1966-67, G 100). Legislation was prepared which would have taxed advertising expenditures heavily but it was rejected by the Cabinet.

The distribution of expenditures by media shows that radio, television, newspaper, and outdoor advertising are the most important, in that order. Over the period, television has gained most, apparently at the expense of newspaper and magazine advertising, which declined relatively though not in absolute terms.

Television was introduced in mid-1955, the first installation on the mainland of Asia. Three years later a second station was added in Bangkok and in 1967 the first color station—another first for mainland Asia. Repeater stations and three regional stations using taped Bangkok material are reported to provide coverage of nearly half the provinces and an estimated peak hour audience in 1966 as high as four million (*Thailand Facts and Figures 1966*, p. 48) for 250,000-300,000 receivers. All TV stations are owned by government agencies or the Armed Forces, as are the more than eighty radio stations, and advertising revenues are an important source for covering operating expenses.

On a typical mid-week night in mid-1968, the two black and white channels operated six hours each, from 5 to 11 P.M., while the color

---

* International comparisons of advertising expenditures related to national income, made by the International Advertising Association and presented in Dunn (1964, pp. 723-77), show Thailand in 1960 at 0.25 percent of her national income, compared with 1.5 percent for Japan, 2 percent for Canada and the United Kingdom, and nearly 3 percent for the United States. Data are available for few developing countries—Turkey with 0.26 percent, and five Latin American countries which range from 0.65 percent to 1.4 percent; no Asian countries other than Japan and Thailand show data. The ratios depend somewhat on the range of media available (France and Belgium, without commercial television, both show 0.8 percent) and are doubly hazardous because of the problem of distortion of national income data which has been mentioned earlier. The ratio for Thailand would be even lower, to the extent that her national income is understated in relation to the developed countries.

channel began one hour later. Of their scheduled time, all three devoted approximately 20 percent to local and world news. All showed American taped programs or films dubbed in Thai live in the studio with the original English soundtrack available over an FM station. One station devoted 29 percent of its time in this fashion ("Mission Impossible," "Big Valley") and the principal block of 42 percent in educational films, programs, and documentaries. The other black and white channel carried "Dragnet" for 12 percent and the majority of its scheduled time in a Thai film, a play, and documentaries. The color channel used 64 percent of its scheduled time in American films ("Please Don't Eat the Daisies," "Suspense Theatre," and a movie) and 12 percent in Thai classical dance. Generously interspersed in these scheduled programs are commercials which occupy 20 percent of total station time in consecutive stretches sufficiently long that viewer complaints are common.

Radio ownership has grown enormously in recent years, spurred by the availability of inexpensive Japanese transistor sets; the *Area Handbook* (1968) estimates 3.5 million sets in use. In the preceding chapter, we saw that the saturation of radios in Bangkok households was 76 percent, compared with 41 percent for television. Import data, which will be discussed in the next chapter, show that in 1956, 126,000 receivers were imported—16 percent of them from Japan; by 1966, the number of sets imported was approximately 265,000 at a total CIF value lower than for a decade earlier and with 71 percent of them coming from Japan. In addition, in the latter year, radios were being assembled in Thailand from imported components. Radio advertising is of course the preferred medium for reaching the upcountry areas with lower-priced consumer goods of mass appeal. However, during 1967 and 1968, the government banned radio commercials because they were suspected of carrying coded messages of the guerrilla terrorists.

Because the Thai are avid movie goers, advertising to the urban market through well made one-half minute or one minute color films shown in cinemas before the initiation of the feature is considered to be quite effective. On the same evening as the television programming described above, twenty first-class cinemas in Bangkok were offering a variety of films—eleven American or English, four Thai, three Chinese, and two Indian. In the best houses unreserved seats in the most expensive section were double or more the price of seats in the less desirable front rows. In a typical program, a series of eleven commercials preceded the feature, advertising such diverse products as house paint, a middle-income housing development, cough drops, a vitamin-enriched milk drink, face cream, bath soap, and Japanese watches and automobiles.

The relative decline in press advertising at the expense of radio and TV is in keeping with trends in other countries. But it appears that newspapers are not widely read in Thailand. Appendix Table 14, which shows some characteristics of residents of the seven principal cities of Asia surveyed by International Research Associates in 1965, indicates that newspapers were read less in Bangkok than in any other city except Manila. At the same time, Bangkok residents had a relatively low level of educational attainment and a high degree of discontent with the amount of their formal education. Tokyo residents were at the opposite extreme and read newspapers more than people in other Asian cities. It is possible then that newspaper reading, and press advertising, will increase in the long run as the Thai educational level rises.

A promotion program of a western manufacturer described in the case study in Appendix B as The Siam Pen Company shows an imaginative adaptation to the conditions of rural and urban markets and to the effectiveness of the available advertising media.

Credit in Marketing

The little information available on the capital market in Thailand suggests some characteristics which are not surprising: what credit there is has been largely employed in marketing; the amount available through unorganized markets is probably much more significant than that moving through organized markets; the importance of the Chinese in this market parallels their importance in commerce generally; and consumer credit is not yet extensively available, particularly in urban areas.

Since the principal activity in the economy has been the export and import trades, it is to be expected that trade financing should dominate the capital markets. A long time is involved in the movement of imports up the channel from the foreign supplier to the Bangkok importer-wholesaler to the retailer and on to the ultimate consumer, and interest rates are high and rising at each stage. The World Bank Mission (IBRD 1959, pp. 205-206) observed that "to the extent that the money market is organized, it is largely confined to commercial bank credit for short-term trading purposes. Interest rates are high, with very little credit available at less than 12 percent, even from the commercial banks. Most financing is done at far higher rates." At the other end of the channel, a survey of credit in rural areas in 1962-63 (Pantum Thisyamondol 1965) found that 17 percent of the loans to farm families were by local storekeepers at an average *monthly* interest rate of 3.5 percent.*

Since trade has been under the control of the Chinese and credit has been available mainly for the trade sector, we would expect the Chinese to predominate in the capital market and to use credit to further their general business interests. Indeed, Silcock (1967, p. 183) describes credit as a "binding factor" similar to kinship and social ties for decentralized Chinese business. Although the principal commercial banks are now Thai but with Chinese participation, their model and philosophy came from the early Chinese banks which were institutions formed to further the business and political interests of the founding group. From this we may infer that credit has been a strong factor in integrating the Chinese wholesaler in Bangkok with the upcountry Chinese network of retailers and a device for maintaining the Chinese control over trade. There are frequent references to Chinese whole-salers offering longer payment terms to their upcountry retailers (see the various market research reports of the U.S. Trade Center, Bang-kok) than the customary thirty—sixty days of the western trading firm. On the other hand, in the marketing of detergents discussed above, the *kongsi* members were extending seven-day credit to retailers al-though they had sixty days extended them by the western trading house—a "gold-coasting" type operation by *kongsi* members.† Another reason for the Chinese predominance in credit as well as trade must not be forgotten; their precarious position as foreigners with a

---

* Among other commercial lenders, crop buyers accounted for 9 percent of loans to farmers, money lenders 5 percent, and landlords 2 percent. Institutional lenders, i.e., the organized market, accounted for only 8 percent of the loans. On the other hand, 56 percent of the number of loans and 49 percent of their value were made with relatives and neighbors, and some of these were at no interest. According to the survey, 26 percent of the loans for less than one year were for living expenses and 35 percent for "productive" purposes, such as buying land, improvements, seed, fertilizer, etc; for longer than one year, living expenses still accounted for 17 percent and "productive" loans for 59 percent.
† Among the measures provided by the first six-year economic development plan for 1961-66 was the provision of "loans on an installment basis to various small retailers. This is to encourage the Thai people to enter into business more and more." (See Appendix D.)

stranglehold on the throat of the economy means a constant threat of discriminatory treatment by the government and hence a high preference for liquidity in the applications of their capital. There is evidence that the Chinese has moved from rapid-turnover or small dose investments in the mercantile, banking, insurance, and real estate sectors to the larger, fixed commitments in industry only when he becomes wealthy and influential enough to be able to risk this exposure or to buy protection (Muscat 1966, pp. 237-38).

We have little information on the role of consumer credit in Thai marketing. Reference has been made earlier to the survey of credit in rural areas which showed that a quarter of the short-term debt of farm families was for meeting living expenses—much of it probably on open account with the village store or itinerant peddler of the area. In Bangkok, open accounts settled monthly are common in the neighborhood grocery and household supplies store, and Thai frequently attribute their loyalty to a particular store over the years to this service of the Chinese retailer and the honesty with which account records are maintained. Clearly, this consumer credit requires a personal and prolonged relationship between retailer and customer which is more likely in rural than urban areas, and which confirms the finding in other developing societies that retail consumer credit is more prevalent in rural areas (Moyer and Hollander 1968, p. 237).

Installment buying of durables has not been extensively used in the past although it is growing in popularity as the availability of incentive goods and incomes and living standards improve. An innovator in Thailand as well as elsewhere in the world was Singer with its sewing machines, which were being sold in 1929 at 160 baht cash or 200 baht on hire-purchase for 15 baht down and 5 baht monthly for 37 months. In that year the company sold 240 imported machines through three Bangkok and three upcountry sales outlets; by 1967, the company was selling nearly 40,000 locally assembled machines annually, together with 1,500 locally assembled television sets and imported refrigerators through 50 outlets in Bangkok and 150 upcountry. The company attributes much of this growth and spread upcountry to installment selling. Typical installment plans available from other firms in mid-1968: a Toyota sedan priced at 48,500 baht for cash was available for 58,000 baht on installments, with a down payment of 16,000 baht and the balance in 24 monthly installments of 1,750 baht. A small Honda motorcycle at 4,500 baht for cash was available for 5,500 with a down payment of 1,000 and monthly payments for ten months. Development homes were being offered with a 10 percent down payment and the balance over twenty years at annual interest of $9\frac{7}{8}$ percent on the unpaid balance.

Human Resources

In recent years, the search for the key to the process of economic development has turned increasingly to human capital. Obviously the thin supply of people with the skills and attitudes needed for business enterprise in general and for marketing development in particular has been a constraint in the Thai case. While the highly developed trading skills of the Chinese merchant class may provide a base for the necessary managerial skills, they do not include the organizational and supervisory competencies which are essential in the modern marketing organization. For example, a private consultant's study has revealed that a large organization, built by its Chinese trader-partners to a position of acknowledged national prominence and with a reputation of great integrity, was increasingly unable to compete with western and Japanese marketing organizations whose structures and policies reflected more dynamic modern methods. The traditional preference of the Thai for government service over industrial and commercial activities also contributes, of course, to the thinness of the supply of human resources for marketing development.

Recent growth in the industrial sector and the arrival of multinational firms has stimulated the demand for managerial personnel and driven salaries in the private firm to multiples of two to four times what a young person with given educational qualifications can earn in government service. The long wait to arrive at the positions of prestige and power on the upper levels of the bureaucracy is increasingly less attractive in comparison with the better immediate rewards in private enterprise, and we have seen in the preceding chapter that training in business administration is increasing in popularity.

University programs in business have been available for some years; although traditionally they have emphasized accountancy, the trend in recent years has been to broaden and modernize the curriculum of these institutions, including courses in marketing. In addition to the public universities, innovations beginning in the mid-1960s include a private university offering only a business program, which has been recognized by the government, and a public graduate school, the National Institute of Development Administration, which has begun a

Master of Business Administration program. A variety of programs and training courses below the university level have also been offered in junior colleges and vocational and technical schools.

Among the less formal programs of human resource development, the work of the Management Development and Productivity Centre, which has technical assistance from the United Nations, has been significant. Finally, continuing education for middle management is provided by the Thailand Management Association through a program of one- to three-day seminars, which have expanded rapidly since the Association's founding in 1964. A similar organization, the Marketing Association of Thailand is more recent; it publishes a journal and sponsors luncheon meetings for its membership of predominantly younger executives in marketing, advertising, and selling. Substantial inputs in such organizations are provided by top management of multinational firms; for example nearly one-half of the current slate of eleven officers and executive council of the Management Association are westerners and two more are Thai executives of western firms. Thus in Thailand as in other developing societies where both the private sector and foreign direct investment are encouraged, industrial plants and commercial offices are some of the most effective schoolrooms the society has for encouraging the skills and attitudes needed for modern management.

**THE ROLE OF
GOVERNMENT IN MARKETING**

In two respects the government acts upon or influences marketing development in Thailand: in stimulating the growth and efficiency of the marketing system and in regulating marketing activities of firms and individuals.

Government efforts toward stimulating the development of the marketing system are evidenced in the policy statements of the national economic and social development plans and in the budgeted expenditures for the sector. In Appendix D selections from the First and the Second Development Plans which relate to marketing are reproduced, together with a table summarizing public development expenditures in the two plans by sector. Abbott (1968, p. 87) has found that the marketing content of most national development plans is very low, and Thailand is no exception. There were no public development expenditures for marketing in the First Plan period and only one-third of 1 percent, by far the smallest of all sectors, was projected for the "Commerce" sector in the Second Plan period. Planned expenditures for agriculture in the Second Plan period were nearly 20 percent of total development expenditures, but only about 1.5 percent of the allocation to the agricultural sector is clearly attributable to marketing, with most of the funds going to irrigation projects, extension services, and crop research and development.

The policy statements of the Plans clearly acknowledge the important role of the commercial sector in raising the standard of living of the people, in accelerating the growth of the economy, and in generating revenues for the government. But it is also clear that, given the commitment to "the growth of a strong and healthy free enterprise system," the government's role in marketing development per se is a limited one. Indirectly, of course, the provision of infrastructure, especially of the transportation system, constitutes a crucial governmental role.

For the five-year period of the Second Plan, 179 million baht or nearly $9 million were projected as development expenditures through budget appropriations to government agencies concerned with the commercial sector. Of this, approximately $5 million were budgeted for export promotion (mostly for trade fairs), one-half a million for marketing research on the country's principal products, and $1.4 million to foster Thaification of the commercial sector. With respect to the latter item, the Plan attributes the failure of Thai nationals to participate more actively in commerce to a lack of capital and inability to obtain prime locations for retailing. Since the problem is so much more complex, as we have seen, it is possible that the Plan's references to marketing disorder, inefficiency and exploitation, and its small appropriations to correct "the problem" are a sop to nationalistic and anti-Chinese elements.

The motivation or philosophy behind government actions which regulate or restrain the marketing activities of firms include consumer protection and, once again, Thaification. Examples of the former motivation would include: regulations imposing an obligation to serve, such as requiring service stations to remain open twenty-four hours a day; protection of the public health, such as prohibiting advertising which exaggerates the properties of medicine or shows the distresses of a sufferer or otherwise uses indecent means or songs and dances in such advertising; and price controls as in the early 1950s when the government exhorted merchants to keep prices down and published lists of "ceiling prices" for their guidance.*

We have referred in Chapter I to the creation of state trading enterprises in each province immediately after World War II as related to control of speculation in scarce supplies and competition to the private (Chinese) sector. By 1965, twenty-four of these were reported as still active and with the government a majority owner, and an additional six where the state had minority ownership (Artamonoff 1965, p. 205). The largest of these had gross sales of 17.5 million baht in 1964 (or about U.S. $870,000) from a wide line of appliances and hardware. In total, however, the gross sales of all *changwat* trading companies were only 133 million baht, or about 1.4 percent of the total sales in retail-only establishments reporting to the 1966 census; Artamonoff found the profit to the government treasury so small it was "probably well below the cost of accounting alone."

In addition to these *changwat* trading companies, the government has other relatively small marketing organizations such as public warehouses, cold storage, and ice plants. Of their function, the Second Plan observed (pp. 114-15) : "The need for commercial or trading enterprises has declined significantly during the First Plan period. . . . They constitute an effective tool of the Government in its regulation and control of the nation's commerce."

---

* Ingram (1955, p. 228) notes that such attempts at government price control were ineffectual and unenforceable, given the great number and small size of retail firms. Blanchard (1958, p. 485) observes that the bureaucracy has inherited the tradition of absolutism from the days of unlimited powers of the king and assumes its fiats will be obeyed unquestioningly. Thai individualism leads however to evasion or ignoring of particularly burdensome regulations. Smuggling of pork and ice into the Bangkok market result from regulations prohibiting their interprovince movement, either from motivations of market stabilization or public health. Muscat (1966, pp. 118-24) refers to the agricultural commodity marketing syndicates, such as in livestock, as the use of government powers for the sole benefit of the syndicate promoters. In the case of illegal ice (*Bangkok World*, 20 April 1968), a heat wave and consequent shortage in the city made it worthwhile for smugglers to truck it from fifty miles away and risk fines for violating the regulation, which was created because the process of manufacture outside of Bangkok was "often unhygienic."

IV
The Development
of a
National Consumer Goods Market

If we conceive of national development as being achieved through the economic, political, and social integration of the national territory, then we may also view market integration as an important dimension of economic integration. Thus the creation of a national market is the end result of a process of progressive integration of the territory into a single interrelated market. If the test of integration is approximate equality of a factor or a phenomenon across the national territory, then the test of market integration is approximate equality in the stock of goods available for trading throughout the national space. While space is an obstacle to all transmission, whether of ideas or values or goods, the development of a transportation system is probably most crucial for the achievement of market integration. We must therefore devote some attention to transportation improvement in Thailand as it is related to the development of a national market.

TRANSPORTATION IMPROVEMENT
AND SPATIAL ASPECTS OF THE MARKET

The primate-city malignancy of Bangkok dominating the Thai society and economy has been described above. Early trade in Thailand was based upon an inland waterway system centered on Bangkok. Descriptions of trading during the first half of the nineteenth century are informative:

Both sides of the river at Bangkok were lined with floating shops for over four miles. These "houses," some thirty to forty feet square in size and ranged in rows of eight to ten, literally floated on the water, though they were anchored to posts. Each was provided with a covered platform on which was displayed the merchandise for sale—both Chinese imports and local products. . . . In those days Bangkok was indeed an Eastern Venice. Most retail trading was done on the water because the populace lived in houses on stilts at the water's edge (Skinner 1957, p. 106) .

That description of the river-oriented trade of Bangkok was for the first half of the nineteenth century. Even a century and a half earlier, when Bangkok was a mere fortified village at a bend in the river protecting Ayutthaya, the more resplendent capital of the Thai kingdom lying fifty miles upriver, the river orientation was also evident (Collis 1965, 46-47). And today, a principal tourist attraction in Bangkok is a trip by boat through rivers and canals to the Floating Market. Only in fairly recent times has the city moved off the water and away from the shoreline; the first city street was built in 1864 and the second and subsequent streets and roads came only after 1895.* This history of Bangkok is repeated throughout the kingdom—water transportation in the river systems if they were available, with all other transportation limited to elephants, bullock-drawn carts, or the legs of humans. Thus the first stage of national integration was based on, and limited to, the relatively small area covered by the river systems and the coasts of the Gulf.

The Inland Waterway System

The rivers and canals of the Central Plain constitute an excellent transportation system. As portrayed in the map on page 113, the area of this year-round waterway system covers nearly 48,000 square kilometers, or about 9 percent of the national territory; the delineation of the area is highly generalized and does not take into account those portions of rivers in the Central Plain which are not navigable year-around by medium-sized paddy boats.

If the coastline of the Gulf of Siam is added to the area of the river

---

* Thompson (1941, p. 506). Skinner (1957, p. 115) observes that "between 1890 and 1910, Bangkok changed from a city on water to one on land."

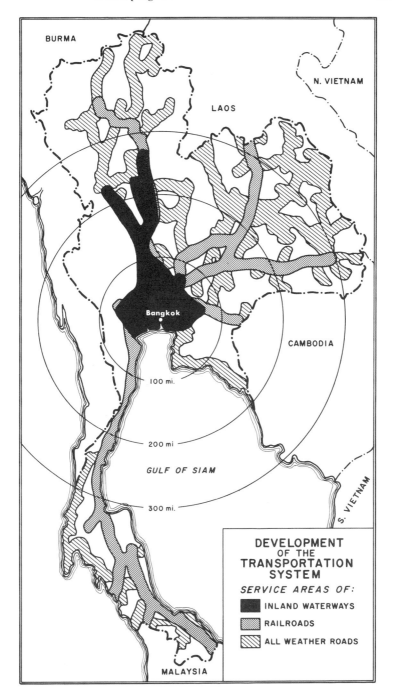

DEVELOPMENT
OF THE
TRANSPORTATION
SYSTEM
SERVICE AREAS OF:

INLAND WATERWAYS

RAILROADS

ALL WEATHER ROADS

and canal system of the Central Plain, a more extensive area served by water transportation is delineated. With the coastline comprising some 1,875 kilometers along the Gulf of Siam and assuming that an area of land 15 kilometers or 9 miles inland from the coast is "served" by the availability of transport over this waterway system, then the area of national integration based on the waterway system becomes 74,000 square kilometers or 14 percent of the national territory. However, it is doubtful if coastwise traffic was ever a significant element in *domestic* transportation.* Commerce in the Gulf of Siam was of course intense in very early times; Chapter I has described the importance of trade with India and China long before the arrival of the first Europeans and of the significant movement of Chinese junks around the coast in the cargo trades and in bringing Chinese settlers to Thailand (Skinner 1957, p. 51). But the ports on the Gulf of Siam were either transshipment points on the China-India route which had to portage across the Malayan Peninsula, or *entrepot* in their own right, gathering local produce and receiving the trinket imports of the world from junk traders whose last stop had been Singapore or Penang.†

Two other transportation systems were in existence during this early period in Thailand's history and before the government embarked on programs of transport investment: the Mekong River with its tributaries in Thailand and overland caravan routes. The Mekong is a river of obvious potential as a transportation system, but in considering marketing in Thailand it has had only the most limited significance. For a distance of 800 kilometers, the Mekong constitutes the border between Thailand and Laos; in addition, the Nam Che and the Nam Mune are substantial rivers which drain Thailand's Korat Plateau into the Mekong. However, although local short-haul traffic between points in Thailand is probably not insignificant, these rivers can hardly be considered to perform an integrating function for the national market since they begin hundreds of miles from Bangkok and flow away from it and from the rest of the heartland.

---

* James A. Hafner, Department of Geography, University of Michigan project on Inland Waterways at the Applied Scientific Research Corp. of Thailand has suggested that at least the eastern shore of the Gulf be included in view of the early activities of some trading houses in the extraction of hardwoods from that area for shipment to Bangkok. I am indebted to Mr. Hafner for the sharing of his extensive knowledge of the waterway system and in delineating its service area.
† Graham (1912, pp. 395-97) describes the meager development of commerce at the ports of southern Siam by the end of the last century.

Overland traffic by oxcart, pack animal, and human carrier has certainly existed for centuries in all areas outside the Central Plain and indeed persists in certain regions today. An early account describes the value of the external trade of the Korat Plateau in 1893 (just prior to the arrival of the railroad) at about £120,000 annually, equally divided between exports and imports and virtually all of it with Bangkok. Imports (over 80 percent of the value of which was in textiles) moved from Bangkok to Saraburi by boat and thence over the mountains by bullock caravan with equal shares of the goods being sold in Korat, moving east to Ubon, and being distributed along the Nongkhai trail to the north (H. Warington Smyth, cited in Ingram 1955, p. 117). A modern reference to this traffic is the following item from the *Bangkok Post* of 10 May 1968:

> One of 10 armed robbers was killed during an attack on a caravan of oxcarts hauling goods through Samangam district in the province of Phichit this week, a police source reported here today.
>
> The caravan, including five men led by Nom Thongrongyai, had bedded down for the night in a defensive formation when the attack began at 9 p.m. Wednesday. The ensuing gun fight lasted 10 minutes, with the robbers finally giving up and fleeing.

Caravans from southwest China criss-crossed the Indochina Peninsula from early times carrying the high-value, small-bulk goods of that low level of commerce. As we shall note later, however, the presence of the Singer sewing machine or even Coca-Cola in remote areas does not evidence economic integration so much as the strength of the propensity to "truck and barter."

The inland waterway system has been a unifying and integrating force within the Central Plain, as "all-weather" or "hard-surfaced" as any alternative system might have been, and offering much lower cost levels.* But the integration of the North and Northeastern regions

---

* International comparisons of "accessibility" or "mobility" understate Thai development when they fail to include the waterway system. For example, Owen (1964, p. 14) presents indexes of freight mobility and of passenger mobility composed of a series of measures of railroad and highway development but notes the exclusion of mobility by air and water. By these indexes, Thailand, which ranked eighth from the last among 53 nations in per capita gross national product, ranked ninth and eighth from the last in freight and passenger mobility respectively. Similarly, Ginsburg (1961), in his various measures of accessibility, understates the Thai case.

which contain half of the nation's land area had to await the development of the railroad system.

The Railroad System

The first efforts toward railroad building began in 1887 with a contract let to a British firm for a survey of a line from Bangkok to the northernmost city of the nation on the Mekong River border with Laos. Apparently British interest in countering French ambitions by building a railroad to connect southwest China with Burma across northern Thailand led to this first Thai survey. However, the first railroad construction (except for a 12-mile private line out of Bangkok completed in 1893) was on a line to the eastern, rather than to the northern provinces; again, the threat was external. As Graham (1912, pp. 416-17) describes it, the "approaching and encroaching" of the French on Thailand's eastern frontier and their plans for draining the trade of the region away from Bangkok and through Saigon convinced Thailand of the immediate need for a railroad to the frontier "in case of military necessity." By 1897, when the first 45 miles of the eastern line was opened to traffic, the plan for a northern line had been revived and soon afterward construction began on a line to the south. The rail network developed in all directions out of Bangkok; by 1921, the northern line reached Chiengmai, the nation's second largest city and 750 kilometers from Bangkok; in the following year, the southern line joined the Malaysian State Railway 1159 kilometers from Bangkok, and in 1926 the eastern line of 255 kilometers reached Cambodia. The lines into the northeast were the last to be completed; Ubol, 575 kilometers east of Bangkok, was reached in 1938 and Nongkhai, 618 kilometers northeast and the frontier crossing to Vientiane, the capital of Laos, was reached only in 1955. Although the main network was completed by 1940, about 15 percent of additional mileage has been added in minor extensions and cutoffs during the 25 years since then, as shown in Table 17 in the Appendix.

While the original impetus to develop the rail system may have come from external threats, the importance of the railway in effective administration and in economic development was soon apparent. In 1907, at the inauguration of a section of the northern line, King Chulalongkorn described the nation's rail policy in these terms:

> The construction of railways has not only the greatest influence upon the development of a country, but is also the most striking evidence of

that development. . . . By bringing the different parts of a country within close communication the railway renders possible that close and beneficial supervision which is necessary to effective administration. By furnishing rapid and easy means of transportation, it adds materially to the value of the land and its products. . . . The railway wherever it goes carries with it enlightenment and encourages the growth of that national feeling which is so important an element in the welfare of a country (Graham 1912, pp. 419-20) .

That the railroad system was viewed by the government more as a means of improving public administration and increasing government revenues than of economic development, is probably the case however.

The beginnings of the railroad building era coincided with a movement in administrative reform which attempted to integrate the provinces with the capital. A reorganization of the Ministry of Interior and of provincial government which began in 1892 under the very progressive Prince Damrong signified a new view of the developmental role of government. Perhaps the motivation was as much to collect tax revenue from the outlying provinces as to unify the nation;* Siffin (1966, p. 68) notes that Prince Damrong was effective on both scores. From the point of view of marketing development, however, the use of the state railway system as a source of government revenues was highly important.

Particularly prior to 1932, government policy with regard to capital improvements appears to have emphasized direct return on the investment as the significant criterion. Ingram (1955, p. 194) found that both irrigation projects and highway construction were retarded by the government, despite their obviously crucial importance for development, because they could not easily be made to pay for themselves. And the highway construction that was undertaken was of feeder lines to improve the railway system revenue; as Thompson (1941, p. 507) puts it, the prerevolution regime had a "cardinal principal—that roads must feed and not compete with the railroads."

Although the evidence is sparse, we may surmise that railroad rates were high during the prehighway stage. Ingram (1955, p. 116) says as much of the period 1890-1920 in the north. Further he notes that revenues from commercial services provided by the government (principally, net revenues of the state railways) increased from almost nothing in 1892 to 13 percent of total revenues of the government in

---

* As late as 1900, the central government received no revenue from the North, part of the Northeast, or the Malay States of the South (Ingram 1955, p. 176).

1926, exceeded only by land and capitation taxes (20-25 percent) and the import and sale of opium (20 percent). Thompson (1941, pp. 504-505) observes that in 1941 "Siam's railroads still run at a profit; but the margin is considerably smaller than formerly, and criticism of them is much louder." By then, of course, the absolute monarchy had been succeeded by the constitutional regime and the nation had been through the depression of the 1930s.

One additional aspect of railway service needs to be taken into account: the Express Transportation Organization (ETO), a state enterprise created by the government in 1947 to operate a freight forwarding business by rail.* Certain privileges were granted the ETO in obtaining empty freightcars and the exclusive right to handle carload and less than carload freight, including pick-up and delivery service at 110 principal railway stations. The organization expanded into over-the-road trucking, mainly in less-than-truckload and contract carriage, and long-haul bus service and by 1957 was operating over 600,000 vehicle-kilometers of service monthly in each of these services.

The result was curious as an example of transport coordination: two state enterprises organizationally lodged in the same Ministry of Communications, with the ETO having powers which were prejudicial to the state railway when it carried out its mandate. Thus the Transportation Consultants Inc. report (p. 131) observed that the ETO had the right to levy unpublished freight handling charges whether it or the shipper unloaded freight cars, and in effect controlled carload and less than carload movements. The result was that "any delays . . . naturally prejudice a shipper against railway service," and the "existing practice . . . offers tempting opportunity of effecting diversions to other transport media."

In summary then, while the railways system of Thailand constituted a large step forward in national integration and today serves the nation well as an efficient transport medium,† government policy in the past and the technology of the present left the creation of a national consumer goods market to highway transportation.

---

* According to one source (Transportation Consultants, Inc. 1959, p. 129) the motivation for the creation of ETO was that "the railway freight transportation fell into the hands of certain aliens or a cartel of foreigners" during and immediately following World War II, "making it difficult for Thai shippers to obtain sufficient railway wagons, which were then in short supply."

† For example, USOM (1957, p. 53) notes that in employees per kilometer of line owned and operated, Thailand in 1957 showed 6.2, against 18.9 for India, 22.0 for Japan, 7.8 for Turkey, and 2.9 in the United States.

The Highway System

The observation that the development of roads changes life in modernizing societies is commonplace. Notes of a Thai interviewer (Joint Thai-USOM 1966, VB 22) studying the impact of roads in the Northeast of Thailand describe the revolution:

> At first the villagers of Ban Non Ta Saeng wanted the road cut around the village. It was cut through instead, but they seem enthusiastic because they have new experiences. When they grow vegetables, fruits, and raise chickens, they know where to sell them. *Everything can be changed into money* (italics added).

The extent of the revolution is shown on the map on page 113 where the increment in the land area which has been integrated by the all-weather highway system is portrayed as the third stage in the process of integration, covering roughly the post-World War II period to the present.

Also shown on the map is the railway system, with a band of 15 kilometers (or 9 miles) on either side of a rail line arbitrarily assumed to delineate its service area. The same convention has been followed in drawing the service area of the all-weather highway system. The purpose of this presentation is merely to illustrate the spread effects of transport network development on the integration of the national space of Thailand. In other terms, the first stage inland waterway system served a total of 48,000 square kilometers or 9 percent of the national territory (or 74,000 square kilometers and 14 percent if the Gulf of Siam coastline is included). The second stage—the railway system—reached another 71,000 square kilometers or nearly 14 percent of the national territory not heretofore served by the waterway system. Finally, the most recent stage—the all-weather highway system—has added approximately 145,000 square kilometers or 28 percent of the nation's land area which had not been reached by the two earlier forms of transport.* The unshaded areas, constituting about half of the national space, are more than 15 kilometers from any form of modern low-cost all-weather transport.

---

* Needless to say, this demonstration is not intended as a rigorous analysis of the service area of any one transport form nor can the increments be added as implied. Further, the assumption of a band of 15 kilometers on either side of any type of facility as its service area is of course arbitrary and disregards the reality that lines are not laid across unobstructed plains and that nodes develop along lines (such as railway stations and road junctions), and so forth.

For a number of reasons, the highway contribution is understated. Roads shown as under construction on the base map (USOM, Capital Projects Division, dated September, 1967) have been excluded although the flow of traffic begins on a segment of a road as soon as it is completed. We have measured here only the increment in service area but a good part of the highway system lies in the area attributed to earlier forms of transport and main highways often parallel the rail lines. Because of the door-to-door service advantages of the motor vehicle, trucking to the rail head for transshipment is probably rapidly disappearing and much traffic originating at and destined to points within the area first served by other modes of transport is now moving by highway carrier. In fact, there are cases where the railroad is feeding truck transportation. The Ministry of Agriculture's study of agricultural marketing in the Northeast (Ministry of Agriculture 1964, p. 7) noted of Korat, the terminus of the Friendship Highway, that "much of the produce is transferred from trains to trucks at this point as trucking to Bangkok is less expensive and quicker. Trucks also reduce further handling in Bangkok."*

Growth of Highways

In view of the government policy to protect the railway system as a source of revenue to the state, it is not surprising that highway development in Thailand was substantially retarded. Thompson (1941, p. 510) notes that in 1936 when a road building policy began in earnest, Thailand had 310 square kilometers of land area per kilometer of road, far inferior to her neighbors such as Malaya, with 8 square kilometers, and Indochina with 22. Of course, these were colonial dependencies, not an independent kingdom whose sovereignty was under threat. Even had the Thai objective been infrastructure development, it clearly could not have endangered its international solvency by borrowing heavily abroad or letting its reserves down when its revenue base was subject to crop failure or other catastrophe.

The early history of highway development is obscure, in part

---

* The study reports a cost of 8 baht per sack of milled rice from Korat to Bangkok by rail, of which 60 percent is in the line haul charge and 20 percent each in local delivery to the warehouse in Bangkok and labor costs of loading and unloading. And a shipper may have to pay more in demurrage if he cannot remove his products from the railway in time. By truck, the delivered cost to the warehouse in Bangkok is 7 baht per sack.

because of the definition of a road,* but since our concern is with motorized road transport, the pre-Revolution period need not detain us. In 1935, the National Assembly approved Thailand's first National Highway Plan for the construction of 14,900 kilometers of road during the eighteen-year period to 1953, at a cost of 153 million baht. At the time, there were probably about six thousand cars and trucks in the Kingdom, or approximately one vehicle for each three thousand inhabitants (*Highways* 1967, p. 64) .† The Plan was overly ambitious; neither financial resources, the trained manpower, nor the bureaucratic organization were equal to such a task. However, some progress was made; the World Bank reported the construction of "2,215 kilometers of roads of fair quality" (IBRD 1959, p. 129) during the 1936-1940 period. Activity was suspended during the war, which was followed by a period of reconstruction and in consequence the development of the highways began in earnest only in the early 1950s. The following tabulation shows the growth in kilometers of the national highway system during the period 1945-1966; of special significance is the growth in paved mileage from 14.6 percent to 52

Year	Absolute	Paved Percentage of Total	Laterite and Stone	Earth	Total
1945	909	14.6	4,912	410	6,231
1950	811	14.0	4,768	253	5,832
1955	1,816	25.5	5,199	100	7,115
1960	2,787	33.5	5,456	84	8,327
1965	5,042	53.1	4,329	122	9,493
1966	5,368	52.0	4968		10,336

SOURCE: Ministry of National Development, Highway Department.

---

* *Highways in Thailand* (1967, p. 64) states that the first "highway" in Thailand, a 40 kilometer road across the border with Malaysia, was built in 1873 to accommodate the carriages of King Chulalongkorn upon his return from abroad. Thompson (1941, pp. 506-507) states that during 28 years (1904-31) prior to the Revolution, a total of 38 million baht had been spent on roads by the government. The National Highway Plan of 1935 projected 30 million baht for construction of some 3,000 kilometers in the first five years of the Plan. For the year 1951, the Government of Thailand budgeted 232 million baht for construction, maintenance, and administration of highways, and for 1967, nearly ten times that amount (*Highways* 1967, p. 32).
† Thompson (1941, p. 510) states that before the 1939 war, "about 4,500 cars existed in the whole kingdom" of which the majority were in Bangkok.

percent of the total. In addition to this national system, nearly 4,000 kilometers of provincial roads under the jurisdiction of local administrations were in existence in 1966.

It would be difficult to overestimate the catalyst role of the Friendship Highway in the development of a national market in Thailand. The vast Northeast, one-third of the country's land area, lies above the Central Plains on the Korat Plateau, almost entirely within the Mekong watershed and draining away from the heartland. Thus the first segment of the nation's rail system which was completed in 1890—the 264 kilometer line from Bangkok to Korat, the gateway to the Northeast, was of great significance. Sixty years later, transport consisted either of a "road of sorts" from Bangkok 90 kilometers north to Saraburi, still in the Central Plains, and from there to Korat which was 300 kilometers of tortuous muddy tracks and rocky mountain trails, impassible four months out of the year "or the railroad which was by then antiquated and in disrepair" (*Highways* 1967, p. 14). An application in 1950 of the Thai government to the World Bank for a loan for construction of a road from Saraburi to Korat was rejected. In 1953, limited funds were made available to start the project from the newly opened office of the Foreign Operations Administration of the United States. A supplement of funds from the Thai and U.S. governments permitted construction to begin in late 1955 by two American construction firms, and two and one-half years later, in mid-1958, the 150-kilometer Friendship highway was completed. Subsequent improvements on the road into Bangkok to complete this model facility relied heavily on the use of newly formed Thai construction companies, a deliberate policy of the American Mission, and the entire road building program became an important stimulus to the private enterprise sector and to the training of a force of engineers and skilled labor (Muscat 1966, 214-16).

A number of studies have carefully documented the economic effects of the Friendship Highway (Jones 1964, and studies cited therein). The highway paralleled the railroad line and caused an immediate and sharp decline in both passenger and carload and less-than-carload freight on the railroad, apparently for reasons of service rather than lower freight rates. In time series comparisons with selected areas beyond the influence of the Friendship Highway, other results are evident, such as substantial increases in cultivated land and in upland crops and vegetable production (although not in rice production). Similar comparisons made for the second large project to be completed after the Friendship Highway—the East-West Highway in north-central Thailand—showed similar results, including substantial increases in the formation of new commercial firms and small manufacturing and processing establishments (Jones 1964).

Growth in Motor Vehicles

The growth in motor vehicles which accompanied the development of highways has been spectacular. During the fifteen-year period 1950-64, while the national highway system nearly doubled in length and the paved mileage increased about six times, the total number of vehicles increased ten times.

It is noteworthy that the greatest increases were registered in those types of vehicles which are most directly related to increasing mobility of goods and people throughout the Kingdom and not simply in Bangkok. The following data, taken from the more detailed Appendix Table 16, show the growth of principal types of vehicles and their concentration in the Bangkok Metropolitan Area:

Type of Vehicle	*Number of vehicles and concentration in Bangkok*	
	1950	*1964*
Private passenger cars (thousands)	9.6	56.8
percent in Bangkok	87	80
Motorcycles (thousands)	1.4	87.4
percent in Bangkok	75	30
Private trucks (thousands)	3.2	53.3
percent in Bangkok	67	31
For-hire trucks (thousands)	3.1	20.0
percent in Bangkok	41	8

The number of private passenger cars increased only about six times over the period and remained largely concentrated in the Bangkok Metropolitan Area. On the other hand, the number of motorcycles increased sixty-five times and the proportion concentrated in Bangkok dropped from 75 percent to 30 percent over the fifteen years. The motorcycle in a society like Thailand's is the minimum-investment motorized vehicle for transporting persons and cargo on land. Although the Japanese advertising in Thailand of the Honda carries out the western image of a sports vehicle for a boy, often with his girl, it is more usually a utilitarian vehicle piled perilously high with cargo or with father taking the entire family for an outing on the weekend. Thus, it should be viewed as transportation for the upward mobile, who probably have already moved up from a bicycle and who will trade up further from two wheels to four when finances permit.* The relative prices of different types of vehicles in mid-1968, in Bangkok at retail for cash, were, in dollar equivalents: bicycle—$40, motorbike—$100, motorcycle—$225 up, lowest-price four-wheeled passenger car (Honda) —$1,600, Volkswagen sedan—$2,825.

The Impact of Highways

We can distinguish several results of the revolution in mobility which have been attributed to the road building program of the past decade. These results may be classified as *cost-reducing,* as *creating alternatives,* and as *change-diffusing.* The cost-reducing results of the highway program are amply documented. A World Bank Mission (Park 1966, p. 7) has estimated interurban motor and railroad freight traffic at about equal in 1955, respectively, 900 and 870 million ton-kilometers. Ten years later, however, railway traffic had less than doubled to about 1,500 million ton-kilometres, while road freight traffic was estimated at a five-fold growth or approximately 4,500 million ton-kilometers. The experiences of nations the world over, both developed and developing, in road and rail competition are now being repeated in Thailand. The increasing average length of haul of carload freight and declining less-than-carload tonnage by rail (see Appendix Table 17) reflect diversion to motor transport. The private trucking industry is highly atomized with the owner-driver firm predominating,† and in the absence of entry and rate control, competition is fierce, and rates are variable with market conditions and probably often driven below cost. We have seen above that the power of the ETO over pick-up and delivery service has constituted an

---

* The widespread ownership of bicycles by rural families was evident in Table 2.2. Except for the Central Plains, where a boat is the more important family conveyance, other regions show as many as half the families owning a bicycle.
† The Transportation Act of 1954 requires that firms hauling agricultural and livestock products must own at least ten trucks and have a minimum of 100,000 baht (U.S. $5,000) in working capital. Apparently it is common for individual owner-drivers to group together by tens to comply with the regulation (Ministry of Agriculture 1964, p. 89).

invitation to truck transportation to divert from rail.* Certainly, it also partly explains the growth of private trucking throughout the nation. Of course, the advantages in the qualitative dimensions of highway transportation would justify diversion from rail or water, even without rate advantages. While rate comparisons for moving high-value consumer goods are not available, we do have comparisons for the rice trade from Usher's study (1967, p. 216 and in 1968, p. 167) which show the cost reductions made possible by truck. He found the following relationships in baht per ton-kilometer:

canal boat (long-haul, 400 km.)	0.1
truck on good roads and rail (for 100 km. and over)	0.2 to 0.5
truck on poor roads or in collecting small quantities at the farm	1.0
jeep (1 ton) or ox-cart (½ ton), used only on short hauls	2.0 to 4.0

On a transport rate comparison alone, truck transport has achieved a dramatic reduction in costs over alternative land transportation in those vast areas outside the Central Plain waterway system. In terms of total transportation costs for higher value goods, the service advantages of trucking because of higher speeds and door-to-door delivery makes its impact truly revolutionary. For consumer goods, uniform pricing to the retailer throughout the country is increasingly coming to be the rule. The impact is also apparent in the decline of regional warehousing; one trading firm no longer maintains inventories at its nine regional sales offices since they all can be reached by a maximum of one and one-half day truck service from Bangkok.

In summary then, the reduction in the cost of overcoming space in the movement of people and goods over the new highways of the nation has constituted a substantial stimulus to the creation of a national market.

The dramatic diversification into new agricultural crops for export in the past ten years may be cited as an instance of the *creating of alternatives* which have been related to the new mobility. The increase in Thailand's exports of maize of ten times over a six-year

---

* As a sidelight, Usher (1967, p. 218) cites the case of truck competition reducing the amount of graft in getting freight cars in certain areas. Offseting this are the frequently cited bribes which must be paid by truckers to officials at the highway checkpoints.

period from 1957, of sixteen times in jute and kenaf in five years, and three times in cassava in six years as a response of the Thai farmer to a new alternative has been thoroughly analyzed by Muscat (1966, pp. 80ff) and Silcock (1967, pp. 231ff). The combination of an international demand for these products and the road system which made the farmer a part of the world market even in areas not suitable for rice production elicited an autonomous response to the new alternatives by the Thai farmer who heretofore had been considered conservative and unmaterialistic.* The role of transportation in this development is described by Muscat (1966, p. 116) in these terms:

> The kenaf and maize experiences have been particularly illuminating because they succeeded in accomplishing the commercialization of non-rice agriculture in wide areas which previously had been either partially commercialized in rice or subsisting in remote near-isolation. The difference between the areas participating in the latest spurt of commercialization and the large areas still excluded came into sharp focus. Principal among these differences was *the cost and efficiency of transport connection with Bangkok. Largely as a result of this lack of low-cost transport, production of agricultural commodities for market was blocked* (italics added).

Both producing for the export market, which Muscat is describing, and for the growing domestic market, was succinctly described in the remote villager's response: *"Everything can be changed into money."*

Finally, we can attribute the *change-diffusing* effect to the new mobility. This effect is closely related to that of opening new alternatives; indeed, all three effects are intertwined. And while the recent Thai experience repeats what has occurred in other countries with improvements in accessibility, an examination of the evidence from the rural areas of Thailand gives us a better picture of how the development of a national market proceeds.

The isolation which is being broken by the road program is, of course, relative and not absolute. Opium from the farthest hills will always get out and the ubiquitous Singer sewing machine will apparently get in, everywhere. But the movement of items of high value in

---

* Subsequent declines in the exportation of these products suggested that autonomous farmer response to export demand was not a sufficient condition and that the lag of the government as the administrator of development must somehow be overcome. See Muscat (1966, pp. 139 ff.) in the section titled "The Role of Government in Technological Change."

relation to their bulk or weight does not evidence an integrated national market. The itinerant peddler has probably roamed every corner of Thailand for centuries, leaving behind him products from the factories of many nations. What has changed with low-cost accessibility is the frequency and variety of the intrusions from the outside on the peasant's world. And, since the peasant must be viewed as the passive element in the process, the ability of the outside to come in is more important than his ability to get out.* Two agents of change diffusion have been particularly important—the travelling middlemen and the village store.

The vehicle of the middleman (outside the area served by the inland waterway system) is the small truck, Land Rover, or Jeep with which he leaves the improved road and strikes out across cart tracks or open country to the dispersed clusters of settlement. Although we know of no studies on the point, we may assume there is a margin somewhere, beyond which it is not worth his while to go. This limit will be nearer if he is buying agricultural produce than if he is selling goods to the peasants because of the greater weight or bulk per unit of value in the former case. In any event, lowering the cost of accessibility increases the market area of the middleman, and for a particular village, increases the number of middlemen, the frequency of their visits, and the quantity of what they can take out or variety of what they bring in.† The effect on stores in isolated villages which gained accessibility through new roads built under the Accelerated Rural Development Program in the sensitive Northeast offers further evidence of the diffusion of change.‡ In the twenty-five villages studied, there was a net gain of about 20 percent in the number of stores in the one-year period before and after the building of the

---

* An evaluation of roads in isolated areas (Joint Thai-USOM 1966, p. 175) found that the villagers who depended on simple transportation for short distances did not feel as isolated from the outside as the government officials, relying on rapid transportation over long distances, felt isolated from the villagers.

† Both Muscat (1966, p. 115) and Silcock (1967, p. 245) comment on the role of the travelling middleman in the transmission of market demand for new products such as maize to potential producers and on the stimulus to the middleman which low-cost road access provides.

‡ The study, by the Joint Thai-USOM Evaluation Team (Joint Thai-USOM 1966) and summarized in Jones and Orr (1966), involved sixty-six village shops in twenty-five villages which were visited in 1965 and in 1966, before and after the breaking of the villages' isolation by the new road. The roads, one in each of six provinces, branch out from existing main roads, and range in length from 20 to 38 kilometers, with laterite surfacing.

road. Where stores went out of business, the explanation frequently was that it was impossible to compete with stores in the nearby larger town to which the villagers could now go to shop. Although the prices of merchandise offered were quite steady over the year between the two surveys, the variety of items stocked increased after the roads were opened.

Other studies in connection with the evaluation demonstrated the villagers apparent satisfaction with the change roads had made in their world. In interviews with fifty respondents, the most common advantages cited were the improvement in transportation and communications in general, the greater ease of exporting the village's produce, improvements in farming practices because of easier access of agricultural advisors, and a favorable reaction to the increased exposure to urban ways—movies, ice, ready-made clothing, beauty parlours, and taxis. Although few respondents were aware of disadvantages, some mentioned increased dust and danger from passing vehicles, the fact that local retail stores lost sales, and that expensive family demands for new goods and services were created (Joint Thai-USOM 1966, II VB).

In summary, we have in this section sketched three stages in the physical integration of the Thai economy, and have attributed to the last stage of highway development a revolutionary impact on the creation of a national market. Rostow's now classic prescription, "How to Make a National Market" (Rostow 1964, p. 137), viewed roads and education as necessary but not sufficient conditions for developing nations in general. In addition, he suggested that developing nations also needed more *technical advice,* especially on markets and marketing, more *credit* resources, and *increased incentives to shift* to new methods of agricultural production or to new crops.

The Thai case is, of course, specific. We have shown in Chapter II that the education factor in Thailand is probably not a significant obstacle. However, the other conditions are not so easily resolved. There has been, and is now, a plethora of technical assistance although little of it on marketing until recently. However, activities which the improved road system has made possible, such as the fertilizer demonstration efforts of the Thai Oil Refinery and Shell, among others, are encouraging. On the other hand, the recent failure of the Thai subsidiary of an American commodity trader—Calabrian Company—to set up, with the participation of AID and U.S. and Thai banks, a streamlined corn production and marketing venture providing hybrid seed, warehousing, and a guaranteed market to the Thai farmer who diversifies out of rice, is discouraging. The question of agricultural credit is also complicated: Muscat (1966, p. 131) terms it a "red herring" as a major impediment to agricultural development. It is possible, however, that further commercialization of agriculture may hinge on the availability of farm credit, which is presently unsatisfactory. Finally, among Rostow's other conditions, incentives to shift loom large as an obstacle to further development. As mentioned above, the special cases of maize and kenaf do not assure the continued autonomous response of the agricultural sector toward diversification. Unfortunately, the three conditions of technical assistance, credit, and incentives put much of the burden on the bureaucracy, and that onus may be too heavy. But our thesis is that a revolution has begun, not that it will be completed to the level of self-sustaining growth of the economy.

THE CHANGING CHARACTER
OF CONSUMER GOODS IMPORTS

The broadening of the geographic market from a base built on the city of Bangkok to encompass more of the nation's space and more of its population should be reflected in the character of goods available in the market. We would expect to find new goods being demanded by the new markets, and in this section, some evidence of such shifts will be examined.

The value of Thailand's imports have grown from 2.6 billion baht in 1950 to about 18.0 billion baht or U.S. $900 million in 1966 (exclusive of over 7 billion baht in foreign aid imports in the latter year) as shown in Table 20 in the Appendix. The two categories, "manufactured goods, classified by material" and "machinery and transport equipment" have together accounted for over half the value of all imports throughout the period. Manufactured goods have declined steadily, from 45 percent of all imports to 25 percent by the end of the period. Machinery and transport equipment have, on the other hand, increased from 14.5 percent in 1950 to 27.3 percent of total imports in 1966, reflecting in large part the equipment needs of industrialization and the transport revolution. The third most important category, "chemicals," has also increased—6.8 percent to 13.6 percent.

These broad classifications, of course, obscure the consumer goods component of imports. In 1966, however, the leading import item was "road motor vehicles," with a value of 2.5 billion baht or 10 percent of total imports (including foreign aid which unfortunately cannot be netted out at this level of detail). The next leading imports in declining order were "mining, construction, and other industrial machinery" —1.7 billion; "petroleum products—1.6 billion; "iron and steel"—1.5 billion, and "manufactured articles, n.e.s."—1.4 billion. The importance in total imports of motor vehicles both for passengers and freight is evident.

Although changing definitions in the Customs publications complicate the analysis, the general trends in the importation of passenger motor vehicles can be described. For the six years 1950-1955, imports averaged about 3,400 vehicles annually, with no clear upward trend. In 1956, a change in the definition included "three-wheeled motor cars" and imports shot up to over 8,000 units; in the following year three-wheeled vehicles were apparently excluded and the units imported dropped to 3,200, almost the same as in 1955. For the three years 1957-1959, imports averaged 2,400 units with a declining trend, ending with only about 1,900 units in 1959 when the Thai economy was going through a depression. For the three years 1960-1962, the annual average was about 3,900 units and trending upward. In 1963, the number nearly doubled over the preceding year to 9,150; in 1964 and 1965, about 11,000 each year, and in 1966, nearly 15,000 units were imported.

Dramatic changes have occurred in the importation of specific consumer goods which demonstrate the thesis of the different goods being required by new markets. Appendix Table 21 shows some evidence of this for twelve articles which, although of significance and interest, cannot be considered as necessarily representative of all consumer goods.* Three trends are discernible in the data which deserve comment: the growing market evident over the eleven-year period, the trend toward the importation of cheaper goods, and the shifts in the origins of imported goods.

---

* The criteria for selection were items (a) principally used by individuals or households, (b) of some importance and hence interest (the value of total imports of the least important, soap, toilet and bath, amounted to over a quarter of a million dollars in 1966), and (c) for which comparison in the two years was possible. More items were examined and abandoned because of changes in Customs classifications of goods. There was no attempt to select those showing the greatest gain in markets for Japan.

Despite the fact that by 1966 there was local manufacture or assembly of all but three of the twelve products (watches, pens, and home air conditioners), the quantity imported of the fully assembled items increased over the period. This is not surprising however. For many items, local production was just getting under way and the government was apparently not using its powers to protect these local industries by quantitative restrictions or increased import duties.* There are two exceptions to the increase in quantity of imports over the period—bath and toilet soap and dentifrices. For these items, local production was probably most highly developed. Soap is an exceptional case among the twelve items in another respect; it is the only item for which the average value per unit (tons) increased, by nearly 65 percent, from 1956 to 1966. Apparently imported soaps shifted to the expensive brands for the luxury market while the local manufacturers took over the bulk of the market. The average value per ton of imported dentifrices in 1966 was only 42 percent of the 1956 average value; "luxury" brands of tooth paste are difficult to imagine. However, the author found in mid-1968 both locally and American manufactured family-sized Colgate Dental Creme stocked in a Bangkok supermarket, and priced respectively at 12.50 baht (62 cents) and 29 baht ($1.45).

The case of ballpoint pens and pencils is, of course, special, since it reflects the enormous growth in the use of throw-away pens the world over; such pens can be considered a different product than that imported in 1956. To a much lesser degree, the same tendency may have occurred in some other products such as refrigerators, where the very small units may have become increasingly important in the mix of imported models. Also, we should note that since the Customs data show the invoice value on a CIF basis, the shift from western to oriental countries of origin would reduce the ocean freight rate somewhat.

The trend toward lower-priced goods is evident throughout the list of goods as the following show:

---

* Corden (1967, p. 163) discusses the government's policy of using import duties for revenue rather than protection. Local industrialists have complained that duty on the components or raw materials they import are higher than the duty on the finished imported product with which they compete. Corden also shows the *ad valorem* import duty rates in 1965 for a variety of consumer goods, including motor cars (60 percent), watches (40 percent), television sets (35 percent), radios (30 percent), and fountain pens (25 percent).

Item	Average CIF Value per Unit, 1966 Imports as a Percentage of 1956
Soap	164
Tires for motor cars	95
Motorcycles	91
Passenger cars	87
Wrist watches[1]	74
Air conditioners[1]	73
Toilet paper	71
Refrigerators and freezers	57
Radios	48
Television sets	44
Dentifrice	42
Ballpoint pens[1]	8

[1] No local production or assembly in 1966.

Finally, the changing origins of imported goods are apparent in Appendix Table 21. For a third of the items, Japan has moved in the eleven years from a minor share of the market to domination: in motor cycles, from 1 percent to 95 percent on a quantity basis; watches, from 0 percent to 84 percent; radios, from 16 percent to 71 percent; and TV sets, 11 percent to 70 percent. In five other items where the market is more atomized, Japan has pulled into the lead, as in passenger cars from 0.7 percent to 29 percent; tires, 16 percent to 42 percent; refrigerators, 0.7 percent to 19 percent; dentifrices, 0.1 to 47 percent; and toilet paper, 0 to 38 percent. Only in home air conditioners (where the United States dominates) and in pens is Japan not a serious competitor.*

If the above analysis were extended to include the importation of raw materials and components for assembly in Thailand, the position of Japan would be further strengthened; Japan dominates the importation of motor vehicle parts for assembly and the same would probably be true of other items such as radios.

---

* With the growth in overseas manufacturing subsidiaries, the "country of origin" of a product will increasingly understate the country share of the market; thus the General Electric factory in Italy accounts for a significant part of Thailand's imports of "Italian" refrigerators. In view of Japan's present restrictive policies on foreign participation in manufacturing, this factor does not affect our conclusions on the importance of Japan in the Thai market.

A broader view of the shifts in imports to Thailand is shown in Appendix Table 20. Data from 1962 on have been shown both gross and net of foreign aid.* The trend toward an increasing share of imports from Japan in clear; from about one-fifth of total value, it increased to over one-third by the end of the period.

CONCLUSION

The case of Thailand in the decade of the 1960s is highly specific and not duplicated in other developing nations, even in other neighboring nations outside the combat areas on the peninsula. The government has been able to pursue with high priority the rapid development of an infrastructure which would integrate the nation and enable the central government to counter insurgency in the least developed and isolated regions of the country. A by-product of this effort has been a lowering of the costs of moving goods and people throughout the country and an increase in the amount of such movement, both in the intensive and extensive dimensions. People respond, even in such a self-satisfied society as that of Thailand. A market develops for locally manufactured goods as well as for imports, but the goods for this new larger market must be attractive, inexpensive, and of reasonable quality. This is not to say that a developing economy needs only a low-cost year-around transportation system to achieve self-sustaining growth. But the crucial role of marketing in national integration is obvious. The conclusions of the Adelman-Morris study of seventy-four underdeveloped countries (1968, p. 1191) suggest that "the underlying influences most conducive to transforming ideas and attitudes in low-income countries are the geographic linking together of the population through the creation of transportation networks and the economic integration of the country by means of the spread of the market throughout the nation."

---

* Subsequent to the preparation of Appendix Table 20, the author learned that the Bank of Thailand had published revised figures making a similar adjustment (see *Monthly Report,* February 1968 with revisions retroactive to 1957). The Bank of Thailand data "exclude military goods" (which apparently include military support items for the commissary which is available to American AID personnel). According to this source, total imports from all countries was 18.5 billion baht after adjustment, and 3.0 billion from the United States compared with 18.0 billion and 2.7 billion shown in the table. U.S. Department of Commerce data show exports to Thailand of $107 million in 1965 and $128 million in 1966, or roughly the same as the net figure in the table.

There are other requisites for nation-building and only time will confirm whether these are present or can be generated in the Thai society. But the important role of a developing national market in the process of economic integration is clear.

V
Conclusions

We may now pull together the main threads which have been traced in the preceding chapters. What are the general characteristics of the marketing system at present, how have they evolved out of the past, and what trends are evident which suggest the characteristics of the system in the future? Since many generalizations must be tentative because of insufficient knowledge of the Thai society and economy, we will point out a number of areas where research appears essential. Finally, we will keep in mind throughout, the broader question of the extent to which the Thai experience corroborates the generalizations from the literature of comparative marketing on aspects of the process of nation building and economic development.

CONSTRAINTS ON
THE PROPENSITY TO CONSUME

There are examples of ascetic societies which place a high value on disinterest in the possession and use of material goods and the enjoyment of services. In such cases, the individual achieves a position of equilibrium at a low level of consumption. The marketing system reflects the limited demands made on it and remains primitive and uncomplicated, more like a marsh on which water stands but does not flow than a stream bed carrying only a trickle. This is not the picture of the Thai society, however; the evidence we have examined suggests it is not significantly deficient in materialistic interests.

Over a century ago, the opening of an export market for rice in-duced the peasant to produce more and to use the cash proceeds to acquire imported consumer goods. Today, the discovery that a com-mercial market exists for untraditional crops such as maize and kenaf elicits a similar response. Throughout this modern period of Thai-land's history, a number of observers have offered evidence that the peasant has increased his level of consumption when a clear oppor-tunity for gain from increased output presents itself. What has con-strained his consumption has been his physical isolation, which limited him to economic self-sufficiency, in other words, the lack of a national market.

A number of forces might be expected to reduce the materialistic drive, particularly among the rural population which accounts for 85 percent of the national total. First, mere survival is not difficult in this tropical land. Rice is grown over substantial areas with intensive labor required only during a part of the year. This staff of life is supple-mented at a minimum expenditure of effort by fish and fruit and vegetables. Hunger has never been a serious spectre in the national history. The tropical climate assures that minimal expenditures will satisfy the basic needs for clothing and shelter. Second, Buddhism, which is more a spiritual philosophy than a religion, reaches far into the lives and actions of the Thai. While Buddhism steers a middle way between the extremes of asceticism and self-indulgence, the mate-rial resources an individual comes to control may be used as gifts to the temple or monks to gain merit for a future life. Third, the psychological make-up of the Thai would tend to reduce the pressures on him toward conspicuous or imitative consumption. Highly noncon-formist and independent of others, he has gone his own way and made his own decisions throughout his life, relatively free of the group pressures westerners are so well acquainted with. Finally, the relative economic classlessness of rural society, where each family owns its own small plot and earns a similar income from similar economic activities reduces the scope for a local demonstration effect. Yet despite these forces, the evidence all points to rising levels of consumption for those in environments reached by the recent revolution in the mobility of goods and people. More research, both in case studies of changing family consumption patterns and of continuing household expendi-ture surveys by the National Statistical Office will be necessary to confirm and measure this response.

The urban Thai is substantially less constrained in his materialistic drives than his rural counterpart. Self-sufficiency is hardly possible in urban areas. Further, there is some evidence that a smaller proportion of urban family income is devoted to merit acquisition, perhaps because of the wider range of goods and services available as alternative demands on income. Finally both the development of a class structure on economic lines and the impact of an international demonstration effect are most apparent in Thai urban society, particularly in Bangkok. It is there where the full force of events of the mid-twentieth century is felt and absorbed—the peninsula wars, the international commitments to planned economic and social development, and the growth in tourism resulting from the development of commercial air transportation. It is there where the traditional values of the Thai people are being challenged and are changing most rapidly.

OTHER CONSUMER CHARACTERISTICS

In addition to materialism, other characteristics of the Thai as a consumer are important in describing the present marketing system and its probable evolution. The low level of personal or family income is, of course, the most important of these characteristics, both for the present and into the foreseeable future. It should be remembered however that the amount of discretionary income is greater than is apparent from the usual international per capita income comparisons because of the downward bias against an economy like Thailand's in the definitions and methods of national income accounting. Thus, the western marketer is often surprised that there is discretionary income available for his product despite the very low published per capita income figures.

Limited incomes of consumers of course impose some restrictions on the kinds, sizes, and qualities of goods and on the way they are marketed. Clearly, the less expensive and simpler the model, the larger the number of consumers—whether for transistor radios, sewing machines, or automobiles. Similarly, the large family- or economy-size package or the pack or carton of cigarettes characteristic of retailing in a developed nation must give way in a developing market to the small unit of sale of a sample-sized box or envelope of detergent or a single cigarette. The evidence on the Thai consumer's price- versus quality-consciousness is conflicting and research studies are necessary. Also, the role of consumer credit in the broadening market is unknown in the absence of any investigations. We may only speculate that this financing will grow rapidly, especially in urban markets. The evidence of a Thai preference for present over future consumption, as seen in the low levels of ownership of insurance and financial assets and relatively high levels of ownership of durable consumer goods in comparison with other Asians, would support this view.

The often-observed improvidence with money of the Thai male suggests irrational or capricious consumer behavior. Counterbalancing this adverse marketing factor, however, is the acceptance of the woman as more other-worldly and materialistic and hence as conserver of family resources, principal shopper, and dominant voice in decisions to purchase. Reisman (in Lerner 1964) has called attention to the importance of equality of the sexes in the process of modernization. With neither the Middle Eastern veil nor Latin American *machismo* to make inferiors of half its population, the Thai society enjoys the full participation of all its members as producers, as consumers, and as receivers of the stimuli to change and improvement.

Finally, the Chinese strain in the society exerts an important influence on consumer behavior. Historically, the value systems of the Thai and of the Chinese immigrants in Thailand contained many opposite elements. The Chinese brought with them the characteristics necessary for survival in their harsh home environment—industriousness, frugality, and an occupational and geographic mobility in pursuit of remunerative activity. Money was more than important; it was everything. Something of these characteristics must have rubbed off on the Thai over the decades of Chinese assimilation, especially in the urban areas. With respect to consumer behavior, it seems likely that at a given income level, the ethnic Chinese historically has spent less on consumer goods and saved more (to invest in building up his commercial activities, and so forth) than the Thai. While we have some data on class-linked consumer behavior, they do not however permit identifying ethnic differences. In any event, ethnic determinants of consumer behavior are of diminishing importance with the closing of large-scale immigration after World War II and the continuing integration of the Chinese into Thai society.

MARKETING AGENCIES AND ACTORS

The development in recent years of an all-weather highway system has connected a significant portion of the settled land area with the nation's capital, which is both the center of industry, commerce, education, and government and the principal interface with the more modern "rest of the world." The resulting revolution in mobility has made possible for the first time in Thailand's history a national market for a variety of consumer goods. It is true that for centuries imported goods have been carried to all parts of the kingdom by itinerant traders but the high cost of transportation by animals, bicycles, and human backs restricted the flow of goods to a trickle. What has changed with lower-cost, year-round road transport is the volume of the flow and, in consequence, the roles of the existing marketing agencies and actors. The marketing structure is now in process of change, adapting to the new conditions of an inchoate national market. We shall examine briefly how each element in the structure seems likely to be affected by the redistribution of the functions performed in marketing. Any conclusions regarding trends must be highly tentative because the time span is so short (the transportation revolution began only in the mid-1950s) and because time series are unavailable for many essential elements for describing marketing (there has been only one household expenditure survey of 1962-63, and one census of industry in 1964, and of trade in 1966). Further research on marketing development requires, above all else, improved government data collection on a regular basis through surveys and censuses.

Beginning with the rural consumer who constitutes four-fifths of the nation's population, we may identify the principal marketing agencies and actors who are involved. The most important output of the farmer—the rice he grows—enters the marketing system only to the extent that his crop exceeds the food needs of his family. The rice surplus, together with any non-food crops, is collected for cash by agents of the Chinese rice mill or processing plant or by the local store owner for cash or in exchange for tools and consumer goods. Assuming a continuation of the traditional small family farm, the function of collecting or bulking these small surpluses for transporting to provincial centers and thence for export out of the region will continue to be performed much as it now is. But the effect of the transportation revolution is to bring larger areas and more farm families within reach of the collecting middleman. Moerman (1968, p. 97) observed of the northern village he analyzed that "with the completion of the railroad [in 1930], rice 'began to have a price' "; the effect of the highway system is to make rice and other crops have a price, or a better price, over a substantially greater portion of the nation.

Peasant marketing, or the trade in goods produced and consumed within an area of a few miles around the larger villages or towns principally involves adjusting household stocks by exchanging small quantities of surplus items for goods in short supply. No bulking operation is involved and the traders are the women of the household —unspecialized, part time, without capital or much market information, and with low opportunity costs and low profits. Although increased mobility permits the Thai woman to reach a somewhat more distant village, it seems likely that this type of trading will remain unattractive to specialized traders such as the Chinese and continue largely unchanged for a long time.

In rural areas, retailing by specialists appears to be undergoing transformation with increasing consumer mobility. This is true of both the fixed location retailer and the itinerant trader. All but the smallest settlements have a store; census data suggest a reporting retail establishment on the average for approximately every two square miles of total area including unsettled land, but since most villages are clustered and many are contiguous in the functional as well as administrative sense, it seems likely that few rural households are more than a mile from a fixed-location retailer. He performs the usual functions of the retailer of breaking bulk down to the very small units which characterize peasant purchases, maintaining a limited stock of the few necessities and the fewer luxuries which combine both utility and prestige, and extending credit. Typically, he is ethnically Chinese, although increasingly assimilated and accepted by his neighbors despite his relative affluence. The increasing discretionary income and increasing mobility of his customers, however, is forcing him to either grow by expanding his line, or, where the accessibility and size of the next larger commercial center in the area make competition impossible to go out of business. A similar trend is probably occurring in urban areas resulting from the parallel growth of incomes and mobility there, although we know of no studies which would provide documentation. In Bangkok, the only observable counterforce which would protect the small neighborhood convenience-goods store would be rapidly increasing traffic congestion. Parenthetically, it can be noted that the explosive increase in private autos, taxis, and trucks far exceeds the small additions in road capacity so that Bangkok shares with other large cities a foreseeable paralysis of street traffic. An index of the increased velocity of traffic is found in Bangkok police prohibitions of slower forms of transport. The ricksha was banned in 1952 and its substitute, the manual pedicab or two-passenger tricycle, in 1960 (Textor 1961, p. 3); by 1967, the samlor, a motorized version of the tricycle, was being threatened with removal from the streets in favor of the four-wheel compact automobile. In each instance, the displaced form of the taxi has moved to provincial cities where it enjoys a brief reincarnation.

The itinerant retailer has summed the small individual demands of many rural households into a volume sufficient to justify his full-time specialization in trading. A traditional figure in upcountry Thailand for centuries, he has performed the functions of breaking the bulk of his purchases from wholesalers in provincial market centers, transporting them to the farm, and on occasion extending credit. We may conjecture that while improved roads and the possibility of his using a truck increases his market area, the number of customers he can serve, and the size and variety of the stock he can carry, he will still not be able to compete with the larger stores in the village or town. His role in the past was based on the peasant's immobility and a willingness to pay a premium for home delivery during the busy seasons of the crop year or when the rains made other supply sources difficult to reach. But he can hardly compete in price or variety with a town store or with all else the town provides—movies and beauty parlors, social contact, and excitement. Other forms of itinerant trading such as the combining of entertainment and advertising with mobile wholesaling and retailing, as exemplified in the cases of the pharmaceutical houses and Bangkok consumer goods manufacturers, are probably also transitional, because as the volume handled by local retail stores increases, such efforts become both less necessary to push the product and more damaging to the manufacturer's relations with his retailers.

Historically, in the flow of imported consumer goods the channel members downstream from the rural or urban retailer have been one or more levels of Chinese wholesalers and the western trading firms. The functions performed at this stage are easily identified: importation, warehousing at the port, regulating the flow of goods out into the channels, breaking of bulk, long-haul transportation from Bangkok to provincial trading centers, and credit extension. However, with the small volume and extent of the market and the consequent low level of functional specialization, much variation existed in the number and mix of functions performed by a particular marketing actor. From the opening of free trade in the mid-nineteenth century, the symbiotic relationship between the western trading firms, which contributed their access to foreign manufacturers, shipping, finance, and insurance, and the Chinese with their control of the domestic distribution net, was particularly important. As the market has grown, the classic stages of increasing manufacturer investment and control in a foreign market has been followed in Thailand as elsewhere around the world. The inadequacies of import-oriented marketing mechanisms for the distribution of products to a growing national market, as described by Sherbini (1968), are clearly evident in the Thai case. The result is increasing control by the manufacturer over the marketing of his products and a declining role for the western trading firm and the Chinese importer/wholesaler as well.

THE ROLE OF GOVERNMENT

The policies and activities of the government sector, including the attitudes of the ruling or bureaucratic elite, merit examination because of actual or potential significance in the development of the marketing system. The modernizing ideals of the elite may be traced back to the goals set for the society during the last half of the nineteenth century by the modernizing kings—Mongkut and Chulalongkorn—and their efforts to achieve accommodation with the West through harmonizing the alien with the traditional values. Extensive use of foreign advisors and stimulation to education and travel in the West have provided the elite with exposure to the modern which Thailand's neighbors enjoyed as colonial areas, but without their relationship of subservience. It is important to remember, however, that what has been imported was usually adapted for local use and that the counterforce of traditionalism has been strong. Evers and Silcock (1967, p. 91) distinguish three elite groups—bureaucratic, power or military, and Chinese—and observe that the most traditional and least westernized are the army cliques which have controlled the government in recent years.

From the publication of the *First Economic Development Plan* in 1961, economic development has been a stated goal of the government and marketing development an aspect of that larger goal. In the First Plan, the objectives of the maintenance of "as much competition as possible among producers and distributors," private control of commercial activities, and encouragement of Thai participation in distribution were mentioned. In the Second Plan, policy objectives included were "to create an orderly and efficient commercial system and to promote healthy competition . . . , discourage monopolistic practices and cartels which are contrary to the best interests of producers or consumers . . . , maintain price stability for both industrial and consumer goods, so as to prevent harmful increases in the cost of living . . . , and . . . encourage wider participation by Thai nationals in commercial and service activities." The government position on its role is clear:

> Policies and measures for the development of Thailand's commerce and services are based on the desire to encourage the growth of a strong and healthy free enterprise system. The Government's role is not one of regulation, but of assistance to the private sector, particularly in the provision of technical assistance and the solution of critical problems and the bottlenecks in commerce and services (Appendix D).

Plan objectives such as these involve the government as stimulator and regulator of the distribution system. Their implementation does not require public investment but rather diagnostic studies of the functioning of the components of the system, followed by legislation or administrative action to correct deficiencies. It is not surprising then that in the First Plan there were no public development expenditures for marketing* and in the Second Plan, only 0.3 percent of expenditures were budgeted for the commercial sector, of which three-fifths were for export promotion, mostly through trade fairs, and another one-fifth was earmarked for price support for rice.

One other observation needs to be made regarding the statements by the government of its objectives for the commercial sector, however. They have a western tone, suggesting that they came from the West or were made for the benefit of the West, or both. For a century, western advisors resident in Thailand have been giving advice which

---

* The report of the World Bank Mission in 1959, which led to the promulgation of the First Plan the following year, contained no references to the marketing system except for the need to control unfair competition to well-known imported branded goods by inferior locally produced or imported products bearing nearly identical trademarks (IBRD 1955, p. 105). The Mission strongly supported private enterprise in industry and recommended the liquidation of state industrial ventures or their operation by private management organizations on contract with the government (pp. 20-21).

has not always been easy to accept.* At the same time, the Thai have initiated reforms which they sensed were expected of them by the community of modern nations. Whatever the source or motivation of the statements of objectives regarding the marketing system, it is doubtful if the government has any deep interest in attempting such reforms, or the capacity as yet to carry them out. Certainly, the past record is not convincing. After over thirty years of attempting to implant the concept of cooperatives to achieve reform in agricultural marketing and credit, relatively little has been achieved. The reasons for this experience are various, but peasant apathy and bureaucratic faith in fiat are probably basic. (See footnote p. 110 in Chapter III.) Other government efforts at reform or control mentioned earlier such as exhorting retailers to hold down prices, the operation of state trading companies, and legitimizing commodity marketing syndicates have been ineffectual if not damaging to the broad public interest.† Finally, the precipitous introduction of color television transmission in 1967 suggests a questionable set of priorities for modernization on the part of the bureaucracy, as well as an example of the showcase mentality so often found in developing societies. Government publicity notes that the Army TV station's first color transmission, which had been expedited to be available for the annual Miss Thailand contest, occurred two days before the introduction of color TV in Hong Kong and two weeks before the British Broadcasting Company took the same step. However, it was estimated that two months after regular color programming began in Thailand, there were only 400 color TV sets in the country, or about one for each thousand black and white sets in use.

SUMMARY

The picture we have described of shifting roles among marketing actors and agencies as the Thai economy and society have developed

---

* Campbell (1902, p. 318), writing at the turn of the century observed of the fate of suggestions of European advisors that "some reforms which do not interfere with vested interests are allowed to go through, others are passed with a flourish of trumpets for the express purpose of throwing dust in the eyes of Europe."
† Although the case is complex and the full story not available, a report of the recent failure of the Calabrian (Thailand) Co., Ltd. venture to modernize corn production and marketing includes among contributing causes "the Thai trading system dominated by Chinese merchants with powerful influence on the Bangkok government" (*Wall Street Journal*, April 7, 1969).

and changed suggests an automatic adaptive response of the distribution system. Such, in fact, has occurred in the Thai environment of fiscal conservatism, laissez-faire, and a symbiosis between the Chinese commercial class and the Thai bureaucratic elite. Whether these automatic adjustments through the mechanisms of prices and profits, and with no more social control than has been exercised, have been the best possible course cannot be judged without more research than has yet been undertaken.* Similarly, conjecture on the future characteristics of the marketing system can only be based on a very inadequate base from which to extrapolate.

Large reductions in transport cost have resulted over that substantial portion of the land area which has been integrated into the national market by the new all-weather highway net. Private ownership and operation of motor vehicles for both private and for-hire transportation has been possible, fortunately, without government attempts at economic regulation of trucking in order to protect its investment in the state railway. Evidence suggests that for consumer goods the traditional pattern of higher prices with increasing distance from Bangkok is giving way to uniform prices to retailers throughout the national territory.

The increased size of the market facing all elements in the distribution system both requires and justifies greater specialization. Product differentiation and the presence of the manufacturer within Thailand rather than in some distant land assures the emergence of a different retailer performing broader functions than the traditional Chinese merchant of the past. Even more, the continued assimilation of this ethnic minority signifies the decline of the Chinese influence as controllers of all commerce and principal purveyors of modernization, with their favored status symbols which were also professional tools—the Parker pen and the Swiss wrist watch.

Marketing development in Thailand in the past decade or two is a highly specific case since it reflects the very distinctive and attractive Thai society and people. Yet there are substantial similarities to other developing countries in the process of modernization and of the development of a national market. People respond to the opportunity to modernize and values change rapidly, even in the self-satisfied Thai

---

* As a start, what is needed is something like the comprehensive diagnostic studies undertaken by the Latin American Market Planning Center (LAMP) at Michigan State University for AID missions in various Latin American cities.

society. This may be a source of sadness to westerners who have known Thailand. But, in David Reisman's words (Lerner 1964, p. 11), we can hardly bring ourselves "to begrudge others the literacies and comforts that no longer wholly assuage us."

Appendix A

Socioeconomic Data for the
Study of Marketing in Thailand

Socioeconomic Data for the
Study of Marketing in Thailand

Table 1 — Percentage Distribution of the Population by Age,
1947, 1966, and Projected 1981

Age Group	1947		1966		Projected 1981	
0-4	15.2		18.2		14.6	
5-9	14.2		15.1		13.8	
10-14	12.9		12.4		13.3	
Sub-total 0-14		42.3		45.7		41.7
15-19	11.1		9.8		11.2	
20-24	8.9		8.1		9.4	
25-29	7.1		7.0		7.8	
30-39	12.4		11.5		11.2	
40-49	8.7		8.3		8.2	
50-59	5.2		5.1		5.4	
Sub-total 15-59		53.4		49.8		53.2
60-69	2.8		3.1		3.2	
70-79	1.5		1.1		1.5	
80 and over			0.3		0.4	
Sub-total 60 and over		4.3		4.5		5.1
Total	100.0		100.0		100.0	

SOURCES: For 1947, *Statistical Yearbook*, 1965, p. 42. For subsequent years, National Economic Development Board, "The Methodology for Preparing the Second Economic and Social Development Plan of Thailand," May 1967, mimeographed, p. 57. The assumed birth and death rates used were as follows:

	1966-71	1971-76	1976-81
Birth rate (per 1,000 pop.)	42.2	39.0	35.7
Death rate (per 1,000 pop.)	9.3	8.8	7.3

149

Table 2 — Literacy of the Population, Age Ten and Over, 1947 and 1960

	1947		1960	
	Male	Female	Male	Female
Total population				
(*thousands of persons*)	6,143	6,184	9,004	9,022
Percent literate	67.4	40.1	80.6	61.0
Both sexes		53.7		70.8
By age groups:				
10-14 years	62.2	60.7	86.6	84.8
15-19	80.5	72.7	91.0	85.8
20-24	79.6	56.0	88.6	79.4
25-29	75.2	39.3	85.7	75.0
30-34	71.9	29.6	86.0	70.3
35-39	67.9	19.4	80.3	51.3
40-44	61.4	11.8	73.5	33.5
45-49	56.7	9.0	69.7	25.8
50-54	52.8	7.0	62.8	13.0
55-59	47.3	5.7	56.8	9.1
60-64	40.8	5.6	52.4	7.4
65 and over	n.a.	n.a.	46.1	6.2
Age unknown	47.6	24.6	63.1	32.1

SOURCE: *Statistical Yearbook*, no. 26, 1965, p. 131.

Note: Literacy is defined as the ability to read and write in any language. The total number of persons with age unknown was approximately ten thousand in 1947 and forty-six thousand in 1960.

n.a.: not available.

Table 3 — Percentage Distribution of Gross Domestic Product by Sector, 1957-1971

	1957	1961	1965	1971 Target	Average Annual Growth Rate[1]	
					1961-66	1967-71
Agriculture	37.4	38.6	32.8	26.0	4.6	4.3
Crops	24.4	27.0	22.1	n.a.	n.a.	4.4
Livestock	7.7	6.6	5.2	n.a.	n.a.	5.0
Fisheries	1.8	1.9	2.8	n.a.	n.a.	4.7
Forestry	3.5	3.1	2.7	n.a.	n.a.	n.a.
Mining and quarrying	1.6	1.5	2.1	2.0	10.9	6.6
Manufacturing	12.1	11.1	12.1	13.6	10.2	10.9
Construction	3.1	3.6	4.8	5.8	12.3	11.4
Electricity and water supply	0.3	0.5	0.7	1.2	18.2	18.0
Transportation and communication	5.9	6.8	7.5	8.6	9.0	11.0
Wholesale and retail trade	19.1	17.2	18.6	18.6	8.0	8.4
Banking, insurance, and real estate	1.7	2.5	3.7	5.7	16.6	17.0
Ownership of dwellings	4.4	4.5	4.2	3.5	3.7	5.0
Public administration and defense	5.4	4.9	4.9	5.9	7.2	12.0
Services	9.0	8.8	8.6	9.1	6.0	9.5
Gross domestic product	100.0	100.0	100.0	100.0	7.3	8.5

SOURCE: National Economic Development Board, "The Second National Economic and Social Development Plan (1967-1971)," mimeographed, p. 41.
[1] At 1965 prices.
n.a. not available.

Table 4 — Value Added in the Manufacturing Sector, 1960, 1966, and Projected 1971

(in millions of baht at 1965 prices)

Industry	1960	1966a	1971 Targets	Average Annual Growth Rate	
				1960-1966 (percentage)	1967-1971 (percentage)
Food	1,902	3,149	4,162	8.9	5.5
Beverage industries	650	1,237	2,417	11.9	14.1
Tobacco manufacturing	889	1,331	1,600	7.3	5.1
Manufacturing of textiles	162	397	759	17.1	13.4
Manufacture of footwear, wearing apparel, and made-up textiles	269	343	481	4.3	7.1
Wood and cork except manufacture of furniture	292	605	884	14.0	7.8
Furniture and fixtures	89	127	223	6.4	12.1
Paper and paper products	24	32	192	6.7	37.8
Printing, publishing, and allied industries	134	236	390	10.6	10.6
Leather and leather products except footwear	120	135	157	2.2	3.2
Rubber products	227	268	413	3.4	9.1
Chemicals and chemical products	426	635	943	7.3	7.5
Non-metallic mineral products except products of petroleum and coal	267	702	1,173	17.6	11.1
Iron and steel basic industries	17	11	35	4.0	26.1
Electrical machinery, apparatus, appliances and supplies	27	39	120	3.6	25.1
Machinery and transport equipment	244	338	545	6.1	10.1
All others	209	978	3,307	31.4	27.4
Total	5,949	10,583	17,800	10.3	10.9

SOURCE: National Economic Development Board, "The Second National Economic and Social Development Plan (1967-1971)," p. 44.
a 1966 estimates are based on incomplete data.

152

Table 5 — Regional Percentage Distribution of Gross Domestic Product by Industry, 1963

| | | *Percentage of Kingdom Total* | | |
| | | *North-* | *Central* | |
Category	*North*	*east*	*Plain*	*South*
Agriculture:	19.9	25.5	36.1	18.5
Crops	18.2	26.2	37.0	18.6
Livestock	22.7	40.2	22.6	14.5
Fisheries	16.2	11.7	57.6	14.5
Forestry	39.8	14.5	19.3	26.4
Mining and quarrying	7.3	4.1	26.0	62.6
Manufacturing	11.3	13.3	67.1	8.3
Construction	12.7	11.5	65.4	10.4
Electricity and water supply	10.3	6.3	77.5	5.9
Transportation and communication	10.7	8.7	72.0	8.6
Wholesale and retail trade	11.3	14.7	62.0	12.0
Banking, insurance, and real estate	3.0	2.0	91.5	3.5
Ownership of dwellings	19.3	29.4	39.8	11.5
Public administration and defense	11.4	13.3	67.5	7.8
Services	15.2	15.2	56.6	13.0
Total gross domestic product	14.7	17.8	53.7	13.8

SOURCE: National Economic Development Board, *Regional Gross Domestic Product,* 1965, p. 40.

Table 6 — Distribution of Employment by Occupation and by Industry

	Percentage Distribution	
	All Thailand, 1966	Urban Areas, 1963
A. Employment by Occupation:		
1. Professional, technical, and related workers	1.4	7.3
2. Administrative, executive, and managerial	0.5	2.5
3. Clerical workers	1.3	6.1
4. Sales workers	6.8	31.6
5. Farmers, fishermen, loggers, miners, etc.	80.1	9.2
6. Workers in transportation and communication	1.5	6.7
7. Craftsmen, production process workers, and laborers, n.e.c.	6.3	24.5
8. Service, sport and recreation	2.1	12.0
9. Workers not classifiable	—	0.1
Total	100.0	100.0
B. Employment by Industry:		
1. Agriculture, forestry, hunting, fishing	79.9	9.0
2. Mining and quarrying	0.3	0.2
3. Manufacturing	4.7	15.7
4. Construction, repair, demolition	0.7	3.8
5. Electricity, gas, water and sanitary services	0.2	0.6
6. Commerce	7.1	32.2
7. Transport, storage, and communication	1.6	6.7
8. Services	5.5	30.8
9. Activities not adequately described	—	1.0
Total	100.0	100.0
Absolute number of persons	12,450,000	1,335,000

SOURCES: Data for all Thailand are from National Economic Development Board, "The Second National Economic and Social Development Plan (1967-1971)," pp. 78-79 and are estimates for the end of the fiscal year, with the labor force defined as the economically active population fifteen years of age and over. Data for urban areas are from National Statistical Office, *Report of the Labor Force Survey (Round 4), July 1963*, pp. 72-73, and cover persons eleven years of age and over. Industry and occupation classifications are of the International Labor Organization.

Table 7 — Some Characteristics of Thai Industry, 1964

Size of Establishment in Number of Employees	Number of Establishments	Percentage Distribution of Total	
		Persons Engaged	Sales
1-4 employees	91.9	55.5	6.2
5-9 employees	5.9	12.3	7.0
10-19 employees	1.0	4.9	7.8
20-49 employees	0.8	7.6	16.0
50-99 employees	0.2	4.7	10.3
100 employees and over	0.1	15.0	52.7

The census was tabulated and is being published by a classification of establishments based on the number of employees and the use of paid employees, as follows:

Size C: 10 engaged persons (paid and unpaid) or more.
Size B: less than 10 engaged persons but with at least one paid employee.
Size A: less than 10 engaged persons and no paid employee.

Since *home industry* is defined as activities conducted within living quarters or area by family members either full or part time, and with no paid employees, we may reclassify the census totals as follows:

	Number of Establishments	Number of Persons Engaged Absolute	Per Estab.	Sales (in million baht)
Large industry (Size C)	3,584	154,956	43	11,277
Small industry (Size B)	16,707	66,259	4	1,238
Home industry (Size A)ᵃ	143,711	259,998	1.8	473
Total	164,002	481,213		12,988

or, in percentages of the totals:

Large industry	2.2	32.3	87.0
Small industry	10.2	13.8	9.4
Home industry	87.6	53.9	3.6
	100.0	100.0	100.0

SOURCE: National Statistical Office, *Report of the 1964 Industrial Census*, vols. I and II.
ᵃ These data are derived by subtraction of the sum of the data for Large Industry (published as vol. I in 1967) and Small Industry (published as vol. II in 1968), from the grand totals for the census, shown in both vols. I and II. Vol. III, on what we have called Home Industry, had not yet been published at the time of writing. The census covered all manufacturing and home industries in the 120 municipalities and in villages with two or more establishments, excluding small rice mills, during the calendar year 1963.

Table 8 — Problems Confronting Thai Industry, 1964

Type of Difficulty[1] or Problem	*Large Industry[2]* No. of Establishments Citing Difficulties Absolute	Percentage of Total Reporting to Census	*Small Industry[2]* No. of Establishments Citing Difficulties Absolute	Percentage of Total Reporting to Census
Shortage of raw materials	1,269	35.5	3,889	23.3
Marketing difficulties	1,115	31.2	4,646	27.7
Problems in transportation	834	23.3	1,597	9.6
Others	659	18.4	2,686	16.1
Out-of-date machinery	609	17.0	1,338	8.0
Not enough energy and water supplies	550	15.4	937	5.6
Lack of skilled workers	462	12.9	1,847	11.2
Competition with imported goods	454	12.7	766	4.6
Unsuitable factory space	332	9.3	1,156	6.9
Lack of good management	236	6.7	747	4.5
Total establishments reporting to census	3,584		16,707	

SOURCE: National Statistical Office, *Report of the 1964 Industrial Census*, vol. I, table 15, and vol. II, table 11.

[1] Type of difficulty listed by declining rank order of large establishments reporting.

[2] Large and small industry are defined in the notes to Table 7.

Note: Number of establishments responding to this question was not published; percentages relate number citing difficulty to number of establishments enumerated in the census.

Table 9 — Commercial and Service Establishments in Urban Areas, 1966

Type of Activity *(in decreasing order* *of receipts)*	*Number of* *Establish-* *ments*	*Number of* *Persons* *Engaged*	*Receipts*[1] *(million* *baht)*	*Value*[2] *Added* *(million* *baht)*
Wholesale only	2,395	20,261	13,902	4,097
Wholesale and retail	5,238	40,748	13,455	3,867
Retail only	51,859	123,965	7,832	3,292
Services only	39,935	136,527	6,514	5,071
Retail and services	10,427	36,626	2,642	1,501
Wholesale, retail, and services	305	6,238	2,632	1,020
Producing and retail	3,849	15,327	558	275
Wholesale and services	153	1,563	383	16
Others and unknown	362	2,158	166	82
Total, all municipalities	114,523	383,413	48,084	19,222

SOURCE: National Statistical Office, *Census of Business Trade or Services, 1966,* Abridged Report.

1 Defined as "sales of goods purchased plus sales of goods produced plus services rendered plus brokerage fees or commissions plus change in inventory."

2 Value added is "Receipts" less "Expenditures" which were defined as "purchase of goods plus operating expenses (excluding rents, salaries, and bonuses)."

Notes: The census consisted of two parts: a complete enumeration of the 120 municipal areas in Thailand and a sample of 650 villages for areas outside municipal areas. The census covers establishments which operate in fixed locations; it excluded all itinerant peddlars operating from boats or on land and traders operating at markets erected at fixed locations only on certain days of the week. Apparently included, however, are traders who operate from the permanent stands of others in market places or elsewhere, where they leave some of their goods and equipment at the end of the day. (See *Enumerators Instruction Book* for the census, pp. 19-20, and enumeration form.)

Wholesale trade was defined as the purchase and resale of goods to retailers, industrial and other commercial establishments, institutions, government organizations, and other wholesalers; retail trade as the sale of goods directly to consumers for personal or household consumption or use. Services covered were of three types: business services, such as legal, accounting, enginering, and architectural; recreational services, such as production, distribution, and projection of motion pictures, radio and television, sports activities, hotels, restaurants, bars and night clubs, and personal services, such as laundry, barbers, tailors, commercial photography, funerals, fortune tellers, and massage services.

Table 10 — The Structure of Trade in Urban Areas, 1966

Type of Activity	Number of Establishments	Number of Persons Employed Absolute	Per Establishment	Receipts[1] Absolute (million baht)	Per Establishment (thousand baht)
Wholesale only					
All municip.	2,395	20,261	8.5	13,902	5,805
Bangkok Met. Area	1,306	14,919	11.4	11,587	8,872
Bangkok Met. Area as percent of total	54.5	73.6		83.3	
Retail only					
All municip.	51,859	123,965	2.4	7,832	151
Bangkok Met. Area	19,990	51,082	2.5	4,020	201
Bangkok as percent of total	38.6	41.2		51.3	
Wholesale and Retail					
All municip.	5,238	40,748	7.8	13,455	2,569
Bangkok Met. Area	2,883	27,188	9.4	11,202	3,885
Bangkok as percent of total	55.0	66.7		83.2	
Producing and retail					
All municip.	3,849	15,327	4.0	558	145
Bangkok Met. Area	1,235	6,020	4.9	353	286
Bangkok as percent of total	32.1	39.3		63.3	

SOURCE: National Statistical Office, *Census of Business Trade or Services, 1966,* Abridged Report.
1 Defined as sales of goods purchased, plus sales of goods produced, plus services rendered, plus brokerage fees or commissions, plus change in inventory.
Note: See Table 9.

Table 11 — Commercial Establishments in Rural Areas, 1966

Type of Activity	Number of Establish- ments	Number of Persons Employed	Receipts (million baht)
Wholesale and retail	2,228	10,651	4,396
Retail only	76,306	194,337	2,053
Wholesale only	2,575	8,731	1,274

SOURCE: Unpublished data of the National Statistical Office.
Note: See Table 9.

Table 12 — Growth in the Number of Commercial Bank Offices, by Regions, 1940-1967

Regions and Principal Provinces (in parenthesis, no. of provinces)	1940	1950	1955	1960	1967
Central Plain (26)	10	33	54	182	288
including,					
Bangkok	9	29	40	105	162
Thonburi	1	1	2	8	20
Chonburi	—	2	5	8	13
Ratburi	—	—	3	11	13
Northern (16)	2	12	21	66	84
including,					
Chiengmai	1	4	5	11	14
Lampang	1	2	4	10	10
Nakornsawan	—	3	4	10	11
Northeastern (15)	—	3	9	31	64
including,					
Khonkaen	—	1	2	7	13
Nakhornratchsima	—	1	3	8	12
Southern (14)	2	14	31	73	99
including,					
Songkla	1	5	9	13	19
Trang	—	1	2	10	12
Nakornsrithamrat	—	4	4	8	11
Yala	—	1	3	7	10
Whole kingdom (71)	14	62	115	352	535
(Number of provinces with no office)	(65)	(54)	(42)	(9)	(0)

SOURCE: Reports of the Bank of Thailand.
Note: Principal provinces are those with ten or more bank offices in 1967.

Table 13 — Distribution of Household Consumption by Types of Goods and Services, 1962-63

A. *Average Household Expenditures Including Value of Home-Produced Goods*

	Percentage Distribution by Location			
Types of Goods and Services	Whole Kingdom	Bangkok Met. Area	Towns	Rural
Food and beverages	44.6	46.2	42.9	44.8
Clothing, materials, and services	15.6	9.2	14.9	17.1
Housing, furnishings, and household operations	15.9	17.5	16.6	15.3
Medical and personal care	6.9	6.9	7.5	6.7
Transportation, own vehicle and public	4.2	6.7	4.6	3.6
Recreation, reading and education	3.9	5.6	6.4	3.0
Tobacco and alcohol	4.4	4.7	4.8	4.2
Miscellaneous	4.5	3.2	2.3	5.3
Total	100.0	100.0	100.0	100.0
Total average monthly expenditure, including value of home produced and goods received free (in baht)	690	1,424	1,003	580

B. *Percentage Distribution of Household Expenditures by Family Income Class for Rural Families*

	Percentage Distribution by Family Annual Income				
Types of Goods and Services	Under 3,000	3,000- 5,999	6,000- 11,999	12,000- 17,999	18,000- and over
Food and beverages incl. value of rice drawn from storage for family use	46.7	42.6	39.2	35.4	28.1
Clothing and materials	16.9	17.2	18.5	17.2	15.2
Housing, furnishings, and operations	10.8	11.6	11.6	12.5	14.4
Medical and personal care	7.2	7.7	7.1	6.6	5.6
Transportation	2.5	3.1	3.9	6.2	11.4
Reading, recreation, education	2.0	3.1	4.2	5.5	6.4
Tobacco and alcohol	4.0	4.3	4.2	4.6	4.0
Misc. household exp.	6.0	5.5	6.1	6.0	7.4
Gifts and contributions	3.6	4.5	4.7	6.2	6.4
Taxes	0.3	0.4	0.5	0.7	1.1

SOURCE: National Statistical Office: *Household Expenditure Survey*, Advance Report, Whole Kingdom, 1963.

Table 14 — Survey of Attitudes and Affluence in Seven Asian Capitals, 1965
(*Tokyo, Manila, Singapore, Bangkok, Hong Kong, Taipei, Seoul*)

Attitudes and Affluence	*Percentage*	Bangkok *Rank Among Seven*	*Percentage of All Seven Cities*
A. Standard of Living			
Interviewees who say that living conditions compared with five years ago are:			
Better	63	3rd	48
By socioeconomic status:			
Upper class	61	4th	59
Middle and lower	64	3rd	46
About the same	14	2nd	20
Worse	19	3rd	30
Households owning:			
Automobiles—one or more	25	2nd	13
—two or more	7	1st	2
Motorcycles or scooters	9	3rd[1]	7
Home radios	77	2nd	63
Transistor radios	41	4th	41
Television	39	3rd	36
Record players	16	5th	25
Tape recorders	8	3rd[1]	9
Refrigerators	27	4th	32
Sewing machines	55	3rd	52
Air conditioners	2	6th	3
Still cameras	24	3rd	27
Home	49	3rd	42
Bank accounts	42	6th	45
Life insurance	13	5th	29
Stocks and bonds	6	5th	12
B. Education and Travel			
Interviewees who finished full-time education under age 18	63	6th	56
Interviewees who would rather have had more education	83	1st	67
Interviewees who had read a newspaper during last 24 hours	68	6th	76
Households with members who traveled abroad in last 3 years:			
Total households:	18	1st	11
Upper class	43	2nd	39
Middle and lower	14	1st	7
Purpose of travel:			
Study/education	56	1st	30
Business	64	3rd[1]	54

162

APPENDIX A

Table 14 — Survey of Attitudes and Affluence in Seven Asian Capitals, 1965 (cont'd)

Attitudes and Affluence	Bangkok Percentage	Rank Among All Seven, Each City Evaluating Its Own Countrymen
C. National Image		
Bangkokians who perceive own country's products as good-quality, inexpensive, well-designed, modern	n.a.	7th
Bangkokians who think of their own countrymen as:		
Energetic	15	3rd
Scientific	less than 0.5	7th
Hard-working	16	7th
Reliable	28	1st
Conscientious	16	4th
Pleasure loving	43	1st
Lazy	39	1st
Excitable	37	1st
Romantic	2	5th
Frivolous	24	1st

SOURCE: International Research Associates, *The New Far East: Seven Nations of Asia* (Hong Kong: Readers Digest Far East Ltd., 1966), 159 pp.
1 Signifies rank shared with another city.

Table 15 — Articles Stocked in Ten Stores in Isolated Villages, 1965-1966

Articles Carried in All 10 Stores	Articles Carried in 9 Out of 10 Stores	Articles Carried in 8 Out of 10 Stores	Articles Carried in 7 Out of 10 Stores
Flour	Canned fish		
Biscuits*	Fish sauce		
Palm sugar	Cane sugar*	Candy*	Cigarettes*
Condensed milk			Cola-type soft drinks
Kerosene*		Oil lamps	Floor mats
Flashlights			
Batteries			
Matches			
Enamelled spoons	Pots, pans		Glasses
Laundry soap*	Pails		Enamelled basins
Dishes	Brooms		
Soap		Headache	
Toothpaste		remedies*	
Hair cream		Hair dye	
Combs*			
Face powder			
Mirrors			
Quilted blankets	Towels		
Undershirts	Footwear		
Hats	Shorts		
Sewing items	Pasin (loincloth)		
Weaving items	Belts		
Pencils*	Paper in ream*	Crepe paper	
Paper pads*			
Rulers*			
Envelopes			
Nails	Wire	Hemp rope	Oxen and buffalo
Nylon rope	Hoes		bells
			Fertilizer
Ceremonial items:			
Joss sticks			
(incense)*			
Candles*			

SOURCE: Interviewers' worksheets covering visits in February-March 1966 to stores which had been surveyed a year before in connection with a study of the impact of new roads. See Second Joint Thai-USOM Evaluation of the Accelerated Rural Development Projects. Evaluation Reports, vols. I and II, Bangkok, July 1966.

Notes: The median number of different types of articles carried in the 10 stores was 73, with a range of 58 to 93. (Note that sewing items, weaving items, and pots and pans, were considered as a single type of article.) *A very small store in Nongkhai province, not included in the group of 10, carried only these 16 types of articles, which are indicated in the above list by an asterisk.

The sample of 10 stores consists of 6 stores located in 2 villages in Amphur Srichiengmai in Nongkhai province and 4 stores located in 3 villages in Amphurs Phana and Amnat Charoen in Ubon province.

Of the 10 store salesmen interviewed in the sample, 6 indicated farming as their major occupation and selling as a secondary occupation; 2 reported selling as a major occupation and farming as secondary, and 2 reported selling as their only occupation.

Table 16 — Motor Vehicle Registration, by Type and Location, 1950-1961 [1]

Type of Vehicle		Number of Vehicles				(Times increase, 1964 over 1950)
		1950	1955	1960	1964	
Personal cars	—whole kingdom	9,627	20,686	33,105	56,835	(5.9)
	Bangkok	8,444	17,427	26,170	45,493	(5.4)
Taxis	—whole kingdom	516	3,601	16,762[2]	12,497	(24.2)
	Bangkok	367	2,508	14,341[2]	8,942	(24.4)
Buses[3]	—whole kingdom	5,001	9,241	12,605	11,306	(2.3)
	Bangkok	689	945	1,993	2,207	(3.2)
Private trucks	—whole kingdom	3,197	10,864	25,615	53,256	(16.7)
	Bangkok	2,138	5,709	11,564	16,549	(7.7)
For-hire trucks	—whole kingdom	3,148	6,469	10,638	19,894	(6.3)
	Bangkok	1,276	2,002	1,802	1,493	(1.2)
Motorcycles	—whole kingdom	1,352	7,661	22,289	87,444	(64.7)
	Bangkok	1,019	5,196	12,679	26,338	(25.8)
Total Vehicles	—all types[4]					
	whole kingdom	25,006	63,073	127,217	260,933	(10.4)
	Bangkok	14,797	36,207	70,908	108,792	(7.4)

Type of Vehicle	Bangkok Metropolitan Area as Percentage of Kingdom Total			
	1950	1955	1960	1964
Personal cars	87	84	79	80
Taxis	71	70	86	71
Buses	14	10	16	20
Private trucks	67	53	45	31
For-hire trucks	41	31	17	8
Motorcycles	75	68	57	30
Total motor vehicles	59	57	56	42

SOURCE: Statistical Yearbook, no. 22 (1945-55), p. 370; no. 24 (1963), p. 224; no. 26 (1965), p. 260.

[1] These data from the Police Department records differ somewhat from data of the Department of Highways; the principal difference appears to be in the understatement of buses (see 3 below). In the Highway Department data for 1964, there were a total of 23,500 buses in the kingdom (over twice the number reported here) of which 2,100 were in the Bangkok-Thonburi municipalities (approximately the same as reported here). Other differences for 1964 were:

	Whole Kingdom	Bangkok-Thonburi
Cars	73,700	58,800
(versus private + taxis, above	69,332	53,435)
Trucks	62,200	19,400
(versus private + for hire, above	73,150	18,042)

Table 16 — Motor Vehicle Registration, by Type and Location, 1950-1964 [1]
(cont'd)

[2] The decline after 1960 is apparently due to a reclassification in that year of *"samlors"* from taxis to "motorcycles" in subsequent years.

[3] Includes only motorbuses imported or constructed for purpose of public passenger transportation under conditions prescribed by the Transport Control Commission. Thus the figures are understated by the exclusion of the many "unofficial" conversions of small and large trucks to jitneys and mixed passenger and cargo vehicles.

[4] Includes, in addition to the above-mentioned, "other motor vehicles" and "motor tricycles."

Table 17 — The Railroad System, 1940-1965

Traffic	1940	1947	1950	1955	1960	1965
Route kilometers operated	3130	3272	3272	3377	3494	3598a
Passenger traffic						
Number of passengers (*millions*)	5.9	18.1	25.6	34.6	39.6	43.9
Passenger kilometers (*millions*)	337	1039	1436	2007	2353	2847
Average distance (*kilometers*)	57.1	57.4	56.1	58.0	58.9	64.8
Revenue freight traffic						
Tons of freight (*thousands*)	1498	858	2023	3153	3684	4435
Carload				2528	3089	3903
Less than carload				625	595	532
Ton-kilometers carload freight (*millions*)	459	224	480	778	1147	1534
Average haul per carload (*kilometers*)	n.a.	n.a.	n.a.	307	371	393
Percentage of total revenues accounted for by:						
Passengers	35	60	56	51	49	50a
Freight	59	38	39	45	47	46a

Composition of Carload Freight Traffic in 1964

Product	Tons Carried (*percentage*)	Revenue	Average Haul (*kilometers*)
Petroleum products	13.9	18.7	485
Rice products	14.4	15.8	482
Lumber, logs, and poles	8.1	11.2	528
Cement	5.6	6.6	480
Clinker and marl	21.9	4.7	64
Metal goods, machinery	1.8	2.7	497
Jute and kenaf	2.3	2.5	475
Livestock	0.8	2.3	409
Lignite	1.5	2.0	587
Maize	2.4	1.9	311
All other products	27.3	31.6	460

SOURCE: *Statistical Yearbook*, no. 22 (1945-55), pp. 328-35 and no. 26 (1965), pp. 249-50. State Railway of Thailand.

n.a.: not available.

aData are for 1964.

Table 18 — Domestic Air Traffic, 1948-1964

I. Routes and Passenger Traffic

Year	Regular Route Kilometers	Plane Kilometers Flown (thousands)	Passengers Number (thousands)	Passenger/ Kilometers (millions)	Average Journey (kilometers)
1948	4,090	485.3	10.1	5.3	525
1950	3,465	622.7	8.5	3.5	411
1952	3,850	1,018.9	21.1	9.3	440
1954	3,225	1,122.9	24.9	10.1	405
1956	3,615	1,243.4	40.8	15.6	382
1958	3,742	1,394.4	42.0	17.3	411
1960	3,562	1,008.7	39.5	16.3	412
1962	3,562	1,202.0	45.3	20.2	445
1964	5,587	1,585.6	55.8	26.5	474

II. Goods Traffic

Year	Tons	Cargo Ton/Kms. (thousands)	Average Haul	Tons	Mail Ton/Kms. (thousands)	Average Haul
1948	122	66.6	546	48	23.1	481
1950	142	60.6	426	37	16.6	448
1952	270	111.0	411	78	41.2	528
1954	334	102.9	308	74	38.0	513
1956	434	130.1	299	73	38.5	527
1958	594	185.9	313	76	44.3	583
1960	476	186.5	392	26	13.4	515
1962	597	252.2	422	30	16.3	543
1964	708	361.7	510	45	27.8	617

SOURCE: Statistical Yearbook, 1956-58, p. 414; 1965, p. 277.

Table 19 — Imports by Commodity Groups, Percentage Distribution of Value, 1950-1966

Year	Food	Bev., Tobacco	Crude Mater., Inedible	Mineral Fuels, Lub.	Animal, Veg. Oils, Fats	Chemicals	Mfgd. Goods	Mach., Transpt. Equip.	Misc. Mfgd. Arts.	Misc. Transact. & Commod.
1950	11.1	2.1	1.5	7.4	0.3	6.8	45.0	14.5	10.5	0.8
1955	8.8	2.1	1.0	9.2	0.4	7.7	36.8	18.4	12.2	3.3
1960	8.2	1.1	1.5	10.6	0.2	9.7	34.2	24.8	5.4	3.8
1962	6.6	1.3	1.8	10.8	0.2	10.3	33.7	27.4	4.9	3.2
1964	6.1	1.3	2.0	10.2	0.2	10.4	30.5	31.7	4.8	2.7
1966	8.6	3.4	2.0	9.1	0.1	13.6	24.9	27.3	8.3	2.7

SOURCE: *Statistical Yearbook*, various, and *Foreign Trade of Thailand 1966*.

167

Table 20 — Value of Imports by Country of Origin,
for the Four Leading Nations,[1] 1950-1966

Year	Total Imports[2]	Japan	U.S.A.	United Kingdom	West Germany[3]
		A. Absolute value in millions of baht			
1950	2,625	529	386	255	33
1952	5,525	1,025	1,096	888	237
1954	7,022	1,522	1,331	934	506
1956	7,655	1,267	1,175	877	462
1958	8,237	1,890	1,418	870	540
1960	9,622	2,463	1,604	967	811
1962 Total	11,504	3,357	1,951	1,024	828
Less: aid	227	11	142	21	10
Net of aid	11,277	3,346	1,809	1,003	818
1963 Total	12,803	4,074	2,184	1,139	888
Less: aid	646	9	458	12	21
Net of aid	12,157	4,065	1,726	1,127	867
1964 Total	14,253	4,704	2,301	1,326	1,093
Less: aid	405	21	282	16	8
Net of aid	13,848	4,683	2,019	1,310	1,085
1965 Total	16,185	5,200	3,015	1,506	1,550
Less: aid	1,215	143	939	19	11
Net of aid	14,970	5,057	2,076	1,487	1,539
1966 Total	25,347	6,744	9,136	1,539	1,458
Less: aid	7,336	194	6,478	33	23
Net of aid	18,011	6,550	2,658	1,506	1,425
		B. Percentage of total imports (excluding aid, 1962 on)			
	(Total of 4 countries)				
1950	45.8	20.1	14.7	9.7	1.3
1952	58.7	18.5	19.8	16.1	4.3
1954	61.1	21.7	18.9	13.5	7.2
1956	49.0	16.4	15.2	11.4	6.0
1958	57.3	22.9	17.2	10.6	6.6
1960	60.7	25.6	16.7	10.0	8.4
1962	61.9	29.7	16.0	8.9	7.3
1963	64.1	33.5	14.2	9.3	7.1
1964	65.7	33.8	14.6	9.5	7.8
1965	68.0	33.9	13.9	9.9	10.3
1966	67.5	36.4	14.8	8.4	7.9

Table 20 — Value of Imports by Country of Origin, for the Four Leading Nations,[1] (*cont'd*)

SOURCES: *Statistical Yearbook*, and *Foreign Trade of Thailand*, various years.
[1] Because of the increasing importance of foreign aid in recent years, the data for 1962-66 are shown gross and net of foreign aid. Data are by country of origin except for the years 1955-61 when the basis of collection was country of purchase.

Beginning in 1960, the four nations shown have been the most important sources of Thailand's imports. For 1950-1960, other nations (especially Hong Kong and Singapore) exceeded the United Kingdom and West Germany in value of imports in many years.
[2] Includes a small amount (2-3 percent of total value) of goods subsequently re-exported.
[3] Data before 1956 refer to Germany.

Table 21 — Changing Origins of Selected Imported Consumer Goods, 1956 and 1966

Item and Country of Origin	1956 Total Quantity	1956 Total Value (thousand baht)	1966 Total Quantity	1966 Total Value (thousand baht)
Passenger motor vehicles (*units*)	3,187	107,975	14,984	434,541
(Percentage distribution by leading countries)				
W. Germany	26.1	28.0	24.2	28.9
Japan	0.7	0.7	29.4	21.3
United Kingdom	31.1	26.7	14.4	13.2
Italy	10.0	7.3	13.5	12.2
U.S.A.	13.8	20.3	7.3	11.8
	(81.6)	(83.0)	(88.8)	(87.4)
Motorcycles (*units*)	7,492	26,638	76,321	247,629
(Percentage distribution by leading countries)				
Japan	0.9	1.2	94.5	92.0
Italy	17.3	19.2	2.7	4.3
W. Germany	41.6	37.2	2.6	3.1
	(59.8)	(57.6)	(99.8)	(99.4)
Tires for motor cars. All weights (*thous. of units*)	141	78,549	306	161,830
(Percentage distribution by leading countries)				
Japan	15.6	14.9	41.8	39.5
W. Germany	20.6	16.0	9.8	8.9
United Kingdom	21.3	23.6	6.5	6.2
	(57.5)	(54.5)	(58.1)	(54.6)
Radio receivers (*units*)	126,188	56,760	264,487	55,818
(Percentage distribution by leading countries)				
Japan	16.4	9.3	71.4	62.7
Netherlands	48.2	45.2	19.5	18.7
W. Germany	24.6	34.7	2.5	11.1
	(89.2)	(89.2)	(93.4)	(92.5)

Table 21 — Changing Origins of Selected Imported
Consumer Goods, 1956 and 1966 (cont'd)

Item and Country of Origin	1956		1966	
	Total Quantity	Total Value (thousand baht)	Total Quantity	Total Value (thousand baht)
Television receivers (units)	3,159	10,764	52,119	77,331
(Percentage distribution by leading countries)				
Japan	10.9	7.7	69.9	63.3
Netherlands	—	—	15.0	18.5
U.S.A.	89.1	89.9	1.3	2.3
Austria	—	—	8.3	8.5
	(100.0)	(97.6)	(94.5)	(92.6)
Wrist watches (units)	134,907	25,481	135,393	19,495
(Percentage distribution by leading countries)				
Japan	—	—	84.3	73.9
Switzerland	91.1	97.5	11.3	25.0
	(91.1)	(97.5)	(95.6)	(98.9)
Air conditioners	1,467	8,293	16,841	68,061
(Percentage distribution by leading countries)				
U.S.A.	93.0	88.9	93.0	92.2
Japan	0.1	0.1	2.8	3.8
Hong Kong	0.7	0.2	2.1	1.1
	(93.8)	(89.2)	(97.9)	(97.1)
Refrigerators and freezers	2,874	11,998	25,791	60,807
(Percentage distribution by leading countries)				
Italy	—	—	54.5	45.2
U.S.A.	61.8	70.8	14.5	29.3
Japan	0.7	0.4	19.4	14.1
	(62.5)	(71.2)	(88.4)	(88.6)
Soap, toilet and bath (tons)	330	6,733	156	5,259
(Percentage distribution by leading countries)				
United Kingdom	19.6	17.1	28.4	23.8
U.S.A.	57.1	45.5	26.9	22.2
France	2.4	9.9	8.9	20.0
Japan	6.4	5.5	10.8	14.0
	(85.5)	(78.0)	(75.0)	(80.0)

Table 21 — Changing Origins of Selected Imported
Consumer Goods, 1956 and 1966 *(cont'd)*

Item and Country of Origin	*1956*		*1966*	
	Total Quantity	*Total Value (thousand baht)*	*Total Quantity*	*Total Value (thousand baht)*
Dentifrices, all kinds and forms *(tons)*	441	18,885	342	6,023
	(Percentage distribution by leading countries)			
Japan	0.1	0.1	47.2	38.5
Taiwan	—	—	19.7	7.8
Hong Kong	13.3	8.2	19.2	27.7
W. Germany	0.6	0.4	12.1	21.0
United Kingdom	45.2	44.5	0.1	0.1
U.S.A.	25.4	35.2	1.2	4.2
Netherlands	14.0	10.2	0.2	0.2
	(98.6)	(98.6)	(99.7)	(99.5)
Toilet paper *(tons)*	70	897	1,626	14,795
	(Percentage distribution by leading countries)			
United Kingdom	59.6	62.5	36.9	44.6
Japan	—	—	37.5	32.3
U.S.A.	29.6	27.0	6.3	7.7
	(89.2)	(89.5)	(80.7)	(84.6)
Ball point pens and pencils *(units)*	164,560	1,549	20,233,923	13,488
	(Percentage distribution by leading countries)			
Italy	0.06	0.03	62.2	33.4
France	14.6	1.9	14.3	21.4
W. Germany	8.8	3.2	12.4	17.9
U.S.A	45.1	83.3	1.1	15.9
Hong Kong	21.6	7.7	0.5	0.6
	(90.1)	(96.1)	(90.5)	(89.2)

SOURCES: Thailand Department of Customs, *The Imports and Exports of Thailand, December 1956,* and *Foreign Trade of Thailand,* 1957 and 1966.
Note: Data for 1956 cover imports at the Port of Bangkok only, and report country of purchase rather than origin. For passenger motor vehicles only, data are for 1957 rather than 1956 and cover all ports.

Appendix B

The Siam Pen Company:
A Case Study in Sales Promotion Techniques

The Siam Pen Company:
A Case Study in Sales Promotion Techniques

The Siam Pen Co., Ltd. is a Thai subsidiary of a western manufacturer of mechanical pencils and ball-point pens. Until 1960, the company was engaged solely in the distribution of the imported product; in that year it began construction of a factory to assemble mechanical pencils using imported metal parts (point and mechanism) and locally made plastic casings. The company developed profitably; local management had substantial freedom to adapt imaginatively to market conditions, and the high literacy and heavy commitment to education of the Thai society were favorable factors. By 1967, The Siam Pen Co. was ready to launch an inexpensive ball-point pen, using local materials except for the metal point which was imported. The pen was to retail at 10 baht (50 cents U.S.). Competition from cheap imported pens was intense, especially in the Bangkok metropolitan area. One, with a clear plastic casing so that the ink supply was visible, retailed at 4 baht, and another with an opaque case sold at 6 baht; neither had the retractable point and pocket clip of the Siam Pen model. Other imported models from Japan and Europe were available in the market from 18 baht up; in the luxury market, imports from internationally known firms sold from 100 baht up.

Siam Pen has developed over the years a system of national distribution into every province. The base of the operation is the Bangkok plant, with no regional sales offices or warehouses. Trucks with a salesman/driver and helper remain a month or more in the field. Sales to retailers are for cash and to wholesalers on thirty-day credit. Along with the stock of pencils, the truck carries billboard and store display materials. As is typical in such lines,

---

Note: The company product has been altered to disguise this actual marketing plan.

replenishing of the truck stock is by common-carrier truck delivery, consigned to the driver in care of various hotels in the territory. In view of its well-developed coverage of the entire national market, the contacts of its salesmen/drivers with upcountry retailers of stationery supplies, and its reputation for a quality product, the Siam Pen Co. believed it could secure a third of the market, by units, in medium-priced ball-point pens within a year after introduction. Of course, much depended on the success of the promotion plan for introducing the new product.

The promotion plan as finally developed reflected the company's experience with earlier promotions, of which there had been about one a year, and the characteristics of the new product. The essence of the plan was a series of prizes, "something for everyone"—consumer, retailer, and wholesaler. For the consumer, an item of great acceptability throughout the country was selected—the Little Honda motor bike, worth 2,800 baht at retail or U.S. $140. A monthly lottery over a period of eight months would award ten motor bikes monthly, or a total of eighty bikes. Management was aware that the fact that the ink supply in its pen was not visible was a product weakness in the local market, since some retailers are not above using a product prior to sale. For example, aerosol dispensers without seals which are destroyed when opened (as in imported shaving cream and deodorants), are subject to substantial abuse in Thai retailing. Therefore, a protective cap had been devised for the pen with an identifying seal which had to be torn on removal. This protection against prior use, along with the retracting point and pocket clip, were the pen's features which were stressed in an advertising of product characteristics. For this contest, the consumer qualified for the monthly drawing by mailing or presenting a torn protective cap and seal.

For distributors, a group of prizes was established which had resale value and which ranged from large to small items so that wholesalers and retailers of widely varying size and turnover would all qualify for some prize. The unit of sale to the retailer was a box containing 12 pens, while at the wholesale level, a carton contained 12 boxes or 144 pens. For the promotion, prizes were valued by flaps from the boxes and by coupons, one of which was inserted in each carton. These prizes, which were calculated at a retail value of about 2 percent of the value of the pens sold, were as follows:

Wholesaler's Participation:

Item	Retail Value (baht)	No. of Coupons
Wrist watch, gentleman's	975	45
Wrist watch, ladies	675	32
Electric table fan	500	25
36 unbreakable plastic beakers	126	6
24 bars Lifebuoy soap	24	1
2 plastic ice buckets	20	1

Retailer's Participation:

Item	Retail Value (baht)	No. of Flaps
Cutlery set (for eight)	200	70
12 tubes Ipana toothpaste	150	52
Ronson Comet gas lighter	125	45
12 unbreakable plastic beakers	42	15
24 bars Lifebuoy soap	24	7
12 pencils (in box)	12	4

It was anticipated that many distributors would simply add their prizes to their stock of goods for sale; consequently, the use of the company's ball-point pens as prizes was avoided because of possible adverse effects on the price structure. Introductory packages of pens in quantities which corresponded to normal orders of retailers were sold at regular price, and inducement to buy was the inclusion of fifteen, thirty, or more free shopping bags. Such bags are highly valued by distributors who sell or use them as gifts to customers. They are made of stiff paper or plastic with reinforced cutout handles, imprinted with Siam Pen advertising, and cost the company the equivalent of 1.7 cents in paper and 15 cents in plastic (imported from Hong Kong).

Advertising of the new pen and the promotion consisted of: introductory letters to wholesalers (written in Chinese and in Thai in parallel columns); the imprinted paper and plastic bags; three-sided hanging mobiles and decals to be placed in each retail outlet as a condition of the free offer of shopping bags; billboard ads in a few selected locations, newspaper advertising in Bangkok and nine upcountry towns throughout the eight-month promotion period; and national radio, thirty- and sixty-second spots, six times daily through the first seven months.

The total cost of the promotion was distributed in percentages as follows:

Prizes	Percentage of Total Cost
Consumers—80 motor bikes	24
Retailers	17
Wholesalers	9
Shopping bags (for retailers)	4
	54

Advertising	
Radio	16
Newspaper	11
Poster, store displays	8
	35

Other	
Entry blanks, leaflets, direct mail	9
Salesmen's incentive prizes	1
Police permit for lottery	1
	11

The promotion was successfully concluded and the pen well launched in the market. However, developments in Thai marketing while the promotion was in progress suggested that this type of program could not have been successfully carried out a year later. Prize contests for consumers became widely used during the period of the Siam Pen eight-month promotion, some promotions were suspected of dishonesty, and police permission for such lottery-type drawings became increasingly difficult to obtain. Also during this period, the government prohibited radio commercials upcountry under the suspicion that they were being used surreptitiously to convey guerrilla propaganda. Finally, the Siam Pen Co. concluded it should restudy its use of outdoor poster advertising affixed to fences and building walls. Again, this media had become so popular that the company might get only a half-hour's exposure before another advertiser came along and covered up its message with theirs.

Appendix C

Measuring Public Opinion:
"Quantifying Thai Opinions"

Quantifying Thai Opinions

by Frederic L. Ayer

The Thai people are justifiably world famous for their cheerful courtesy. The inbred abhorrence of being the cause of anyone's displeasure or discomfort gives some credence to the ages-old and often repeated story of a stranger travelling on foot from Bangkok to Chiengmai, some 900 kilometers to the North. On reaching one of the ancient capitals about half-way between the two cities, he became confused in the market place and started back along the road by which he had arrived. Not sure of his direction, he asked a local inhabitant, "Is this the way to Chiengmai?" Seeing that the stranger was heading in the opposite direction, the villager could not bear to offend him by implying that such a grand and wealthy person could be wrong, and replied, "Certainly, sir." Continuing on the way but still somewhat unsure, he asked again and received the same reply. To verify this, he further questioned, "How far is it?" "Very far" was the response.

Whether or not this tale has been exaggerated over the years of being told, it is illustrative of two characteristics of Thai culture which bedevil the opinion researcher: an inherent courtesy bias and a reluctance to commit oneself to a statement of fact which may later prove to be untrue or inaccurate. Some of the earliest modern public opinion research work was done in Thailand in the mid '50's in connection with an industrial trade fair. The sponsors, eager to correct any deficiencies, commissioned a survey designed, among other things, to disclose dissatisfactions experienced by the

Reproduced with permission from *United Asia-International Magazine of Afro-Asian Affairs* (Bombay), Nov.-Dec. 1964, vol. 16, no. 6 (Special number on Thailand).

visitor. They found, according to the survey, glowing satisfaction expressed by the Thai, and the only criticisms coming from the foreigners . . . yet most of the exhibit presentations were in English, understood with difficulty by the majority of the Thai visitors, who had privately been disturbed by this but who would never say so to a stranger.

In nine years of experimenting with various kinds of research requiring the assessment of local opinion, the author has come to the conclusion that courtesy bias is not an insurmountable obstacle but requires only careful attention to questionnaire design and question framing. Once it is accepted by the researcher that courtesy bias exists and the respondent hates to offend it is relatively easy to ask questions so that his answer cannot be construed as offensive. Often this is as simple as introducing the questions with an explanation of the importance of critical answers to the research sponsor, and expressing his eager desire for the "true" reply. Sometimes it may involve the conscious introduction of a negative bias in the question, or an inverted ranking scale where all alternatives are conceded to be "good," but some are "not so good as others." Results can easily be interpreted by ranking from "best" to "worst."

A much knottier problem is that of inducing precise answers, particularly in respect to reasons for opinions or preferences. A Thai respondent is quick to express his preference for "A" over "B" but when asked why he likes it or what is better about it, he is inclined to reply, "Because I like it," and "I don't like "B" as well as "A." The usual expressions for time and distance are almost always vague and lack the precision required if one is to utilize answers in tabular form. The expression for "a long time ago" can mean anything from one hour to 500 years past . . . and more often than not the context in which the term is used provides no clue. On the other hand the Thai term meaning roughly "in a moment" is applicable for any period from a few seconds to 24 hours. In determining biographic data for respondents in up-country areas particularly, it is easy to find out that a person was born on Monday at 9:56 a.m. in the Year of the Dog, for these are important to astrological predictions, but the month and date of birth may be completely unknown, and with older people, it may be impossible to determine which of the twelve-year cycles was responsible for their Year of the Dog birth.

Nearly related to the above is the difficulty that many Thai people have in dealing with abstractions which, of course, include many opinions and attitudes. Questions of the order, "How do you feel about the idea of. . . ?" are likely to be greeted with a blank look and no response. Cross-cultural research poses its own problems, not completely restricted to language translation. Concepts which can be expressed by a single word in English may require a complete explanation and definition in Thai, and conversely a question may be answered by a single word in Thai which requires a long description in English. For instance, a farmer in a small Thai village expressed some disappointment that a foreign-aid official who had visited his recently, had not noticed that the village needed a new water supply. When an interviewer, in probing this dissatisfaction, asked if he had called the deficiency to the official's attention, he said he could not because he felt *kreng-chai*. In Thailand where vertical status is extremely important in the social structure and is clearly defined, the single word *kreng-chai* describes the emotional syndrome experienced in the presence of a person of higher status than oneself, when one is critical of this higher person's actions or attitudes but cannot show this for fear of offending him, or of appearing to be impolite in his eyes. The usual translation of embarrassment fails completely to do it justice.

The Thai politeness works in favour of the researcher when it comes to obtaining interviews, however. A refusal rate of above one or two per cent is highly unusual, and where Western interviewer training emphasizes methods of getting into a house for an interview, Thai interviewers need extensive training on polite methods of getting out after the interview is finished. It is not unknown for an interviewer to spend two or three hours on a fifteen minute questionnaire, unable to decline gracefully the hospitality of the respondent. Even the few refusals are likely to be continued postponements, especially with those of upper socio-economic status, so that while the prospective respondent never flatly turns down the interview, no appointment convenient to both interviewer and respondent can ever be made within reasonable field work scheduling limitations.

As with most of the industrially developing nations, much of the social and public opinion research work is somewhat limited in scope because of the lack of definitive or complete statistics from public sources. Thailand is fortunate in having an unusually complete population census for the year 1960, and the National Statistical Office is conducting and publishing a series of special enumerations in the interim period before the next full census in 1970. Published to date have been a Household Expenditure Survey for a sample of 1,000 Bangkok households, and an Agricultural and Land Use Survey covering all farm operations in 1963 throughout the country. An Industrial Census is now in process, as is a survey of Tourist Expenditure. The Department of Customs maintains and publishes a complete record of imports and exports, and the National Statistical Office publishes a quarterly Bulletin of selected statistics from a variety of government sources.

Much of the other material available from public sources, however, is subject to considerable and unpredictable collection error, and it is impossible to estimate with any accuracy how much has been omitted or reported only by estimate, yet some of the reported figures have continued to be used as bases for other research. The Bureau of Psychological and Educational Research of Chulalongkorn University discovered in 1958, for example, that the birthweight norms used by most of Bangkok's obstetricians were compiled in 1932 by one obstetrician from some 200 babies born in one hospital in a single year. All hospitals in Bangkok had been recording birthweights and lengths for many years, but the statistics had never been compiled.

With such basic demographic information often lacking, it is to be expected that there is also a complete dearth of past research studies on human attitudes, opinions, and behavior, so that opinion research now conducted must necessarily report only what obtains at present, without any attempt to relate it to past conditions.

With such lack of up-to-date basic statistics, it might be assumed that numerous sampling problems would occur. In practice, this has not been a serious problem. It is obviously impracticable to develop valid stratified sample designs, since there are few reliable universe data from which to determine the allocations to the various strata, simple random start, fixed take samples of people are rarely possible, for existing lists or files of the pertinent population are either not in existence, are hopelessly out of date, or are inaccurate. An example is one listing of certain respondents in Bangkok by a foreign government department which assured the research agency that its records were complete to the end of the month preceding a scheduled survey. An accurate sampling of this directory revealed fourteen per cent moved to up-country addresses, five per cent abroad, one per cent deceased, and six per cent unlocatable within a six-week period of investigation—a quarter of the universe thus erroneously listed.

On the other hand, Thailand is fortunate in having complete and precise map coverage of almost all of the Kingdom, and although maps for some sections of the country have not been revised for more than ten years, and some villages are somewhat misplaced or have moved en masse since the mapping date, on the whole these provide a solid base for area probability samples. Maps of the major towns and the capital city show in accurate detail the exact location and type of construction of dwelling units, commercial and government buildings and other structures. Since streets and footpaths often follow an irregular pattern, and probably three-quarters of the buildings in Bangkok do not have a street frontage, these maps are invaluable in selecting sampling units and ensuring that samples conform to the basic principle of each unit's having an equal probability of being chosen, regardless of its location or accessibility.

Procedural difficulties are not the only ones encountered by the public opinion researcher in this country. While on the whole, the value of research is recognized and applauded by government agencies, commercial enterprises and other institutions—in principle—this is not always the case in fact. There exists an attitude far too prevalent, that it may be better to know nothing than to have solid proof of an unpleasant fact. In one study a few years ago, the interview schedule included one or two questions aimed at ascertaining what knowledge university students had of various political systems. Authorities required deletion of categories dealing with Communism and Socialism, on the grounds that if a significant proportion of students were found to be conversant with Communist tenets, this would look bad for the educational system. Implied, but not expressed, was the idea that concrete evidence of such a situation would require some kind of action. Actually, a similar study run under different auspices about the same period showed conclusively that students at that time knew practically nothing about the subject which was a matter of such concern to the authorities.

A similar attitude is encountered in commercial sponsorship, where a businessman may feel he is wasting money to sponsor research which proves his decisions are correct, and refuses to believe research results which may indicate his decisions have not been of the best. With so many deterrents, can public opinion research be profitably undertaken, and can valid results be obtained? The answer can only be an emphatic "Yes!"

Adaptations of methodology to the local situation can be and are being made. Relatively low labour costs make it feasible to design precise samples on an area-probability basis, and to maintain a supervisor for teams of as few as five interviewers. Travel costs in general are reasonable enough that it is not prohibitive in cost to send trained teams from the capital city to any area of the country to conduct interviews, thus not requiring reliance on a remote field crew under practically no home-office control. In Bangkok, we find it completely feasible to require interviewers to report daily to the Study Director, and their completed interview schedules are edited on the spot and in their presence by a supervisor. Omissions and errors are quickly detected, and can be corrected or supplemented by re-interviews within time limits practical to study requirements. The same circumstances permit the field verification by supervisory personnel of as much as one-third of the reported interviews—an impossibly high figure for many other countries.

In questionnaire design, conscientious workmanship, a sound knowledge of the Thai culture, and a fair sprinkling of inspiration combine to develop lines of questioning which can eiicit most of the opinions and attitudes for which measurement is desired. Questions framed in Thai, with full understanding of the study objectives, can lead a respondent to an abstract generalization, even if he does not appear to have the requisite vocabulary; or a series of questions can establish a concrete response pattern from which the analyst can make the generalization.

In one study we found that village people in a remote area had words for only the colours black, white, green, yellow, and red, yet probing revealed that they could distinguish such colours as orange, blue, and purple. Questions concerning colour preference thus had to be phrased to include such expressions as "grass-green" and "sky-green," and "faded-work-clothes-black." Fairly short questions may follow one or two paragraphs of explanatory introduction, couched in concrete terms about things or experiences which are part of the respondent's daily life.

Formal questioning of some unsophisticated groups may be completely out of the question, but an interviewer with an "interview guide" or check-list can meet in a bull session with a small group of four or five people and inject his questions at appropriate times during the conversation, unobtrusively checking off his records as he receives direct replies, and interpreting indirect answers to other areas on his schedule from the context. Such procedures are often purely qualitative, but when carried out with a proper sample of such groups, can be effectively and accurately quantified within predictable limits of sampling error.

Even though the culture may be occasionally radically different from Western culture patterns, the principles of human behavior remain the same, and the same principles of interpersonal contact apply, even though the manifestation may be shown in other ways. It is often virtually impossible to obtain an interview in privacy, since neither physical surroundings nor patterns of living are conducive to any person's being all alone. Culture standards do, however, inhibit a person lower on the status scale from interrupting or interfering with the conduct or conversation of his superior. This works to the advantage of the researcher when the subject of his interview is the highest status person present, but can be a detriment if the chosen respondent is outranked by some one else on the interview site.

One solution to this situation has proven practicable: to enlist the assistance of the high status person present in conducting other interviews with other respondents—the results of which are charged off to expendiency and examined for interest only. But the interview for the record has been accomplished without the restricting presence of higher authority.

Attention must be paid to status differentials as well in selecting and assigning interviewers. If the differential is too great, the interview will seldom be successful. An assistant lecturer from a university may be unable to obtain satisfactory replies from an illiterate farmer, and a university student may not be able to probe effectively open-ended questions directed to a Cabinet Minister. Many well-educated people make poor interviewers, because they cannot even temporarily suppress their own status-consciousness while talking with people of limited education and means, and thus cannot gain effective rapport. Some of the most successful interviewers are young men of rural origin, who have attained vocational or technical training school certificates in the city. They find it easy to adapt themselves to respondents either above or below them in social status. Girls of the same general background have proved exceptionally successful in interviewing high government and business officials.

The best measure of the practicality of measuring public opinion in Thailand is the extent to which it is being done. In 1955 not one full scale public opinion research project had ever been carried out in the Kingdom. In 1964 there are three private commercial research agencies devoting a major share of their time to studies of this kind, and at least five academic institutes, departments, or faculties each carrying out several projects annually. Recently the National Research Council, a division of the Thai

Government, has established an independent organization devoted to social research, which is scheduled to allocate much of its efforts to the opinion area.

In spite of some inherent limitations, and deficiencies in basic information which are rapidly being made up, Thai public opinion can be measured, is being measured, and effective quantification accomplished.

Appendix D

Selections from
Thailand's Economic Development Plans
Which Relate to Marketing Development

Selections from Thailand's Economic Development Plans Which Relate to Marketing Development

I *The First Economic Development Plan, 1961-66*

Except for agricultural marketing, including the stimulation of cooperatives and improvement of warehousing, the First Plan provided for no development expenditures specifically for the commerce sector. In the statement of overall economic policy, a section entitled "Improvement of Merchandising Methods" set the objectives of price stabilization and grading of agricultural products, promotion of exports and of cooperatives, and

"(4) Promote commercial interest among the Thai people

(5) Maintain as much competition as possible among producers and distributors."

In the statement of proposed implementation steps ("VII Commerce") except for those concerned with agricultural marketing, cooperatives, and warehousing, only the following were mentioned:

Item 2: "General commercial activities are to be left in private hands."

Item 6: (6) "To provide loans on an installment basis to various small retailers. This is to encourage the Thai people to enter into business more and more."

(Quotations from unofficial translation of the Plan reproduced in Mayer 1962.)

II *The Second National Economic and Social Development Plan, 1967-1971*
Chapter XIII—Development of Commerce and Services

1) The development of commerce in Thailand is an important factor in raising the standard of living of the people, in generating revenue

191

for the government, and in accelerating the growth of the economy as a whole. Since Thailand is still basically an agricultural economy, domestic consumption and the export of agricultural products are important to the economic welfare of the country. In this respect, an efficient and freely functioning commercial system, with equitable treatment for those who are engaged in the production and distribution of goods and services, is necessarily a primary force in the economic development of the country.

2) At present there are approximately 20,300 registered business firms in the country. The rate of increase in number has been on the average about 9 percent per annum. In addition to the registered firms, there are numerous unregistered business establishments in the Bangkok-Thon Buri area and the provinces. Most of these are small retailers, and research is being conducted to obtain reliable data and information on them. The rate of growth in the number of firms is expected to continue. The government intends actively to promote the development of an efficient commercial system, so as to facilitate the flow and the exchange of goods within the domestic market and as exports to overseas markets. Encouragement will also be given to greater participation by Thai nationals in commercial and service activities.

3) The growth of external trade has been phenomenal during the First Plan period. From 1961 to 1965, exports increased from 9,997 to 12,941 million baht and imports from 10,287 to 16,185 million baht. Equipment and other types of capital items accounted for over one fourth of total import value. This relatively large percentage reflects the dependence of capital formation on imports. Chapter Five explains that the rapid increase and the absolute size of capital goods imports have not created balance of payments problems because of the increased receipts from invisible items and the inflow of private capital and foreign assistance.

4) The services sector [private transportation, construction, and tourism] has experienced a rapid rate of growth in the past few years. Most of the activities in this sector are undertaken by private efforts and initiative. In consultation with the private sector, the government will seek to assist the development of this sector so as to ensure steady growth and to promote healthy competition within the sector and vis-à-vis other sectors.

Policy Objectives

5) The Government will seek to create an orderly and efficient commercial system and to promote healthy competition so as to enable the commercial sector to serve the public interest more fully. Subsidiary objectives are to promote exports and to encourage wider participation by Thai nationals in commercial and service activities. To achieve these objectives, the government will:

(i) Promote healthy and orderly competition in private commercial activities, so as to secure equitable treatment for the producers, the distributors, and the consumers.

(ii) Discourage monopolistic trade practices and cartels which are contrary to the best interests of producers or consumers.

(iii) Develop and promote export trade so as to achieve growth in terms of export volume and value, as well as diversification of export products.

(iv) Maintain price stability for both industrial and consumer goods, so as to prevent harmful increases in the cost of living.

(v) Support and stabilize the domestic price level of important export commodities, such as rice, and other agricultural and industrial products, in order to provide equitable treatment for the producers, the distributors, and the consumers of the country.

(vi) Encourage Thai nationals to participate more fully in commercial and service activities by designing new and more effective measures than in the past.

(vii) Issue and enforce standard and quality specifications for import and export products.

(viii) Promote the tourist industry in Thailand.

(ix) Encourage private initiative and employment in the service sector.

[Items 6-16 omitted, which specify export targets for individual crops and products.]

Development of Commerce

17) Total government expenditures on the development of commerce during the Second Plan period will amount to 180 million baht, financed entirely from the government budget. Programmes will be implemented for market expansion, market research, and price stabilization.

18) In a programme of market expansion, the Government will:

(i) Study and analyze domestic and foreign market situations in order to design measures to assist domestic producers in the marketing of their products. Special efforts will be made to expand the volume and value of exports in new overseas markets. Furthermore, marketing advisory services will be made available to agricultural and industrial producers.

(ii) Promote consumer preference for Thai products in the domestic and overseas markets by means of participation in domestic and international trade exhibitions and by sending trade missions abroad.

(iii) Promote the export of Thai products by organizing an efficient export system and by discouraging competitive price cutting among exporters when it is contrary to the best interests of the country. Exporters will be encouraged to meet their export commitments, and quality standards will be specified and maintained.

(iv) Encourage Thai nationals to participate more effectively in commerce through the provision of educational facilities in business administration and marketing advisory services.

(v) Improve the marketing system so as to give agricultural producers a fair share of the retail price paid by the consumers.

(vi) Encourage the establishment of an efficient warehousing system throughout the country in order to reduce the costs of distribution.

19) In a programme of market research and forecasting, the Government will provide technical assistance to the nation's marketing system by conducting market studies of the major domestic products. Marketing facts and intelligence will be made available to producers and distributors so as to enable them to make their business decisions on as sound a basis as possible.

20) The objective of the price support programme is to stabilize the prices of basic agricultural commodities, such as rice, so as to benefit both producers and consumers. At the same time, the Government will improve the wholesale and retail price indices as well as the cost of living index, in order to assist the formulation of economic policy and the consideration of price stabilization measures.

[Items 21-30 omitted, which concern private transport services, construction and tourism.]

Problems and Future Outlook

31) Policies and measures for the development of Thailand's commerce and services are based on the desire to encourage the growth of a strong and healthy free enterprise system. The Government's role is not one of regulation, but of assistance to the private sector, particu-

larly in the provision of technical assistance and the solution of critical problems and the bottlenecks in commerce and services. The key problems and the proposed solutions are as follow:

32) The existing disorder and inefficiency in Thailand's commercial system have resulted in unnecessarily high marketing and production costs. This facilitates the exploitation of rural agricultural producers by the middlemen and commodity speculators, as well as creating economic losses for the country as a whole. To improve the functioning of the marketing system, the Government will take the necessary measures, including the revision of existing laws and regulations and the introduction of new legislation in fields, such as that of company law, where there is lack of coverage. Reorganization of government agencies responsible for the administration of commercial laws and for the collection and distribution of commercial intelligence will also be effected, particularly at the provincial and regional level.

33) Quality control and improved standardization of production will strengthen the reputation of Thai exports in foreign markets. During the Second Plan the Government will take steps to implement suitable export regulations in order to assure better quality of export products.

34) Lack of capital and the inability to obtain prime locations for retail activities have so far been the main obstacles to a more active participation by Thai nationals in commercial occupations. The Government will coordinate inter-ministerial efforts to overcome this problem.

35) Coordination among government agencies at the planning and the operations levels will become increasingly necessary in order to give effect to policies which cut across ministerial responsibilities; for example, the policy to encourage farmers to take a more active role in the marketing of their products will directly involve the Ministry of Agriculture and the Ministry of Economic Affairs.

36) In a longer perspective, the growth of the commerce and service sectors will be inevitably tied to the growth of the economy as a whole. As the measures to eliminate monopolistic and other unhealthy trade practices become more effective, an orderly and competitive commercial system will become a prime force in economic development.

Second Plan Development Projects Financed by Budgetary Appropriation—Commerce and Services Sector

(millions of baht)

Projects	1967	1968	1969	1970	1971	Total	
Ministry of Economic Affairs							
1) Export Promotion	29.2	18.5	18.1	18.1	18.0	101.9	(U.S. $5,095,000)
a. Organization of the export system	—	1.5	1.5	1.5	1.5	6.0	
b. Protection and expansion of overseas markets	—	1.9	2.0	2.0	1.9	7.8	
c. Promotion of the export of manufactured products	—	2.5	2.0	2.0	2.0	8.5	
d. Internal and external trade exhibitions	29.2[1]	12.6	12.6	12.6	12.6	79.6	
2) Marketing Research	—	3.0	2.2	2.4	2.6	10.2	(U.S. $510,000)
3) Promotion of Thai Nationals in Commercial Activities	2.2	7.0	6.0	6.0	6.0	27.2	(US. $1,360,000)
a. Loans for commercial activities	2.2	5.0	5.0	5.0	5.0	22.2	
b. Marketing service for small commercial establishments	—	2.0	1.0	1.0	1.0	5.0	
4) Price Support for Paddy[2]	—	10.0	10.0	10.0	10.0	40.0	
Total	31.4	38.5	36.3	36.5	36.6	179.3	

[1] Including 21.1 million baht for First Asian International Trade Fair.
[2] May be expended on farmers' assistance.

The First and Second Plan Public Development Expenditures by Sectors
(millions of baht)

Sector	Estimated Actual Expenditures 1961-1966	%	Planned Expenditures 1967-1971	%
Agriculture	3,900	13.9	11,310	19.8
Industry and Mining	2,340	8.3	915	1.6
Transport and Communications	7,360	26.1	17,000	29.7
Energy	4,740	16.8	4,970	8.6
Commerce	—	—	180	0.3
Community Facilities and Social Welfare	5,560	19.7	10,270	17.8
Public Health	1,060	3.8	2,570	4.5
Education	2,080	7.4	6,605	11.5
Unallocated	1,140	4.0	3,550	6.2
Total	28,180	100.0	57,520	100.0

SOURCE: National Economic Development Board, "The Second National Economic and Social Development Plan (1967-1971)," mimeographed, pp. 59, 241-52.

Bibliography
and
List of References Cited

Abbott, J. C. 1968. Marketing issues in agricultural development planning. In *Markets and marketing in developing economies*, eds. R. Moyer and S. C. Hollander, pp. 87-116. Homewood, Ill.: Richard D. Irwin.

Adelman, I., and Morris, C. T. 1967. *Society, politics and economic development: A quantitative approach.* Baltimore: Johns Hopkins Press.

_____. 1968. An econometric model of socioeconomic and political change in undeveloped countries. *American Economic Review* 58:1184-1218.

Andreski, S. 1968. *The African predicament: A study in the pathology of modernisation.* London: Michael Joseph.

Andrews, J. M. 1935. *Siam, second rural economic survey, 1934-1935.* Bangkok: Bangkok Times Press.

Area handbook for Thailand. 1968. Foreign Area Studies of the American University. Washington, D.C.: USGPO. DA Pamph. no. 550-53.

Artamonoff, G. L. 1965. State owned enterprises of Thailand. Mimeographed. Bangkok: U.S. Operations Mission to Thailand, Agency for International Development.

Ayal, E. B. 1963. Value systems and economic development in Japan and Thailand. *Journal of Social Issues* XIX:35-51.

Bangkok Bank. 1967. *Monthly review.* August.

Bangkok Post. 1968. *Central Department Store.* Special Supplement. April 12.

Bangkok World. 1967. *Highways in Thailand.* Special Supplement. Bangkok: World Press Co.

_____. 1968. *Central Department Store.* Special Supplement. Bangkok: World Press Co. April 12.

Bartels, R., ed. 1963. *Comparative marketing: Wholesaling in fifteen countries.* Homewood, Ill.: Richard D. Irwin.

Bauer, P. T. 1954. *West African trade.* Cambridge: Cambridge Univ. Press.

_____, and Yamey, B. 1957. *The economics of underdeveloped countries.* Chicago: Univ. of Chicago Press.

199

Benedict, R. 1952. *Thai culture and behavior. An unpublished war-time study, dated September 1943.* Ithaca: Cornell Univ., Southeast Asia Program, Data Paper no. 4, February.

Blanchard, W. et al. 1958. *Thailand: Its people, its culture.* New Haven: Human Relations Area Files, Country Survey Series, HRAF Press.

Boyd, H. W., Jr.; Iffland, C. P.; Gibson, D. M. T.; Travis, L. A.; Wadia, M. S., eds. 1966. *Marketing management: Cases from the emerging countries.* Reading, Mass.: Addison Wesley Publishing Co.

Business Research, Ltd. 1966. *Bangkok profile: Selected characteristics of households in Bangkok and Thonburi.* Bangkok, September.

Cady, J. F. 1966. *Thailand, Burma, Laos, and Cambodia.* Englewood Cliffs, N.J.: Prentice-Hall.

Caldwell, J. C. 1967. The demographic structure. In *Thailand: Social and economic studies in development,* ed. T. H. Silcock, pp. 27-44. Canberra: Australian National Univ. Press.

Campbell, J. G. D. 1902. *Siam in the twentieth century. Being the experience and impressions of a British official.* London: Edward Arnold.

Collis, M. 1936. *Siamese White.* London: Faber and Faber. Paperbound ed. 1965.

Corden, W. M. 1967. The exchange rate system and taxation of trade. In *Thailand: Social and economic studies in development,* ed. T. H. Silcock, pp. 151-69. Canberra: Australian National Univ. Press.

Coughlin, R. J. 1960. *Double identity: The Chinese in modern Thailand.* Hong Kong Univ. Press and Oxford Univ. Press.

Crawfurd, J. 1915. *The Crawford papers. Journal of an embassy from the Governor-General of India to the courts of Siam and Cochin-China.* Bangkok: Vajiranana National Library.

Dewey, A. G. 1962. *Peasant marketing in Java.* Glencoe: Free Press.

de Young, J. E. 1955. *Village life in modern Thailand.* Third printing 1963. Berkeley and Los Angeles: Univ. of California Press.

Drucker, P. 1958. Marketing in economic development. *Journal of Marketing* XXII:252-59.

Dunn, S. W. ed. 1964. *International handbook of advertising.* New York: McGraw Hill Book Co.

Ebasco Services, Inc. 1963. *Report on the feasibility of manufacturing electric appliances in Thailand.* New York: Report prepared for the United States Operations Mission to Thailand and the Ministry of Industry and the Board of Investment of Thailand. February.

Embree, J. F. 1950. Thailand—A loosely structured social system. *American Anthropologist* 52:181-93.

Exell, F. K. 1960. *The land and people of Thailand.* London: Adam and Charles Black; New York: Macmillan.

Fforde, J. S. 1957. *An international trade in managerial skills.* Oxford: Basil Blackwell.

Freyn, H. 1961. Culture and economics in Thailand. *Far Eastern Economic Review,* January 12, pp. 48-49, 52-53.

Friedman, J. 1967. Regional planning and nation-building: An agenda for international research. *Economic Development and Cultural Change* 16:119-29.

Ginsburg, N. 1961. *Atlas of economic development*. Univ. of Chicago Press.

Golay, F. H.; Anspach, R.; Pfanner, M. R.; and Ayal, E. B. 1969. *Under-development and economic nationalism in Southeast Asia*. Ithaca: Cornell Univ. Press.

Goldsen, R. K., and Ralis, M. 1957. *Factors related to acceptance of innovations in Bang Chan, Thailand*. Ithaca: Cornell Univ. Southeast Asia Program, Data Paper no. 25, June.

Graham, H., and Graham, J. 1957. *Some changes in Thai family life*. Bangkok: Institute of Public Administration, Thammasat Univ.

Graham, W. A. 1912, 1924. *Siam: a handbook of practical commercial and political information*, 2 vols. London: A. Moring.

Hanks, L. M., and Hanks, J. R. 1963. Thailand: Equality between the sexes. In *Women in the new Asia*, ed. B. E. Ward, pp. 428-51. Paris: UN Educational, Scientific, and Cultural Organization.

Hayden, H. 1967. *Higher education and development in South-East Asia*, vol. I. Director's Report. Paris: UNESCO and the International Association of Universities.

Hirsch, L. 1961. *Marketing in an underdeveloped economy: The North Indian sugar industry*. Englewood Cliffs, N.J.: Prentice Hall.

Hon-Chan, C. 1964. *The development of British Malaya 1896-1909*. Kuala Lumpur: Oxford Univ. Press.

IBRD. 1959. *A public development program for Thailand*. Baltimore: Johns Hopkins Press.

————. The current economic position and prospects of Thailand. Report no. FE-53b, 19 May 1966. Mimeographed.

Ingram, J. C. 1955. *Economic change in Thailand since 1850*. Stanford: Stanford Univ. Press.

International Research Associates. 1966. *The new Far East: Seven nations of Asia*. Survey for Readers Digest Far East, Ltd. Tokyo: Charles Tuttle.

Jones, J. H. 1964. *Economic benefits from development roads in Thailand*. Bangkok: SEATO Graduate School of Engineering, Technical Note no. 15, 15 April.

————, and Orr, J. A. 1966. *Exploratory study of economic effects of selected village roads in northeast Thailand*. Bangkok: SEATO Graduate School of Engineering, Technical Note no. 25, 30 June.

Kirsch, A. T. 1962. Buddhism, sex-roles, and the Thai economy. Mimeographed. Bangkok.

Klausner, W. J. 1966. Ceremonies and festivals in a northeastern Thai village. *Bangkok Social Science Review* 4:1-11.

Kraft, R. J. 1968. *Student background and university admission*. Publication no. 6, Education in Thailand Series. Bangkok: Ministry of Education, with the Institute for International Studies in Education, Michigan State University.

Kunkel, J. H. 1965. Values and behavior in economic development. *Economic Development and Cultural Change* 13:257-77.

Lerner, D. 1958. *The passing of traditional society: Modernizing the Middle East*. New York: The Free Press. Paperbound ed. 1964, with an introduction by David Reisman.

Liander, B.; Terpstra, V.; Yoshino, M. Y.; and Sherbini, A. A. 1967. *Comparative analysis for international marketing.* Boston: Allyn and Bacon for the Marketing Science Institute.

Litchfield, Whiting, Bourne & Associates. 1960. *Greater Bangkok plan.* Bangkok: Thai Ministry of Interior.

Liu, G. V. 1967. The overseas Chinese now: Wanderers no more. *The Asia Magazine,* 12 March 1967, pp. 3-8.

Longhurst, H. 1956. *The Borneo story: The history of the first 100 years of trading in the Far East by the Borneo Company, Limited.* London: Newman Neame.

McGee, T. G. 1967. *The southeast Asian city: A social geography of the primate cities of southeast Asia.* New York: Frederick A. Praeger.

Mayer, P. A. 1962. *Thailand—A market for U.S. products.* Washington, D.C.: U.S. Department of Commerce.

Ministry of Agriculture, Division of Agricultural Economics. 1964. *Marketing margins and marketing channels of major agricultural commodities and livestock in the northeastern region of Thailand, 1963-1964.* Bangkok.

Ministry of National Development. 1966. *Thailand Facts and Figures, 1966.* Bangkok.

Mitani, K. 1968. Key factors in the development of Thailand. In *Economic development issues: Greece, Israel, Taiwan, Thailand.* Supplementary Paper no. 25, pp. 159-215. Committee for Economic Development. September.

Moerman, M. 1964. Western culture and the Thai way of life. *Asia* no. 1, Spring 1964, pp. 31-50.

Moffat, A. L. 1961. *Mongkut, the King of Siam.* Ithaca: Cornell Univ. Press.

Mousny, A. 1964. *The economy of Thailand: An appraisal of a liberal exchange policy.* Bangkok: Social Science Association Press of Thailand.

Moyer, R. 1965. *Marketing in economic development.* East Lansing, Mich: Institute for International Business Management Studies, Michigan State University, Occasional Paper no. 1.

_____, and Hollander, S. C. 1968. eds. *Markets and marketing in developing societies.* Homewood, Ill.: Richard D. Irwin.

Muscat, R. J. 1966. *Development strategy in Thailand: A study of economic growth.* Praeger Special Studies in International Economics and Development. New York: Frederick A. Praeger.

Myrdal, G. 1968. *Asian drama: An inquiry into the poverty of nations.* 3 vols. New York: Pantheon.

Nairn, R. C. 1966. *International aid to Thailand: The new colonialism?* Yale Studies in Political Science, 19. New Haven: Yale Univ. Press.

National Economic Development Board. 1965. *Regional gross domestic product.* Bangkok.

_____. n.d. The second national economic and social development plan (1967-1971). Mimeographed. Bangkok.

_____. 1967. The methodology for preparing the second economic and social development plan of Thailand. Mimeographed. Bangkok.

National Statistical Office. n.d. *Thailand population census, 1960 (whole kingdom).* Bangkok.

_____. *Statistical yearbooks of Thailand*. Various. Bangkok.

_____. 1963. *Household expenditure survey* (1963). Advance Report, Whole Kingdom. Bangkok.

_____. 1963. *Labor force survey*. Bangkok.

_____. 1963. *Report of the labor force survey* (round 4) July. Bangkok.

_____. 1966. *Census of business trade or services, 1966*. Abridged Report. Bangkok.

_____. 1966. *Survey of buying and shopping habits*. Bangkok.

_____. 1968. *Report of the 1964 industrial census*, vols. 1 and 2. Bangkok.

Office of the Board of Investment. 1966. List of recipients of promotion certificates, expired and currently operating, as of 31 December 1967. Mimeographed. Bangkok.

_____. 1968. 1968 investment outlook. *Investment Newsletter* 2:1-8.

Omana, C. J. 1965. Marketing in Sub-Sahara Africa. In *Marketing and economic development*, ed. P. D. Bennett, pp. 128-39. Chicago: American Marketing Association.

Owen, W. 1964. *Strategy for mobility*. Washington, D.C.: Brookings Institution.

Pantum Thisyamondol; Virach Arromdee; and Long, M. F. 1965. *Agricultural credit in Thailand*. Bangkok.

Park, Sei-Young. 1966. Report on the transportation sector of the Thai economy. Mimeographed. May. An annex to the IBRD report *The current economic position and prospects of Thailand*.

Pendleton, R. L. 1962. *Thailand. Aspects of landscape and life*. An American Geographical Society Handbook. New York: Duell, Sloan and Pearce.

Perera, W. ed. 1966-67. *Thailand year book, 1966-67*. Bangkok: Temple Publicity Service.

Phillips, H. P. 1965. *Thai peasant personality: The patterning of interpersonal behavior in the village of Bang Chan*. Berkeley and Los Angeles: Univ. of California Press.

Purcell, V. 1965. *The Chinese in Southeast Asia*. London: Oxford Univ. Press.

Prot Panitpakdi. 1967. National accounts estimates of Thailand. In *Thailand: Social and economic studies in development*, ed. T. H. Silcock, pp. 105-127. Canberra: Australian National Univ. Press.

Raksasataya, A. 1968. The political role of Southeast Asian women. *The Annals of the American Academy of Political and Social Science* 375:86-90.

Riggs, F. W. 1966. *Thailand: the modernization of a bureaucratic polity*. Honolulu: East-West Center Press.

Rostow, W. W. 1964. *View from the seventh floor*. New York: Harper and Row.

Sharp, L. 1968. Cultural differences and Southeast Asian research. New York: The Asia Society, Special Report of a conference of the Southeast Asian Development Advisory Group.

Shaw, A. B., and Buasri, T. 1968. *Teachers in Thailand's universities: An analysis and forecast*. Publication no. 4, Education in Thailand Series. Bangkok: Ministry of Education, with the Institute for International Studies in Education, Michigan State University.

Sherbini, A. A. 1968. Import oriented marketing mechanisms. *MSU Business Topics* 16:70-73.

Siffin, W. J. 1966. *The Thai bureaucracy: Institutional change and development.* Honolulu: East-West Center Press.

Silcock, T. H. 1967. Outline of economic development 1945-65. In *Thailand: Social and economic studies in development,* ed. T. H. Silcock, pp. 1-26. Canberra: Australian National Univ. Press.

Skinner, G. W. 1957. *Chinese society in Thailand: An analytical history.* Ithaca, New York: Cornell Univ. Press.

_____. 1958. *Leadership and power in the Chinese community of Thailand.* Ithaca, New York: Cornell Univ. Press.

Sonakul, S. 1967. Getting to know your Thais. A series of eight articles. *Bangkok Post,* June-September.

Soonthornsima, C. 1949. The relation of college education and pay levels in Thai civil service. M.A. thesis. Mimeographed. Bangkok: Institute of Public Administration, Thammasat Univ.

Stifel, L. D. 1967. Income distribution in Thailand. *Economics Journal of the Economics Society of Thailand* 1:125-31.

Sutton, J. L. 1962. Political and administrative leadership. In *Problems of politics and administration in Thailand,* ed. J. L. Sutton, pp. 1-22. Bloomington: Institute of Training for Public Service, Indiana University.

Textor, R. B. 1961. *From peasant to pedicab driver.* A social study of northeastern Thai farmers who periodically migrated to Bangkok and became pedicab drivers. New Haven: Yale University Southeast Asia Studies, Cultural Report Series no. 9.

Thompson, V. 1941. *Thailand, the new Siam.* New York: Macmillan.

Transportation Consultants, Inc. 1959. *A comprehensive evaluation of Thailand's transportation system requirements. A report to H. E. the Minister of Communications, Government of Thailand,* June 1959.

Trescott, P. B. 1967. Measurement of Thailand's economic growth, 1946-1966. Mimeographed. Bangkok.

United Nations. 1967. *Monthly bulletin of statistics.* New York: January.

United States Operations Mission (USOM). 1966. A cost-benefit study of roads in North and Northeast Thailand. Mimeographed, with annexes. Bangkok: USOM Research Division.

_____. 1966. Second joint Thai-USOM evaluation of the accelerated rural development projects. Evaluation Reports, vols. I and II. Unpublished, Bangkok. July.

_____. 1957. Master plan for primary highways. Unpublished. Bangkok: USOM.

Usher, D. 1967. The Thai rice trade. In *Thailand: Social and economic studies in development,* ed. T. H. Silcock, pp. 206-230. Canberra: Australian National Univ. Press.

_____. 1968. *The price mechanism and the meaning of national income statistics.* Oxford: Clarendon Press.

Vella, W. F. 1955. *The impact of the West on government in Thailand.* Publications in Political Science, vol. 4, no. 3. pp. 317-410. Berkeley: Univ. of California.

Wigglesworth, E. F. and Brotan, J. 1966. Retailing trends in Thailand. *Journal of Retailing*, Summer 1966. pp. 41-51.

Wijeyewardene, G. 1967. Some aspects of rural life in Thailand. In *Thailand: Social and economic studies in development*. ed. T. H. Silcock, pp. 65-83. Canberra: Australian National Univ. Press.

Wilson, D. 1969. Empires of the rising sun. *Management Today* (London) July 1969, pp. 79-81.

Wilson, D. A. 1962. *Politics in Thailand*. Ithaca: Cornell Univ. Press.

Wisit Kasiraksa. 1963. *Economic effects of the friendship highway*. SEATO Grad. School of Engineering.

Wit, D. 1968. *Thailand: another Vietnam?* New York: Scribners.

Index